Empirical
Theories
About Courts

Empirical Theories About Courts

Edited by
Keith O. Boyum
California State University, Fullerton
Lynn Mather
Dartmouth College

Longman
New York & London

Empirical Theories About Courts

Longman Inc., 1560 Broadway, New York, N.Y. 10036
Associated companies, branches, and representatives
throughout the world.

Developmental Editor: Irving E. Rockwood
Editorial and Design Supervisor: Joan Matthews
Production Supervisor: Ferne Y. Kawahara
Manufacturing Supervisor: Marion Hess

Library of Congress Cataloging in Publication Data

Main entry under title:

Empirical theories about courts.

    (Longman professional studies in law and public policy)
    Bibliography: p.
    Includes index.
    1. Courts — Research — United States — Addresses,
essays, lectures. 2. Courts — Research — Addresses,
essays, lectures. I. Boyum, Keith O. II. Mather,
Lynn M. III. Series.
KF8719.A2E46 1983 347.73'1'0724   82–17194
ISBN 0-582-282179   347.30710724

MANUFACTURED IN THE UNITED STATES OF AMERICA

Contents

Preface

Each of the essays in this volume stems from work that was sponsored by the National Institute of Justice under the rubric, "A Research Program to Develop Empirical Theories about Courts." As that title makes clear, the product sought was explanatory generalization and theory development, not the collection of data or the solution of specific court problems. As such, these essays may seem an unusual choice for National Institute of Justice sponsorship. A few words about the genesis of these essays are thus in order.

A number of voices had been heard in 1977 urging the National Institute of Law Enforcement and Criminal Justice (NILECJ, predecessor of the National Institute of Justice) to reform its programs of sponsored research. A goal urged by many in the research community was theoretically well-founded research that might lead to integrated understanding of issues involving crime and the administration of justice. In early 1978 the Adjudication Division of the NILECJ sponsored a one-day conference to which a number of researchers from various parts of the United States and Canada were invited. The question posed was how best to respond to these calls for reform; a consensus reached in the conference was that the time was ripe for explicit theorizing about courts.

Awards were made in 1978 for research that was in each instance underway by 1979. Although several different awards were made, coordination among grantees was sought and facilitated through the good efforts of Dr. Carolyn Burstein of the National Institute of Justice. Principal events in the coordination effort were two meetings attended by all of the grantees at Northwestern University in May 1979, and at Stanford University in November 1979. At these seminars, participants exchanged views that gradually moved from the stage of preliminary sketches to the stage of relatively well-developed ideas, and the unanimous opinion among participants was that the seminars were especially helpful.

As the essays were completed, commented on, and revised, some apparent coordination among them emerged. Occasionally explicitly, but in fact more frequently implicitly, the essays began to speak to each other. In view of that, a mutual decision was reached to jointly publish the essays in an edited book. Subsequently, the essays were further revised, edited, and assembled in the forms presented here.

Interestingly, the initial NILECJ research solicitation did not specify particular approaches to empirical theory building, nor did it limit the scope of topics to be covered (except in requiring some pertinence to trial courts). But if variety, all else equal, is to be sought, it was achieved in good measure in these research efforts. Represented in this volume are scholars from eight different institutions and from four different disciplines—political science, law, sociology, and anthropology. The perspectives of legal history and organizational theory are also developed in several of the chapters.

For conceptualizing, initiating, and, in the early stages, shepherding this project we owe thanks to Carolyn Burstein. There would have been no such project as this without her interest and energy. We are also very grateful to Jonathan Katz for ably picking up the administrative reins on our projects after Dr. Burstein left the National Institute of Justice. This may be an appropriate place to note that this book, like the individual essays, represents the views only of those to whom they are attributed, and do not necessarily represent the views of the National Institute of Justice or the U.S. Department of Justice.

For their special efforts in hosting our seminars we are grateful to Professors Herbert Jacob and Lawrence Friedman. Our stays and our sessions at Northwestern University and at Stanford University were pleasant and productive, but would not have been so without their good offices.

Our editor at Longman, Irving Rockwood, has been patient, affable, and helpful, and we are grateful. We also thank our production editor at Longman, Joan Matthews, for her assistance. The substantive editing was shared equally to the extent possible between the co-editors. Thus our names are simply listed in alphabetical order. If there is any merit or credit that should accrue to the editors, it is equally shared, but should any demerit or criticism be offered to one of the editors, it will cheerfully be attributed wholly to the other.

Keith Boyum would like to acknowledge the good help he received in preparing manuscripts at California State University, Fullerton. Bea Halphide and Dorothy Daversa of the Department of Political Science were willing in every instance, and were always especially competent. Lynn Mather is similarly grateful for the help in manuscript preparation she received at Dartmouth College. Deborah Hodges, in particular, provided excellent assistance, and proved especially graceful under pressure. We also appreciate the financial support of the Faculty Research Committee at Dartmouth College.

Keith O. Boyum
Lynn Mather

About the Authors

M. P. Baumgartner, who holds a Ph. D. in sociology from Yale University, is a Research Associate at the Center for Criminal Justice, Harvard Law School. With Donald Black, she is currently engaged in a cross-cultural survey of dispute settlement and social control. Results of one of her earlier projects, an investigation of conflict and its management in a suburb of New York City, will appear shortly in a book entitled *The Moral Order of a Suburb* (to be published by Academic Press). She is also co-editor of the second edition of *The Social Organization of Law* (with Donald Black; Academic Press, 1983).

Donald Black is Lecturer on Law and Sociology at Harvard Law School and Research Associate at the Center for Criminal Justice, a research facility of Harvard Law School. His publications include *The Behavior of Law* (Academic Press, 1976), *The Manners and Customs of the Police* (Academic Press, 1980), *The Social Organization of Law* (Academic Press, second edition with M. P. Baumgartner, 1983), and *Toward a General Theory of Social Control* (Academic Press, 1983).

Keith O. Boyum is Professor of Political Science at California State University, Fullerton. His research has centered on the influx and processing of civil cases in courts. With Samuel Krislov, he co-edited *Forecasting the Impact of Legislation on Courts* (National Academy Press, 1980). Recent articles he has written have been on that topic as well as on understanding delay in trial courts.

Malcolm M. Feeley is a political scientist teaching at the University of Wisconsin. He has also taught at New York University, Yale, and the University of California at Berkeley. He is the author of *The Process Is the Punishment* (Russell Sage Foundation, 1979), *The Policy Dilemma* (with Austin Sarat, University of Wisconsin, 1981), and other studies of court processes. Most recently he edited (with Roman Tomasic) *Neighborhood Justice: Assessment of an Emerging Idea* (Longman, 1982).

Lawrence M. Friedman is Marion Rice Kirkwood Professor of Law at Stanford University. He is the author of *A History of American Law* (Simon and Schuster, 1973), *The Legal System: A Social Science Perspec-*

tive (Russell Sage Foundation, 1975), and many other books and articles on law. His recent work has included a number of quantitative, historical studies of the work of courts. He is a recent former President of the Law and Society Association.

Marc Galanter, Professor of Law and South Asian Studies at the University of Wisconsin, Madison, has been Editor of the *Law and Society Review* and is President-Elect of the Law and Society Association. He has written a number of articles about courts and litigation in India and in the United States.

Herbert Jacob is Professor of Political Science and Urban Affairs at Northwestern University. He has written extensively about courts and criminal justice. Among his recent monographs are *Felony Justice* (with James Eisenstein, Little Brown, 1977), *Crime and Justice in Urban America* (Prentice-Hall, 1980), *Crime and Governmental Responses in American Cities* (with Robert L. Lineberry, National Institute of Justice, 1982), and *Crime in City Politics* (with Anne Heinz and Robert Lineberry, Longman, 1983).

Samuel Krislov is Professor of Political Science at the University of Minnesota, and formerly was department chairman. He is a past President of the Law and Society Association and of the Midwest Political Science Association, and at one time edited the *Law and Society Review*. As a Guggenheim Fellow in 1979–80 he devoted considerable attention to court case loads. His present interests include problems of compliance with emerging European Economic Community law, which he pursues as a Bush Fellow and as a Senior Fulbright Research Fellow.

Mark Lazerson is a graduate of the New York University School of Law, and practiced criminal defense work in New York City for several years before studying sociology at the University of Wisconsin. He is the author or co-author of several articles, including "In the Halls of Justice the Only Justice is in the Halls," in *The Politics of Informal Justice* (Academic Press, 1982). He has conducted research on law and labor unions in Italy as a Fulbright Fellow.

Lynn Mather is Associate Professor of Government and Chair of the Urban Studies Program at Dartmouth College. She is the author of *Plea Bargaining or Trial?* (Lexington, 1979) and various articles on the administration of criminal justice. Her most recent research and writing has been on the transformation of disputes.

Barbara Yngvesson, Associate Professor of Anthropology at Hampshire College, has published articles on dispute processing, law in nonindustrial societies, small claims courts, and the transformation of disputes. She is currently engaged in ethnographic research on dispute transformation in a lower criminal court.

Empirical Theories About Courts

1

Introduction: Toward Empirical Theories About Courts

Keith O. Boyum

The title of this volume includes three crucial terms: empirical, theory, courts. While most readers have some previous acquaintance with these terms, not all may be familiar with the special meanings for the terms that social scientists intend. To illustrate special meanings and also to set the stage for the chapters that follow, we begin with a review of the terms in our title.

The term *empirical* refers to observed phenomena. *Empirical theory* in turn means that the theory in question seeks to explain observed phenomena. (By contrast, normative theory seeks to prescribe preferred behaviors, based upon explicit value judgments.) Empirical theory explains by defining concepts at a suitable level of abstraction and employing those concepts to describe regularities of human behavior.

The contributions in this volume are not fully developed empirical theories, however. They are, in each instance, precursors to empirical theory, conceptual work that proceeds from empirical studies and builds toward more comprehensive empirical theories. The selections included here are fairly representative, both of the state of the empirical theory building enterprise and of the range of issues and approaches that command current scholarly attention among those who study courts.[1]

Empirical theory seeks to explain observed phenomena by reference to concepts that intentionally simplify reality. Such a concept is referenced in the third major term in the title of this book—*courts*. The single concept of a court encompasses a range of observable phenomena over which there is considerable variation. The Supreme Court of the United States is included along with a storefront justice of the peace in some rural American setting, and included as well may be processes for tribal or clan dispute settlement that anthropologists have reported. The crucial challenge in defining concepts is to ensure that the simplifying—necessary for reasons of economy in explanation—is appropriate to the explanatory task at hand.

THE EMPIRICAL THEORY BUILDING ENTERPRISE

Two important issues are involved when boundaries are marked for the sets of observable phenomena (behaviors) that define concepts. These are, first, whether the boundaries are distinctly marked and, second, whether the boundaries are accurately marked in accord with core meanings of concepts. Perfectly distinct concepts that perfectly demark core meanings may not be achievable in practice, but the theory building exercise critically depends on defining concepts, for only then may associations be determined and approaches to causal understanding be attempted. It is therefore no surprise that scholars labor over issues of definition. The question of what is a court has confronted each of the contributors to this book, although some have expressed themselves on the issue explicitly while others have done so more implicitly. The range of issues in concept definition may be illustrated through a brief review of the contributors' views of the concept of a court.

What Is a Court?

Lawrence Friedman's contribution to this volume is an important theory building effort because it challenges and tests the concept of a court. Friedman's review of the development of courts over time informs the debate that Krislov observes between "nominalists" and "essentialists" on the matter of whether a core meaning for the concept of a court is discoverable. Nominalists argue that "court" has no central meaning. Courts, in this view, are merely whatever observers agree to call courts. To a nominalist, observers could justifiably agree to call more things courts or fewer things. Essentialists argue, to the contrary, that there is a definable core meaning of courts. Further, given the existence of a core meaning, the boundaries of the concept of courts must be drawn with reference to and in conformity with that core meaning.

Nominalists may find in Friedman's review certain support for their position. Institutions that observers have agreed to call courts have, over time, undertaken a remarkable variety of tasks, and have done so while operating through a variety of structures. Those various structures, moreover, have differed perhaps more than in mere detail. On the other hand, essentialists may also find Friedman's review helpful, for if one takes on the task of finding commonality at a core, Friedman provides a field in which to undertake the search.

Even as Friedman's essay concerns itself with courts over time, the essays by Yngvesson and Mather and by Black and Baumgartner focus on observable phenomena across space. In both instances, the contributions virtually discard the concept of a court. Implicit and, to an extent, explicit in the essay by Black and Baumgartner is the view that "court" is simply not a useful concept to employ, even when theorizing about observable behavioral phenomena that take place within settings we commonly call courts. The effort by Yngvesson and Mather to understand the transformation of disputes is not confined to the set of institutions that we in contemporary Western culture refer to as courts. In this one might find support for the view (as Galanter has informally suggested) that "court" is nothing more than a folk concept (albeit *our* folk concept).

In understanding the work that courts do, Krislov comes down on the other side of that fence, declaring himself to be largely in the essentialist camp. It seems suitable for Krislov both to raise the issue in explicit terms and, given his explanatory interest, to resolve it in the way he did. Krislov's interest in the case loads of courts takes him into the realm of concept definition. What is a case? What is case load? What is a court? Krislov could have developed an argument for discarding all three ideas, but instead he sees hope for the eventual development of theoretical understanding, given care in concept definition. For their part, Galanter and Boyum are, like Krislov, interested in understanding the work that courts do. Yet, unlike Krislov, their approaches are not very dependent on an agreement that there is such a thing as a court. The effects that Galanter sees radiating from courts could as easily radiate from institutions sharing crucial characteristics but conceptualized differently. The concepts that Boyum offers for developing understanding of the earliest stages of dispute processing, claim-definition, would presumably serve as well for dispute processors conceptualized as something different from courts.

Even the authors who have concentrated on explaining how courts do their work face the issue of the concept of a court. Recognizing the importance of the issue, Jacob (even as Krislov) addresses the point squarely. The pertinence to Jacob's goal is apparent: if one is to proceed with the application of group theory to courts, a very clear idea of that to which one is applying group theory is crucial. One would not wish to test for goodness of fit (of the theory to courts) on an organization later determined to be outside of what commands our interest. One would not wish to hazard possible modifications to the theory that preexists on the basis of observations drawn not from courts but instead from something else. And if fit is assessed, and if possible modifications to group theory are put forward, one must know how far the measurements with regard to fit apply, how far the modifications to group theory are intended to reach. Further, in one view, the analysis by Feeley and Lazerson of "loosely coupled systems" is exactly concerned with a kind of boundary problem, i.e., what phenomena ought to interest us at the point where (the conceptualized) court system interacts with another (conceptualized) system.

We may recapitulate this way. Concept definition is crucial to empirical theory and also is necessary prior to other exercises of defining associations and approaching causal understanding. That is why scholars interested in developing empirical theoretical understanding labor over concepts, and that is why scholars respond with concerns of definition (instead of, say, concrete plans for action) in the face of apparent social need. On the one hand, even scholars would think it inappropriate in the face of a call for the fire department to respond with an inquiry as to the usefulness of that concept. But on the other hand, some careful thought as to how to arrange responses to physical and chemical emergencies might include some conceptual considerations and also result in better care provided more quickly in the long run. With this we have raised the broader issue of how empirical theory can inform policy choices.

THE USEFULNESS OF EMPIRICAL THEORY

Let us imagine (rather plausibly) that prominent policy makers harbor concerns for the well-being of judiciaries, and that prominent policy makers harbor some fears that the wrong sorts of persons and issues are being brought to courts in numbers too large for comfort. Several responses might be put forth, including (let us say) these. First, let us build local institutions designed to resolve disputes without formal adjudication. Let us call these neighborhood justice centers. Second, let us strip away some of the kinds of disputes and cases and other work that courts presently do, in the hope of giving extra time to judges and others involved in court processes for bringing forth more thoroughly considered decisions. Third, let us add not only more judges to courts but also let us make substantial use of new positions in court organizations. Let us add auditors, magistrates, referees, judges pro-tem, judicial administrators, and systems engineers.

To accomplish the first task seems plainly to require some fundamental understanding of the nature of courts, and this is a central aim of the essays in Part I of this book. To accomplish the second task requires a fundamental understanding of how cases arise (Boyum), how they are treated as "loads" (Krislov), and any broader significances that decisions made and announced might have for the society served by courts (Galanter). To accomplish the third task requires an understanding of how the preexisting network of social relationships in courts will be altered with the introduction of new professionals to the work team. Thus we need to know something about courts as organizations (Jacob); and we need to ask how loosely coupled systems interact (Feeley and Lazerson) in order to inform ourselves of different organizational options in adding our new individuals to the work team.

Most importantly, good scholarly work on institutions enriches evaluations of those institutions by furthering understanding of their nature, use, and consequences. Our argument and our conclusion is that the contributions to theory included here have potential relevance to policy choice. With further work, and in tandem with the contributions of other scholars, we may legitimately expect better understanding and, eventually better courts. But to that strong affirmation we must couple, by way of conclusion, a disclaimer.

Policy questions such as whether courts should be expanded, whether access to courts should be widened or narrowed, whether new functions might usefully be grafted onto courts, and a host of other important questions cannot be simply and unambiguously answered on the basis of theoretical research such as that represented in this volume (even though we believe that significant insights toward such policy issues do emerge from these chapters). Theory requires elaboration, testing, and, frequently, translation before it can be directly useful to policy makers. This has yet to be done. As these essays reveal, a long developmental process of theory building has in many ways only just begun. We hope that these essays will help to stimulate as well as contribute to further development, and to eventual elaboration and translation.

NOTES

1. We note, however, that the approach that is grounded in economics is absent. This is by design, for two reasons. First, examples of the economics-based approach are easily available elsewhere. Interested readers are invited to compare the selections in this book with those found in any recent issue of the *Journal of Legal Studies*, or the *Journal of Law and Economics*. It does not seem to us, by contrast, that empirical theorizing about courts from the standpoints of other social sciences in quite as easily available (although journals such as *Law and Society Review* carry good examples of such theorizing from time to time). Second, econometric work may be understood as having a primary interest in the development and exploitation of tools or methods that draw on theoretical relationships that in fact have been identified in other work. Compare Boyum and Krislov (eds.) observing "two important limits of structural modeling: a lack of well-grounded theory . . . ." (1980:96) and observing further that "the quest for identifiability [in a structural model] ends only when the substantive experts (. . . those in the fields related to court processes) are satisfied that an equation, and the corresponding assumptions about the rest of the system, represents a reasonable statement of causality . . . ." (Boyum and Krislov, 1980:112).

Part I

Comparing Courts Across Time and Space

2

Courts Over Time: A Survey of Theories and Research

Lawrence M. Friedman

This paper is an attempt to sum up one part of the literature on courts—studies with a historical, developmental, or evolutionary focus. Of course, these terms are not very precise, but they do have a fairly clear meaning at the core. Most studies look at courts at one point in time. Some of these studies talk about past situations, but usually without presenting any data. Here, however, we deal with those essays or studies in which time (or the passage of time or change from one period to another) is a variable. We also consider a few studies old enough to be of historical interest, even though they do not use time as a variable themselves.

Our concern is with the behavior of courts. We leave aside any primary focus on the litigants and their lawyers, though of course this comes up incidentally. We also take for granted the functions of courts, such as dispute settlement, and we dodge the issue of what a dispute is anyway. (See Abel, 1974:217; Gessner, 1976:170–183; Mather and Yngvesson, 1981:776.) We also focus on courts, not on judges as such. There is a special literature on judges, some of it historical (for example, comparing the backgrounds or educations of judges over time) (Heiberg, 1969:901; Guice, 1972; Ewing, 1938; Blaustein and Mersky, 1978). In theory, these studies are relevant to our subject; in fact, most of them are of only marginal interest. Many of these studies try to explain differences in the behavior of judges on the same court. They do not study "courts" as institutions, or the output of courts, which are our primary interests.

Also, we are concerned primarily with *empirical* studies. By this we

Author's Note: This chapter was prepared under Grant Number 78-NI-AX-1036 from the National Institute of Justice, U.S. Department of Justice. Points of view herein are those of the author, and do not necessarily represent the position of the U.S. Department of Justice.

9

mean, roughly, studies that approach the courts systematically, often (though not always) quantitatively or which make a significant contribution to theories about court behavior. And, for the most part, we leave out case studies of events or purely institutional studies of courts. We omit the literature on particular landmark cases (such as Kutler, 1971; Fehrenbacher, 1978), and most court histories, including the tremendous body of literature on the history of the U.S Supreme Court[1].

Why should we be interested in historical studies, or studies of courts over time? Social science searches for general propositions. To get anywhere, it must go beyond case studies and single instances; it must try to frame theories or knit together chains of propositions that are not tied to single instances. Such theories or propositions can best be tested by comparative studies. Work on court A may suggest a general proposition; this can then be checked by looking at B, C, and D. Sometimes it may be better or more telling to test the proposition not by looking at courts B, C, and D, but by examining court A at times 1, 2, and 3. And indeed, this may be the only way to test certain propositions, such as those that are themselves developmental or historical, i.e., those which suggest that change takes place over time—that courts do more of this or less of that.

For our purposes, we will divide historical studies into two broad, rough categories: *macro-studies* and *trend studies*. There is nothing magic about the line we are drawing. By macro-studies we mean studies of changes (or stabilities) in courts or court systems over very long periods of time; all others are trend studies. To put it another way (equally rough), macro-studies are studies of legal evolution. Because they deal with the big picture, they concern themselves with gross sorts of change and are more "comparative" in the sense of straddling different cultures and societies. Trend studies by and large are confined to one place or jurisdiction. We begin with a look at some macrostudies, then turn to trend studies.

COURTS AND LEGAL EVOLUTION

Legal evolution is a subject with a distinguished lineage. A convenient beginning is Sir Henry Maine's *Ancient Law*, published in 1861 (although there were important precursors, especially in the German "historical" school of the early 19th century) (See Pospisil, 1971; Stein, 1979). Maine, like most evolutionary scholars, dealt with the legal system as a whole, not merely the courts, but his thesis can well apply to courts. The thesis, stripped of detail, is about the relationship between two variables: social structure and the organization of the legal system. In his most famous passage, Maine describes the evolution "from status to contract" in "progressive" societies, an evolution that ran parallel to an evolution in social organization. Older societies were family-centered, patriarchal; in newer ones, individuals (not families or clans) were the basic carriers of rights and duties—men and women dealt with each other freely and voluntarily on the basis of contract.

An echo of this general thesis can be found in Durkheim (1964), and his famous distinction (in *The Division of Labor in Society*, first published in 1893) between "mechanical" and "organic" solidarity. In primitive society, according to Durkheim, there was little division of labor. Society held together because everyone adhered to the same general norms, which were universal within the society. The main task of the legal system was to punish deviance—to mark off the moral boundaries of society and constantly to show where these boundaries lay. Division of labor and interdependence ("organic solidarity") are characteristic of modern society (compare Tönnies, 1957). The law now emphasizes civil sanctions; it is restitutive rather than penal. The court system has also become more complex: specialized tribunals and agencies develop that are adapted to different kinds of transactions. Durkheim's theory thus predicts a shift in the business of courts as society modernizes. He also predicts that the primeval court system—simple, undifferentiated—will grow into a whole battery of courts, with varied jurisdictions, to take care of the varied businesses of modern society.

Schwartz and Miller (1964:159) studied a sample of societies, searching for the order in which "characteristics of a fully developed legal system" evolved. They noted three characteristics of such a developed system: counsel ("regular use of specialized non-kin advocates in the settlement of disputes"), mediation ("regular use of non-kin third-party intervention in dispute settlement"), and police ("specialized armed force used partially or wholly for norm enforcement"). Certain simple societies lacked all three. Among more advanced societies, the three seemed to emerge in a definite order—first mediation, then police, then counsel.

Our main interest is in what Schwartz and Miller call "mediation." This broad term includes (in addition to what we usually call mediation) most institutions we label "courts." It is not always easy to draw a line between courts and other mediating institutions, but a go-between is conventionally described as a mediator, not a judge, if he has no power to *impose* a solution on either party. A *judge* who sits on a *court*, on the other hand, can impose his will on the parties; he can invoke some sort of coercion to see that his judgment or decision is carried out (cf. Black and Baumgartner, chapter 4).

Howard Wimberley (1973:78) took hold of this distinction and added another stage to the three in Schwartz and Miller. This was the stage of "true" courts, which some societies develop after mediation but before police or counsel. Wimberley tried to relate this particular evolution to stages of *social* development. Mediation, Wimberley argued, was effective only within small groups, groups tied together by blood or marriage. Presumably, social norms (without "force") would be strong enough to make mediation stick. But mediation did not work for disputes between members of *different* clans or groups. Here one needed force or the threat of force to back up the decision. Dispute settlement, then, evolved in a consistent direction, that is, toward giving ever more power to the third-party decision maker. It moved, in other words, in the direction of courts.

The work of Vilhelm Aubert is also relevant to legal evolution. In an important essay, Aubert (1963:2) distinguished between conflicts of interest and conflicts of value or (see also Eckhoff, 1966; Sarat and Grossman, 1975). A conflict of interest arises out of a situation of scarcity: both A and B want the same thing but cannot both have it. A and B do not necessarily disagree over values. Commercial disputes (over terms and prices, for example) are conflicts of interest. A conflict of interests arises, in short, *within* a community (or among individuals) who do not disagree about norms (or facts). The best way to resolve it, in theory at least, is by bargaining or, if necessary, by mediation leading to some sort of compromise. The best way to resolve conflicts of value, on the other hand, is authority, that is, a third party who has the moral or physical strength to force a solution on the parties. In some cases, this is the only way to resolve the conflict. Aubert argues that compromise is hard to achieve in conflicts of value. One must bring "law" (general norms) to bear. The institutions that do this are courts. Aubert's ideas, then, are evolutionary, even though he does not actually cite historical data. As societies grow bigger and more complex mediation loses its bite. Formal law emerges, and with it the coercive power of courts[2].

The classical problem of Durkheim and Maine was also a concern of Max Weber (Rheinstein, 1954). Weber drew a central distinction between the "rational" and the "irrational" in law-finding and law-making. These concepts ran somewhat parallel to Durkheim's two kinds of solidarity and to Maine's domains of status and contract. Weber is not literally evolutionary; he does not say in so many words that there is a definite progression from the irrational to the rational. But the very choice of words implies progress. What is rational certainly *seems* higher on the ladder of evolution than the irrational; and none of the oldest legal systems were "rational" in Weber's sense. Some sort of movement, or progression, has taken place, at least in the West. Formal rationality, the style of courts in the developed, capitalist west replaced irrational justice, informal justice, kadi justice.

Weber was not the sort to leave important terms undefined. Legal process was "formally irrational" when it was such that its means of decision could not be "controlled by the intellect." Oracles and ordeals are good examples. Process is "substantively irrational" when "concrete factors of the particular case" influence decision—factors evaluated on an "ethical, emotional or political basis" instead of by "general norms." Law-finding (decision) is "rational" when it follows general principles. It is "formally rational" when it looks for "legally relevant characteristics of the facts," which it finds through "the logical analysis of meaning." It is "substantively rational" when it takes into account political, social, or economic principles as grounds for decision. (Rheinstein, 1954:63, 79; see also Friedman, 1966:148; Trubek, 1972:720).

As we said, Weber's scheme is not dogmatically evolutionary. Moreover, it is quite possible for all four types to exist within a single society. We can certainly find all four currently in the United States. The draft lottery is (in Weber's terms) irrational[3]; appellate courts, on the other hand, use formal rationality. In simple societies, however, there is no hint of formal rationality. Formal rationality at its dizziest heights is conceptualism; it is the way high courts decided cases (or were supposed to) in Weber's Germany. There is no necessary movement from one stage to any other stage. Formal rationality was, for Weber, probably the most advanced of the four, though he knew it had its faults and its paradoxes. Nor is the movement to formal rationality necessarily the end of the line. Scholars now see, or think they see, a retreat from formal rationality, at least in the direction of substantive rationality. Formal rationality is characteristic of Western courts, but some find this legal trait cold and repressive. In a just society, formal rationality may therefore wither away, and the law will move on to a more "responsive" stage (Nonet and Selznick, 1978; cf. Black, 1976:131–137).

We have set out a few of the major themes in evolutionary studies of courts. These studies go back more than a century. The older studies (notably Maine and Durkheim) were based on assumptions of fact that are no longer totally accepted. We can argue whether Durkheim drew the right picture of primitive law, or whether it is possible to prove or disprove his theory at all (see Baxi, 1974:645; Schwartz, 1974:653; Spitzer, 1975:613). Each evolutionary theory has its problems. Aubert, for example, assumes that conflicts of interest can be compromised more easily than can conflicts of value, but this is by no means self-evident. It is a conflict of interests, not values, when both husband and wife in a divorce want sole custody of a child; but such a conflict may nonetheless not be easy to compromise.

Despite their many differences, the various authors share a common perspective. They all see a definite connection between at least *gross* forms of social organization and *gross* forms of dispute settlement. Mediation precedes courts in time; courts come later and are more formal than mediation bodies. Courts tend to use norms, rules, principles—they decide, in other words, according to "law." They become necessary in complex societies because disputes cut across family, clan, or tribal lines. There is no common authority figure, like the ones that mediate *inside* a family, tribe, or clan. In the big societies, there are too many tribes, too many points of view, too many warring interests. These societies are, in short, too pluralistic. Only courts and only "law" will work.

Advanced societies do indeed have courts, but perhaps it is not right to say that these courts "work" in any ethical or instrumental sense. Indeed, the literature is, on the whole, very critical of courts in Western societies. A constant theme is what a poor job they do after all. On the other hand, anthropologists describe tribal courts in glowing terms (see, for example, Gluckman, 1967 [1955] and 1965; chap. 5). These courts seem so different from those far off at the other end of evolution. In a way, the anthropologists have turned 19th-century notions of progress upside down. The modern literature is still strongly evolutionary, but the path now leads downward (or sideways), not upward. Western courts of law are no longer labeled "progressive," nor are tribal courts brushed off as "primitive." Law has been expelled, as it were, from the Garden of Eden. Western courts are painted as stiff, formal, antidemocratic. They ignore or oppress the poor; they are legalistic and hidebound. They are useless in dealing with disputes of ordinary people. Worst of all, they are expensive. Tribal courts, on the other hand, are cheap, open to all, informal. And they restore social harmony—they "make the balance," in Laura Nader's phrase (1969b:69). They do broad justice among people; they knit a torn social fabric together again.

This raises an interesting question of legal theory. One assumes, perhaps naively, that every society generates a court system that is functional for it in *some* sense. But then why, for example, should the Fiji Islanders (Arno, 1979:411) be more successful at producing suitable courts than the English or French? It may be, of course, that tribal law has been romanticized.[4] Moreover, not everyone would agree that the question has to be answered. Why not simply abandon the notion that courts must suit society as a whole? Clearly, courts must fill *somebody's* needs and functions, but the "somebody" may be a narrow group—a small elite or upper class. In other words, courts need not do justice in the broadest sense to "work" in Western societies; perhaps they serve a tiny but distinctive group, the group which has its hands on the levers of power.

Yet even the far left finds this point of view too crude. We hear a good deal these days about the ideological functions of courts, which they could not perform if they served the rulers of society too brazenly. In fact (so runs the argument), courts fly the banner of justice for all; they may even behave fairly in the individual case. But high cost and legalism put justice out of reach for the average citizen; there is no real "access" to law. (See Nader, 1980.) Stiff, expensive, inaccessible courts are "functional" in an ironic way—a way no court system on the tribal model could hope to be if magically transported to Western society.

There are other ways to approach the (apparent) mismatch between courts and society. Modern Western societies are extremely complicated, much more so than the societies anthropologists usually study. Perhaps the courts are the court of only one tribe, the white middle-class tribe, or the business tribe; perhaps they literally speak a different language from the working-class tribe, or from black and brown minority tribes. Perhaps the mismatch is just another case of *conflict* of legal systems or of norms, of legal pluralism, or a species of colonialism (Burman and Harrell-Bond, 1979).

It has, indeed, been observed that courts in colonial settings sometimes play a perverse, disruptive role. In some societies, the law of the colonial power is a kind of alien invader. Villagers and natives often simply ignore it. Occasionally we find the opposite situation: the natives use the courts heavily, but not for genuine dispute-settlement. Rather, they treat the courts as another weapon in local feuds and quarrels. Legal process becomes an instrument of harassment and struggle, used by vindictive litigants. This point has been made, for example, to explain why India under the British was so litigious (Cohn, 1959:79). The local population took to the British courts "with great enthusiasm," manipulating litigation to their own ends, treating it as "a form of speculation and entertainment" (Kidder, 1979:292).

The same point can be made about societies which are not colonial in the strict sense but in which Westernized law was slapped down on top of older customary norms—for example, modern Turkey (Starr, 1978:275–278) or Mexico (Collier, 1973). We can make the point without denying that law is organically related to society, and that it changes as society changes. Colonial and Westernizing societies are in the process of rapid social change. Different parts and segments of society change at different speeds. Evolution is telescoped. It is a mistake to impose a more "advanced" court system on traditional sectors of society. The mistake is compounded when the advanced court system is the formal, traditional system of colonial or Western powers. For then it will be useless in the village except as a way for people to make trouble, capitalizing on its intricacy, its sloth, its capacities for frustration and cost. We will return to this theme when we discuss trend studies.

Other common threads run through the evolutionary studies. In all of them the idea of progress or progression casts at least a small shadow. History begins with simple societies, in which disputes are settled through mediation or the invisible sword of public opinion (see Schwartz, 1954: 471). More complex societies use courts. At first, courts decide cases rather informally; in Weber's famous image, justice is Kadi justice, the justice of an elder or wise man sitting in the marketplace and deciding cases seemingly in a completely free evaluation of each particular case (Rheinstein, 1954:x1). Of course, the Kadi used norms, but they were general norms of society; there was nothing specifically or technically "legal" about them.

Modern, complex societies have moved on to another phase. These societies cannot rely on "shared experience" (which permits effective mediation), nor do they have father-like authority figures who can get away with Kadi justice. They need formal courts, with force to back them up if necessary. Adjudication splits into two varieties, adjudication proper and arbitration. Adjudication proper is the realm of "judges," who are specially trained in "law," and who apply norms set off from those of the general population. Arbitration is more *ad hoc*; but even arbitration is enforced or can be enforced by real courts.

Some such evolution, it is assumed, actually took place in human history. It is also assumed that this kind of evolution still goes on. In our own society, for instance, when an institution (school, church, business, club) reaches a certain size and complexity, it will find that informal ways to handle grievances or disputes will no longer do; its mechanisms will become more "legal." Sheer size makes it almost inevitable that face-to-face authority will not work, and "shared experience" and "public opinion" will become attenuated.

Is this line of development inevitable? Once it begins, is it reversible? Does it result in patterns of dispute settlement that are just or good for society? Recent literature has raised these issues, and a cluster of others, on privacy and personal integrity, social justice, access to courts, neighborhood courts and peoples' courts, law reform, and so on. But to consider these current issues merges the focus on evolutionary studies with the focus on trend studies, to which we now turn.

TREND STUDIES

Trend studies, as we defined them, are simply studies with a less grand perspective. They measure time in years and decades, not in centuries or periods. Practically speaking, we confine ourselves to studies of recent history. There is, of course, no reason why one could not write about changes in the work of courts over a 50-year period (or a century or two) in medieval times, and there are some examples (see Kagan, 1981). But most of the studies deal with the last 100 years or so. We call them "trend studies" because their main concern, generally speaking, is in what goes on now and how it got that way and how it might continue or change in the future.

Partly for this reason, trend studies tend to define "courts" in quite a different way than do evolutionary studies. To say anything sensible about changes between ancient and modern law or to compare dispute settlement in nomadic tribes with dispute settlement in bureaucratic Germany, a scholar is almost forced to define "court" broadly. A "judge" is any third party who decides cases or disputes between individuals with some sort of force to back up his decision. His institution (or even what he does) makes up a "court" (see Hoebel, 1961:22–26). Trend studies, on the other hand, can get away with narrower definitions of judge and court (when they define these at all). Since trend studies are studies of particular court systems, they usually take the courts for granted—a court is what people in their society call a court.[5] Trend studies are thus studies of courts in the historical, limited, formal sense. They are often studies of how useful or useless these particular institutions are, or they are studies of their work, their position, and their fate. The focus may be on whether they are doing a good job or whether parts of the job should be taken away from courts and parceled out to somebody else. We find suggestions, for example, that it would be better to hand over some kinds of cases to, say, arbitrators. In the long view of history, this would be nothing more than exchanging one kind of court for another. But that does not mean that it is foolish or unimportant to ask if it ought to be done.

Litigation Rates

To study courts empirically we need data, preferably quantitative data. Modern students of courts can observe, interview, send out questionnaires. Trend studies usually have to make do with documents and files. This is of course a rather severe limitation. It confines these studies, inevitably, to certain subjects, bounded and shaped by the data.

A number of studies have tried to measure the rate of litigation. This is a measure which, in theory at least, can be obtained wherever court records are preserved. Of course, litigation rates are only indicators. It is fair to ask what they indicate. Some studies use litigation rates as indicators of the functions of courts; others use them as indicators of disputes or conflicts in society. In other words, some scholars want to know the volume (and type) of work the courts do in order to say something about society itself. We could count divorce cases over time and treat this as an indicator (rough, to be sure) of processes going on within the family. Or we could use data on what courts are doing to suggest how courts are affecting society. We might, therefore, study whether courts handle a large volume of eviction cases and whether landlords win these cases. We could then make (or jump to) conclusions about how courts support (or do not support) landlords in their struggle against tenants. And of course we might use litigation figures or similar data to tell us about trends within the courts themselves, whether they are overworked or underworked, efficient, inefficient, speedy, slow, or the like.

It hardly needs to be said that the study of litigation rates is full of traps for the unwary. To begin with, court statistics are notoriously bad. There is also the question of what the "cases" represent. Litigation is arguably pathological, which makes it risky to deduce much about the "normal" state of society from what we find in court records. We will, again, take divorce rates as our example. Divorce rates have risen steadily and dramatically over the last century. This certainly tells us *something*, but it is not clear what. Divorce rates are not to be trusted as indicators of marital breakdown. A high divorce rate certainly suggests instability in marriages. A low divorce rate, on the other hand, tells us little or nothing in itself. It may only mean (as in 19th-century South Carolina or modern Paraguay), that the legal system does not allow (or severely represses) divorce. If marriages collapse, people will have to make some arrangement outside the normal law. The divorce rate tells us how many people (or couples), at a given state of the law and at given "prices" of divorce, wish to legitimize their status by legally getting rid of their partners. There are all sorts of economic and social reasons why people want to do this. This makes the divorce rate an interesting figure (see Friedman and Percival, 1976:61), but not a reliable guide to family stability or to behavior within the family. Before no-fault divorce burst on the scene, the petitioner in a divorce case had to allege one or more "grounds" for divorce. Adultery, desertion, and cruelty were probably the most common of these. Yet it would be absurd to use these allegations to measure "real" rates of adultery, desertion, or cruelty.

This does not mean that we cannot use litigation rates at all. Any indicator presents problems. In fact, one could say (at the risk of sounding banal) that figures about age, birth, death, or whatever, never mean anything in themselves. They are always indicators, demanding an inferential leap for proper interpretation.

The work of Jose Juan Toharia (1974) illustrates one important use of litigation rates. Toharia studied Spanish courts in the period 1900–1970. He measured the volume of business in formal courts. He also measured the volume of business done by notaries. (Notaries play an important role in the legal system of civil law countries; many important documents—documents used in forming corporations, for example—go through the hands of the notary).

Toharia's findings can be summed up briefly as follows. In Spain, in a time of rapid economic growth, in those centers of economic growth (urban, industrial areas) where one might expect to find the business of courts growing very fast, relative to other times and places, one found the opposite. Case loads were stable, even declining (in proportion to population). On the other hand, notarial acts behaved much more as predicted. These rose, both absolutely and in number of acts per thousand population. The increase was most pronounced in the big industrial centers. For example, in Barcelona, Toharia counted 42.5 notarial acts per 1,000 population in 1910; in 1967, the number of acts was about four times as great (165.5 per 1,000). In the less developed province of Avila, for example, there were only 14.3 acts per 1,000 in 1910; the rise was somewhat slower, too—to 44.7 in 1967—a bit more than three times as great.[6]

The big surprise in Toharia's study, of course, is the failure of litigation rates to "explode" with economic growth. With the tremendous surge in modern economic life, we might expect a flood of commercial cases, but it did not happen in Spain. Each country, of course, has its own peculiarities of legal culture. But studies in other countries—some inspired by Toharia's work—have found support for his thesis. For example, the volume of civil litigation at first instance in Sweden and Denmark was measured between 1930 and 1970. In both countries, volume of litigation did not increase in proportion to the population (Blegvad, Bolding, and Lando, 1973:102–105).[7]

What are we to make of the Toharia thesis? First of all, we must remember that he studied the formal courts of Spain, that is, "courts" understood in a particular sense—courts whose work was shaped and constricted by a long tradition. What he investigated was the relationship between economic development and social change, on the one hand, and *these* courts on the other. The relationship was inverse—one might almost say perverse. In a developing country, perhaps also in a developed country, the number of disputes funneled into court seems to be static or even declining in proportion to population; it certainly lags far behind the growth in sheer *volume* of economic activity.

Of course, we have not put forward a definition of "dispute," and we have no way to measure the number of disputes in society. Perhaps disputes declined in Spain during the period Toharia studied. We have no proof one way or the other. But this we do know: in a modern economy, there are certainly shipments that come late, damaged goods, goods that fall short of what the parties expected, not to mention problems of credit, bank loans, business failures, partnership and corporation squabbles, and so on. There is no reason to assume that the sheer volume (or proportion) of business disagreements has gone down over time. On the contrary, there is every reason to believe that this sort of disagreement *has* to rise, and steeply, with increasing economic tempo and pace. We certainly expect personal injury claims (or potential claims) to rise with industrialization. Industrial machinery, trains, and cars produce almost all of the serious personal injuries in society. In light of this, it seems likely that the court's share of the work of dispute settlement must have fallen off sharply, even if the work load of courts stayed quite stable.

We must not, of course, forget Toharia's figures on the work of notaries. Here he found no stagnation or decline at all; quite the contrary. Hence, he could say, and rightly, that the legal system (or, as he put it, the "juridical system") responded in exactly the expected way to economic growth and social change. Any decent theory of how the legal system (in the broadest sense) meshes with the socioeconomic system predicts growth in the legal system as economic traffic grows and as the engines of social change churn on. There is no need to assume "lag" between the legal system *as a whole* and social change; indeed, there are good arguments against any theory of "lag" (Friedman and Ladinsky, 1967:50). The suggestion that flows from Toharia's work is quite different. Western court systems (or at least courts in Spain) are brittle. They are bound into a specific historical tradition and it is not easy for them to shift their habits to meet the needs of modern society. We will have to look more closely at this thesis.

Before we do, however, we should note some problems of method. I speak here chiefly about the United States because I do not know enough about court records in other countries. The notary does not cut much of a figure in the United States and there is no exact equivalent for the data Toharia gathered on notarial acts in Spain. This means we cannot measure as neatly as he did the relationship between law, in the broadest sense, and economic change.

As for judicial statistics, they are shockingly poor in the United States. No two states gather data the same way; most hardly gather data at all. Trial courts do not keep accurate figures on cases and case loads even today. Their past performance has been equally wretched or worse (Lepawsky, 1932:192–196). There is a movement to do something about judicial statistics (National Center for State Courts, 1975, 1978), but it comes too late to help us historically.

A handful of case studies have tried to look at the work of civil courts over time (Laurent, 1959; Ireland, 1972; Friedman and Percival, 1976— for a critique see Lempert, 1978; Hindus, Hammet, and Hobson, 1979; Daniels, 1981; McIntosh, 1981; see also Brown, 1979; Clark, 1979). Friedman and Percival studied the flow of business in two California trial courts over the course of a century (1890–1970). One court was in urban Alameda County, the other in rural San Benito. The main focus was on the courts' business, the kinds of cases they handled. The authors wanted to test Toharia's thesis as well. They were of course able to measure yearly filings in the courts, and they could compare filings with population figures. The study had five sample points: 1890, 1910, 1930, 1950, and 1970. In Alameda, there were 7.6 filings per 1,000 in 1890, 13.5 in 1910, 11 per 1,000 in 1970. In San Benito, filings were 4.8 per 1,000 in 1890, 10.2 per 1,000 in 1970—slightly less than the 10.4 per 1,000 of 1950. The figures were rather skimpy; the authors worked directly with raw case files and these take a lot of time and effort to handle. Friedman and Percival did not feel that their figures contradicted Toharia, but neither did they provide overwhelming confirmation. One thing did seem clear: there was no evidence for an "explosion" in filings, certainly not up to 1970.

The problem, however, is more complex than this. Their figures were based on *filings* in court. Filings are easy to count, since every time a litigant enters a complaint a number is assigned to the case (the numbers run consecutively), whether the case is trivial or important, contested or uncontested, path-breaking or totally banal. In the 1970s, divorce actions were the single biggest source of filings in California counties.[8] Almost all were rubber-stamp affairs in which everything of moment had been decided ahead of time by the parties and their lawyers, and nothing much happened in front of the judge. Yet each time a person files for divorce, the case gets a number and the number becomes part of the county's statistics. "Cases" of this sort do not take up much energy or time, yet published court statistics usually lump together *all* filings, contested or not, in a grand numerical soup.

Friedman and Percival could hardly help but notice that hundreds of cases in the courts they studied were routine and uncontested. They felt that contested litigation had declined in the counties since the 19th century. What was rising (if anything was) were administrative and routine matters. Some of the routine matters are processed in courts simply because of history or tradition. An uncontested divorce is now almost as cut-and-dried as registering a deed, but deeds are not funneled through the courts. It is also routine to probate a will, which does go through court. Other cases in the two counties (including most tort actions) began as real disputes, but faded out of the docket and were resolved outside of court.[9]

Wayne McIntosh (1981) studied the courts of general jurisdiction in St. Louis, Missouri, from 1820 to 1977. He found a rather marked decline in litigation rates between 1850 and 1900 (filings dropped from 13.9 to 6.9 per 1,000 population). Then the rate rose (it was 14.9 in 1920–1929). Recent figures have been static or slightly rising (12.36 in the decade of the 1940s, 16.85 in the 1970s). But 45% of the cases in the 1970s were family law cases, almost all of them divorces, and probably almost all of these were uncontested. There is certainly no evidence in McIntosh's study for a "litigation explosion"; the "true" litigation rate in St. Louis today is very likely less than it was in 1850.

The studies suggest—one can hardly say "prove"—the following conclusions. For whatever reasons, courts in Western industrial societies do not seem well suited to resolving certain kinds of disputes. They thus fall far short of the ideal of "justice for all," if by justice we mean a cheap, fair, effective tribunal close at hand. This, we recall, is the way tribal courts are often described. Note that we are talking here mainly about private disputes. We are not talking about great constitutional cases, environmental disputes, or major labor cases. We are talking about ordinary bread-and-butter cases, disputes between neighbors, family squabbles, small personal injury cases, actions about rent, complaints about the way the roof was fixed, or quarrels between two partners who own a car-wash business. We are talking about most business disputes—late delivery of a car load of lumber, or a bank loan gone sour. The courts are stiff, formal, and expensive. Ordinary people do not like to use them, or they find them too costly or too remote. There are good reasons, too, for business to avoid litigation. It is disruptive to go to court. A business will try to iron out difficulties without bringing in lawyers and judges whenever its relations with the other side are valuable and continuing (Macaulay, 1963).

The few studies of litigation rates have mostly come out of so-called developed countries. This makes Richard Abel's (1979) data for Kenya all the more interesting. Between 1931 and 1971, filings in the basic trial courts of Kenya declined dramatically, from 7.8 per 1,000 in 1931 (9.1 per 1,000 in 1948) to 2.9 per 1,000 in 1971. This, Abel felt, was as "expected." "Modern courts disvalue litigation, are less attractive to members of tribal societies, and are less accessible to individuals" (1979:180).

His figures, however, show that the decline was greatest in rural areas. In the cities, civil litigation rates were between two and ten times the national average. This is of course exactly the opposite of what Toharia found. Abel's explanation for the high rate in cities is that urban areas are "characterized by high population density, heterogeneity, large African and non-African populations, rapid urban migration, and significant social and cultural change" (1979:184). All well and good, but one could also describe Barcelona and Madrid in similar terms. Why the difference between Kenya and Spain? Again, the definition of "court" may be the key. People in rural Kenya do go to court, but not the courts that publish statistics. Declines in litigation rates, whether in Spain or Kenya or anywhere, occur when courts become more formal and less "popular." It is not disputes that decline, but the use of one particular kind of institution.

The evidence, then, is that many, perhaps most, disputes never go to (formal) court. Where *do* these disputes go? Some may simply evaporate. Some may turn into other forms of behavior that are less desirable (street riots, cheating at business). Some may be decided by "courts" in a broader sense. In some societies, they may go to tribal courts, which are outside official structures. Or society may evolve bypass institutions, which do the work done by courts in other societies, leaving the courts behind, high and dry so to speak. British judges, for example, resplendent in their robes and wigs, have been bypassed by dozens of "tribunals." Many key decisions come out of the tribunals, which do much of the adjudication (on town planning, rent control, and public health) in this centralized welfare state. The tribunals are not "courts" in the wig-and-robe sense, but any anthropologist would recognize them instantly as such. He or she would also recognize as courts the "administrative law courts" of the United States. And these are only the most obvious bypass institutions, the ones that most closely resemble traditional courts. "Cases" are handled by a broad range of bodies, from zoning boards to chambers of commerce.

Still, we have hardly answered the question, why formal courts lose ground, absolutely or relatively. Wolfgang Kaupen (reported in Blankenberg, 1975:312) studied litigation frequencies in Germany. The highest litigation rates, he found, were not in densely populated areas, as one might expect, but in regions with *medium* density (where there were many small business firms). Kaupen thought litigation belonged to the stage of "classical" capitalism, in which small firms compete vigorously with each other. The big oligopolies of more mature economic systems, he felt, avoided litigation. Erhard Blankenburg, on the other hand, read

Kaupen's figures differently. His own trend figures for Germany—unfortunately, they covered only the period after the Second World War—show fairly stagnant rates of litigation. Kaupen's theory demands, for confirmation, better figures and longer periods of time. More recent work by Kaupen and Langerwerf (1980) has returned to the subject in a more ambitious attempt to connect German and Belgian litigation rates with the "socioeconomic setting" in these countries.

Friedman and Percival (1976) make a somewhat different point. Policy in the United States in the 19th century (and no doubt elsewhere) pushed strongly for rapid economic growth. Litigation was not favored because people believed that too much suing might damage the economy. In a "vigorous market" people "absorb losses in the short run, and continue to trade." They do not lightly break off "commercial relationships" or "funnel transactions through courts" (Friedman and Percival, 1976:299). The costs of litigation rose in the 19th century; this discouraged people from bringing lawsuits. No one *planned* it this way, but it happened (or was allowed to happen) nevertheless. Small and medium-sized disputes were gradually frozen out of courts. People had to compromise their disputes somehow or simply swallow them—"lump it" in Felstiner's phrase (1974).

If this explanation is right, we would expect decline (or stagnation) in litigation rates in countries that moved or are moving from traditional to modern economies. At least this would be true of Western-style courts in industrial nations, their colonies, and their former colonies. Such a development would not of course be an iron law of nature; courts *might* become so efficient, so fast on the draw, that they could avoid their standard diseases. A modernizing society would have no need to make detours around them. But traditions die hard; courts find it hard to adapt. Also, judges are lawyers; they have no skills in other fields. They lack any special feel for commercial transactions and do not deal in a sure-footed way with business affairs. At one time, in England, courts used special juries of merchants in commercial cases. The practice was especially associated with Lord Mansfield in the late 18th century. But the special juries are now extinct and there is no chance of resurrecting them.

Of course, the history of the courts in any country is a complicated tale. A thesis as broad as the one proposed by Friedman and Percival can only carry us so far. It does seem true that many legal systems in the 19th century came to discourage ordinary litigation, but not absolutely by any means. We must remember, too, that we are talking about *specific* kinds of courts. Tribunals, for example, are surely courts. They too might damage ongoing, harmonious relationships, but for the most part they are not concerned with such relationships; their share of the game is administrative.

We could shed light on the inner history of courts if we knew more about the history of their rivals—arbitration, for example. It would be good to know the quantity of arbitration, also how parties feel about arbitration and how they react to the experience. An arbitrator, as we said, is an *ad hoc* judge. Arbitrators certainly do not ignore "the law," yet somehow they are less disruptive and abrasive than "real" judges. Indeed, arbitration is often used for grievances that pop up in the midst of ongoing relationships (between unions and management, for example).

So far we have accepted the negative picture of our Western courts without much question. But are these courts really so hidebound? In some ways, courts have become rather efficient, at least at the lowest levels. They have developed, or accepted, new, fast ways to help creditors collect from debtors, and they have learned or adapted techniques that fit the needs of a mass market. Millions of routine cases, in which merchants repossess goods sold on time, foreclose chattel mortgages, or garnish wages have passed through the courts (Silverman, 1980). Transactions have been handled in the mass, quickly and cheaply. Of course, these were not cases in the usual sense; they are routine and trivial, taken one by one. In the aggregate, though, they are vitally important to economic life.

Nonetheless, costs (of all sorts) effectively drove many kinds of cases out of court. For these, the chief solutions are compromise or simple avoidance. This is the situation for ordinary civil actions between parties who are social and economic equals (a dispute between neighbors, for example). Access to court is also too costly for the small man with a small or middle-sized grievance against business (a defective television set, shoddy furniture, and so on). The contingent fee makes lawsuits by middle-cass and poor persons possible, but this device, which is both old and controversial (Auerbach, 1976:43–50), only works when there is a large potential fund out of which the lawyer can be paid, as is true in personal injury cases.

Is the decline of ordinary litigation something to worry about? That is, should we care that our court system is not equipped to deal with small matters between individuals, or between consumers as individuals and businesses, or between tenants and landlords? It is hard to tell. Some scholars feel we should look on this development as part of a larger issue— access to justice (Nader 1980). Access is, or can be, a problem in any society that takes justice seriously and in which courts are expensive and rather formal. Clearly, Western courts are not a cheap, effective forum for ordinary civil actions. Whether this is a serious problem depends of course on whether there are decent alternatives.

If we look at colonial court records in the United States, especially in the first half of the 17th century, we are struck by how much these courts did, how deeply they penetrated into the life of the community.[10] In these small communities huddled on the coastline, it was almost literally true that everybody's name could be found at some point in the court records.

In three years (1633–1636) of county court records in one Virginia county, a researcher found the names of 695 different people as plaintiffs, defendants, witnesses, or applicants for registration of land patents. This was a most "impressive figure" in a "society whose adult population can be approximated at eight hundred people" (Curtis, 1977:287). The range of court matters in the colonial courts was enormous—debts, petty crimes, disputes over land, slander, wills and estates, the behavior of servants. Amounts and subjects often seem, by our reckoning, quite trivial. At least in this regard, the county courts were more like tribal courts than like the courts of modern cities. Moreover, these "courts" were not purely courts. Legislative, judicial, and administrative duties were not shut up in tight, waterproof compartments. The county courts basically governed; they did whatever the law required of local government (McCain, 1954).

Of course, society in 17th-century Virginia or Massachusetts was different from American society in the 20th century, and in dozens of ways. One difference is particularly pertinent. The colonial settlements were tiny. They lacked institutions other than courts for settling disputes. For example, colonial towns did not have full-time, professional police forces; constables and night watchmen were not "dispute settlers," which the police are on a vast scale today. Police intervene in countless crises —husbands beating wives, heads getting cracked in a barroom, neighbors playing their radios too loud, and so on. In 1650 or so, churches handled some disputes between members, but most people in the community were not church members (Konig, 1979:126–128; on the relationship between "community" and colonial litigation, see Mann, 1980; Nelson, 1981). Nor did the colonies have marriage counselors, psychiatrists, newspaper action lines (see Palen, 1979), and so on. All of these are ways of doing for everyday disputes what courts seem incapable of doing today. Hence the discussion (and research) on alternative systems of handling disputes, that is, on ways to fill in the gaps.

We have seen that there is not much evidence of rising litigation rates in the United States and other Western countries. Quite to the contrary, common, ordinary disputes are effectively frozen out of court. Yet, oddly enough, we hear shrill cries from all sides about a "crisis" of litigation, an explosion of lawsuits. The country is supposed to be suffering from some dread disease called "hyperlexis," which has "overloaded" all "legal circuits," including the courts (Manning, 1977; see also Hufstedler, 1971; Rosenberg, 1972). Hyperlexis is a sign, we are told, of a grave rip in the social fabric. But if there is no litigation explosion, why all the fuss? Perhaps there is a dramatic increase in *some* kinds of cases, while others decline, and a change in the style or behavior of courts (and ancillary institutions such as the jury) in a small but important group of cases. It is, in other words, a selective explosion. To assess this hypothesis, we turn now to studies of shifts over time in the business of courts, particularly in civil law matters.

The Business of Courts

What kind of cases do courts actually handle? Once again, our information is surprisingly weak and thin. We are somewhat in the dark even about present-day courts. Judicial statistics give little help. The states are very sloppy about gathering and publishing information; no two states classify cases the same way and the categories they use (such as "contract") are often too broad to be helpful. A handful of studies try to look at the work load of trial courts in some detail (see Wanner, 1974, 1975; Galanter, 1975), but a lot more research is needed.

Another problem stands in the way. The meager statistics do not tell us, by and large, *how* cases are handled, but this is a vital fact. It does not mean much to learn that family law cases make up x or y percent of the case load unless we know how many of these cases are actually contested. Most trial court cases (divorce, debt collection) in fact are uncontested, routine, totally perfunctory. Most tort cases drop off, by way of settlement, before reaching trial.

The dominance of the uncontested case goes back quite far in time. Laurent's (1959) study of the lower courts of Chippewa County for the late 19th and early 20th centuries shows an enormous number of default judgments. Silverman's (1980) study of Boston courts in the late 19th century draws the same conclusion. Trials have been the exception, not the rule, for a century or more in the typical trial court. Vast numbers of cases were settled out of court or processed through default or other perfunctory process. Wherry (1931) counted 1,795 trials in 1927 in the trial term of New York County's Supreme Court out of 16,675 cases disposed of. All the rest were dismissed, settled, or discontinued. Among contested cases, land cases and debt cases once predominated. In Tachau's (1978) study of the federal courts in Kentucky, 1789–1816, half of the civil cases dealt with land. Most of the rest were ordinary debt cases.[11] There has been a shift in the last century or so away from such cases, in the direction of tort, family law, and public law.

What we have so far, sketchy though it is, does not rule out the possibility that the rate of contested cases per 1,000 population has declined since, say, 1800. Certainly, there has been a decline in use of the jury in civil cases. This parallels, as we shall see, a drastic decline in jury use in criminal cases. The phrase "trial by jury" brings to mind a picture of elaborate procedures, but this can be misleading. Criminal trials (in the days before plea bargaining) were usually quick and nasty affairs; the same was probably true of civil cases. What else are we to make of the fact that in the 1780s and 1790s the county court in Davidson County (Tennessee) *averaged* 6.9 "trials" per day? (Brown, 1979:349, 373, 410).

These findings warn us to be careful. "Contested" and "tried" are themselves slippery concepts. Still, some cases do go to trial; the uproar over litigation is because of *these* cases and the way courts handle them.

Critics of litigation are often so blustery and vague that it is hard to tell exactly what is bothering them. But a message does come through, that courts are not playing by the rules any more, that they are breaking out of traditional limits, inventing novel causes of action, extending old ones outrageously, meddling in affairs that are none of their business. They thereby bring disorder and confusion into social and business life.

We will take a look, briefly, at a few areas of law in which courts seem to be moving rapidly, hacking away at inherited doctrines. We begin with tort law. In malpractice law and products liability, to take two examples, the most recent generation has been one of (legal) revolution. With regard to *amounts* of recovery, some sort of invisible cap has popped off the bottle; the same seems to be true for the doctrinal ceiling or cap that kept the scope of liability controlled. At least so it is said. Research on the size of tort recoveries is certainly feasible, and awards certainly could be compared over time if somebody had the patience to dig through old case files. I am not aware of any such studies. There are, however, a few scraps of suggestive data about awards in personal injury cases.

It seems clear that top awards in tort cases have climbed much faster than the inflation rate. (We have no systematic information about average awards.[12]) Probably no 19th-century jury ever awarded more than $50,000 to a plaintiff. A California case (in 1892) awarded $30,000; this is one of the highest I came across.[13] In modern terms, 19th-century awards were quite modest.[14] Awards continued to be rather low by modern standards far into the 20th century. In 1954, a painter—a married man with five children—lost both legs, an arm, and part of his other hand in a terrible accident in a railroad yard. The jury gave him $420,000, an amount considered a record at at the time (*NACCA Law Journal*, 1954:282). In constant dollars, such a verdict today would perhaps be worth something over a million dollars. Top awards, however, have gone far beyond this. Nobody blinks at awards of $2 or $3 million. In November 1979, a New York jury awarded almost $5 million to a child in the Bronx who suffered irreversible brain damage after an incident in the hospital. This was a medical malpractice case. In another, in 1978, a jury awarded $7.6 million to a woman whose spinal cord was destroyed by radiation (*New York Times*, 1978, 1979).

In short, the trend toward higher awards has accelerated in the last twenty years or so. It is important to keep in mind that this is not just a matter of generous juries. Attorneys ask for astronomical sums; juries award them; trial judges allow them; high courts affirm the judgments. Appellate courts have always been reluctant to set aside verdicts on the ground that damages were "excessive"; they still are reluctant. They accept amounts undreamt of even a generation ago.

The biggest awards, of course, are for awful, permanent, disabling injuries—lifetime paralysis, for example. People live on today who would have died in the 19th century, but they may need total lifetime care at staggering cost. Still, recoveries go beyond even the largest out-of-pocket costs. Awards for pain and suffering are also inflated. Pain and suffering were recognized as legitimate aspects of tort recoveries in the early 19th century; by 1850 they were taken almost for granted, but the amounts recovered were usually small. This is no longer true. Medical costs and economic loss are more or less fixed; often, it is pain and suffering, a "protean" category in the hands of shrewd lawyers (O'Connell and Simon, 1972), that makes the recovery swell.

Most important, judges' attitudes toward tort awards have changed over time. Whatever the technical theory, tort recoveries in the 19th century did not really aim for what we would consider full compensation. Nobody tried to make up in money for the misery, poverty, and suffering of a crippled life, or to make amends for as long as life still glowed in its battered shell. Piles of money never make a plaintiff whole, but today the jury will at least want to try.

The second trend, which seems equally real, is harder to show in any systematic way. This is the erosion of ceilings of doctrine. The two developments are linked. Tortfeasors have lost important defenses, and when they lose their cases, they have to pay more. But the links, let us note, are not logical or doctrinal links. No shift in doctrine really explains explosions in the *size* of awards. Doctrine lets victims win where they would have lost before, but doctrine says little about amounts. That is left to a subtle social judgment.

The doctrines that eroded dated mostly from the early 19th century. Judges in that period were eager to protect and encourage young business. It was an age of expansion of enterprise, an age that sought to promote economic growth. The legal system tried to protect and encourage new ventures (Hurst, 1956; Scheiber, 1973). Tort law was essentially a product of the industrial revolution; it was the machine (and especially the railroad engine) that mass-produced personal injuries. The new tort law was a network of rules and defenses, which insulated enterprise against lawsuits for personal injury. The fellow-servant rule, assumption of risk, contributory negligence, charitable immunity—all of these began or were revived in the 19th century (see Friedman, 1973:261–264; 409–427; Malone, 1948, 1965; Friedman and Ladinsky, 1967).

Perhaps the most important doctrine was the fault principle itself. It is a commonplace of legal history that the principle of negligence or fault replaced the older principle of absolute liability in tort. The essence of the fault principle is this. It is not enough to show that plaintiff was injured and that defendant made the injury happen. (This is itself at times a difficult problem). The plaintiff must also show that defendant was "negligent." That is, plaintiff must show that defendant's conduct fell short of some standard in his line of business or in whatever activity he was engaged in (Shearman and Redfield, 1869:5).

In this century, the defenses have been gradually eliminated. Every state abolished the fellow-servant rule and replaced it with workmen's compensation. Wisconsin and New York, just before the First World War, began the process. The immunity of charities in tort actions is virtually gone (on the process, see Canon and Jaros, 1979; but cf. Rabin, 1979). Contributory negligence and assumption of risk are fading fast. Indeed, the whole fault principle is in decay, especially in such rapidly growing fields as products liability. Absolute liability has made a comeback. A new web of doctrines is growing up—complex, difficult, and full of subtle distinctions. The general thrust is plain. This is plaintiff's law; business defendants are fighting a long, losing battle. Liability is imposed beyond anything the 19th century could imagine.

Indeed, legally speaking, liability is sometimes hooked on to rather flimsy grounds. One example will do. In *Reyes v. Wyeth Laboratories* (498 F. 2d 1264, 1974), a little girl in Texas was vaccinated against polio, as state law required. She came down with the disease and was crippled for life. Her family sued the lab that prepared the vaccine. The company tried to show it had done all it could, that no one could make a vaccine safe in every respect, that the girl was simply unlucky, the victim of an accident that strikes, say, one in a million. In 1850 or 1900—perhaps in 1950 as well—a judge would have thrown out such a case, though perhaps with regrets. But the Reyes family won. The grounds were obscure and tenuous. The company had violated a rather farfetched duty to warn ultimate users of the slight but real danger. At the end of the opinion, the judge dropped his mask. A theory of negligence hardly mattered, he said, since losses should fall (whatever the theory) on the maker, not the victim; it should be treated as a "foreseeable cost of doing business."

Malpractice law is another striking area of growth. This too is quite recent. Medical malpractice advanced swiftly after 1950, throwing doctors into panic and touching off a flurry of legislation. Other forms of malpractice—lawyer malpractice, even teacher and preacher malpractice—have sprung up. Changes in doctrine certainly help explain what happened; but here too there is obviously more to the story than doctrine.

The rise of insurance, mass production of goods, changes in the doctor-patient relationship—all these are obvious reasons for the revolution in tort law. Even more important, perhaps, are changes in attitudes toward the rights and duties of enterprise. Social change, it seems clear, directly shapes the work of courts. In the long run, the outputs of elected legislatures and the outputs of the "independent" judiciary run along amazingly parallel lines, in tort law at least. Courts are *not* tightly bound (whatever they say) by the chains of old doctrine. They may find themselves a bit constrained in manner, style, and pace, but so are legislatures. Besides, when courts expand liability in some field or other, they set off a chain reaction. New doctrine can be infectious: one plaintiff sneezes and a dozen others catch the bug. An outburst of lawsuits in turn puts pressure on courts to respond, a pressure they do not long resist when their own inner voices tell them plaintiffs are right, or when plaintiff's situation touches the heart. The cases feed on themselves. A social force and a pliable legal institution make an unbeatable combination.

Yet in certain other fields liability has shrunk, not grown, or been reduced to a formula, choking off litigation. Oddly enough, one of the best examples also comes from tort law. At one time, no type of case was more common in trial courts than industrial accidents. Workmen's compensation took almost all of these cases out of the courts. Under workmen's compensation laws, companies became absolutely liable for almost all accidents on the job. There was no need to worry about fault. The few remaining cases went mostly to a bypass institution, that is, a workmen's compensation board or industrial accident commission. Courts still had a small but important role to play as a kind of board of super-review, and they have made policy at the margins. But courts and boards are not needed to handle the overwhelming majority of accidents.

Divorce is another example. Its routinizing was a long-term process; no-fault laws have now capped off this development. Basically, no-fault ratifies a process that has gone on for almost a century, by which divorce became collusive and consensual, though still formally a dispute between husband and wife. Now cases of divorce are rare if by "case" we mean disputes that actually demand a judge's time and brains. The change here is somewhat masked because shriveled vestiges and forms still go through court.

"Fault" is going out of business in many areas, then. We have strict liability for manufacturers of defective products, divorce almost at will, strict (but limited) liability in work accidents. No-fault is making great headway, too, in auto accident law. Society is still interested in blame and in rewarding good conduct. But in the areas mentioned, society is reassessing the role of courts. The court's role is shrinking in places, and even where it is expanding (products liability), the net social result might be, in the long run, to drive cases out of court.

We have looked at the decline of ordinary business and commercial disputes in court. The general trial courts (we are not speaking here about petty courts, small claims courts, and the like) handle some criminal cases, some tort cases, and some public law cases. But there are a few cases that do represent some sort of "explosion." They break new ground. In these cases, judges seem less committed to precedent, to firmness and consistency, more willing to experiment and innovate than they were a century ago.

Changes in judicial culture are hard to prove. As we will see, there is some information at the appellate level. On the trial court level, we are left with impressions. It is dangerous to look at extremes—at "freak" cases. But these are sometimes important clues to changing attitudes. In one recent incident, a man threatened to sue a woman who stood him up on a date. Another man tried to sue his parents for malpractice in bringing him up. Grandparents have sued for the right to visit their grandchildren. A grouchy Yale graduate wanted a federal court to wipe his degree off Yale's records (*New York Times*, 1979). Most of these freak cases are thrown out of court; but not all. In one case in Minnesota, in 1972, a fourteen-year-old girl went to court to keep her parents from taking her along on a round-the-world trip; she wanted to stay behind with her friends. The judge listened and she won at least half a loaf: she could stay behind, but with her aunt.[15]

What these cases show—win or lose—is a desire to litigate on issues once beyond the pale (matters of personal life and family affairs). There is a vague, half-formed idea that courts should be able to redress any injustice, regardless of the state of prior law. These cases reach out for a new kind of judge, a more activist judge (Chayes, 1976; Galanter, Palen, and Thomas, 1979), and one does find courts that are somewhat sympathetic to the notion of justice untrammeled by strict "law." That is, if somebody asserts a claim that seems just, or sound as policy, judges feel they *should* grant relief. Doctrine or precedent must not block the way without good reason. In the Minnesota case, the judge expressed this attitude quite plainly: "surely no American seeking protection of her real, or even her pretended rights will be barred from at least posing her plea to the courts." In Weberian terms, the courts are moving toward substantive rationality.

Side by side with a decline in the ordinary case, then, may be some increase in the use of courts for the extraodinary case, but the extraordinary case is by definition uncommon. Hence this trend can coexist with stable or declining litigation rates—the Toharia thesis, in short.

Is there evidence for an increase in the big, path-breaking, unusual case? More cases are decided on constitutional grounds than was true in the past (see Kagan et al., 1977). Judicial review is clearly more common than it was a century ago or even twenty years ago. This reflects, of course, an increase in rights consciousness. There is a fresh, vivid sensitivity to human and individual rights and to the abuses of government.

Obviously, judicial review has its plusses and minusses. It is particularly good for stopping or delaying government action. A court cannot build a bridge; but it can keep one from getting built. Courts can protect and conserve; this makes them fine for caribou, but rather hard on pipelines. In any event, cases of judicial review tend to be big, consequential, and controversial. Another piece of evidence is the one clear-cut "litigation explosion"—the explosion in *federal* courts. Federal courts keep better statistics than most state courts, and there is no question that their filings are rising faster than the population is growing. Federal cases are by no means all earth-shaking, but on average they deal in bigger figures and broader issues than state court cases. Some kinds of "big case" (civil rights cases, antitrust cases) are almost exclusively federal (Grossman and

Sarat, 1975; see also Baum, Goldman, and Sarat 1978; Cavanagh and Sarat, 1980; Clark, 1981).

Another kind of case worth mentioning here is the "monster" private suit. The best examples are the great antitrust cases. What makes them unusual is their scale. They run up staggering costs—millions of dollars on either side. The amounts at stake are also staggering, hundreds of millions of dollars, even billions. These are monumental cases in still a third sense. They drag on for months or years, enhausting the judge, the lawyers, and the poor trapped jury.

The Sherman Antitrust Act was passed in 1890. Section 7 of the Act allows private lawsuits against violators. Plaintiff can recover three times actual damages. This provision for treble damages makes it easy to run up big claims, and gives plaintiffs a nice incentive to sue. But private antitrust cases were not common in the early days of the Sherman Act. By all accounts, the big jump in such lawsuits took place recently. Between 1937 and 1954, about 100 cases were filed in federal court each year. In 1974, 1,162 cases were filed, more than ten times as many (Posner, 1976:34). In 1977, there were about 1,600 (Administrative Office of the U.S. Courts, 1977:208). There have been legal and procedural changes in antitrust law, to be sure, but nothing that would adequately explain this huge increase. No doubt there are sound business reasons why it pays to bring these cases, although plaintiffs generally lose. Still, to ask for a billion dollars in damages, or the dismantling of a billion-dollar business, takes a certain amount of gall—not to mention the feeling that the judge will not shy away from drastic consequences. In an age of the "imperial judiciary," that expectation is not unjustified. Hence, this class of case may also be connected to changes in judicial culture.

It is cases like these that explain why people talk about a litigation explosion. Real litigation rates are hidden; not even scholars are sure what they are. Big cases make news. Tort cases do because damages run into millions, antitrust cases because the millions turn into billions, constitutional cases because they touch so many lives. One monster case against a great corporation takes up as much energy and time as thousands of uncontested divorces—and makes headlines too. This is the reality behind the litigation explosion. If courts find it hard to cope with case loads, it is not because of volume but because a handful of cases have inordinate appetites.

Appellate Court Studies

In one sense, there is an enormous literature on appellate courts. The bulk of American legal scholarship concerns itself with these courts and these only. But most of the literature is about doctrine; very little of it is either systematic or quantitative and almost none of it is both systematic or quantitative *and* historical. (For a picture of the appellate process in one state fifty years ago, see Harris, 1933). An exception is the study of sixteen American high courts, 1870–1970 by Kagan et al. (1977, 1978), which shows how the case loads of these courts changed over the years. A century ago, high courts heard mostly appeals in contract and property cases. Today, the center of gravity has shifted to nonmarket cases (criminal cases, tort, public law). Another aspect of this study looked at changes in judicial culture over time (Friedman et al., 1981). Judicial culture of course is not easy to measure. The study used a number of indicators, for example, citation patterns of the sixteen courts over the century. In the late 19th century, appellate courts, on the whole, stuck closely to traditional sorts of authority. They cited cases (mostly their own), state statutes, and rather narrow, technical treatises. There were no university law reviews until almost the end of the 19th century. Practically speaking, courts never cited nonlegal sources.

Appellate courts today still cite cases, statutes, and an occasional treatise. Most cases do not cite law reviews, but the percentage that does is growing. In the period 1905–1935, less than 1% of the cases (in a sample of about 2,000) cited one or more law review articles. This rose to 7.2% in 1940–1970 (11% for the decade 1960–1970). Even fewer cases cited nonlegal sources (newspapers, books about economics or politics, and so on), but for these too the habit is slowly growing (Friedman, et al., 1981; see also Merryman, 1954; 1977). The findings suggest a certain amount of change in the way judges look at their roles. A century ago, most judges held what we might call a traditional concept of judging. They felt they had to decide cases according to strict law, following principles and doctrines laid down in the past or pressed on the court by its legislature. Innovation, except in dramatic and novel instances, was not their province. This was indeed the classic common law view. The civil law idea about judges was, if anything, even more extreme in denying the judges were or ought to be creative (Goutal, 1974).

This style or attitude seems to have changed somewhat over the years, as citation patterns suggest. Courts have moved toward what we might call the realist concept of judging—more skeptical about rules and principles, less deferential to precedent, more concerned with a decision's social consequences. Other indicators, too, point to this evolution in judicial culture. There is, for example, a greater tendency among judges to dissent or to file separate concurring opinions (Canon and Jaros, 1970:175; Glick and Vines, 1973: Ducat and Flango, 1976:58). In the U.S. Supreme Court, the unanimous opinion seems well on its way to extinction. No state court is as extreme, but the percentage of non-unanimous cases is growing almost everywhere. Concurrences and dissents, particularly when they get a bit touchy, personal, or raucous, strongly suggest that there is no one right legal answer, that judges' personal values, not to mention outside social forces, influence decision making. Hence they blur or impair the traditional image of courts.

It is easy to exaggerate how "traditional" judges were in the 19th century, and how "realist" they are today. Some 19th-century judges made policy rather boldly. It was these judges who inspired Karl Llewellyn to concoct his theory of "period-style." Llewellyn (1950, 1960) divided the work of American judges into three periods. The first period (early 19th century) was the period of "grand style." In this period, judges boldly and freely made use of the basic principles underlying the common law, building up a sensible, practical body of law. In the latter part of the 19th century, "grand style" gave way to "formal style"—rigid, conceptual, legalistic, and doggedly faithful to precedent. Llewellyn saw (or hoped for) a return to grand style in the 20th century.

Conceivably, one could test this theory empirically. Llewellyn himself did not test it and it remains a mere guess. The evidence for "grand style" is the work of a handful of famous judges. Whether their lesser contemporaries were also "grand" is a question. There is evidence for the shift to what we called the realist style between 1870 and 1970. Changes in tort law point in the same direction. This shift takes place quite raggedly, however. Judges today still express rather conservative, formalistic attitudes. For example, they draw a line between "law" and "policy" and insist that policy is only for legislatures (Daynard, 1971; Glick, 1971). Lawyers rarely argue "social facts" or present empirical data to courts. This is partly because they feel that lawyers who push too hard with this kind of material would be "chastised by the judges" (Glick and Vines, 1973:79).

Another confounding factor is what we might call the local judicial culture. By any standard there are marked and rather mysterious differences among states—mysterious because the usual variables (urbanization, party politics, and so on) cannot account for them. Glick and Vines (1973) studied dissent rates in the highest state courts at three points in time: 1916, 1941, and 1966. In 1916, the dissent rate among states ranged from zero to 36.5%. The zero percent was in Massachusetts. Nebraska led the pack, somewhat surprisingly. Massachusetts was still rated the lowest in 1966; its dissent rate was a pitiful 1.2%. Michigan was now the most dissent-prone (46.5%). As these figures show, the *range* has increased. So has dissent in general, but variations among states are more striking than variations between periods, at least for the years Glick and Vines studied. The patterns for particular states are also striking (and baffling). In 1916, New York's dissent rate was 34.1% in 1941 it was 15.8%; in 1966, 41%. Clearly, there are many factors at work, probably including state judicial traditions. In some high courts, there is and has been an understanding, as a Virginia judge put it in 1923, that "we are expected to agree and not to disagree" (Morris, 1975:82).

Still, there clearly is *some* relationship between dissent rates and judicial structure. Dissent rates tend to be highest in states with intermediate appellate courts, and in which the highest court has power to choose its own cases (Glick and Vines, 1973:81). This factor also helps explain details of court business and judicial culture. Of course, changes in structure do not take place at random. States with big populations are the ones that feel forced to rearrange their court systems, since otherwise caseloads would become intolerable. Most of these states, in turn, are urban and industrial. Typically, they deal with heavy case loads by creating a new layer of intermediate courts and making these the end of the road for most appeals. They also tend to give their top court more freedom—or total freedom—to choose cases. Usually the two changes go together (Kagan et al., 1978). In 1870, in almost all states, any litigant had the right to appeal to the state's highest court. By the 1970s, most states with big populations had changed this policy. The Supreme Court in a state like California sits on top of the judicial pyramid with great freedom to pick and choose its cases. It will select cases that are (in its view) consequential and important. These cases are the ones most prone to dissents and concurrences. They also tend to be something other than routine commercial or property cases. The California Supreme Court hears many constitutional cases, especially about defendants' rights, and other public law matters. It is plausible to suppose that judges who spend all their time on "important" cases come to have a different perspective than their brethren in small states (see Beiser, 1973) who have to take any appeal that comes along. Certainly, behavior changes. When the North Carolina Supreme Court got docket control, and a buffer of intermediate courts, its opinions grew longer, the case load dropped, and dissents became more frequent (Groot, 1971).

In any event, in federal and big-state appellate courts, judges seem to be turning away from formal rationality in the direction of substantive rationality. They are blurring the line between "legal" and "nonlegal" premises of decision. It is easy to exaggerate the movement, however. And we must also remember how easy it is to confuse style and substance in appellate decisions. Formal opinions do not necessarily betray the grounds that actually lie behind them.

Does the development we describe go beyond style? Constitutional law suggests that it does. There is, quite clearly, a dramatic rise in judicial review. It was uncommon before the Civil War, but has grown steadily ever since (Field, 1941a, b; Nelson, 1947; Hickman, 1954; Swindler, 1969:344–345). Of course, the need is also great. Government does more than ever before and this generates demands for external control.

Tort law also suggests that the new style of judicial work goes beyond form. A recent study looked at patterns of adoption of new doctrine in tort law over time and found a quickened pace of innovation in the 20th century (Canon and Baum, 1980). There is, we suspect, a general retreat from formalism.

Criminal Law

Modern legal systems draw a sharp line between criminal law and the rest of the law. The line, of course, is more than a matter of theory. Criminal justice has its own doctrines and procedures, sometimes even its own courts. Trend studies, on the whole, stick to one or the other, criminal or civil. The historical literature on criminal courts and their work is quite flimsy. Walker (1980), in a general account of the history of criminal justice, spends only a few pages on what happens in courtrooms. There is some material on the colonial period (e.g., Goebel and Naughton, 1944; Greenberg, 1974; Spindel, 1981), a few studies on the 19th and early 20th centuries (Williams, 1959; Monkkonen, 1975; Hindus, Hammett and Hobson, Hindus, 1980; Friedman and Percival, 1981; Ferdinand, 1981); and large gaps everywhere. Most of the literature is unsystematic; rigorous or quantitative studies can be counted on one's fingers (with fingers left over). There is also a small literature on Great Britain and on other countries. We will confine our discussion to the United States, with some references to British experience. Even so, the literature touches on more themes than we can handle here. We will discuss a few of them.

The first theme is the shift from *private* to *public* enforcement. By this we mean that the state has taken over more and more of the job of catching criminals and running them through court. The state pays for the process and calls the tune; the role of the private citizen fades into the background.

British criminal justice, at the beginning of the 19th century, represented the opposite extreme. Ordinary criminal prosecution depended almost entirely on private prosecutors (Kurland and Waters, 1959; Philips, 1977: chap. 4; Tobias, 1979:117–128). If a man was caught stealing hams from a butcher, it was the butcher who prosecuted. If the butcher decided not to prosecute, or dropped the case for any reason, that was the end of the matter. It cost money to prosecute, and this burden too fell on the butcher. A system of this sort obviously discouraged poor people from using criminal courts to punish people who stole from them or assaulted them. During the 19th century, the British gradually reformed the system to remedy this failing. Prosecutions were subsidized and the public role in enforcement of the penal code increased. Still, to this day, the prosecutor in England is technically "always a particular named person," and it is a dogma of English law that "anyone may prosecute" (Jackson, 1971:84–85).

Private prosecution was not the norm in the United States.[16] Even in the colonial period, prosecution was carried out by *public* officers. Indeed, this was one way in which American criminal justice, at an early stage, deviated from its English model. The prosecuting officer was called the district attorney or state's attorney. The practice may have begun in New Amsterdam (later New York) under the Dutch, who of course were free from the peculiarities of English law (they had their own). Still, the Dutch inheritance in colonial law was otherwise obliterated. The district attorney survived, flourished, and spread, which shows that the office filled a social need.

The shift from a private to a public prosecutor paid by the state is part of a larger trend: the professionalization of criminal justice. In 1800, it would be fair to say that the system was run by amateurs, people who did not make a living out of criminal justice. There were no police forces, no public defenders, no full-time prosecutors. The grand jury (made up of laymen) set the process in motion by returning bills of indictment, and the process usually ended when the jury (more laymen) convicted or acquitted the defendant. The judge was a professional, to be sure, but he probably spent only part of his time on criminal cases. The lawyer for the state no doubt practiced law on the side. As for the defendant, typically he had no lawyer at all. In England before the 18th century, the defendant was not even allowed to have counsel (Langbein, 1978:263). The police themselves were basically a 19th-century invention (see Lane, 1967; Richardson, 1974; Miller, 1977; Fogelson, 1978). A rather haphazard collection of constables and night watchmen guarded the cities and enforced the laws (if anybody did). Amateurs even played a part in catching criminals. Any fan of Western movies knows about the posse. In England, a victim of robbery might raise a "hue and cry," that is, call generally on the bystanders to chase and catch a thief.

The layman is in full retreat in modern law. Some states have stripped the grand jury of most of its functions.[17] Prosecutors, especially in the cities, are full-time professionals. The defendant's lawyer is also probably a full-time professional—either a public defender or an attorney who specializes in criminal defense. The jury has the merest sliver of its former role. Every city has a full-time police department. Other professionals work throughout the system—social workers, probation and parole officers, psychologists, ballistics experts, and so on. Most of these roles were unknown a century ago.

The long, slow decline of trial by jury is part of the shift to a more professional system. On the surface, the picture is clear. Trial by jury was at one time the norm. Bench trials were rare and unimportant before this century. Few states allowed a defendant to waive a jury. But in the 20th century, this "right" became generally available (Bond, 1927:699; Kalven and Zeisel, 1966:22–30). The main alternative to the jury, however, is the guilty plea. These pleas have been common for more than a century. In New York state, in 1839, they accounted for a quarter of the felony dispositions. The percentage rose to about half by 1850. By the 1920s, the guilty plea was even more dominant; it accounted for 88% of the convictions in New York City, 85% in Chicago, 70% in Dallas, Texas. It was common even in rural areas—74% of the convictions in rural counties in New York state and 58% in rural Georgia stemmed from guilty pleas

(Moley, 1929:163–168; see Jackson, 1937 for data on England). In the 1970s, guilty pleas accounted for as many as 90% of all conviction in some jurisdictions.

Why do defendants plead guilty? Some plead guilty because they *feel* guilty. Or their case is hopeless and they want it over quickly. But a far more important explanation is plea bargaining. The term covers a number of practices. What these have in common is the guilty plea entered in exchange for some benefit or promise. The prosecutor (sometimes the judge) agrees to drop charges, recommend or give a lighter sentence, grant probation, and so on.

Studies of the history of plea bargaining have begun to appear only recently (Wishingrad, 1974; Heumann, 1975; Alschuler, 1979; Friedman, 1979). These studies show that plea bargaining is at least a century old and probably older. There was, for example, plea bargaining in the Superior Court of Alameda County (and in other California counties) from the very first years this court began business in 1880. Between 1880 and 1910, about 14 percent of the felony defendants in Alameda County changed their pleas from not guilty to guilty; about half of these changed their pleas to guilty of fewer or lesser charges. This was done with the consent of the prosecution and are unmistakable examples of plea bargaining (Friedman and Percival, 1981:176).

There was also a good deal of what Milton Heumann (1975) has called "implicit" bargaining, though this is somewhat harder to show. Implicit plea bargaining takes place when a defendant pleads guilty without an explicit promise or deal, but knowing (or assuming) that better deals go to those who "cooperate" and spare the public the bother and expense of a trial. Defendants who plead guilty will get lighter sentences than stubborn ones who hold out for trial (and lose). Of course, there is always *some* hope of acquittal, while a guilty plea means certain conviction. There has to be some "payment" to induce a guilty plea. No doubt defendants do believe and have believed in this "paymnent." Occasionally, even the judge speaks openly about giving "credit" (that is, leniency) in return for a guilty plea (Friedman, 1979). Mostly, of course, implicit bargaining leaves no traces. High rates of guilty pleas, however, strongly suggest implicit bargaining, and these rates have risen dramatically over the years.

But why is there bargaining at all? How can we explain it? The best explanation may be that there is nothing much to explain (at least in a common-law system) (see Langbein, 1979, on Germany). Plea bargaining is an effect, and a rather natural one, of professionalization (but cf. Mather, 1979a; Haller, 1979). Trial by jury is a crude, amateurish way of sifting the guilty from the innocent. At one time there was no better way. Even routine cases went before a jury. This was the case in England, as Langbein (1978) has shown; it was also the case in the United States.

Trial by jury evokes a particular image—a dramatic struggle between rival lawyers, a battle of wits with each side using all the tricks of the trade. A shrewd and dedicated lawyer protects the defendant's rights. This image, it hardly needs to be said, is a romantic exaggeration. Most trials in 1800 or 1850 were not like this at all. The typical trial was a quick, slap-dash affair; it was arguably little better than a plea-bargaining session as far as defendants' rights were concerned. In England, for example, in the 17th and 18th centuries, juries were not selected case by case. A single jury typically decided a whole series of of cases, in "batches, with extraordinary rapidity" (Langbein, 1978:274–277). This remained more or less true in the 19th century for the typical case, and for parts of the United States as well. Cases sampled from the 1890s in Leon County, Florida (Tallahassee), show remarkably similar practices (Friedman and Percival, 1981:194).

The situation, then, in criminal justice can be compared to the situation in civil courts. Routine cases get routine treatment. The big criminal cases usually go before a jury, and are like big, contested civil cases. Plea-bargained cases are like the default cases that march through trial courts in droves. A "routine" case, of course, may be routine only as a *case*—hours and hours of painful negotiation may lie behind an uncontested divorce that takes up ten minutes of the judge's time.

There was and is what we might call a two-faced system of criminal justice (like the double standard in civil justice). The average or typical criminal trial is no trial at all; it is an administrative procedure or a deal hammered out by lawyers. Some deals are elaborate, some are perfunctory. An important case means a carefully crafted bargain. A dull, ordinary case—a nineteen year-old from a slum neighborhood caught holding up a gas station—gets perfunctory treatment, especially if an overworked public defender handles the case. Routinization goes far back in time; but in the days before the professionals, it was the trial itself that was routinized. The old-time trials, like plea bargains today, do not pass strict tests of due process. Careful sifting of evidence, meticulous concern for defendants' rights—this was and is saved for the big case, the exceptional case. On the other hand, it is from these big cases that the public gets its idea of what criminal trials are "really" like. The information is decidedly misleading. The everyday case was and is buried in obscurity.

We saw in the last section that some aspects of civil justice have been atrophying while others suffer from elephantiasis. One can make a rather similar point about criminal justice. Indeed, the point almost cries out to be made. On the one side we hear howls of outrage about courts coddling criminals, judges who care more for murderers than their victims, dangerous people let loose because of clever technicalities. On the other hand, we hear anguished protests that criminal justice is not justice at all, that due process is a joke, that the presumption of innocence is consistently ravished. Both sides can be right.

Although plea bargaining rates and guilty pleas have risen dramatically, other indicators suggest close attention to defendants' rights. To take one example, the assertion of constitutional rights in criminal trials has clearly risen over the years. There were about 100 criminal appeals in Alameda County, California, between 1870 and 1910. Hardly any of the cases, three or four at most, raised constitutional issues, state or federal (Friedman and Percival, 1981:283; also see Sherrill, 1930:33, 36–42). But today, criminal cases make up a high percentage of the case load of state supreme courts—about 30%, for example, in Illinois and California. And many of these raise constitutional issues. In California, between 1940 and 1970, over half of the criminal appeals in the Supreme Court posed issues of procedural due process (54.3%). Constitutional issues were prominent in criminal appeals in other states, too (Kagan et al., 1977:147–148).

The Warren court expanded the rights of defendants and forced these rights on the states. The Warren court cases gave defendants more chances; they also gave the defendant the right to a lawyer, who could take advantage of these chances.[18] The new constitutional cases were mainly federal. In the 19th century, on the other hand, federal courts played a negligible role in American criminal justice. They handled a few cases of tax cheating, smuggling, mail fraud and illegal immigration, and little else. The Mann Act, motor vehicle theft laws, and prohibition swelled the total in the 1920s. But the increase in rights-consciousness on the state level is much more than a matter of federal pushing. Some states (particularly in the south) have dragged their feet, but others have been only too eager to follow the federal lead or even to lead on their own, making use of their own constitutions.

Roscoe Pound (1930) complained about the "hypertrophy" of procedure in the late 19th century. Criminal cases (he claimed) were reversed on trivial, technical grounds; legalism had run wild. Pound had little or no systematic evidence of "hyperthrophy," though it was easy to find examples here and there. "Hypertrophy" (if there was such a thing) would be a sign of a bifurcated system, in which a few, highly visible cases enjoy full legalistic treatment and the rest are disposed of in a quick, routine way. Some courts did have the habit of reversing many criminal appeals. But few cases were appealed to begin with. In Alameda County, 1870–1910, about one of seven defendants convicted by a jury appealed. The percentage today is much higher—not surprisingly, since free counsel is often available and defendant has nothing to lose. If it becomes easier to appeal, we would expect the percentage of reversals to decline. Some studies have indeed shown declines in the reversal rate between, say, 1850 and 1930 (Vernier and Selig, 1928; Kimball, 1965). Unfortunately, we do not have have much in the way of recent figures.

In a classic essay, Herbert Packer (1968:149) distinguished between two "models" of criminal justice—the "crime control" model and the "due process" model. The difference is one of emphasis. To crime control people, the main job of criminal justice is deterring criminals, while due process people worry about fairness and the rights of defendants. The struggle between the "models" is a continuing theme in the history of criminal justice.

Packer was thinking mostly of the United States and mostly of appellate court doctrine. The founding fathers had worried about King George, and criminal justice as a tool to destroy dissent. Criminal justice has indeed often been the vehicle for repression. The Bill of Rights was, to a remarkable degree, a miniature code of criminal procedure, and much of the history of criminal justice in the United States is, in the 20th century, a history of how these rights have been more and more elaborated and infused with more finely grained notions of what makes process fair.

But the rarefied "rights" of defendants are one piece in a big jigsaw puzzle. Criminal justice, in reality, is harsh and complex. The real world includes police brutality, plea bargaining, slapdash public defenders, and crowded, subhuman prisons. There is also a long history of criminal justice (so to speak) outside the law—vigilantes and lynch mobs, for example. Formal legality in this country means that stern, summary justice is difficult to achieve *inside* the law. Other countries are not so squeamish. In England, Star Chamber won for itself an unenviable name. In 18th-century Mexico, there was the "acordada," which dispensed swift, efficient, final justice to bandits (MacLachlan, 1974). Special tribunals, states of siege, courts martial—there is no end of examples. Depending on circumstances, culture, traditions, the sensibilities of the legal profession, and the politics of the situation, governments will be more or less open to suppressing opposition through *legal* forms. The Soviet Union prefers trials; Argentina prefers to make people "disappear." All systems are two-faced, but in some the second face is more hideous than in others.

Bifurcated systems have both instrumental and symbolic functions in criminal justice. Douglas Hay (1975) explored the subject in a remarkable essay on English criminal law in the 18th century (see also Thompson, 1975). The criminal justice system, Hay argues, was "critically important" to English society. It maintained "bonds of obedience and deference"; it legitimized the "structure of authority which arose from property" and in turn protected and sustained that structure. How did criminal justice perform these tasks? Property crimes, mostly theft, dominated criminal justice. Theft could be, and often was, treated very severely. A person could hang for stealing. This severity served the interests of people who owned property. Yet the legal system was also sometimes cautious and legalistic; it showed a "punctilious attention to forms." This gave out the message "that those administering and using the laws submitted to its rules." The very inefficiency and "absurd formalism" of law was "part of its strength and ideology" (Hay, 1975:33).

Still another aspect of the system was the space it left for discretion and mercy. The terror of the gallows was tempered by mercy and pardon, part of a "tissue of paternalism." The "peculiar genius" of the law "allowed a prosecutor to terrorize the petty thief and then command his gratitude." This "encouraged loyalty to the king and the state" (Hay, 1975:48–49).

Hay's essay is an invitation to look at the *kinds* of crime a legal system punishes, as indicators of what that society (or its leaders and elites) consider dangerous, what values they want to protect, and what behavior they are anxious to control. In England, during the period Hay studied, and in the first half of the 19th century as well, there was enormous emphasis on theft and related crimes. In the United States, in the colonial period, there was heavy stress on crimes against morality. In Massachusetts Bay, in the 17th century, fornication was the most commonly prosecuted crime. The colony began as a small, tightly-knit, theocratic society; its courts punished, by the hundreds, men and women charged with sex outside of marriage, or blasphemy, idleness, and failure to go to church (Nelson, 1967; Friedman, 1974; Hindus, 1977; an important revision of Nelson's work is Hartog, 1976). In the 19th century, in booming, enterprise-minded America, theft and other property crimes moved to center stage, just as they had in England.

Class conflict and class domination can be used to explain why English law would emphasize property crimes so much (and so neglect crimes of violence and crimes against morality). What is particularly interesting is seeing how the work load of criminal courts changed in the course of the 19th century. Friedman and Percival, in an unpublished study of the central criminal courts of London, looked at a sample of serious crimes tried in the 19th century. At the beginning of the century, the distribution of offenses was what one might expect from reading Hay. Overwhelmingly, defendants were accused of crimes against property. Of the cases in 1810, 86.1% fell into this category; only 11.1% were crimes against the person, 1.9% public order crime, and less than 1% were crimes against morality. In 1840, one crime—larceny—accounted for 79.4% of the major prosecutions in this metropolitan system!

The picture was quite different in 1900. The criminal justice system no longer played a single note so relentlessly. Crimes against property had fallen to 54.3% of the total; crimes against the person were now 31% of the case load, crimes against morality, 13.8%.[19] There had been, of course, changes in the governing law. England lowered its age of consent. This criminalized sexual behavior that had not been taken seriously before. But noting this fact merely pushes the inquiry back one step. Presumably, changes in social structure and social ideology that affected criminal case loads were also at work on Parliament.

There is no obvious explanation for the trend. The law was perhaps more responsive to middle-class interests and morality. In the 18th century, the landed gentry and the merchant class controlled the legal system. It operated for their benefit. British society was transformed, however, in the course of the 19th century. The franchise was extended, and the middle class gained considerable power. The legal system (including, of course, criminal justice) was still class-bound, but it responded to a richer, more varied, more complex set of interests. It aimed to protect not only property but also bourgeois morality. It abhorred violence, even among members of the lower orders, which hardly troubled the law in the 18th century. To explain the system in 1900, we need to call back the ghost of Emile Durkheim; Marx (or at least vulgar Marx) is no longer enough.

These are guesses, to be sure. We need more information. The studies are few and are hard to compare with each other. Comparisons, even between courts in the same country, suffer because jurisdiction refuses to sit still. Offenses move from one court to another, or higher or lower in the scale of courts. When we talk about American colonial law, for example, we are talking about courts that dealt with both serious and petty crimes (crimes that only the lowest courts, police and justice courts, handle today). In some ways, then, colonial courts are best compared to modern felony courts, in some ways to justice courts and police courts. Our data from 19th-century America comes from courts that handled serious crime. Literature on the lower courts—police courts, justice courts—is slim indeed.[20]

The criminal courts have had their own version of the litigation explosion. Here too, there are serious problems of measurement. We can make the explosions as large as we like—by counting traffic offenses, for example. But most of these are "cases" only in the sense that a no-fault divorce or a repossession of a TV set are "cases." If we stick to serious crimes (murder, armed robbery, deadly assault, rape, burglary), it seems clear enough that the number of cases in court has increased sharply, at least since the end of the Second World War. Very likely, an increase in the true crime rate underlies this increase in the business of criminal courts. Crimes rates themselves are notoriously hard to measure, but the evidence, crude as it is, points in a single direction. Serious crime declined in the late 19th century, rose slowly in the 20th until about the middle of the century, then took off in an almost demonic fashion (Ferdinand, 1967; Lane, 1969; Gurr and Grabosky, 1976; on homicides, see Lane, 1979:chaps. 4 and 5).[21]

The increase in serious crime does crowd the courts, and while crowded dockets do not explain why plea bargaining started, it does explain why it is so useful today. Overloading also gives weight to the movement to "decriminalize"—to get drunkenness, prostitution, non-canonical sex between consenting adults, and minor drug crimes out of the courts. After all, if we chase out these victimless offenses, courts can spend more time on "real" crime. But obviously more is involved. Some victimless crimes were never seriously prosecuted. The movement to get them off the books is a movement to legitimize behavior more than it is to ease the burden on courts or prevent these acts from being punished. In this regard, decriminalization is part of a trend toward making criminal justice more "rational," more in tune with "modern times" and less "hypocritical."

SUMMARY

We have discussed a grand melange of studies covering different periods and vastly different kinds of "courts," lower and higher, trial and appellate, civil and criminal, in all sorts of societies and settings. Is there any way to sum up what we found? It would be too much to expect simple formulas to hold true. Close inspection is likely to reveal all sorts of leaks in any general propositions. But overall trends are worth noting.

First of all, there is a definite flight among modern courts away from formal rationality in Weber's sense and in the direction of substantive rationality. Formalism and legalism are losing their grip. Medieval law was a maze of legal fictions, a wonderland of technical rules. Even in the 19th century, courts were "legalistic," with stubborn emphasis on precedent, craft, legal logic. Conceptual arguments and technical formulas are not likely to persuade or influence contemporary courts. Even the most conservative court today seems broad-minded by comparison with courts of the past. And at least some courts tend to look toward social and moral norms (as the courts conceive them) for premises of decision. It is not enough that a rule or a doctrine is "law"; it must also make good sense or good policy or both. The tendency seems particularly strong in the United States, and particularly in the federal courts. Creeping "activism," however, has reared its head in other places as well. It is an age of rationalism, not an age of tradition, ritual, and ceremonies. Judges (and people in general) look on law as *instrumental*, that is, as a man-made tool used to achieve human ends (Friedman, 1969). People feel similarly about the work of the courts.

This general hypothesis has to be qualified in a number of regards. First of all, in some ways courts are more, not less, legalistic. On the criminal side, the rights of criminal defendants are taken more seriously than they were a century ago. Hope of acquittal, or for dismissal on technical grounds, burns brighter today than ever before. There is a massive, technical body of rules about defendants' rights.

On both the civil and the criminal side, we have a bifurcated system. For 90% or more of people accused of crime, "rights" are clipped and bypassed in reality. Most civil cases are routine. A few are big, carefully crafted, and demand enormous amounts of time and energy.

In general, we must not confuse substance and style. Style today is rationalistic. Modern law does not easily tolerate fictions. This is not because of absurd results (they were never absurd), but because legal fictions look bizarre and are out of place in an instrumental world of law. It is the technique that has gone out of style; the underlying doctrines often survive.[22]

We should, probably, draw a line between macro- and micro-evolution. No doubt there are massive, long-term trends. In the long course of history, adjudication moved from an informal style (we might call it tribal style) to formal rationality. Some sort of high water mark may have been reached in the late 19th century. The style has now receded, more or less, in favor of substantive rationality.

Styles of legal reasoning are not matters of accident. They depend on theories of legal legitimacy that prevail within a society. In some systems (we can call them "closed"), courts can legitimately use only a fixed, finite set of premises in their reasoning. The extreme example would be a sacred-law system, with a single sacred text which is the only legitimate starting point for legal reasoning. Since judges cannot actually solve all legal problems by deducing meaning from a text (especially when the text is centuries old), courts in closed systems find themselves stretching and straining, twisting meanings, behaving legalistically—indulging in Talmudic reasoning, to use an appropriate phrase. The classic common law was also, in a way, a closed system. Reasoning under Civil Law codes has elements, too, of this style. In all these systems we find legalism because society denies to courts the right to add openly to the stock of premises (Friedman, 1975; see also Wetter, 1960).

The evolution in the United States has been generally away from the style of a closed system toward substantive rationality in word and deed. But it would be rash to consider this a "natural" or inevitable development. There is no single, uniform line of development. Nonet and Selznick (1978) express the hope—or belief—that our legal system is moving toward a more "responsive" stage. That might be true for some parts of it—the Supreme Court, perhaps. But some subsystems may be heading in the opposite direction. There is, after all, a push to control official discretion through more and tighter "rules." No one can say that closed systems are always less just than open systems. And the Supreme Court manages to combine substantive rationality, responsiveness, and an adherence to the Constitution, a closed set of premises if there ever was one.

Assessing the Courts

American courts are controversial. They stir up mischief and they seem to be doing too much. This is the theme of a chorus of critics. Our survey has shown that some of the complaints rest on mythology. Others are unjustified because they pin the tail on the wrong donkey. Courts are not independent, autonomous bodies; they are in and of society. Social influence on courts is constant, universal, and so obvious that the point is, or ought to be, banal—yet it is amazing how often critics (and defenders) of American courts miss the point.

For example, those who gripe at the way courts meddle in government affairs, in race relations, business matters, moral issues and so on, tend to forget that Congress and the state legislatures are at least partly responsible. Civil rights cases, a sizeable and controversial class of cases in federal courts, barely existed before the 1960s. The *Brown* decision and what came after encouraged a cycle of social change. But Congress, too, joined in. New civil rights legislation is the immediate source of most of the civil rights work in the courts. Also, laws do not and cannot create court cases; they are prerequisites at most. The social demand so palpable in civil rights cases was not created by courts; it exists out there in society.

Courts also respond to internal pressures. Courts are more than judges sitting on a bench. They are organizations and have organizational structure (Eisenstein and Jacob, 1977; see also Jacob, chapter 8, and Feeley and Lazerson, chapter 9). Appellate courts sit in panels. Group dynamics accounts for some of their behavior. Courts also have relationships with the outside world. Internal structure and external relations may explain certain peculiarities in the way courts move and in the way doctrine is shaped, at least in its formal aspects. Martin Shapiro (1964) has suggested that courts will naturally move "incrementally." Friedman (1967) put forward the idea that judicial rules tend to become quantitative, objective, and hard and fast over time. This is because objective rules help protect courts from challenge, from demands for definition, and thus from uncertainty and endless litigation. Courts as organizations have become more complex and have had to respond to a more and more complex environment. Demands from outside are sometimes impossible to meet, are contradictory, or pose dangers to the organization. Organizations try to avoid trouble; they build routines and spin cocoons around themselves.[23]

The message here is that a longer view of courts, together with an organizational perspective, tempers the notion that the institutions are running amok. Yet this is not, of course, the whole story. Not every court is "incremental," timorous, and withdrawn like some of the European systems. There really are "activist" courts, of the kind that so outrage legal conservatives. This is no surprise, even from an organizational perspective. After all, studies of organizations and bureaucracies lead us to expect red tape and timidity, but also a certain amount of imperialism, struggles for turf, and so on.

More important, "activism" in courts confronts "activism" in government—that vast, powerful, blind, sometimes ruthless Leviathan. It is true that judicial power now extends into nooks and crannies where one never saw it before—the insides of schools, clubs, prisons, and hospitals, for example. Some cases are startling and innovative; some try to stretch due process into unexpected territory. This is no simple grab for power. After all, it runs parallel to (and reacts against) an even greater extension of power and range by government in general. Executive and legislature have gone into places where they never dared set foot a century ago. Power does corrupt and abuse is real enough. Society needs all the watchdogs it can get.

The final point is this. Over the years, the boundary between the public and the private domain has blurred and is tending to vanish. The line between "law" and "non-law" is similarly smudged. If courts turn their backs on formal rationality, it is partly because formal rationality depends on crisp, sharp definition of "legal" norms (as opposed to social or ethical ones). When criminal justice is professionalized, this means, among other things, that the norms that determine decisions are professional, not merely legal. Even in civil cases, the pretrial stage threatens to eclipse the formal trial stage (witness the rise of discovery process). "Non-law" does not mean lay rule in other words; it may mean bringing to bear a wider, richer body of expert norms.

In any event, our generation finds it harder and harder to draw the line between law and non-law. Also, the doings and achievements of a few exceptional courts mask the real place of courts in modern society, compared to, say, a century ago. Other lawmakers have stepped up production, as far as we can tell, far more than the courts. A century ago, a single fat volume held the statutes of a typical state. Administrative regulation was rudimentary. There were no zoning ordinances, architectural controls, elevator inspection rules, wool labeling requirements. Tax law was a tiny chip compared to today. The total volume of law in society, however one measures it, has grown enormously. The relative position of courts may have actually diminished.

Nonetheless, courts are powerful institutions. As far ahead as we can see (which is not very far), they will probably stay that way. This is true even of the formal, traditional courts. Over the last century or so, events in society built up the power of these courts and created a constituency for them. That constituency gets larger and larger. In a sense, it now includes the whole country. Everybody belongs in some way to some group that is a potential litigant. Most people do not go to court themselves, yet their lives have been touched, and deeply, by litigation in which they were a hidden or silent party. Indeed, the activist role of courts has helped drive away "ordinary" cases. Courts are more specialized than they were a century ago. They are still quite central in this society. The exact details are peculiar to the United States. Still, the social conditions that gave rise to this development are far from unique. The court customs of the American tribe may well spread throughout the world, like Hollywood movies or Coca-Cola.

NOTES

1. Some of the literature is valuable, of course. Charles Warren's (1922) classic work on the United States Supreme Court, though about sixty years old, is still worth reading for its careful attention to the social context in which the court worked. Good state court histories are exceptionally rare, but see Bond (1928) and Dimond (1960). For England, see Stevens (1978).

2. William Felsteiner (1974:63) makes a similar distinction between "adjudication" and "mediation." He also distinguishes two types of society— the technologically complex rich society (TCRS) and the technologically simple poor society (TSPS). The TSPS is organized around families or clans. Mediation suits it better than it suits the TCRS. Mediation depends for its success on "shared experience," which, in complex, pluralistic societies, the parties probably do not have to the right degree. As a group or community grows in size, mediation yields to adjudication, which becomes "the dominant form of dispute processing." For any particular dispute, we are not likely to find "occupants of specific social positions" who know and understand the point of view of the parties, who are aware of their personal history. But without this knowledge, it is hard to do an effective job of suggesting "acceptable outcomes." Adjudication is the only answer.

3. So, too, is the jury, which does not give reasons, decides mysteriously and privately, and (to Weber) resembles an oracle (Rheinstein, 1954:79).

4. A small, stateless society may be, in fact, violent and full of conflicts, which certainly implies that its institutions are not such a raving success at keeping harmony among members. Moreover, "systematic continuity" is not the same as peace. A society can be both stable (in general structure) and unstable in particular role-incumbents; there are, for example, governments plagued by palace coups (Moore, 1980; see also Yngvesson and Mather, chapter 3).

5. In historical or anthropological terms, an arbitrator is a full-fledged judge. He is, after all, a third party with power to decide cases brought to him, and he can back up decisions with force. Yet in the United States, for example, people draw a sharp distinction between arbitrators and judges. In general, when modern writers talk about judges and courts, they are thinking of specific traditions and definitions.

6. Civil matters filed in courts of first instance rose from 56,485 in 1906 to 82,983 in 1969, but this modest growth did not keep up with population growth. The number per 1,000 population actually declined slightly, from 2.92 per 1,000 to 2.53 per 1,000. There were many fluctuations along the way, but from 1950 on, the figures show remarkably little change; what change there was, was in a downward direction (Toharia, 1974:171–172).

7. Toharia (1974:211) also shows figures that demonstrate a sharp decline in Italian litigation since 1900. Over the last century or so, German litigation rates have declined, while Belgian rates have risen (though quite slowly in the 20th-century), as shown by Kaupen and Langerwerf (1980).

8. Langerwerf (1978), who found a rise in rates per 1,000 in Belgian courts, also ascribes the increase to the large number of divorces in recent times.

9. Toharia (1974:173) also has figures on contested matters, compared to uncontested. The figures are somewhat sketchy. There were 1.44 contested cases per 1,000 population in 1906 and 1.83 per 1,000 in 1969, but the numbers have been virtually static since the Second World War and, if anything, show a slight decline. Litigation rates in six countries (Chile, Costa Rica, Peru, Colombia, Spain, and Italy) for the period 1945–1970, are charted in Merryman, Clark and Friedman (1979); see also Gutierrez (1979) (Costa Rica).

10. There is a vast literature on colonial courts. See in general, Haskins (1960); Konig (1979); Nelson (1981). Compare, in addition to various tribal systems, the description in T. Stone (1979) of miners' meetings in the Yukon in the late 19th century.

11. Kentucky need not be taken to be typical, however. There were, for example, no admiralty cases in Kentucky. Maritime cases were the largest category of civil cases in the Federal Circuit Courts, 1790–1815, and indeed in the U.S. Supreme Court at that time (Frank, 1948:3, 16, 17). On the early federal courts, see also Henderson (1971).

12. Clark and Shulman (1937) reported on the size of jury verdicts in the Superior Court of New Haven, Connecticut, for 1919–1928, but they did not break down the verdicts by type of case. There were 244 jury verdicts. The median verdict was somewhere in the $1,000 to $2,000 range; only 11.5% were over $5,000. They did report that most (about three-quarters) of the jury trials were "of the negligence type," and over two-thirds of these were auto cases. Less than 10% of the cases "were in the contract group"; the rest were scattered among other causes of action. There is little historic work on tort litigation in general. A noteworthy exception is Posner (1972).

13. *Smith v. Whittier*, 95 Cal. 279, 30 Pac. 529 (1892). Plaintiff was severely injured in an elevator accident. The court held, among other things, that the damages were not excessive. This indeed was the usual outcome in cases of personal injury. The appeals court rarely disturbed the jury's verdict. In the hard-fought case of *Shaw v. Boston & Worcester Rr. Corp.*, 74 Mass. 45, 81–85 (1857), a verdict for $22,250 was upheld, against the argument that the verdict was clearly excessive; defendant's lawyer claimed that only three cases were on record with a verdict of more than $10,000 and that the highest of these verdicts was for $16,000. *Silberstein v. Houston, W. St. & P.F.R. Co.*, 4 N.Y. Supp. 843 (1889), is an example of the exceptional case in which an award was overturned as excessive. An eight-year-old boy was run over by the horsedrawn car of a street railway. He lost his right arm. The jury returned a verdict of $15,000; the court, on appeal, felt that $10,000 "would be as large as the jury should render in a case of this description."

    It is, of course, impossible to tell much about the work of the trial courts, since only a handful of cases were appealed. Those that were appealed do give us some notion about awards considered so high that they risked reversal.

14. I sampled personal injury cases in the Oxford Circuit, 1883–1885 (England), and found no award larger than £1,150; the second highest award was only £350. Personal injury cases were far from common, in general.

15. *In the Matter of the Welfare of Lee Anne G.*, State of Minnesota, County of Hennepin, District Court-Juvenile Division, Fourth Judicial District, judgment filed August 11, 1972. Michael Wald brought this case to my attention. (See also "When Children Sue Parents," *New York Times*, 1980.)

16. Even in the United States, of course, it is vital to have a complaining witness; if the witness fails to come forward, the case will probably be dropped. But in theory (and, in some cases, in practice), the complainant is not a necessary party. The case can go forward without him or her.

17. This happened a century ago in California (Cal. Const. 1879, Art. 1, sec. 8.) From this time on, *information* (complaint brought directly by a prosecutor) largely replaced *indictment* as the normal way to begin a felony case. The U.S. Supreme Court upheld the system in *Hurtado v. California*, 110 U.S. 516 (1884). In the 1880s, indictments began about one-ninth of the felony cases, falling to about 3% in the period 1900–1910 (Friedman and Percival, 1981:167) and to about 1% today.

18. California gave defendants the right to a lawyer, free, at trial, as early as 1872; but this right did not extend to appeal.

   Legal aid dates from the late 19th century (Maguire, 1928). Public defender systems did not come into being until much later, and only in the last two decades has government been willing to spend much money on free lawyers.

19. This mix of types of case was probably typical of common-law jurisdictions in the late 19th century, see Friedman and Percival (1981, chap. 5). It continued into the 20th century; see, for example, Marshall (1932:5).

20. The exceptions include Wunder, 1979; Friedman and Percival, 1981, chap. 4. Starting in the 1920s, there is information in various crime reports (for example, Pound and Frankfurter, 1922) and in a few empirical studies such as Douglass (1933); see also Moley (1932).

21. Since crime itself is hard to measure, crime rate studies are usually studies of arrests or (more generally) prosecutions. Ebbs and flows in prosecutions of other than serious crimes, of course, may reflect "crackdowns" of one sort or another, based on factors which have little or nothing to do with the actual rate of commission of crime. This is especially the case with victimless crimes, such as gambling, drunkenness, and drug addiction. For these crimes, there is the hypothesis that the commission rate remains stable and that what changes is society's reaction. (Erikson, 1966: chap. 4).

22. And, of course, some "fictions" of enormous importance survive. In England there is the pleasant fiction that the country is run by the Queen. No bill becomes law without her signature. In the United States, constitutional law rests in its own way on fiction: that "the constitution" (or its text, or even its spirit) decides the hundreds of constitutional cases that federal courts hand down every year.

23. This is a message, too, of Nonet's (1969) study of the California Industrial Accident Commission. He traced the history of this body over a half century, watching it move from "policy" to "law" (cf. Johnson, 1979).

3

Courts, Moots, and the Disputing Process

Barbara Yngvesson and Lynn Mather

In this chapter, we develop an analytic framework for comparing dispute processing cross-culturally, focusing on dispute transformations and on contextual features that circumscribe the transformation process. Using this framework, we explore similarities and differences between court and noncourt dispute processing. Our approach plays down the distinction between tribal and modern processes and underlines the importance of the forum in which disputes are argued: its physical and social accessibility (open or closed arena), its cultural accessibility (specialized or generalized language and procedure), and the organizational levels through which a dispute must pass as it is dealt with (simple or complex organization). Our aim is to explore how these features affect the ways in which power is distributed among participants in a dispute and the ways in which outcomes are shaped.

Current theory in dispute processing typically contrasts "modern" courts with adjudicated, norm-based, coercive judgments on the one hand, and tribal moots using mediation to reach negotiated, noncoercive outcomes on the other. Variation in these processes is explained by references to variation in social structure (Friedman, chapter 2). We criticize that paradigm here. An emphasis on distinctions between types of third party and styles of dispute management (e.g., mediation, adjudication),

Authors' Note: Contributions of authors were equal. This chapter developed out of our earlier research, "Language, Audience, and the Transformation of Disputes" (Mather and Yngvesson, 1981), prepared under grant number 78-N1-AX-0138 from the National Institute of Law Enforcement and Criminal Justice, L.E.A.A., U.S. Department of Justice. Points of view stated in this chapter are those of the authors and do not necessarily represent the official policy of the U.S. Department of Justice. We are grateful to the Faculty Research Committee of Dartmouth College for support to manuscript preparation.

while important in describing the form of dispute processing (Black and Baumgartner, chapter 4), is less useful in explaining outcomes or in considering the relation between dispute outcomes and social order. Indeed, strategies of mediation and adjudication are often remarkably similar and the outcomes of these processes hard to distinguish from one another. Outcome is closely related to the ways in which the object of a dispute is defined; thus it is important to examine who controls the definition of a dispute and how this control is developed and maintained. In exploring this question, we consider the relations and interaction of a range of participants—disputants, supporters, relevant publics, and third parties—in defining and transforming disputes.

A second emphasis in the paper is on continuities between dispute processing and other social and political processes in both tribal and modern settings. The processing of individual disputes involves negotiations over the meaning of relationships, acts, and events. The imposition and transformation of meaning is always a political transaction, affecting not only the outcome of a particular dispute but shaping basic perceptions of order in society as well. For example, classification of an act of physical assault as a "family problem" rather than a "criminal offense," or of verbal assault as "harassment" rather than "threats" affects the options and power of particular victims and abusers. Additionally, it serves as a more general statement about the relative power of certain categories of persons (e.g., husbands and wives, policemen and ordinary citizens) and about the insulation of certain institutions (e.g., the family) from public scrutiny and public sanction. Elsewhere (Mather and Yngvesson, 1981), we have discussed more extensively how the transformation of disputes links disputing processes to the maintenance (and occasionally change) of political order. Here we simply reiterate that transformation—that is, *change*—in the object of individual disputes is of particular interest because the nature and implications of such change are so intimately connected to fundamental relationships in society.[1]

In the next section of the paper, we review some of the works that employ models of tribal and modern courts, and then critique these characterizations of tribal dispute processing, of tribal social organization, and of modern courts. Throughout this section the emphasis is on the continuities between tribal and modern processes. Following that discussion, an alternative framework for analyzing dispute processing is presented. We focus on forum characteristics that cross-cut tribal and modern distinctions and suggest how these characteristics affect the capacity of participants to define and transform disputes. The final section suggests directions for further research, building on a transformational approach.

THE TRIBAL/MODERN PARADIGM

Much of the empirical and theoretical literature on dispute management, and particularly on the role of courts in handling disputes, draws on a paradigm in which "traditional" and "modern" dispute management are seen as opposite poles of a developmental continuum. Traditional dispute processing is seen as more consensual than dispute processing in urban industrial society. A third party, if present, is a "facilitator" or mediator rather than a judge; thus traditional dispute processing is perceived as inherently more dyadic and dominated by negotiation, modern dispute processing as more triadic and characterized by imposed judgments. The object of the dispute is broadly defined in traditional settings, including elements of the relationship of the disputants, rather than narrowly construed as a specific act, a feature more characteristic of litigation in modern courts. Corresponding to these differences in style of dispute processing are postulated differences in social organization. Tribal society is typically described as a face-to-face, relatively egalitarian community in which there is consensus about values; urban industrial society is conceptualized as a society of strangers dominated by hierarchical relationships, in which consensus is lacking.

As tribal societies develop in complexity, their disputing processes are said to become more coercive, formal, and legalistic, moving toward the prototype of the modern court.[2] For example, Friedman (chapter 2:00) summarizes key evolutionary studies:

> History begins with simple societies, in which disputes are settled through mediation or the invisible sword of public opinion (see Schwartz, 1954:471). More complex societies use courts. At first, courts decide cases rather informally; in Weber's famous image, justice is Kadi justice, the justice of an elder or wise man sitting in the marketplace and deciding cases. . . . Modern, complex societies have moved on to another phase. These societies cannot rely on 'shared experience' (which permits effective mediation), nor do they have father-like authority figures who can get away with Kadi justice. They need formal courts, with force to back them up if necessary.

The emergence of modern courts, in this view, is thus related to levels of social development. With development comes greater power for the third-party decision maker (and more force or threat of force behind the decision), more regularized and formal settlement procedures, and use of norms, principles, and rules in decision making (Friedman, chapter 2).

The contrast between tribal and modern dispute management is also raised by Abel (1979). Abel suggests that "modern courts characteristically handle disputes by rendering coercive decisions based on narrowly focused issues, and these tend to destroy any relationship between the parties" (1979:182). He contrasts these "legalistic" courts with tribal dispute institutions, which lack coercive powers and thus must obtain consent of the parties, in which fault is not unilaterally assigned, behavioral reform is a goal, and "the norms employed by the institution are particularistic, flexible, vague, inconsistent, familiar, and supported by widespread consensus" (1979:170). One of Abel's principal points is the demonstration of a fit between dispute institutions and social structure. In brief, he argues that tribal dispute institutions are suited to a relatively egalitarian society in which norms are widely shared and to relationships that are multiplex, affective, and enduring (1979:170). "Tribal litigation is integrative; it preserves and even strengthens those relationships," Abel suggests (1979:196). These images of tribal society and tribal modes of disputing are admittedly exaggerated ideal types. Nevertheless, as we will discuss below, they are too distant from actual practice to be useful for understanding social relations and disputing in the nonindustrial world.[3]

Sarat and Grossman's (1975) article "Courts and Conflict Resolution" provides another example of the developmental paradigm. They focus on the level of formality and the degree of "publicness" to distinguish among four major types of dispute processing institutions: private-informal, public-informal, private-formal, and public-formal. Private-informal dispute management, they note, is "relatively most extensive in primitive or underdeveloped societies" (1975:1203). In these settings disputants accept the decision of the third party out of respect for his position or loyalty to the close-knit social community. As societies develop in complexity, social relationships tend to become more impersonal and single-stranded, and conflict management tends more toward public-formal adjudication (1975:1209–1210).

Sarat and Grossman qualify the social development model with the important caveat that public-formal modes of conflict management do not necessarily replace the processes characteristic of simpler societies. Instead, as societies develop, various types of dispute institutions are incorporated into a society's system of conflict management. Kidder (1975) similarly argues—in one of the earliest critiques of the tribal/modern dichotomy—that recent research "may help us to disabuse ourselves of the misconception, a too-prevalent legacy of Weberian and Durkheimian analysis, that modernization (or the increase of complexity) necessarily and uniformly obliterates older (or simpler) social forms" (1975:387). It is increasingly clear that modern Western dispute processing is characterized by a multiplicity of conflict management practices, despite the cultural emphasis on the dominance of public-formal institutions. But the complexity of tribal dispute processing practices has been less widely acknowledged.

Particular features of this tribal/modern dichotomy have been recently reexamined,[4] but the paradigm as a whole continues to influence research on dispute processing. The paradigm has also become an important component in the debate over policy changes in court usage both in this country and elsewhere (Danzig, 1973; Fisher, 1975; Sander, 1976;

McGillis and Mullen, 1977; Abel, 1979; Burman and Harrell-Bond, 1979). In view of a range of criticisms and qualifications of the paradigm, however, we suggest moving away from the stereotypes. Table 3–1 summarizes key features of the ideal-typical concept of tribal and modern dispute processing; we will draw on these features in our critique.

TABLE 3-1 Key Features of Tribal/Modern Paradigm

Tribal Dispute Processing	*Modern Dispute Processing*
Informal	Formal
Dyadic (or, if triadic, third party is mediator)	Triadic (Third party is arbitrator or judge)
Coercive process	Consensual process
Compromise decisions	Either/or decisions
Broadly framed issues	Narrowly focused issues
Individualized outcomes (interests of disputants primary)	Outcomes determined by legal norms

Few of those who use this paradigm view it as other than an ideal type, useful as a measuring stick for discussion of empirical studies or as a simple abstraction to aid in theoretical analysis. But as Shapiro (1975:321) noted of court studies, when the prototype fits almost none of them, it is time to begin again "without worrying about where 'true courtness' ends and something else begins."[5]

Critique of the Tribal Model

Analysis of dispute processing, whether in tribal or modern societies, requires close attention to the differences between a particular ideology of dispute management and the actual strategies and decisions made by individuals as they manage a dispute. Classic descriptions by anthropologists emphasize the consensual and compromise aspects of dispute processing in nonindustrial societies, but details of case analyses contradict this conclusion. For example, Gluckman's (1967) descriptions of Lozi *kutas* are for many a model of tribal court operations. The kuta is informal, dealing with broadly framed issues, reaching compromise outcomes in accord with the interests of the disputants. It has limited powers and is dependent on shared values to support its decisions. Examination of some of Gluckman's cases, however, suggests that, while the kuta emphasizes consensus and *talks* about compromise, its actual operations are less conciliatory.

The *Case of the Biased Father* (Gluckman, 1967:37–52) is brought by three brothers against an elder kinsman, who is also headman of their natal village. The brothers argue that although they reside elsewhere, they are entitled to use village land, but the headman will not allow them to do so. In his analysis, Gluckman emphasizes the efforts of the judges to reconcile the disputants. He suggests that, through the process of re-iteration of shared norms (obligations toward kinsmen, keeping villages united), disputants are led to see the error of their ways and a mutually agreeable outcome can be reached. In this way, Gluckman maintains that although decisions of the kuta involve the application of normative rules, these rules are not imposed but agreed on, and the outcome of court action is a compromise. There is considerable evidence in this case, however, that one of the disputants does *not* share the commitment articulated by the judges to maintaining kin ties and keeping villages united; instead, he is seeking to found an independent village and is using this quarrel as a means of furthering his ambition (1967:44,47). The decision of the kuta that the brothers must return to their village was a clear loss for them and a win for the headman who was defendant in the case.

Gibbs' (1963:1–10) analysis of a Kpelle moot is another extensively cited example of dispute processing in a non-Western setting. The moot involves an informal airing of a dispute before an assembled group that includes kinsmen and neighbors of the litigants. One of the kinsmen—typically one who also holds political office—serves as mediator in the proceedings. The *Case of the Ousted Wife* was brought by Wama Nya against his second wife, Yokpo, whom he inherited upon the death of his older brother. Wama Nya accused Yokpo of staying out late at night, harvesting rice without his knowledge, and he admitted having a physical struggle with her. Yokpo denied these accusations and complained that Wama Nya had assaulted her and expelled her from his house. The mediator, a brother of Yokpo, decided, in conjunction with the public present at the moot, that Yokpo was the offended party. Wama Nya, the husband, and the children of both his wives were at fault and "had to apologize to Yokpo and bring gifts of apology" for the disputants and participants in the moot.

Gibbs describes in some detail a variety of conciliatory elements employed in the processing of disputes by a moot, not the least of which is a full and open airing of a situation that most frequently involves complex relationships. He argues persuasively that these conciliatory mechanisms are therapeutic, serving to reconcile disputants, and particularly the one deemed in the wrong, to the outcome. As in the case described by Gluckman, however, accommodation of a range of interests and verbal emphasis on harmony should not mask our understanding of what in fact was happening in this case: a judgment was made; a third party, in collaboration with a broader group, was instrumental in reaching this judgment; and one party was deemed to be at fault (see Felstiner 1974:87 for a discussion of this point).

These examples illustrate the discrepancies between descriptions of tribal courts, which emphasize the ideology of consensus and reconciliation, and some of the actual case data. Starr and Yngvesson (1975) provide a more systematic reexamination of cases in Gluckman's (1967) study of the Barotse court, in Gulliver's (1963) material on Arusha dispute processing, and in Nader's (1969b) study of dispute processing in a Mexican village court. Their analysis suggests that in a significant percentage of the cases (indeed, in 71 percent of Gluckman's cases [Starr and Yngvesson, 1975:556]) the data do not support the model of the tribal court, at least with respect to compromise outcomes that reconcile the disputants.

The stereotype of widespread mediation in tribal and village societies is also challenged by Felstiner (1974:78–79). Felstiner's review of the literature on the occurrence of mediation and adjudication cross-culturally indicates that *both* of these forms of dispute processing are found in the relatively small, face-to-face contexts typically studied by anthropologists. "Whether groups in any particular society will use both institutionalized adjudication and mediation, or one more than the other, may then be a function of considerations other than social organization" (1974:78). Studies such as Moore (1972), Peters (1972), Bailey (1971), Colson (1974), and Li (1977) also document marked coercive and zero-sum features of some of the processes used to handle people perceived as offenders or potential offenders in tribal and village contexts. Forms of coercion can be seen in the public pressure created by gossip, ostracism, and avoidance, in pranks by youths or youth groups against moral offenders, in decisions by oracle or ordeal, and so forth. There is also a strong adversary component to many of these procedures: an offender is identified and defined by a community (through a variety of mechanisms and often over time) as a problem for the community (Yngvesson, 1976).

To summarize, "simple" societies in fact demonstrate many different forms of dispute management. Some of those are quite coercive, with authoritative either/or judgments which do not reconcile the disputants and which do not emanate from a shared set of values. This picture stands in marked contrast to the typical images of consensual decision making in tribal society.

A second point is that the concept of "mediator" itself encompasses a wide range of variation. Further, empirically distinguishing adjudication from mediation is difficult at best. Yet the distinction between these two types of third-party involvement is integral to the tribal model of dispute processing, since many "simple" nonindustrial societies are said to lack the formal process of authoritative judgment that characterizes adjudication. In his recent work on disputes and negotiations, Gulliver (1979:chap. 1) discusses various features suggested by the literature to characterize adjudication versus negotiation (including mediation as a variation on negotiation). These include values versus interests, either/or versus compromise decisions, rule-using versus rule-making, etc. Gulliver rejects the notion that these features effectively distinguish the two procedures. He argues, however, that there is a fundamental difference in the *locus of decision making* in negotiation (a process of joint decision making by disputants) and adjudication (unilateral decision making by an authoritative third party), with mediators acting simply as "facilitators" of the negotiation process (1979:3–7).

Despite his emphasis on this fundamental difference between mediation and adjudication, Gulliver's discussion suggests to us that even this distinction is of questionable empirical value. He focuses explicitly on the varying strategies of the mediator in negotiation, distinguishing a series of mediator roles. These range along a continuum from the most passive role to that of chairman, enunciator, prompter, leader, and "virtual arbitrator" (1979:220). Gulliver points out that, while mediators are "facilitators" and not adjudicators (1979:200), it is nevertheless clear that "the mediator exercises influence in some degree, whether he remains largely passive or *virtually controls the exchange of information*" (1979:213, italics ours). Gulliver adds that the mediator "not only affects the interaction but, at least in part, seeks and encourages an outcome that is tolerable to him in terms of his own ideas and interests" (1979:213–214). To the extent that the mediator controls the information exchange in the light of his own interests, he is certainly acting in a unilateral, authoritative way. An enunciator-mediator, for example, "directs and interprets the information exchanged, influencing the perceptions, preferences, and demands of the parties and implying certain lines of coordination and agreement" (1979:223). In playing this role, the enunciator "represents the wider community and the rules it embraces" but "is not, as such, making judgments" (1979:223).

Gulliver persuasively argues the point that some mediators "virtually take control and make effective decisions" (1979:209). Nevertheless, he does not take the additional step of questioning the usefulness of the mediator/adjudicator distinction. Since mediators lack the overriding authority of adjudicators, the two roles "are analytically distinct, and in actual situations they are effectively different" (1979:210). Yet in Gulliver's description of adjudication he notes that "the degree of authority held and exercised by an adjudicator ranges from the virtually absolute to no more than the ephemeral, accepted ability to propose an outcome" (1979:4) a range that is nearly identical to that he had described for mediators. The analytical distinction seems to be (although this is not explicitly stated) between a third party who is legitimately entitled to speak for a community and one who must skillfully *persuade* disputants that his proposals are based on community norms and thus would ultimately receive public support. Clearly, any third party, to be effective, will operate in terms of an assumed relationship or alliance with some broader group or community.

Indeed, it is the relation between the mediator and powerful others that often leads to the coercive nature of mediation as it typically operates in small, face-to-face communities. Contrary to the popular image of tribal mediation, the ethnographic literature clearly demonstrates the coercion behind mediated settlements, as Merry's (1982) review of this literature suggests. This coercion may come directly from the mediator (or his kin group, allies, or supernatural sanctions), or it may come from the community itself, as it exerts social pressure to settle and abide by the agreement. Such pressure may carry with it the same (or even greater) force than that which accompanies a court judgment in Western society. Coercion would, in practice, seem to be related to whether people expect that they must comply with an agreement or decision and to the nature of the pressure that can be brought to bear to create this expectation, whether the third party is called a mediator or a judge.

A final weakness in the tribal model of dispute processing lies in its overemphasis on individualized dispute outcomes, failing to note the influence of general rules or norms, especially in negotiated and mediated disputes (e.g., Gulliver, 1969:18–19). Gluckman (1967:49) carefully documented the ways in which normative frameworks shaped judicial decisions in Barotse dispute processing, but underlined the breadth and generality of the concepts and rules applied and the flexibility of the decision-making process. The implied contrast, in much of the work on tribal dispute processing, is with a more strictly norm-determined process in "modern" courts. This point has received considerable attention in the literature, with more recent work illustrating both the ways in which norms are used in a variety of dispute processes (tribal and modern) and the ways in which these norms are manipulated by disputants, supporters, third parties, and others in order to achieve desired outcomes (Abel, 1974:234–237; Kidder, 1975; Eisenberg, 1976; Gulliver, 1979:8–13). Comaroff and Roberts (1977) illustrate how disputants invoke norms in tribal disputes through the way in which they define their conflicts; these definitions describe "relevant events and actions *in terms of one or more (implicit or explicit) normative referents*" (1977:86). These definitions are often crucial to dispute outcome and thus struggles over definition help us to understand both the dynamics of conflict management and the use of norms in that process.

Comparative analysis of dispute processing would do well to abandon the stereotyped tribal model of litigation. Likewise, the all-too-frequent portrayal of harmonious social relations in tribal and rural societies requires comment. Since this issue has been addressed elsewhere (Moore, 1972; Yngvesson, 1977; Kidder, 1979), we will simply summarize the major points in the next section.

Tribal Social Organization

The idea that face-to-face societies are characterized by relationships that are affective and enduring, that norms are shared and there is consensus about how they should be applied, and that there is little social differentiation is a legacy of Maine's and Durkheim's theories of primitive society. Maine argued that "primitive groups" were organized "on the model or principle of an association of kindred" and that "all thought, language, and law adjusted themselves to the assumption [that all were kin]" (1963:127). This meant, in part, that in these settings "[m]en are regarded and treated, not as individuals, but always as members of a particular group" (1963:177). In modern society, in contrast, the individual, not the group, is the basic unit of social life (1963:168). Durkheim proposed a model of social development in which mechanical solidarity (cohesion based on a shared or collective conscience) is replaced by organic solidarity (cohesion based on the division of labor) (1964:109, 111 ff.). He argued that the former type of society "can be strong only if the ideas and tendencies common to all the members of the society are greater in number and intensity than those which pertain personally to each member" (1964:129). "It is quite otherwise with the solidarity which the division of labor produces. Whereas the previous type implies that individuals resemble each other, this type presumes their difference. The first is possible only in so far as the individual personality is absorbed into the collective personality; the second is possible only if each one has a sphere of action which is peculiar to him" (1964:131).

Maine's and Durkheim's concept of the importance of kinship and of group identity in "primitive society" has value. There is no question that in many tribal and village contexts kinship-based corporate groups provide the dominant conceptual scheme for organizing social relations. It does *not* follow from this, however, that most social ties in these settings are affective ones, that there is little social differentiation, or that the political system in such groups assumes a "mystical form" that "reflects the common interests of all members of the society in the interconnected rights, duties, and sentiments which make it a single community" (Gluckman, 1965:280). The model of tribal and village society as "family writ large" is further undermined by recent literature on the family that questions our assumptions about the nature of social relations in this unit (L. Stone, 1979).

In contrast to this harmonious model, numerous studies point to the pervasiveness of hostility, aggressiveness, and fighting in tribal and village contexts (Evans-Pritchard, 1940; Foster, 1960; Gluckman, 1963), to the existence of marked social and political inequalities (Balandier, 1970; Bourdieu, 1977; Yngvesson, 1978; Collier and Rosaldo, 1981), and to the aggressive pursuit of individual interests over broader considerations of community welfare (Moore, 1972:63–67; Starr and Yngvesson, 1975). It is just as simplistic to conceptualize a single view of "tribal social relations" as it is to portray modern industrial society in terms of a single ideal type. There are many kinds of social and political forms in the nonindustrial world (Sahlins, 1963) evidencing different degrees of centralization and of social and political hierarchy. The important point, however, is that the prototype of a "tribal society" seems to characterize almost none of these.

The question of whether tribal and village social organizations are egalitarian or in some degree hierarchical is a particularly important one and is central to our understanding of dispute processing in these settings. A number of studies point to the public emphasis on equality (Foster, 1965; Bailey, 1971; Yngvesson, 1978) in face-to-face communities and to the range of mechanisms that disguise differences in rank and power. At the same time, data from these communities reveal pronounced inequality, evident in patterns of male–female interaction, in institutionalized personal service obligations (sons-in-law to fathers-in-law, daughters-in-law to mothers-in-law, junior males to clan elders) and in distinctions between the ritually initiated (possessors of "knowledge") and others (Koch, 1974; Bourdieu, 1977; Collier and Rosaldo, 1981). Inequality is also evident in the more obvious disparities in control over material resources such as land, pigs, cattle, and so on.

It is from such disparities, which foster conflicts of interest between individuals and groups, that many of the disputes in tribal societies arise. Thus, siblings dispute over property divisions (Collier, 1973:173–176), neighbors dispute over money or crops owed (Collier, 1973:219–222), classificatory kinsmen dispute over garden land (Koch, 1974:125–127; Moore, 1977:161–187), and affines dispute over bridewealth claims (Van Velsen, 1964:133–139). Some of these disputes mask other conflicts over power and privilege, providing "an easily definable and legal basis for claims which are otherwise not so easily defined" (Van Velsen, 1964:133). As this suggests, questions of definition of disputes and changes in those definitions assume considerable importance in tribal, as well as in modern, disputing.

Critique of the Modern Model

There is wide recognition today that very few disputes in modern Western society are settled according to the ideal of full-blown adjudication in court. Research by the Civil Litigation Research Project (*Law and Society Review*, 1980–1981) builds on earlier studies (Ross, 1970; Felstiner, 1974; Sarat, 1976; Best and Andreasen, 1977 Macaulay, 1977; Steele, 1977) to examine how disputes are actually handled and to place court processing in the context of noncourt alternatives. Studies of police and prosecutorial discretion, as well as material from the victimization surveys, likewise suggest the extent to which many potential criminal cases are dealt with outside the formal court process (Ennis, 1967; Wilson, 1968; Cole, 1970; Black, 1980;). Indeed, the whole question of how one even comes to define a problem as a "dispute" is currently under investigation (FitzGerald, Hickman, and Dickins, 1980; Felstiner, Abel and Sarat, 1981; Boyum, chapter 6; Yngvesson, forthcoming).

Not only do most disputes never reach court, the handling of cases within court is characterized more by informal negotiation, mediation, or "routine administration" (Friedman and Percival, 1976:270) than by formal adjudication. The extensive plea bargaining literature (Heumann, 1978; Utz, 1978; Mather, 1979b; *Law and Society Review*, 1979) supports this, as does literature on civil litigation (Wanner, 1974, 1975; Macaulay, 1977; Mnookin and Kornhauser, 1979). Thus, as Galanter (chapter 5:00) writes, "We should not assume that courts are places where cases enter and (subject to attrition) proceed normally and typically to a trial, with genuine adversary contest and a decision according to formal rules."

At least with respect to dispute processing in American society, then, features of the modern model outlined at the beginning of this chapter do not reflect present practice. Considering the full range of noncourt and court processing, one finds that disputes are more likely to be handled informally than formally, developing compromise decisions as well as either/or ones, and working with broadly defined issues at certain stages, while focusing on narrow issues at other stages.

In addition, the central emphasis in the modern model on the authoritative third party who judges disputes is misplaced. The distinction between dyadic and triadic dispute settlement is not all that clear in practice, particularly when lawyers are assisting in two-party negotiation. Discussing the role of legal specialists in consumer protection cases, Macaulay (1979:117) notes that "lawyers often mediate between their client and those not represented by lawyers. They seek to educate, persuade and coerce *both* sides to adopt the best available compromise rather than to engage in legal warfare" (see also Eisenberg, 1976). In the context of criminal courts, Blumberg (1967b) first explained the defense lawyer's role as agent–mediator between his client and the court (also see Skolnick, 1967). When both disputants have lawyers as their representatives and when these lawyers share ongoing relations with each other (e.g., as in plea bargaining), then the extent to which lawyers essentially "judge" the dispute is quite striking. Just as lawyers do a lot of judging, so do judges "do a lot of nonjudging" (Shapiro, 1975:332). Lempert (1978:131, 99–100), for example stresses the mediative activity of trial judges and discusses a number of ways judges contribute to the settlement of cases other than by adjudication.[6] The point is that third-party intervention may be called mediation, arbitration, or adjudication, but it still largely consists of two-party negotiation between the disputing parties—negotiation that is "facilitated, but not controlled, by the intervener" (Abel, 1978:190).

The extent to which judges in modern society rely on coercion to enforce case outcomes may also be questioned. For example, litigants in small claims courts—especially individual and unrepresented plaintiffs—cite collection on their court-awarded judgments to be a major problem with the courts (Yngvesson and Hennessey, 1975:254–255). Studies of child support and alimony orders likewise show a rather significant lack of coercion behind the judicial decrees (Eckhardt, 1968; Nagel and Weitzman, 1972). The literature in political science on the impact of court decisions is replete with examples of evasion and defiance of judicial orders (Wasby, 1970; Becker and Feeley, 1973). As we mentioned earlier, coercion then, is not an intrinsic attribute of a third-party adjudicator, despite what legal ideology might proclaim; the words of a judge are not final simply because they are spoken by someone called a "judge." What finality we do observe in adjudicated outcomes may be explained by the relative power of the disputants (and attendant ability to mobilize support to enforce the outcome), rather than by the legitimacy or authority of the courts (Kidder, 1975:389).

Finally, although the ideology of dispute processing in modern courts holds that case outcomes are unambiguously determined by legal norms, the reality of case dispositions shows more individualized outcomes, which reflect the interests, knowledge, and relative strength of various parties involved (disputants, third party, audience, supporters, etc.). Legal norms do play a role in the disputing process, but as Galanter (chapter 5) suggests, it is most often the indirect role of providing "bargaining chips" for disputants to use in their negotiations with one another (see also Mnookin and Kornhauser, 1979). While the norms of contract law seldom actually resolve disputes over contracts, the law provides a "normative vocabulary" affecting expectations about what is fair and thus indirectly influencing the settlement process (Macaulay, 1977:519). In criminal courts, the legal definitions of crimes also provide a "normative vocabulary," but these normative definitions are transformed by court personnel into working definitions of cases to reflect the court's own knowledge and values on the importance of various elements of an offense (Sudnow, 1965; Mather, 1979b).

Just as descriptions of tribal and village dispute processing have over-emphasized the ideology of harmony and compromise, so have observers of modern courts accepted too readily the ideology of an impartial third party imposing judgment according to predetermined legal rules. Examination of the strategies actually used and choices made by disputants and third parties suggests a far more complex, varied set of disputing processes in *both* tribal and modern societies (see also Shapiro, 1980). Conflict management in tribal societies includes elements of coercive third-party judgment, with either/or outcomes, just as processes in modern societies include dyadic negotiations, with noncoercive, compromise outcomes.

CONTEXT AND CONTROL IN THE DISPUTING PROCESS

In view of the shared range of processes and third-party roles in societies of varying degrees of social development, we suggest a focus on dispute transformations and on contextual features that constrain the transformation process as an alternate way to compare dispute processing in diverse socio-cultural settings. Disputes are not simply static events that just "happen," but they also reflect individual conflicts that change or are transformed as others become involved in the disputing process. The participation of others—friends, neighbors, witnesses, lawyers, third parties, and so on—reinforces some perspectives and adds other interests to a case. Change in the form or content of a dispute as a result of the interaction and participation of others constitutes the *transformation of a dispute*. As examples, we point to the rephrasing of an auto accident into a tort lawsuit over money damages; the change in a quarrel between two neighbors into a dispute over town zoning policy; a marital dispute into a child custody case; a conflict between brothers into a dispute between kin over property; a quarrel between co-wives into a dispute between affines over bridewealth. Negotiations over what a dispute is about are a critical dimension of the disputing process; indeed, the importance of these negotiations holds "irrespective of the type of relationships underlying the dispute or of the structural features of the dispute processing context," as Santos (1977:20) suggests.

To reconceptualize dispute processing in this way, we draw on our previous discussion of dispute transformation (Mather and Yngvesson, 1981) to emphasize the following points.

1. *Defining disputes.* Once disputants bring their dispute to a third party (whether the third party is a supporter or settlement agent; see Black and Baumgartner, chapter 4), a critical process begins of fitting particular people and relationships into categories of right and wrong or into certain abstract rules. This process of dispute definition is a significant political process, whether it occurs in a tribal moot, community gossip network, urban police station, corporate law office, or trial court. Understanding the factors that shape the definition process will aid in explaining individual dispute outcomes, as well as provide an important linkage between routine processes of conflict management and broader considerations of legal order and change. A dispute case is not a "given" that someone does something to. Rather, the development of what kind of case it is—and whether it is really a case at all—must be seen as problematic.

2. *Agents of dispute transformation.* Various participants in the disputing process may act as agents of transformation, through their superior ability to maintain control, or trigger changes in the way issues are defined. Disputants, representatives for either side, groups of supporters of one of the parties, a broader community public, or a third party may act in this role. The third parties typically emphasized in the literature on dispute processing (judges, arbitrators, mediators, and others) frequently act as agents of transformation, and it is in this role—as *transformers*, rather than as spokesmen for "authoritative" decisions—that third parties perform their most influential function in the disputing process. A skillful

third party must be able to shape a dispute without appearing to force a value choice; rather, he will construe the facts in such a way that norms seem to relate to them inevitably (Barkun, 1968:147). Faced with other skilled or powerful transformers (lawyers or an organized interest group), the most powerful third parties can only hope to negotiate a mutually acceptable definition.

Focus on agents of transformation opens the range of inquiry to a broader set of participants than is often studied. Specifically, while the two disputants and a third-party settlement agent are obviously important actors, others (such as representatives, supporters, or audiences) may in fact be more significant in shifting and fixing the definition of the dispute. Lawyers are, of course, critical participants in this regard, as discussed by Cain (1979), Ladinsky (1976), and Lempert (1976). We would also underline the importance of the audience to a dispute. Expectations and perceptions of the audience(s) to a conflict may change the issues involved, change the balance of power between the adversaries, or constrain the options available to the third party. As Schattschneider (1960:2) argued, "the spectators are an integral part of the situation, for, as likely as not, the *audience* determines the outcome of the fight." This point is also developed by Carter (1979:227) in the context of judging, and by Santos (1977:18–20, 99) in the context of mediation.

3. *Public and private dispute processing.* As others besides the two immediate disputants act as agents of transformation and, in so doing, add their own concerns and values to the dispute, it is apparent that "public" issues may surface in the dispute negotiations. In our society the line between private and public disputes is often blurred, shifting, and subject to manipulation (e.g., see Shapiro, 1972; Myers and Hagan, 1979). Just as elsewhere in the political process, during informal dispute negotiations or through formal litigation in court, individuals may seek to redefine their selective interests in terms of a broader collective interest, or they may try to avoid the public implications of their dispute and confine discussion to specific "private" issues.

To contrast dispute processing in tribal and modern societies as to the degree of "public-ness" of the dispute institution is misleading, however. Tribal and modern conflict management clearly involves both "private" and "public" processes. Indeed, what is notable about tribal disputes is that, unlike those in modern industrial society, they cannot easily be insulated and kept "private" (Moore, 1972:67–79; Shapiro, 1975:338). "In the small corporate groups of pre-industrial societies and in their relationships with one another, disputes between individuals are far more likely to be disruptive to the social fabric than in impersonal, large-scale societies. In part, this is inherently so because of the small numbers, but it is the more so because of the way in which *structurally determined partisan commitments spread the effects of what start as individual disputes*" (Moore, 1972:74, italics ours). Thus, the disputing process, through which individuals seek to improve their position vis-à-vis others, may serve as an occasion for broader political and economic confrontation, with a view to altering the distribution of power. On the other hand, an offense by one individual against another, or a misunderstanding between two individuals, may provoke concern and interference by a broader group that perceives its security or welfare to be threatened by the "private" conflict.

While in both tribal and modern settings matters of "public" and "private" concern overlap, ironically the connections between the two may be more visible, and may affect the disputing process more markedly, in tribal societies. In many ways, the forums that traditionally have been considered most "public" (the courts of modern industrial society [Sarat and Grossman, 1975]) may in fact insulate the disputing process from participation by a broader community in ways that would not be possible in the more open disputing arenas of tribal society, where a wide range of people can often take part in the handling of a dispute.

4. *Contextual constraints in dispute transformations.* As the above comment indicates, key differences between dispute management in various social settings may lie in the contextual features that circumscribe the bargaining process.[7] That is, while continuities are apparent in the importance of defining disputes, in the range of possible agents of transformation and in the interaction of public and private dispute processing, the processes of dispute transformation will be significantly shaped by the circumstances, or content, in which the process takes place. We will consider three contextual variables. Restricting the *arena* for dispute processing, for example, will influence the number and nature of actors who can participate. The concept of arena includes both physical (or geographic) elements and social elements (FitzGerald and Dickins, 1981:687). *Open* arenas allow for participation by a broad array of actors; conflict management in a village square, in a marketplace, or in any accessible public setting are examples of open arena dispute processing. *Closed* arenas, in contrast, restrict involvement in a dispute to a few actors. Often these are official dispute processors or others with economic and political resources that give them an advantage in controlling dispute definition. Restricting the arena for dispute processing will affect the ability of disputants or others to mobilize an audience supportive of a definition challenging that of more powerful actors. Some closed arenas exclude one or both of the original disputants (e.g., plea conferences, gossip networks). Santo (1977:68) argues that "in camera" (i.e., closed) proceedings not only exclude public participation, but facilitate the imposition of a "foreshortened perspective" on a case.

A second contextual variable involves the extent to which *language and procedure* are specialized in the disputing forum. Where there is a specilized language and/or other forms of specialized symbolic behavior (administering of oaths, ordeals, ritualized gestures, dances) for dispute processing, those who are familiar with the proper forms have a clear advantage in the disputing process. Specialized language requires intermediaries who are able to translate, but who may also transform (Cain, 1979) a dispute in accordance with their own needs. In addition, where the intermediaries and legal officials work regularly together over a period of time, they may develop their own operational meanings of legal codes or normative rules and follow their own informal procedures for processing cases. Transformation of disputes may then emphasize issues relevant to the informal norms and local working environment of the disputing forum rather than to the disputants or the broader community. We consider the language and procedure of dispute processing as varying along a continuum, with everyday discourse and behavior at one end and a highly specialized language and procedure of law at the other. We explore the effect of variation in language and procedure on the ways in which disputes are transformed and on the roles of participants in the disputing process.

Kidder's (1979) model of external law suggests a third variable, *organization complexity*. In Kidder's critique of studies of imposed legal systems, he develops the concept of "externality" of law to deal with the interaction of varying legal levels. An increase in the layers of organization complexity leads to relatively more external law, according to Kidder's model. Further, "by definition, the more external the legal system, the more any conflict introduced into it or induced by it will take on meanings not originally relevant to the conflicting parties" (Kidder, 1979:297). Dispute transformations occurring in legal systems with such organization complexity[8] will reflect other (and most likely different) interests than those originally brought by the disputants. Focus on changes in the definition of a dispute as the result of the involvement of diverse organizations and groups should then clarify what Kidder (1979:299) calls "the details of struggle between different levels of [legal and political] authority."

These three contextual variables may point to key differences in dispute management processes in diverse social settings, but we should not assume that they will always be found together, collapsed into an ideal type. In the next two sections, we will discuss cases that illustrate the ways in which variation in arena, language and procedure, and organization complexity shape the disputing process. The cases will point to similarities across the tribal-modern continuum, as well as illustrate how the contextual features give certain participants an advantage in controlling dispute definition and transformation.

DISPUTE TRANSFORMATIONS IN TRIBAL AND VILLAGE SETTINGS

Drawing on case materials from New Guinea, Africa, and Western Europe, we first consider transformation processes in tribal and village dispute processing. Our focus here and in the next section (on modern disputing) will be on (1) the problematic nature of the object of the dispute, (2) the roles of various agents of transformation and degrees of public participation in the process of dispute definition, (3) the public implications of individual disputes, and (4) variation in the contextual features of dispute processing.

In the following case, drawn from Koch's (1974) study of dispute management in highland New Guinea, a broad community public comprised of supporters of the two disputants plays a critical role in the definition/transformation process, casting what was initially a private quarrel in terms that underline its significance for the group as a whole. The dispute (Koch, 1974:125–127) began when two men from neighboring wards in the same village were clearing brushwood on contiguous garden plots. As their work progressed, one began to object that the other was trespassing on his land, but by nightfall the matter was still unresolved and both left. The following day the two men returned to the site with supporters, and the dispute escalated into a shouting match, then subsequently into a scuffle involving kin and ward-mates of each.

With the participation of the broader group, the men aired grievances over the unresolved pig debts of one of the men and over the actions of one of the men's sons in a recent war. As the shouting continued, the supporters became concerned that neither disputant should alone impose his own definition on the matter, since this would jeopardize the relationship of the wards. Consequently, they took an active role in mediating the conflict and persuaded the two men to reach a compromise. The man accused of trespassing agreed to cultivate the garden he had cleared for one season only, and the other man withdrew his claim on the land. The supporters accomplished this in part by shifting the definition of the dispute to include a broader array of issues: unfulfilled obligations of one of the disputants to his ward-mates and the controversial role played by this man's son in a recent inter-village war.

Arena: This case was argued in a totally open community arena—the actual site of the conflict. This setting allowed for broad participation by members of the larger group encompassing both men.

Language and procedure: The procedure and the language used were unspecialized and comprehensible to all, facilitating the involvement of a more general public in the case. Even with the use of a general discourse, however, it is important to note that much of the discussion was over the terms in which the dispute should be phrased—as a conflict over land rights or over pig transactions. Phrasing of the dispute in one set of terms rather than another would be advantageous depending on the ways in which one's debt network (an important source of power in this community) was built (Mather and Yngvesson, 1981:785). Redefinition of the case in terms of its impact on village security served as a framework for finding a compromise solution that balanced the separate interests of different groups.

Organization complexity: Complexity of social organization characterizing the disputing process in this case was minimal. Participation of the supporters (and their actions as implicit third party) occurred directly with no intervening level of organization. In addition, the various interests that emerged were all shared by, and centered in, the immediate community.

Much of the village and tribal disputing described in the literature conforms to the pattern described in this New Guinea trespassing case, with open community arenas, unspecialized discourse, and few or no layers of intervening organization complexity. Nevertheless, there are a number of traditional settings that deviate in one or more dimensions from this pattern. Study of dispute processing in these settings points to some of the similarities between traditional and modern processes, as illustrated in the next two examples.

Evans-Pritchard's (1937) work on the Azande provides a fascinating look at dispute processing that involves active audience participation (like the New Guinea case above) but that also has some highly specialized layers of processing and restrictions on participation. The Azande use oracles and witch-doctors to handle quarrels between intimates such as spouses, co-wives, and neighbors. Through public accusations of witchcraft, oracles are used to control the behavior of a person who is causing difficulty. The ostensible grounds for consulting an oracle or a witch-doctor may be any one a number of misfortunes (Evans-Pritchard, 1937:261–262). However, as a recent reexamination of Evans-Pritchard's study suggests, "the selection of the misfortune to be used as validation of a consultation would appear to be as whimsical as the misfortune itself"; significantly, however, while "misfortune is haphazard[,] the selection of names is deliberate" (Peters, 1972:145). The oracle or witch-doctor can thus be used by an individual to transform a specific misfortune into an accusation of an intimate against whom one has a grievance.

There are several levels of oracles, ranging from the lesser oracles of the rubbing board and the three sticks to the termites oracle, and finally to the most important, the poison oracle. A fifth type, seance with a witch-doctor, is another important alternative, though of lesser status than the poison oracle.[9] Each of these oracles may be used as an end in itself or may serve as a first step in a longer process in which several procedures are consulted. Choice of a procedure, Peters suggests (1972:148), is determined by the kind of public an individual wants to involve in his case. The rubbing-board oracle, for example, is used in a private setting with a small group of close friends or kin chosen by the aggrieved individual. While the rubbing board may be the principal means for handling relatively minor grievances, it is also a way in which more serious matters may be aired, prior to consulting a poison oracle. Both the rubbing-board and the three-sticks oracles thus provide a first test of public opinion before one proceeds with more serious charges against an enemy (Peters, 1972:149). These charges can be made through the termites oracle, a process that, in contrast to the previous two oracles, must take place in a fairly public place—namely, where there is a termite mound. Successful use of the termites oracle, in effect, requires one to convince a wider range of people than the small selected groups whose reactions were already tested by one of the lesser oracles (Peters, 1972:150).

Even broader public involvement in Zande dispute processing occurs when one asks a witch-doctor to conduct a seance, attended by a "large crowd of spectators" (Evans-Pritchard, 1937:160). Employment of a witch-doctor's services involves feeding, entertaining, and presenting gifts to the witch-doctor (or doctors, as there may be several involved), in addition to the client's gathering the necessary apparatus for the seance. Before this open, public seance, the client meets privately with the witch-doctor and some of "the more influential spectators" (Peters, 1972:151) to go over the names of those the client has in mind as the suspect parties. At the seance the witch-doctor leads an elaborate ritual involving song, dance, and verbal declarations. The client advances questions to the witch-doctor, which are then answered in ritualized forms of speech involving innuendo, braggart tones, or the voice of a medium (Evans-Pritchard, 1937:169). Only the questioner, "who alone has a full understanding of the situation," is able to interpret these utterances according to his own particular social circumstances and frame of mind (Evans-Pritchard, 1937:172–173). The client or complainant thus influences the outcome of his case in important ways—through the information he provides the witch-doctor and by the flexibility he retains in interpreting the revelations that emerge.

The witch-doctor himself, however, by virtue of his special training and esoteric knowledge, also plays a significant role in processing disputes. His knowledge of stock enmities in Zande culture allows him to provide a general framework for dispute definition, while the client, through his questions, can fill in the details. Beyond this, through his performance, the witch-doctor skillfully molds public opinion "to proselytize for a client's cause, to play the piper and lead his client's co-residents towards a consensus of support for one man against another of the same community" (Peters, 1972:152).

This interaction between the witch-doctor and the public is of considerable interest, particularly in view of the fact that some of the public "decisions" emerging from the ritual are to an extent orchestrated in private prior to the seance. A similar type of interaction characterizes the most important of Azande oracles, the poison oracle. With this oracle the principal interaction is between the questioner (who may be the aggrieved complainant or someone standing in for him) and the public in attendance. The two principal types of dispute taken to the poison oracle are adultery and witchcraft; for these the oracle is "in itself the greater part of what we know of as rules of evidence, judge, jury, and witnesses" (Evans-Pritchard, 1937:267). Misfortunes of various kinds—illness, a wife behaving in an unusual manner—are taken to the oracle in order to learn the identity of, in the former case, the witch responsible for illness, and in the latter, the wife's lover. Thus the oracle is able to transform perceived misfortune into a more concrete source of grievance that can be dealt with in the open. A verdict from the poison oracle against an individual is a ritual way of expressing public disapproval of the guilty party and public support for the accuser.

The poison oracle is costly, in part because of the cost of the fowls to whom the poison is administered, but more because of the difficulty and cost of acquiring the poison. Unlike any of the other oracles, use of the poison oracle is restricted to married men with households. Women, younger men, and poor men cannot consult it directly; for the older men who control it, therefore, "it gives them great power over their juniors and is one of the main sources of their prestige" (Evans-Pritchard, 1937:283). Consultation of the poison oracle requires not only senior status, but highly specialized knowledge of language and ritual as well.

Arena: Dispute processing arenas for Azande oracles vary from the most "closed" (private decision making by senior men at a poison-oracle seance or prior to consulting a witch-doctor) to restricted arenas involving disputant(s), kin, neighbors, and an oracle operator, to the open community arena of a witch-doctoring seance. Significantly, the arenas that appear most open are also those in which the most careful preparations are made—at a closed session—to direct the nature of public participation in a case.

Language and procedure: Oracles are consulted by the Azande as a means of making decisions for a range of problems of everyday life. Evans-Pritchard has argued that use of oracles is an integral part of life for many Zande, and that even though some special procedures are involved, oracles such as the three sticks and rubbing board, or even the termites oracle, require no great specialization of knowledge or technique. Clearly, however, witch-doctoring and the poison oracle do require highly specialized rituals and language. In both cases the services of trained or experienced specialists are a significant part of the seance or oracle, and the skilled performances of these specialists are a critical element in case definition, particularly in the process of managing and manipulating a public toward accepting and backing this definition (Peters, 1972:151–153). In this sense they are important agents of transformation in Zande dispute processing and perhaps not so unlike lawyers, who are the trained advocates in modern dispute processing. It is noteworthy that witch-doctors of the same area tend to form local corporations (Evans-

Pritchard, 1937:202–204), groupings that may be analogous in some way to lawyers banding to form county bar associations.

Organization complexity: There are several potential layers in the processing of disputes at oracles and witch-doctoring seances. Some grievances may be dealt with solely at a private or semi-private session using less important oracles such as the rubbing board or three sticks. Others, however, are handled initially—as a kind of sounding-out mechanism—at the lesser oracles, and subsequently taken to the termites oracle or to the poison oracle for confirmation or for greater specificity in the answer sought. Cases taken to witch-doctors may also be dealt with subsequently at a poison oracle. As noted above, the various levels of oracle also involve different publics. While all in attendance come from the local community and share the same Azande culture, the broadest audience will include interests more distant, and perhaps divergent, from those of the original disputants and their close kin and neighbors who attended the earlier, more restricted sessions.

A final example of dispute processing in a traditional setting, which shares characteristics identified for the Azande, is provided by gossip networks in certain European rural villages. Ethnograhic studies of gossip describe how decisions reached "in camera" are subsequently legitimized and ratified through a more public airing. Gossip proceedings tend to have highly limited access, and those who are present substantially control case definition and outcome. Through gossip, cases are defined in accordance with criteria set by the gossipers—a group that typically excludes one or both of the disputants—and responsive to their interests. Yngvesson (1976) discusses ways in which different networks of gossipers, representing central and more marginal individuals in a European fishing community, act to define and redefine the meaning of behavior in intra-community disputes. Behavior which at one point in time is defined as "normal" becomes a basis for ostracism and exclusion at a later date. Typically, definitions imposed by the more central network prevail; these are circulated through the use of pivotal persons (such as the postmistress), who link networks of gossipers and who can relay information to a broader island public. In addition, gossip may serve as a means of "preparing the ground" for an explicit public statement that can mobilize community opinion regarding a case (Yngvesson, 1976; Mather and Yngvesson, 1981: 811–812). In this way, gossip acts in a manner similar to that of the rubbing-board or three-sticks, oracles, or even witch-doctoring seances among the Azande. The gossipers function as agents of transformation, acting in the interests of specific community members who cannot proceed without marshalling more widespread support.

Peters' (1972) account[10] of the social control activities of a youth group in a Welsh country parish also illustrates the importance of a relatively closed network of gossipers in articulating norms and defining behavior in parish disputes. The group, composed of fifteen to forty unmarried young men, gathers nightly to drink, gossip, and discuss moral infractions by parish members. These discussions sometimes lead to action by the group, such as harassment, ridicule, or other proceedings, against the offender. In one of the youth group cases described by Peters (1972:112), a man had denied rumors that he was responsible for the pregnancy of an unmarried young woman. The man was the son of one of the larger, wealthier farmers in the area, and the youth group decided that his irresponsibility could not go unpunished. "One night the youths removed the babe from its mother's care, took it to the farm of the mother's alleged lover and placed it in bed with him. The return of the child had to be made publicly, thereby forcing the man to acknowledge that his denial of paternity was not accepted" (1972:112). Although the man still did not admit publicly to his paternal role, he did begin privately providing for the mother and her child and continued to do so for many years. In this and other cases described by Peters, the youth group defines the meaning of controversial behavior, and then takes the necessary steps to make this definition public.

Arena: The gossip networks of the European fishing community and the Welsh youth group are both characterized by a closed arena for dispute processing. Although the gossipers have numerous links to the broader community, their deliberations are closed to those who are not members of the group.

Language and procedure: Gossipers speak in the general discourse of the community, without the specialized meanings utilized by the Azande witch-doctors or oracle operators. Gossip often does rely on imagery and metaphor, however, to redefine an individual case in the terms of, and to the advantage of, specific group interests in the community. Procedure in gossip networks is relatively unspecialized, although there is an element of skill involved in successful gossiping.

Organization complexity: There appear to be few layers of organization complexity between disputants and dispute processors in gossip cases, although there are clear differences of interest between at least one, and perhaps both, of the disputants and those who deal with a case. Gossip networks present more layering than we found in the highland New Guinea setting, but less than in oracular dispute processing in Africa.

Summary of Tribal Section

The bargaining context for redefining and transforming individual disputes in at least some tribal and village settings thus may be characterized by restrictions on participation, specialized language and procedures, and various layers of organization involved in dispute processing. It is these contextual features that often allow for those of higher social status to dominate in the handling of individual disputes and, in so doing, to reinforce broader patterns of social order. For example, closed arenas (such as gossip networks, pre-seance meetings, private oracular seances) seem to lend themselves to control of dispute definition and transformation by an elite that may exclude one of the disputants or portions of the community at large. In the European fishing village discussed above, despite its ostensibly egalitarian nature, differences in social rank are apparent and these differences are reflected in the ways in which gossip circulates. Because of the relatively closed circle of gossipers, it is difficult for those of marginal status (or their supporters) to assert their own interpretations of events and to define their own interests.

Similarly, the existence of specialized procedures (such as the poison oracle or witch-doctoring seances) and the need for specialists (in ritual, language, esoteric knowledge) to conduct these successfully seem to lend themselves to a process that is typically controlled by more prestigious community members. The more specialized and esoteric the procedure and the greater the expense involved in organizing it the less likely it is that a broad array of interests will be introduced in the processing of disputes. As various layers of dispute processing organization are introduced between an initial dispute hearing and a final outcome, greater familiarity and knowledge of the entire process may be required if one is to achieve a particular outcome. This organization complexity will be an advantage to those who have a continuing stake in influencing case definition—namely, those of highest political or social status, or those whose job it is to perform the specialized rituals (Galanter, 1974b).

In the next section we will discuss dispute processing in settings in which closed arenas, specialized language and procedure, and organization complexity are more marked. We will argue that the differences between dispute management in the courts of urban industial society and dispute management in tribal and village contexts are differences in *degree*, not in *kind*. An interesting consequence of these differences, however, may be that as the dispute processing context becomes more restricted, specialized, or complex, direct participation in the process by a broad public becomes more difficult. In the New Guinea trespassing case a public acted very directly as the actual agent of transformation, with the audience of supporters and both disputants struggling openly over meaning. In other cases (the Azande witch-doctors and oracle operators, the Welsh youth group and the fishing village gossip circle) a separate agent mobilized a public around a particular definition of a case, allowing the agent to influence the course of the dispute in light of his or its own interests as well. As specialized agents of transformation come to dominate dispute proceedings in modern settings, and as their ties to the broader society become attenuated, the identity and role of the "relevant public" becomes problematic and the issue of control over the agent of transformation becomes central.

DISPUTE TRANSFORMATIONS IN MODERN SETTINGS

Conflict over how to define a dispute and participation by a range of parties all attempting to influence the process of definition are important features of dispute negotiations in modern settings as well as in the so-called "simple" societies. Dispute transformations in courts are of particular interest because it is here that restrictions and specialization of the disputing context seem the most pronounced. The two examples below involve courts in the United States. While we clearly cannot generalize to courts in other advanced industrial countries, we suggest that some of our analysis of dispute transformation would apply there as well.

The first case was reported in a study[11] of hearings by a clerk of a misdemeanor court in a suburban community in the Northeast. For criminal cases brought by individuals against one another ("civilian-signed complaints"), a clerk's hearing is required before a formal criminal complaint is issued. Studies of police discretion (Skolnick, 1966; Wilson, 1968) describe how police response to individual disputes is shaped by diverse factors, especially institutional needs of the police department and the working environment of the individual officer. Likewise, one finds the court clerk responding to cases in ways that reflect the concerns of the court organization. Thus, it is the policy of the clerk's office to dismiss as many of these civilian-signed complaints as possible, since they are regarded as "neighborhood," "family," or "garbage" cases that are not sufficiently serious to warrant court time. Consequently, after listening to individuals describe a dispute in their own terms, the court clerk either rejects the case on the grounds that it is not a criminal matter, or he redefines it in legal terms and issues a criminal charge against the respondent.

In this case a rather unusual shift occurs in the definition of the object of the dispute so that at the conclusion of the hearing, the original complainant becomes redefined as the respondent to a new complaint. The critical agent of transformation is a representative of the town police force, permanently based at the court as a police prosecutor. The case involved a complaint filed by an 18-year-old woman against a man of the same age for threats and harassment. The complaint stemmed from an intimate relationship of several years' duration. The man had been trying to terminate the relationship for some time, but the woman was unable to accept this. The previous year, the police had been called by the man's parents when she allegedly hit him; the police recommended that the family file a complaint with the court. The case was referred at that time to mediation, and although an agreement was reached, the problem was not resolved. The present complaint was thus simply one of the stages in an ongoing dispute.

Since the complainant did not appear for the hearing, the clerk announced he would dismiss the case, but before doing so, he asked the respondent and the people accompanying him to tell their side of the story. This was not unusual behavior for the clerk who, as a member of the local community, defined his own role at the court, in part, as a peacemaker. He also recognized his obligations to the court, however, and thus while he frequently spent a considerable amount of time in efforts to settle neighborhood disputes, he rarely issued complaints for such cases. Present at the hearing were the respondent and his mother, his sister, his employer (the owner of a local gas station), another gas station employee, and the police prosecutor.

At the hearing, the owner of the gas station explained that the complainant kept calling the respondent at work; she also drove around the block and harassed him at the gas station. In spite of requests that she stop, her annoying behavior had continued. The police prosecutor added that the police had become involved because the gas business had been affected. The mother of the respondent proposed that they file a new complaint against the woman for harassment, and when the clerk stated that "there is no such crime," the police prosecutor suggested they file a claim for assault instead. The clerk described this as "ridiculous." He added, "We only issue a complaint if someone gets hurt. Just getting slapped or shoved—we have these all the time. Can't send them upstairs." The police prosecutor argued, however, that "it would be nice to have her here before you—I would like to see her here with S [the respondent]. He should be the complainant." The clerk stated that they should wait to see if perhaps the dispute would be resolved on its own, but the mother of the respondent pointed out that the behavior had been going on for a long time—"We called the police last summer." The employer concurred that the woman's behavior was a genuine problem: "I'd be willing to come in as a witness. My opinion of this girl—she's a little sick and needs help. This has been going on a long time. It affects his work." Finally, the police prosecutor said to the clerk, "I think, Mr. G, we should schedule a hearing on the Assault and Battery committed by [the woman] against [the man]." The clerk asked them to get a form, and the young man (the new complainant) produced one already filled out. The police prosecutor said, "We need Miss S to know she can't go around shouting these things, harassing him. [Filing a complaint] is her way to harass him. Apparently she hasn't been called to task by the authorities. Then if she does do something, she can't say she hasn't been warned." The clerk continued to object to the way in which the complaint procedure was being used, but finally agreed to a new hearing. He warned them, however, that "I think you should know ahead of time—I can't issue a complaint on this. I send this case upstairs, the judge will say, 'What's the matter with him?'"

The role of the police prosecutor in this case was particularly interesting. As a member of the town police, he explained his advocacy role for the respondent on the grounds that a local business was being bothered (suggesting that this made the case more a matter of public concern and justifying police involvement, although they had not made an arrest). At the same time, he was a regular participant in the court and his opinion carried some weight; he knew how to bring pressure on the clerk to accomplish what he wished and was familiar with the legal terminology ("assault" rather than "harassment") necessary to define the dispute in an acceptable way. Without his involvement, the case would surely have been dismissed by the clerk, although he would have listened to the respondent's story and advised him to stay away from the complainant in the future. Although finally agreeing to a new hearing, the clerk made it clear that this was simply a threat and that he would not issue a complaint. Thus the clerk was able to balance the pressures from both the community and the court regarding how cases of this type should be handled.

Arena: The arena in this case was a restricted one, in that only people immediately involved in a case were admitted to the hearing. However, "involvement" was defined broadly, allowing various supporters of disputants to attend, and the decision maker was himself a member of the local community.

Language and procedure: Although much of the hearing itself was carried out in everyday discourse, the use of specialized language to classify cases as appropriate or inappropriate for court action ("assault" rather than "harassment") was an important factor influencing the course of the hearings. Skill in manipulating the language was an advantage, and this advantage typically lay with the clerk, unless participants such as the police prosecutor or another specialist (such as a lawyer) were present. Procedure was relatively unspecialized. The process of filing a request for a complaint hearing required some guidance in proper use of the complaint form, however, and the hearing itself was conducted by the clerk, who instructed participants as to when they could speak and what information was relevant.

Organization complexity: The fact that the court hearing was simply one stage in a larger organizational process introduces perhaps an additional degree of organization complexity beyond that in the cases we considered in the last section. While local community values continued to play a role through the police prosecutor and the clerk himself, the values and pressures of the court organization strongly shaped decision making so that this case would ultimately be rejected as a "case."

In the next case, taken from Mather's (1979b) research on felony case processing in Los Angeles, the effects of a restricted arena, specialized language, and organization complexity are much more evident. In this court, as in others in the United States, a limited group of prosecutors, defense attorneys, and other regular participants rephrases disputes according to its own "folk legal categories," categories which are developed by actors within the forum as they process cases and which may differ significantly from those of the broader society. Criminal court research has shown how statutorily defined categories of crime are modified by the subculture of justice in local courts to produce the working definitions of "normal crime" and "real" criminals used by court personnel. These working definitions shape plea bargaining as well as other discretionary decisions in the criminal courts (Sudnow, 1965; Rosett and Cressey, 1976; Mather, 1979b). As might be expected, in many cases heard in these forums, the impact of a local community public is hard to detect. Nevertheless, other kinds of relevant publics contained within the court shape the case definition process; occasionally, as in the following case, the definitions used within the court are questioned when the case is subjected to more public scrutiny.

In a Los Angeles homicide case (Mather, 1979b: 113–116), a prosecutor described what was "*legally* a first-degree murder" committed by a 22-year-old: "The defendant had told friends that he was going to shoot his stepfather. Then he went to San Francisco, got a gun, and returned to his stepfather's house with a friend" (1979b: 114). During a scuffle the stepfather was shot four times, with several shots in the head; the defendant's friend (who had witnessed the shooting and had fired one of the shots) testified against the defendant in court (in exchange for immunity for himself). The prosecutor explained, however, that this was not *really* first-degree murder because of what he called the "equities" in the case: "The victim was a very bad guy. You know, he wasn't the kind of guy you'd take home to mother. In fact [laughing], you wouldn't want him near your mother 'cause he'd probably beat her up! He was a wife beater. ... The son watched him beat her. ... *It's more like a second degree ...*" (1979b: 114). In many criminal courts prosecutors are relatively free to define cases as *they* see them in the course of plea bargaining with defense attorneys. In some courts, however, others within the office bureaucracy must concur with the bargain arranged by an individual prosecutor. In Los Angeles, especially for very serious crimes, prosecutors did not have full discretion. In this murder case, the office superior rejected the plea bargain to second degree and insisted that the assistant district attorney prosecute at first degree and even seek the death penalty. At trial the public defender argued it was a self-defense shooting and persuaded the jury to see the "equalities" involved in evaluating the defendant's motives and the victim's character. The trial ended with a conviction for voluntary manslaughter, a verdict that surprised even the defense attorneys in its leniency and that illustrates how juries also exert influence in defining cases to reflect their values.

Note that, as was the routine practice in this court, the two attorneys, in plea negotiations prior to trial, had mediated the two versions of the case (a cold-blooded murder—"first-degree murder"—versus a self-defense shooting by a man protecting his mother—"voluntary manslaughter") to converge on a compromise of second-degree murder. Because of the gravity of the crime, however, this agreed-upon definition by the legal specialists had to go through another layer of the organization, the prosecutor's boss. In rejecting this definition of the case, the prosecutor's office was in effect responding to their "relevant public," a particularly conservative, law-and-order set of interests. In contrast, the jury (a group composed of many inner-city, minority residents) was persuaded by the defense attorney's definition of the issues at trial. Juries thus provide one link between community norms and the more specialized norms developed by the regular courtroom participants.

Arena: In the informal plea bargaining sessions at which most felony cases are settled, participation is highly restricted; only the legal specialists participate, with even the immediate disputants—the defendant and the victim—excluded. The public hearing that ratifies these dispositions, however, occurs in a more open arena, but still one at which roles for speaking are carefully defined. At a full court trial, as in this case, the public or supporters may attend in the audience, but the legal specialists control the discussion.

Language and procedure: The language of dispute processing in criminal court is highly specialized, involving not only detailed legal categories, but also the operational meanings of those categories as they are commonly used by court personnel. Similarly, procedures draw both on the specialized rules and motives of the formal criminal procedure and on the informal norms of the courtroom workgroup (or, in this case, the informal values of the jury).

Organization complexity: Resolution of a case in an urban court such as the one discussed here requires a number of different stages of processing. As cases move through the various standard screening (or decision) points, different sets of people become involved, all attempting to define issues in ways consistent with their own interests and in terms of constraints on the interactions of various offices. How a case is defined then (or re-defined) will reflect patterns of cooperation and conflict between different organizations (e.g., district attorney and public defender offices) and between individuals within the same organization (e.g., the two prosecutors in this case).

Summary of Modern Section

These cases share with the earlier ones the characteristic that supporters of one of the disputants either on their own or linked to legal specialists (the police prosecutor in the first case, the public defender in the second case) played the active role in transforming cases. The third party, by comparison, played a somewhat lesser role in the first case. In the second, while the bulk of material on plea negotiations points to the more passive role of the third-party judge, cases at jury trial provide the unusual opportunity for more active transformation of issues by the jury as third party.

Because these cases, and others in the literature on American courts, point to the prominence of the role of a legal specialist, it is tempting to argue that this is a primary difference between tribal and modern courts. The role of these specialists is certainly a significant one in our own society. As Kidder (1979: 299) suggests, "law creates one or more interest groups (lawyers, judges, prosecutors, police, legal scholars) whose purposes are not totally consistent with any other group or institution in society. Legal groups have specialized goals and special abilities to manipulate the symbolic and institutional artifacts of law. They respond *in part* to the need to maintain these special symbols and artifacts as justifications for their separate existence." Yet the material discussed earlier suggests that highly specialized functionaries similar to those Kidder describes are also found in the disputing forums of the nonindustrial world. Similarly, closed arenas and complex layers of organization in dispute processing can also be found in tribal and village contexts, although these contextual features may not always appear in combination.

Even in the most open arenas (such as that represented in the New Guinea trespassing case, with no legal specialists and no organizational complexity) the most powerful participants in a dispute will tend to dominate in defining a case so as to influence an outcome in their favor. This power will be reinforced, however, the more restricted is the access to a disputing forum, the more esoteric are the language and procedure required to process a dispute, and the greater is the number of layers of organization involved in the disputing process. That is, where access to the disputing forum is limited, those who control access will be at an advantage in imposing a meaning on disputed events. Similarly, where dispute processing is characterized by organizational complexity, layers of "new meaning" may be easily imposed by those entering the dispute. Limiting access and increasing complexity of organization are thus important mechanisms for institutionalizing political control. Study of them should aid in learning more about the processes through which disputing is linked to political order in a range of social and cultural settings.

DIRECTIONS FOR FUTURE RESEARCH

Future research in this field should focus on some of these as yet little understood processes for controlling the definition, and hence the potential public impact, of disputes. We have argued that an important feature of dispute processing, in tribal as well as in modern court settings, can be explained by asking who controls dispute transformation, how this control is effected, and what social and political variables contribute to the exercise of control. Thus, we have discussed negotiations among a range of participants over the object of a dispute, focusing especially on the roles of relevant publics and on less conventional "third-party" roles such as those played by supporters of disputants, or by specialists such as lawyers, witch-doctors, police prosecutors, and others. Important differences in the context of dispute processing, we suggest, do affect the process of dispute transformation. In this discussion (Table 3-2), we have focused on three particular dimensions for comparison, although it is likely that others may also prove useful.

TABLE 3-2   Contextual Features of Dispute Processing Forum

(general)	⟵———————	DISCOURSE ———————⟶	(specialized)
		(Language and procedure)	
(open)	⟵———————	ARENA ———————⟶	(closed)
(simple)	⟵———————	ORGANIZATION COMPLEXITY ⟶	(complex)

These contextual features frequently overlap so that, as we have mentioned in an earlier example, dispute processing in the New Guinea community described by Koch (1974) occurs in a relatively simple organizational setting, with general discourse for discussion and an arena open freely to others. In contrast, modern American court processes are often characterized by the reverse extreme. However, the fact that these features may frequently be found together does not mean that we should collapse them into a single dimension of tribal versus modern dispute institutions. There are important exceptions to any single dimension of differentiation of the dispute processing institution from the wider society, as we have noted above.

In planning for the reform of tribal and modern forums, it is important to understand the similarities of the disputing process in diverse cultural and institutional settings and the commonalities in the way tribesmen and modern strangers use this process. Replacing moots with courts, or formal tribunals with informal justice centers, is more likely to change the ideology of dispute management than change the actual process through which cases are managed. In both settings, dispute management will typically involve a complex process of bargaining in which the object of the dispute is an important focus of discussion. *Who* becomes involved in this bargaining may well be affected by the complexity of the society, as well as by the structure of the dispute processing forum. This in turn will influence the kinds of interests introduced into the disputing process. Thus, in planning institutional reform, we may want to focus more on accessibility and on local control than on changing the ideology (mediation or adjudication) or the form of the process (more dyadic or more triadic). Available research suggests that ideological and formal differences mask processes which tend to merge in practice.

NOTES

1. Compare this aspect of our analysis here (and in our earlier paper, Mather and Yngvesson, 1981) with comments of Lempert (1981:711–715), Kidder (1981:718–725), and Trubek (1981:740–744).
2. We are not concerned here about the next stage of development (i.e., the Toharia thesis), in which formal courts are said to become routine administrative bodiesl displaced in their conflict-resolving functions by other, more specialized institutions (see Friedman and Percival, 1976; Friedman, chapter 2).
3. Abel's use of ideal types in this analysis (1979) is somewhat surprising in view of his earlier work (1974) in which he criticized ideal types of disputing processes as unhelpful stereotypes (1974:241).
4. Problems in assumptions about mediation and adjudication have been discussed by Felstiner (1974), Kidder (1975), Eisenberg (1976), Lempert (1978), and Merry (1982). Third-party roles have been re-examined by Shapiro (1975) and Gulliver (1979). The nature of tribal social relations has been questioned by Moore (1972), Yngvesson (1977), and Kidder (1979), while Starr and Yngvesson (1975) have critized assumptions about "compromise" outcomes in tribal courts.
5. See also Shapiro's (1980) more recent work in which he fully develops a critique of the court "prototype," drawing on comparative and historical studies of courts in England, Western Europe, Imperial China, and Islam.
6. Lempert's (1978:99–100) thoughtful listing of court contributions to dispute settlement is quoted in this volume by Galanter (chapter 5: footnote 1).
7. Our focus on "contextual variables" is somewhat similar to Abel's (1974:251–262) discussion of "structural variables" that influence disputing processes. Key structural variables in Abel's analysis are specialization, differentiation, and bureaucratization. These variables are of particular interest in his analysis, however, insofar as they define the role of the third-party intervener.
8. Kidder (1979:297) initially uses the term "structural complexity" to analyze the particular example he gives of external law. His explanation however, refers to the number of "layers of intervening organization complexity between the lawmakers and the governed" (1979:297). We use the term "organization complexity" to avoid confusion between social structure and structural complexity.
9. According to Evans-Pritchard (1937), the order of ascending importance is: rubbing-board oracle and witch-doctors (equal), the three-sticks oracle, the termites oracle, and the poison oracle (the poison oracle being supreme). However, Peters (1972:150–153) persuasively argues that the witch-doctor's seances were actually more significant than the three lesser oracles and second only to the poison oracle in status. We refer to these oracles in the ethnographic present, although some of these rituals are no longer practiced.

10. This work by Peters (1972) is a reexamination of the classic monograph by Rees (1961), *Life in a Welsh Countryside.*
11. This unpublished study of court clerks' hearings was done as a pilot project in 1981 by Barbara Yngvesson in preparation for a larger research project, "The Transformation of Disputes in a Lower Criminal Court," now underway with N.S.F. funding.

4

Toward a Theory
of the Third Party

Donald Black and M. P. Baumgartner

In this chapter we present a classification of the various roles through which people intervene as third parties in the conflicts of others. Such a classification, or typology, is a first step toward a general theory of the third party, since it specifies the primary range of variation that a theory of this kind must confront. Although our typology is the product of an extensive review of anthropological, sociological, and historical materials on the management of human conflict, it will undoubtedly need revision and refinement in light of future inquiry. What follows, then, should not be construed as definitive. Even so, it is intended to be comprehensive.

The theory of the third party—which necessarily refers to a typology such as ours—seeks to understand when and how people intervene in the conflicts of others, and with what consequences. It thus builds upon existing formulations that specify how the social characteristics of the principals in a conflict, including the nature of their relationship with one another, predict and explain what happens to their case (such as whether it is taken to a court of law and, if so, who wins). It is already known, for example, that the relative status of the principals, their intimacy with each other, and the degree of their organization are all relevant to how their

Authors' Note: This chapter was prepared in the course of a larger project supported by the National Institute of Law Enforcement and Criminal Justice, Law Enforcement Assistance Administration, U.S. Department of Justice, and by the Program in Law and Social Science of the National Science Foundation. An earlier version of the chapter was presented to the Disputes Processing Research Program, University of Wisconsin, and to the Center for Criminal Justice, Harvard Law School. We thank the participants at these sessions for their helpful comments. We also thank Mark Cooney, Lynn Mather, and Sally Engle Merry for comments on an earlier draft.

dispute is pursued and processed (see especially Black, 1976, for pertinent formulations). The theory of the third party addresses the relevance of analogous characteristics of any other parties who play a role in a conflict. Although not every conflict results in the intervention of third parties, in all societies a great many do, including most of those that become public.

The range of conduct embraced by our typology, and advanced here as a subject matter for the theory of the third party, is very broad. In this respect our approach departs quite radically from earlier efforts of a comparable nature. In particular, we include in our concept of third parties virtually all individuals or groups who intervene in any way in an on-going conflict, including those who are overtly and unabashedly partisan from the outset, such as lawyers, champions-at-arms, and witnesses. In contrast, earlier typologies have treated as third parties only those who are, or who claim to be, nonpartisan, such as mediators, arbitrators, and judges (e.g., Galtung, 1965; Eckhoff, 1966; Koch, 1974:27–31; Shapiro, 1975:323–325; Sander, 1976; McGillis and Mullen, 1977:4–25; but see FitzGerald, Hickman, and Dickins, 1980).

We include partisans as third parties because, in the first place, a distinction between partisans and nonpartisans, though useful for some purposes, is by no means absolute. On the one hand, many third parties who claim to be neutral in a conflict are actually biased in favor of one side or the other. That this is a possibility is known to every lawyer who goes to court, and it may also be the case in more informal modes of conflict management, such as mediation in a tribal society, a private association, or a family. Apart from bias apparent during the settlement process itself, moreover, the whole point of resorting to a third party is often simply to determine which principal the settlement agent will ultimately support. A modern judge typically chooses which side of a conflict the state will take, for example, and arbitrators frequently decide to throw their weight entirely behind one party as well.

On the other hand, people who intervene as supporters rarely if ever do so without first assessing the merits of a case. Lawyers, for example, do not automatically accept the business brought to them by potential clients, but first evaluate the issues in question in much the same way that a judge or arbitrator would (see, e.g., Macaulay, 1979). The same applies to kinfolk and friends who come to the aid of their fellows. There is a limit to the conduct that they will defend, and there are alleged offenders whom they may be reluctant to oppose. Even under the pressure of collective responsibility, wherein all the members of a group are held liable for the conduct of each, cooperation depends upon an assessment of each matter at issue, and there is a point beyond which any group will refuse to be identified with one of its wayward members (see Moore, 1972; Posner, 1980:43–44). In short, supporters commonly relate to conflicts partly in the manner of settlement agents, and vice versa. For this reason alone it would seem unwise to ignore partisan intervention in a theory of the third party.

Beyond these considerations, another reason for including supporters in a typology of third parties is that they may play an important role in the actual management of conflict. In some cases, they may be the deciding factor in how the issues in dispute are defined at the outset (see Fitz-Gerald et al., 1980:14–15; Mather and Yngvesson, 1981:807–810), and in whether and how they are subsequently resolved. At every stage, the social status and other characteristics of each supporter, as well as the number and organization of the body of supporters as a group, contribute to the structure and process of the conflict situation. Not only do their attributes have significance for the conduct of the principals, but also for that of any settlement agent who might become involved. In fact, the relationship of a supporter to a settlement agent may prove critical in the ultimate fate of a dispute.

Because the typology that follows is so inclusive, the body of theory which applies to it is necessarily very general in scope. It predicts and explains much about what transpires during fights and feuds, in the offices of attorneys and psychiatrists, and in village moots and modern courtrooms. It thus subsumes aspects of more limited theories ordinarily viewed as complete unto themselves, such as theories about vengeance, feuding, negotiation, litigation, or adjudication. Viewed against the broad range of phenomena contemplated by the typology, every pattern of conflict appears as one of a spectrum of possibilities, each of which, we assume, occurs under specifiable conditions. One aim of our typology, then, is to cast a theory about third parties at a universal level. In the concluding pages of this essay, we present several propositions that illustrate the kind of theory of the third party we envision.

A TYPOLOGY OF THIRD PARTIES

Our typology is designed to classify third parties along two major dimen-sions: the nature of their intervention—whether partisan or not—and the degree of their intervention. It identifies a total of twelve roles, including five support roles (informer, adviser, advocate, ally, and surrogate) and five settlement roles (friendly peacemaker, mediator, arbitrator, judge, and repressive peacemaker). Each is ranked according to the degree of intervention it entails, with the extent of partisan involvement featured in the case of the support roles and authoritative involvement in the case of the settlement roles (see, e.g., Gluckman, 1968:222; Sander, 1976:114; compare, e.g., Abel, 1974; Griffiths, forthcoming). In addition, we include one role that combines partisan and nonpartisan elements (the negotiator) and one that lies beyond these categories entirely (the healer). The 12 roles are graphically represented in Figure 4–1.

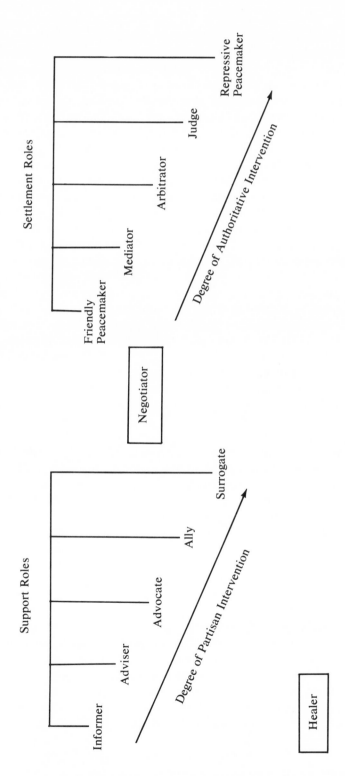

FIGURE 4-1 Typology of Third Parties.

In the remaining pages we describe our typology in further detail, illustrating each role with examples from diverse settings across time and space. As we proceed, the reader should bear in mind that the typology does not describe a set of discrete categories, but rather a number of spans along each continuum of intervention, partisan and authoritative, with every role shading into the next.

SUPPORT ROLES

Although impartial arbiters are likely to come to mind as examples of third parties, and although they receive a disproportionate amount of scholarly attention, it seems clear that most people who interpose themselves in the conflicts of others make no claim to neutrality. Instead, they act entirely on behalf of one side, and are generally recognized as doing so by all concerned from the beginning. These actors, performing support roles, are distinguished among themselves by the amount of assistance they give and by the extent of risk and hardship they assume as a result. Put another way, they differ in the extent of their investment in the conflicts that they make their concern. In the following pages, the five major support roles—the informer, the adviser, the advocate, the ally, and the surrogate—are discussed and illustrations of each are given. The section closes with a note on opposition, the obverse of support.

Informers

Among the various supporters of people in conflict, the smallest investment is generally made by the informer. People who assist others in this way provide information or facts but do not participate in resolving the conflict to which their information pertains. Their contribution is usually restricted to an early stage of the conflict, and is more likely than other kinds of support to be provided in secret.

Informers may be recruited by a principal or by another supporter, or they may step forward on their own. Often, in fact, the informer is simply a gossip. In intimate communities of all kinds, frequent chatter about the activities of others seems to be a prominent feature of social life (see, e.g., Gluckman, 1963; Merry, forthcoming). Some individuals even become specialists in transmitting information about their fellows, well known as town or village gossips. Those who exchange information casually, and all the more those for whom doing so approaches an avocation, may communicate directly to people a piece of information pertinent to their conflicts. Still other informers may be paid for their services. In modern American police work, for example, informers are often paid, in money or other consideration, for information about narcotics offenses (see Skolnick, 1966:chap. 6; Gould et al., 1974: 72–76). In ancient Athens, where prior knowledge of an opponent's arguments in court was considered especially valuable, there were many successful attempts to bribe attorneys or friends into divulging confidential information of this sort (Chroust, 1954a:375–376). Others are neither gossips nor merchants in information, but step forth from a sense of moral outrage against an offender, sympathy or affection for one of the principals, or dislike of his or her opponent. Finally, people are occasionally coerced by threats or violence into giving information relevant to a conflict.

In some instances an individual may invest time and energy in the task of uncovering information relating to another's grievance or offense. Active participation such as this defines the role of the partisan investigator, a subtype of the informer. The prototypical partisan investigator is perhaps the modern private detective, a professional who, for a price, invests considerable resources in discovering and reporting what a client wants to know. Partisan investigators may be amateurs as well— "snoops" and "spies" of various kinds.

An exotic variant of the informer, also worthy of brief notice here, is the diviner. In many societies, aggrieved parties can bring their questions about the identity or intentions of offenders to individuals skilled in the use of supernatural methods of discovery. Usually in return for material compensation, such specialists may read leaves, cards, or animal entrails, enter trances, perform rituals, or take other measures designed to uncover facts useful to someone else. Among the Azande of the Sudan, for example, witch-doctors drink potions and dance themselves into frenzies so that they can determine who is responsible for a person's misfortunes (see Evans-Pritchard, 1937:part 2). In 17th-century England, "wise women" and "cunning men" used a variety of techniques to reveal who had stolen something from their clients (Thomas, 1971:212–222). And similarly, among the Qolla of Peru, skilled *maestros* are believed to be able to discover thieves (Bolton, 1974).

In some cases, informers appear to be crucial to the conflict process, focussing the diffuse anger of a victim or enabling a party to gain decisive advantage over his or her opponent. Yet in comparison with other kinds of supporters, they have, as a group, a small involvement in the conflicts upon which their activities bear. Having imparted their information, they retreat from the conflict itself, leaving others to act upon the facts they have provided.

Advisers

Advisers give opinions about how to manage a conflict to one of the principals involved. Accordingly, they are third parties who assist in devising the strategy by which a dispute will be prosecuted. Unlike more involved partisans, however, they do not participate in executing such a strategy. In many cases, in fact, their contribution is made behind the scenes and remains unknown to the opposition.

In societies where they have evolved, attorneys frequently adopt the role of adviser. Giving advice to clients occupies a great deal of the time of contemporary American lawyers, for instance (see, e.g., Carlin, 1962; Smigel, 1964:chap. 6). In the Soviet Union, lawyers dispense advice from storefront "consultation offices" or from their posts as "jurisconsults" to enterprises and organizations (see Barry and Berman, 1968; Giddings, 1975). In an earlier period, Greek and Roman attorneys also advised clients on what to do about their interpersonal tensions (see Chroust, 1954a, b).

Other advisers are frequently found in the persons of those empowered to adjudicate disputes. Thus, one anthropologist who studied the Tiv of Nigeria has noted that "the sort of advice which we in the West have come to associate with legal counsel is, in Tivland, usually given by the persons who are going to judge one's case" (Bohannan, 1957:29). Many Tiv approach judges informally to ask them what course of action they recommend in a dispute, and, as a result, numerous cases are settled without further ado. It is not, however, only in traditional societies that designated judges perform this function. In an affluent suburb in modern America, for example, it is not uncommon for the municipal judge to dispense advice to aggrieved individuals who come to him privately for consultations (Baumgartner, 1981). In some societies, there are also specialized individuals who, for a fee or other consideration, give legal advice in the capacity of "broker." These are people with no official position and no formal training, but who nonetheless have a certain amount of influence in official circles and who have become experts in the operation of a legal system. Because of their unusual knowledge about how to manipulate the law, they are frequently approached for their opinions by fellow villagers. In a village of Lesotho, for example, a man in this position routinely helps others decide matters such' as whether or not to initiate litigation and, if so, how best to manage their cases in court (Perry, 1977).

Traditional patron-client relationships also constitute fertile ground for the transmission of advice. The terms of such social arrangements generally include assistance to the client by the patron in times of difficulty—assistance which often amounts in practice, so far as conflicts are concerned, to the giving of advice. In ancient Rome, for instance, a powerful *patronus* might give his *cliens* legal advice as a way of discharging his obligations (Kelly, 1966:27). Less formally, local gentry not specifically related to their lower-status neighbors as patrons appear nonetheless to be frequently approached for their advice.

Family members, friends, and other associates often assume the role of adviser when one of their number becomes involved in a conflict. Surveys of the contemporary American public, for example, reveal that intimates are especially likely to be called upon for advice and moral support when trouble arises (see, e.g., Schulman, 1979). Thus, one student of consumer problems in the United States notes that "the complainants' sense of outrage and injustice is often validated by friends, colleagues, and even supervisors who empathize with and may urge them to complain" (Addiss, 1980:172). In other societies as well, intimates appear to play a crucial role in determining how offenses will be dealt with and peace restored (see, e.g., Ekvall, 1954; Jones, 1974:67–68). Often such advice is situational and spontaneous. Among the Yanomamö of Venezuela and Brazil, fellow villagers are reported to give their opinions freely about quarrels in progress (Chagnon, 1977:92), and the same is true of the Kapauku of highland New Guinea (Pospisil, 1958:254–255).

Advisers may shape the character of a conflict considerably by urging moderation or by agitating for a forceful response to a grievance. At the same time, some simply help plan the execution of a strategy, as was true of the ancient Greek specialists known as "logographers." These individuals, for a fee, served as ghostwriters of the impassioned speeches that litigants were required to make before the courts (Chroust, 1954a:345–350). Regardless of the substance of the opinions provided, however, advisers invest comparatively little in the conflicts about which they comment. More active support is found in several other roles.

Advocates

Advocates are third parties who step forward publicly and plead the cause of the people they support. They range from spokesmen or spokeswomen, who simply present a principal's position, to sponsors, who invoke their own reputation and social standing to secure advantages for someone else. As is true of informers and advisers, they may voluntarily seek to give this assistance, or they may be paid for their services. In some tribal societies, an advocate might step forth on behalf of an aggrieved individual simply to publicize the complaint for all to hear. Among the Hopi Indians of the American Southwest, for example, an elder esteemed for his oratorical abilities may air a villager's complaint by climbing to a rooftop and giving a stylized chant, in which he pleads with an alleged offender to desist from a particular activity or to make amends for a misdeed. His performance is known as a "grievance chant" (Black, 1967). Similarly, the Cheyenne Indians of the American Plains have a "camp crier" who presents complaints when the offender is unknown, in hopes of ending the offensive behavior or possibly gaining a more specific form of satisfaction for the complainant, such as the return of a stolen article:

> Appropriation of another's property seems not to have been too uncommon. Calf Woman says that lots of times she heard the crier haranguing about the loss of an article by somebody . . . . As an example, Deaf Ear lost his entire

buckskin suit. A crier made the announcement. Still, no suit. A second crier offered a horse [as a reward]. "It is a well-marked suit. Any member of the family will know it. You'll feel badly if you are caught with it on," he warned. The suit was returned (Llewellyn and Hoebel, 1941:226).

In modern societies, advocacy is one of the principal functions of attorneys. It is also undertaken by various other participants in legal life. Character witnesses, for instance, who vouch for the integrity of a disputant as a human being effectively perform an advocate's role. In the Soviet Union, organizations of citizens are encouraged to appoint one of their number to appear in court as "social defenders" if, in their experience with a defendant as a neighbor or co-worker, they have found the individual to be a good associate (see Feifer, 1964:chap. 4). One of the most developed forms of advocacy, compurgation, played a major role in the trials of early Germanic and Celtic societies. The compurgator was an individual who swore a supporting oath to substantiate the claims of a principal, and, in sufficient numbers (as determined by the circumstances of a case) and provided all gave a perfect recitation of the required formulas, their combined backing was decisive (see Lea, 1892:13–99; Pollock and Maitland, 1968:vol. 2, 634–637; Berman, 1978:561–562). Early Roman courts had advocates of several kinds:

> Hearsay evidence was permitted and any number of prominent persons might be heard on their opinions. The social prominence of such "witnesses," who went by the significant name of *laudatores* (praisers), in itself was considered an adequate substitute for real knowledge of the facts on their part. To have less than ten such laudatores was considered an outright disgrace (Chroust, 1954b:131).

During the same period, Romans might hire claques to appear in court during their trials, and, at appropriate moments, support their testimony with applause and cheers or assail that of their opponents with hoots and whistles (Chroust, 1954b:132–133).

Advocacy also stands with advice as one of the principal kinds of support provided by patrons to their clients. Thus, in Japan:

> If a *kobun* [client] got in trouble with the police—caught for gambling, say, or fighting—his family would turn to the *oyabun* [patron] as the obvious one to go and *moraisageru* him—a curious word meaning "to secure release from custody on the informal guarantee of a social superior," literally, "to get back down" (Dore, 1978:291).

Patrons in Latin America (Tumin, 1952:126) and Thailand (Engel, 1978:22) similarly engage in advocacy on behalf of their clients. Among the Tiv of Nigeria, however, advocates for someone whose case is being aired in a moot are likely to be members of that person's age group, or peers (Bohannan, 1957:168). The same general pattern appears to be widespread. Siblings speak up for siblings, co-workers for co-workers, and friends for friends. In fact, while less dramatic than other forms of advocacy, informal support of this kind seems to be far more common.

The investment made by advocates on behalf of those they support is generally greater than that made by informers or advisers. Advocates are directly involved in the process of conflict management, and, especially as they move toward active personal sponsorship, may come to stake their own reputation for the benefit of the principal they support. Even so, their role does not often require them to make significant material contributions to a conflict or to assume significant material risks because of it. For a higher degree of commitment, a principal must turn to an ally or a surrogate.

Allies

Of all the people who give support to others, the ally is perhaps the most celebrated. Allies are a striking manifestation of partisanship, taking up personal burdens for the good of others. They may render themselves vulnerable to physical injury, for instance, or contribute from their own resources to help secure an advantageous outcome for the person or group whose cause they espouse. While they share the jeopardy of a party in conflict, they do not, however, take principally upon themselves all of the risks involved. Their support thus stops short of the maximum.

In tribal societies, alliance usually arises from kinship. In the typical scenario described in many accounts, a group of relatives assembles upon learning of an incident involving one of their number. After discussing the matter, they decide upon a course of action and approach the opponent, who is likely to be buttressed by supporters of a similar kind. In the ensuing confrontation, the family members may be prepared, if necessary, to exert force against the person or property of the opponent. If, on the other hand, a peaceful settlement emerges as a possibility, they may contribute goods—livestock, shells, or whatever—to enable their kinsman or kinswoman to conclude the affair. At the same time, they stand to benefit materially should the ultimate settlement be in favor of their side. This widespread pattern of kin alliance has been noted among the ancient Germans (Berman, 1978) and their descendants in feudal times (Bloch, 1964b:chap. 9), the Jalé of highland New Guinea (Koch, 1974), the Ifugao of the Philippines (Barton, 1969), the Nuristani of Afghanistan (Jones, 1974), the nomads of Tibet (Ekvall, 1954), the Nuer of the Sudan (Evans-Pritchard, 1940), the Ndendeuli of Tanzania (Gulliver, 1969), the Yanomamö of Venezuela and Brazil (Chagnon, 1977), the Bedouin of Libya (Peters, 1967), the Sards of Sardinia (Ruffini, 1978), and among many other peoples. A well-developed alliance system is found among the nomads of northern Somalia, who maintain organizations called "dia-paying groups" (literally, bloodwealth-paying groups) expressly designed to handle complaints by or against their members. A dia-paying group is composed of men who are genealogically related, though it also involves a contract specifying how much compensation the group will demand in case of a homicide, injury, or insult against a member by an outsider, the proportion to be kept by the organization, the proportion that the organization will pay if a member commits an offense against an outsider, and so on (Lewis, 1959, 1961).

Allies are also frequently found beyond the family circle. In feudal Europe, for instance, it was the obligation of vassals to assist their lords in times of conflict (Bloch, 1964b:chap. 16). Circles of friends often act as allies for one another, too. Among the Pokot of Kenya, an aggrieved wife may call upon her female friends and neighbors to form a "shaming party" to humiliate her husband publicly by, for example, tying him nude to a tree, beating him with sticks, and urinating upon him (Edgerton and Conant, 1964). In modern America, an observer of the Hell's Angels motorcycle club has noted that in conflicts between an Angel and an outsider, club members "have a very simple rule of thumb .... a fellow Angel is *always right*. To disagree with a Hell's Angel is to be *wrong*— and to persist in being wrong is an open challenge" (Thompson, 1966:71). In support of their fellows, moreover, Hell's Angels are quite willing to resort to violence (Thompson, 1966:chap. 6). In ancient Athens, adult males of consequence usually belonged to a club or fraternity expressly designed to provide assistance to members in legal difficulty. One's fraternity brethren might donate from their own funds in order to hire the best professional assistance for their comrade, or they might use their personal funds to bribe the authorities on his behalf (Chroust, 1954a:352–353).

Like other supporters, some allies expect to be paid for their services. Thus, mercenary soldiers may be hired by a nation or faction to fight alongside its own members in a violent conflict with another group. Or people may be bribed to hide and supply parties operating against their opponents in secret, even when this exposes them to the risk of punishment should they be discovered. Allies may also be recruited by coercion, a pattern often seen when people fight for another's cause or shelter fugitives.

Regardless of how they are mobilized, however, allies—by definition —always invest heavily in the conflicts that become their concern. What they do on behalf of a principal greatly exceeds what is done by informers, advisers, or advocates. Even so, their involvement remains secondary to that of the principals themselves. In this respect they may be distinguished from those supporters who go further still and assume the primary risks and burdens of a conflict, making it, for all practical purposes, their own. Such are the most supportive of all supporters: surrogates.

Surrogates

The surrogate substitutes for another person or group in the management of a conflict, largely or totally relieving a principal of responsibility and risk in the whole affair. Substitutes of this kind appear to comprise a significant portion of all third parties, though they may be the least common of the several support roles we include in our typology. Surrogates come in a variety of forms, distinguished among themselves by the precise nature of their conduct and their liability, and by the circumstances surrounding their mobilization, whether voluntary or not.

One variety of surrogate, for example, is the avenger or champion who prosecutes another's grievance as if it were his or her own. In many societies, relatives of murdered or incapacitated victims of violence routinely assume a role of this kind. Thus, among the Cherokee Indians of southeastern America, the nearest relative of the person slain was expected to take the life of a member of the slayer's clan (Reid, 1970:90–91). Among the Ifugao of the Philippines, a close male relative of a murder victim is expected to retaliate by killing the murderer or someone in the murderer's family, and, until this is accomplished, the would-be avenger must wear his hair long as a visible symbol of his unfulfilled mission (Barton, 1969:68–76, plate 11). Not infrequently, vengeance follows upon vengeance in a continuing exchange of violence, a pattern of conflict known as the feud (see, e.g., Thoden van Velzen and van Wetering, 1960; Otterbein and Otterbein, 1965).

There are also societies in which people who are not physically incapacitated occasionally seek the help of a champion better able than themselves to deal with an opponent. Among the Comanche Indians of the American Plains, for instance, an aggrieved party might approach a renowned warrior for these purposes, and the warrior was under considerable pressure to accept this responsibility:

> A war leader who refused to accept the request for aid in prosecution was to be deemed unworthy of his rank, for it was imputed that he feared the defendant. No war leader could admit fear (Hoebel, 1940:64).

Similarly, in feudal Europe, the code of chivalry dictated that able-bodied knights should not refuse to take up arms on behalf of any weak and needy person (Bloch, 1964a:chap. 23), while more prosperous citizens could have recourse to professional champions who would fight the battles of others for a price (Lea, 1892:179–198). In modern societies, legal officials may be said to perform the role of champion when a citizen's grievance is prosecuted by the state as a crime (see below).

Another variety of surrogate makes an advance commitment (or is committed involuntarily) to satisfy any claims that might arise in the future from the misconduct of someone else. Hostages, for instance, perform this role in many societies, including those of the ancient Germans and Celts, among whom it was common practice for one or both parties to give up hostages when forging an important agreement of some sort (such as an agreement to settle a dispute through composition). For as long as the agreement was honored, each principal was required to provide for any hostages held in a manner befitting their rank. Should a party renege, however, the hostages that he had given might be injured or reduced to slavery (see Berger, 1940a, b). A related practice, still seen in the commercial life of the modern West, is the institution of suretyship, whereby a third party pledges to repay a debt if the original debtor should fail to discharge his or her obligations (see Berger, 1940a, b).

Yet another kind of surrogate is the scapegoat. This is an individual or group who, without having been appointed in advance, is compelled to bear punishment for the offense of someone else. Thus, where collective responsibility prevails, so that any member of a wrongdoer's group may be sanctioned for the misdeed, revenge is frequently taken against a relative or associate rather than against the original perpetrator. Scapegoats may also be selected along racial or ethnic lines. In the American South, for example, traditionally any black might be seized and punished for the transgression of another black against a white person. And during the Nazi occupation of Poland in the 1940s, it was Nazi policy to punish randomly selected Poles whenever an offense was committed by a Polish national against the Nazi regime (Gross, 1979: chap. 9). Scapegoats are not always selected because of their similarity to the offenders, however. Among the Suku of the Congo, for instance, victimized individuals often bypass the offender and members of his or her family, retaliating in kind against someone from a third group altogether. This new victim may seek satisfaction by taking revenge against someone from a fourth group, and so on (Kopytoff, 1961). A further illustration is provided by the Tlingit Indians of the American Northwest Coast, who punished a scapegoat when a high-status individual was discovered in the act of theft. It was commonly decided that such misbehavior arose because the thief had been bewitched by a slave, who was thereupon executed and the matter closed (Oberg, 1934:149, 155).

Some scapegoats voluntarily give themselves up for punishment on behalf of an offender. In modern society, such people are known colloquially as "fall guys." It is widely alleged that certain individuals serving time in American prisons are there because they have confessed falsely to misdeeds actually committed by higher-ranking associates in organized crime. Similarly, in traditional Thailand, men often accepted the blame for the misconduct of their higher-status patrons (Engel, 1978:74). In Manchu China, where witnesses were commonly hired to testify to one party's innocence or another's guilt, surrogation was also available for a price:

There were . . . some who made a living by confessing guilt and submitting on behalf of real offenders to corporal punishment, and we hear of "a band of devoted men" in the neighborhood of Canton prepared to risk transportation and even death for the sake of payment to their families (van der Sprenkel, 1962:71).

And, lastly, in a famous fictional account of a surrogate in revolutionary France, Sydney Carton substituted himself for Charles Darnay on the guillotine and lost his head (Dickens, 1859).

Whether given willingly or not, for free or for pay, the support provided by surrogates defines the extreme of partisan aid. Although, from the point of view of a principal, the surrogate's contribution is enormous, whether it is the most likely to result in an early and enduring settlement of a conflict is another question altogether. Much of the remainder of this essay pertains to the roles through which third parties strive primarily to end conflicts in which they become involved, but first we comment briefly upon another dimension of support roles, namely, opposition.

Opposition Roles

In situations of human conflict, one side's supporter is another side's opponent. All five of the support roles, when seen from the perspective of the principal on the other side, may be understood as opposition roles. Opponents act to force concessions from a party to a dispute, to inflict injury, or to thwart efforts to obtain satisfaction from an adversary. Their conduct may help, ultimately, to make one party lose.

In a few cases it is possible to find concepts in the practical world that designate the reverse of a support role. Thus, informers may be labelled by those against whom they inform as "stool-pigeons," "rats," or "tattle-tales." In the Soviet Union, citizens who step forward during a trial to denounce a defendant are called "social accusers," in contrast to citizen advocates who are called "social defenders" (see Feifer, 1964:104–106). In other cases, there is no special vocabulary to distinguish support from opposition. In the course of an on-going dispute, however, the distinction between supporters and opponents is usually sharp and significant.

Often it is possible to discern whether a given third party is primarily a supporter or an opponent. People in the former category are drawn into conflicts through their relationship with the principal whose cause they espouse, those in the latter group, through their relationship with the principal whom they seek to undermine. Thus, enemies or competitors of one principal may assist the other side in order to advance their own interests. In ancient Athens, for example, where paid advocates were despised and the usual excuse for assisting a litigant was a preexistent bond of intimacy, a lawyer might openly admit his own hostile interest in the case:

As an additional justification for his appearance the lawyer could always make the unusual plea that he did so because he was an enemy of the opposing side or the opposing lawyer and therefore had a personal interest in the outcome of the case (Chroust, 1954a:359).

In many other settings, the best chance poor and powerless people have in their conflicts with a more influential antagonist is to enlist the support of any of the latter's peers who happen to be the antagonist's enemies as well. In at least one part of traditional India, for instance, one "means of redress for an aggrieved lower-caste person, if his dispute was with his own patron, was to seek the help of his patron's enemies within the dominant caste" (Cohn, 1965:92). In 17th-century France, a royal edict of Louis XIV accused low-status persons of actually fomenting and exacerbating discord between aristocrats for similar reasons:

> It does appear that there are persons of ignoble birth . . . who have never borne arms, yet are insolent enough to call out gentlemen who refuse to give them satisfaction, justly grounding their refusal on the inequality of the conditions; in consequence of which these persons excite and oppose to them other gentlemen of like degree, whence arise not infrequently murders [i.e., duelling fatalities], the more detestable since they originate from abject sources (quoted in Baldick, 1965:60).

In political and international arenas as well, where numerous competing factions are commonly found, opponents frequently ally themselves with their enemy's enemies. "Politics makes strange bedfellows" is a colloquial expression which speaks to the unlikely associations often forged on the basis of nothing more than a common opposition to the same people or groups.

In some instances, neither the role of supporter nor that of opponent seems primary—the third party's ties to both principals are equally important. It is always true, moreover, that the distinction between the two categories of roles ultimately breaks down, with each constituting only a different perspective on the same partisan conduct. A fundamentally different kind of third-party intervention (even if it has points of convergence with partisan action—see above) is seen in the behavior of people who adopt a settlement role, placing themselves between the principals and directing their energies toward a resolution of the conflict. The next section examines these roles in some detail.

SETTLEMENT ROLES

Although most conflicts in all societies appear to have a bilateral character—with one side opposing another and any third parties assuming the role of supporters—all societies also seem to have at least occasional conflicts in which third parties intervene without taking sides, thereby imparting to the matter a trilateral character. Where a third party acts in a predominantly nonpartisan fashion, we may classify the behavior involved in terms of the several settlement roles in our typology (see Figure 4–1). We now consider these roles, proceeding in order of the amount of intervention each entails.

Friendly Peacemakers

A widely found settlement role is that of an individual or group who simply tries to influence parties in conflict to abandon their hostilities or, at least, not to escalate them. This is the role of the peacemaker. It is distinctive among settlement roles in one major respect. Unlike other third parties who relate to both sides of a conflict, peacemakers manage to do this without in any way addressing the matter at issue between the people involved. They strive merely to bring an end to the dispute, outwardly at least, regardless of its causes or content. However, there are two radically different ways in which the pacification of a conflict may proceed—one friendly, the other repressive. The first entails the least intervention of any settlement role, the second the most. Here we discuss the friendly variety of this phenomenon, returning to the repressive variety after surveying the roles that lie between them on the continuum of authoritative intervention.

A friendly peacemaker acts in the interests of both sides of a conflict and is, in effect, supportive of both without taking the side of either. Often this entails an effort to separate the antagonists from one another, by physical restraint if necessary, while in many cases the same result may be achieved simply by distracting them from their hostilities. In either case, the peacemaker may seek to convince the parties that their conflict is doing more harm than good for all concerned, that it is foolish, futile, or even funny, and that it should be brought to an end without further ado. Among the Cheyenne, for example, who stigmatize murderers as "putrid" and believe that they bring misfortune to the entire tribe until a purification ritual is performed, bystanders commonly try to persuade angry people to restrain themselves:

> People intervened when men quarreled violently. What they said was "You must not." "You must not be a murderer." "You will disgrace yourself." "It is not worth it" (Llewellyn and Hoebel, 1941:134; also see page 133).

The Shavante of central Brazil consider only disputes between men to be worthy of a hearing in their informal court (the "men's council"), whereas those between women are viewed as "laughable and unworthy of serious attention" (Maybury-Lewis, 1967:179). If women become violent to the point of seriously endangering each other, however, the men will pull them apart (see, e.g., Maybury-Lewis, 1967:180). Among the Yanomamö of Venezuela and Brazil, women often throw the leaves of a magical plant on men who threaten to use their war clubs, since this allegedly "keeps their tempers under control and prevents the fight from escalating to shooting" (Chagnon, 1977:37).

The Mbuti Pygmies of Zaire have an unusually well-developed system of friendly pacification, specialized in the role of the camp clown:

> The only individual who might be recognized as occupying a special political position in the life of the hunting band, on any ground other than age, is the camp clown. . . . His function is to act as a buffer between disputants, deflecting the more serious disputes away from their original sources, absolving other individuals of blame by accepting it himself. . . . The clown, however, never passes judgment or exerts authority (except through ridicule) (Turnbull, 1965:182–183).

The camp clown, it would seem, is not wholly unlike the court jester of the European Middle Ages. Still another example of friendly peacemaking is provided by the religious leaders (*sheikhs* and *wadaads*) of northern Somalia, who resolve many disputes simply by insisting that each party swear an oath to be peaceful toward the other (Lewis, 1961:217). Friendly peacemakers are found in modern as well as in tribal and other traditional societies. Bartenders may play this role, for instance, and so may lifeguards at public beaches (see Edgerton, 1979:47–49), and the friends, relatives, and peers of people in conflict from all walks of life. Indeed, in some situations, peacemakers of this kind are so near at hand and so quick to intervene when trouble occurs that those with complaints can hurl themselves at their opponents without fear of retaliation, knowing full well that they will be restrained before any harm can be done. A pattern of this sort has been observed in Japan:

> It's amazing, really, how some people change when they're drunk and surrounded by a lot of people. They seem to go out of their mind, sometimes, but they know really that they're safe, because if they provoke the other chap to violence there are enough people there to keep them apart. And the next morning they'll all be smiles and greet each other as if nothing happened. But the one who spoke his mind will know the other one will remember what he said. He'll have got his point home. In fact people—you could see it—often used to come to a party with the express intention of picking a quarrel and getting something off their chest (quoted in Dore, 1978:266).

It thus seems that friendly peacemakers not only keep hostilities from escalating but may sometimes help create a kind of forum for the airing of grievances, however little they intend to do so.

Mediators

In scholarly as well as popular thought, the roles most associated with the idea of the third party seem to be those of the mediator, the arbitrator, and the judge (see, e.g., Eckhoff, 1966; Koch, 1974:27–31; Shapiro,

1975:323–325). Such roles are actually found in only a limited range of social settings, however, and they include some of the most developed and specialized manifestations of social control that have ever been observed. The literature pertaining to them is quite extensive, but for present purposes a brief overview of each should be sufficient.

On the continuum of intervention portrayed in our typology, mediators appear just one step beyond friendly peacemakers (see Figure 4-1). Like peacemakers, mediators in their pure form refuse to take sides, but they differ from peacemakers in their willingness to acknowledge and, often, to delve into a problem existing in the relationship between those in conflict. Mediators seek to facilitate a solution of the problem by encouraging the parties to reach a mutually agreeable settlement, typically a compromise. Since theirs is essentially a role through which the disputants themselves are led to negotiate an outcome, mediation has been described simply as "supervised negotiation" (Hart and Sacks, 1958:655) and, similarly, as "negotiation by brokerage" (Koch, 1979:4). It may nevertheless include a broad spectrum of activities, ranging from complete passivity—so that a mediator's mere presence is the only contribution made—to highly aggressive conduct in devising and promoting the terms by which a conflict might be resolved (see Fuller, 1971; Gulliver, 1977). Ultimately, however, mediators defer to the principals with respect to the terms of a possible resolution of the conflict. Beyond that point, when a third party unilaterally decides on the proper outcome, the degree of intervention reaches a level associated with the more authoritative roles of the arbitrator and the judge.

Social scientists, especially anthropologists, have described mediators at work in a number of societies (for overviews, see Witty, 1980:chap. 1; Merry, 1982). But the scholarly literature may inadvertently overrepresent the more active forms of mediation, if only because the varied behavior of active mediators may seem especially worthy of detailed description. Passive mediation—in which the principals are quietly encouraged to discuss their differences—is probably far more frequent, and it has a force of its own that should not be underestimated:

> By his very presence a quite passive mediator can encourage positive communication and interaction between the parties, stimulating the continuation or the renewal of the exchange of information. Because he is there, the parties are often constrained to observe minimal courtesy to each other, to reduce personal invective and to listen and to respond with some relevance. . . . This has been a quite deliberate strategy on occasion, for example, by some American industrial mediators. They attend a meeting between the two parties, but sit and say nothing and seek to show no particular reaction to what is said and done (Gulliver, 1977:26–27, including note 13).

Passive mediation is also commonly used by police officers when handling interpersonal disputes (see Black, 1980:chap. 5, especially 132–133). Thus, an American officer made the following observation about a colleague:

> One police officer I really admired, he'd come into a family beef with a hus-
> band and wife throwing and yelling at each other. Then he'd set down on the
> couch and take his hat off, and he didn't say a word. Sooner or later the
> couple felt kind of silly. He'd take 45 minutes in each of these situations, but
> he never had to come back (quoted by Muir, 1977:82).

Mediation among friends is likely to be very passive as well, and so is the
sort of mediation—usually not recognized as such—often performed by
children when a conflict erupts between their parents (see Baumgartner,
1981:chap. 2).

Many of the mediators portrayed in the anthropological literature fall
so far toward the other extreme that they might almost be said to make
authoritative decisions, and so cross the line into arbitration (see below).
This applies, for instance, to the *monkalun* of the Ifugao, a tribal people
of the Philippines:

> To the end of peaceful settlement, [the monkalun] exhausts every art of Ifu-
> gao diplomacy. He wheedles, coaxes, flatters, threatens, drives, scolds, in-
> sinuates. He beats down the demands of the plaintiffs or prosecution, and
> bolsters up the proposals of the defendants until a point be reached at which
> the two parties may compromise. If the culprit or accused be not disposed to
> listen to reason and runs away or "shows fight" when approached, the mon-
> kalun waits till the former ascends into his house, follows him, and, *war-knife
> in hand*, sits in front of him and compels him to listen . . . . The monkalun has
> no authority. All that he can do is to act as a peace making go-between. His
> only power is in his art of persuasion, his tact and his skillful playing on
> human emotions and motives (Barton, 1969:87).

Although the monkalun is one of the most frequently cited examples of a
mediator in the anthropological literature, the description above suggests
that he might reasonably be viewed as an arbitrator or even—in light of
his threats of violence—as a kind of judge. Consider first the role of the
arbitrator.

Arbitrators

Along the continuum of authoritative intervention, arbitration appears
between mediation and adjudication (see Figure 4-1). Unlike a mediator
but like a judge, the arbitrator pronounces a resolution to the conflict in
question, sometimes even designating one side as right and the other as
wrong. Also like a judge, the arbitrator makes a decision without regard—
outwardly at least—to the wishes of the parties involved. In contrast to
a judge, however, the arbitrator does not have the capacity to enforce a
settlement if it is subsequently violated or ignored. Accordingly, arbitrators give opinions rather than verdicts.

Arbitrated opinions nevertheless operate as effectively as judicial verdicts in many instances. Often the principals agree in advance to abide by
whatever an arbitrator decides, as happened, for instance, when Spain

and Portugal agreed to let the Pope of the Roman Catholic Church determine how South America would be divided between them. In addition, the arbitrator's decision may be effectively enforceable by someone external to the arbitration process itself, such as close associates of those in conflict or members of the community at large. Considerable pressure to accept arbitrated decisions is commonly present, a pattern especially well documented in tribal and other simpler societies, where traditional leaders may be mobilized to resolve disputes by arbitration. When arbitrators make a decision in northern Somalia, for example, enforcement typically depends upon the response of the principals' relatives:

> If their kinsmen wish to reach a peaceful settlement, either through fear of war or pressure from the [British] Administration, and if they consider that the [arbitrators'] decision is a reasonable one, they will see that it is executed. If necessary, pressure will be put upon the parties directly concerned to force them to accept the award. But the panel of arbitrators, in itself, has no punitive sanctions with which it can coerce litigants into accepting its judgments (Lewis, 1961:228).

In modern societies, arbitrated decisions may be enforceable by a court of law, as in the American process known as "binding arbitration" (for overviews, see, e.g., Mentschikoff, 1961; Getman, 1979). On the other hand, much arbitration also occurs without any mechanism of enforcement at all, other than a desire on the part of the disputants to avoid the displeasure of those making the decision or, possibly, of supernatural spirits. It has even been proposed that supernatural spirits are themselves used as arbitrators in some cases, such as when an ordeal or oracle is employed to resolve a dispute (Koch, 1979:5).

One earlier society with a highly developed system of arbitration was ancient Ireland, where the practice has come to be known, somewhat misleadingly, as "*brehon* law." The brehon was among the most esteemed of men:

> The brehon was an arbitrator, umpire, expounder of the law, rather than a judge in the modern acceptation. . . . [His] position resembled that of an eminent Roman jurisprudens, whose opinion was eagerly sought and paid for by people in legal difficulties. He heard the case, gave it the necessary consideration, and pronounced a decision in accordance with law and justice. This decision, though called a judgment, and eminently entitled to that name, was not precisely what the word judgment means with us. It was rather a declaration of law and justice as applied to the facts before him, rather an award founded in each particular case on a submission to arbitration. There was no public officer whose duty it was to enforce the judgment when given. The successful party was left to execute it himself (Ginnell, 1924:51).

Although the party favored by a brehon's decision was theoretically "left to execute it himself," in fact the pressures of kinship and popular opinion were usually entirely equal to the task of gaining compliance:

These combined forces went far to render executive officers of the law, as sheriffs, bailiffs, and police, unnecessary. They were practically irresistible, for they could go the length of outlawing a man and rendering his life and all he possessed worthless to him if he dared to withstand the execution of what a brehon had declared to be the demands of law and justice. They were quite as effectual as is what we now call the arm of the law (Ginnell, 1924:51).

Much "international law" is also arbitration, since most international tribunals have no capacity to enforce their rulings.

Judges

Even if most arbitrators know that their decisions will ultimately be enforced through one means or another, the fact remains that they do not have the capacity to see to this themselves. Hence, they are forever dependent upon someone else, and so have considerably less authority than judges. Judges do not merely give opinions; they give orders. They are dependent upon no one, except in the limited sense in which those with authority always must depend upon their subordinates for obedience (see Simmel, 1960:part 3, chap. 1). Judges, then, address the matter separating the principals (like mediators), make a settlement decision (like arbitrators), and, if necessary, enforce it.

Many variants of adjudication appear in social space, each with different procedures, personnel, and jurisdictions (see Fuller, 1978). Some judges, for instance, are empowered only to hear complaints brought to them by citizens, whereas others can initiate cases on their own. Some are called upon only to decide whether specific charges are justified or not, while others delve into the details of an allegation. Some routinely decide which of two parties is in the right, while others commonly find both sides to have merit. In practice, these and other dimensions combine in a number of different ways.

Among the Tarahumara Indians of northern Mexico, for example, the *gobernador*, or mayor, holds public trials and punishes those he defines as offenders, but has no power unless a specific complaint is brought to him. Thus, one gobernador commented:

> There are many bad things, but people do not complain. If they complain to me, then I must do something. If not . . . , we can only give advice and warn the people not to do these things (Fried, 1953:295).

Among the Kpelle of Liberia, too, the chief's court will hear only specific complaints brought to it by citizens, and it normally ascribes blame to only one side (Gibbs, 1962). The same is true of most courts of law in modern society. The Lozi judges of Barotseland (now Zambia), however—the first tribal judges to be observed systematically by an anthropologist— also seemed to hear only specific complaints, but they often resolved cases by declaring both parties at fault to some degree (see Gluckman, 1967). Still another pattern was followed by the courts of Manchu China, where one party had to be found wrong and to suffer accordingly in virtually every case. There could be no dismissals:

> The unavoidable consequence of a legal case once started was punishment for at least one person. It could end in punishment for the accused, if judged guilty; if he were not, punishment would be assigned to the unjustified accuser (van der Sprenkel, 1962:69; for a closely related process among the Ashanti of Ghana, see Rattray, 1979:chap. 22).

Another variable altogether is the number of judges. While modern trial courts in the United States and similar societies typically have only one judge (unless there is a jury), for example, so-called popular tribunals have several (e.g., Berman, 1969), and the Lozi court—or *kuta*—appears to have had about 20 (see Gluckman, 1967:9–14). The kuta, in fact, provided an unusually elaborate mode of settlement. After the plaintiff, defendant, and their witnesses had spoken at a hearing, the numerous members of the court took over:

> The kuta, assisted by anyone present, proceeds to cross-examine and to pit the parties and witnesses against one another. When all the evidence has been heard, the lowest induna [an official] gives the first judgment. He is then followed by councillors [sitting] on the three mats (indunas, princes, and stewards) in ascending order of seniority across from one mat to the other, until the senior councillor-of-the-right gives the final judgment. This is then referred to the ruler of the capital, who confirms, rejects, or alters it, or refers it back to the kuta for further investigation and discussion. It is this final judgment by the last induna to speak which, subject to the ruler's approval, is binding (Gluckman, 1967:15).

As possibly the best known of all third parties, judges may not need further description. In the popular mind, however, judges are associated strictly with law, or governmental social control (Black, 1972:1096), and so it should be noted that the concept of the judge advanced here is somewhat broader, including as it does any third party who resolves a conflict with an order backed by sanctions. Adjudication in this sense occurs in a wide variety of social settings, even in stateless societies that have, by definition, no law on a permanent basis. The nomads of northern Somalia, for example, traditionally adjudicate disputes within their lineage organizations ("dia-paying groups"):

> Fighting between individual members of a dia-paying group when several members are present, leads to prompt and concerted action. The disputants are separated; if necessary they are seized by young men on the instructions of the elders, and brought for trial before a dia-paying group council. When compensation has been determined . . . or a fine imposed it must be paid, or at least promised, or punitive action will be taken by the group as a whole. A recalcitrant member of a dia-paying group is bound to a tree and several of his best sheep or a coveted camel slaughtered before him until he agrees to the judgment of his elders. The slaughtered stock are eaten by the elders (Lewis, 1961:232)

Adjudication in our broad sense may also be seen in families, particularly those with a highly patriarchal structure, and in organizations such as business firms and voluntary associations in which judgments against members may ultimately be enforced by their expulsion ("firing," "black-balling," "excommunicating," etc.). It should thus be clear that from the standpoint of our typology, courts of law are but one among many settings where judges may be observed.

Repressive Peacemakers

We now reach the phenomenon of repressive pacification, a mode of conflict management involving the greatest exercise of authority by a third party that is ever seen. Paradoxically, it shares with the gentlest mode— the friendly version of pacification—one major characteristic: an indifference to the issues dividing those in conflict (see above). Here, however, this indifference does not express an overriding concern for the well-being of the parties but rather a total lack of concern, if not contempt. Whatever grievance one or both principals might have against the other is likely to be dismissed, if it is noticed at all. The process is negative rather than positive in spirit, hostile, and possibly even wantonly destructive toward those involved. The point is simply to end the conflict as quickly as possible, violently if necessary, without regard to the consequences for the parties. If neither side is allowed to get the better of the other, it is only because, by dint of their conflict, both are deemed wrong and possibly worthy of punishment. Indeed, the conflict itself is regarded as a kind of offense against the third party.

Colonial settings give rise to much repressive pacification, since under these conditions the foreign administration often seeks to eliminate the use of violence by the native population. Traditional modes of social control such as blood vengeance, feuding, and fighting are therefore outlawed and subject to penal measures. That such traditional practices constitute the pursuit of justice for those involved is ignored entirely. The British, French, Germans, and other Western Europeans commonly related to their colonial populations in this way, and so have other conquerors. In northern Albania, for example, repressive pacification was employed during the Turkish and Austro-Hungarian occupations:

> Friends were not the only interveners. Occasionally the Turkish government took a hand, declaring on penalty of imprisonment, internment and burning out that all feuds more than seven years old were to be compounded by a money payment and not reopened. When during the 1914–18 war Austria-Hungary was in occupation of all north Albania, she also ordered blood feuds to be ended with a money payment (Hasluck, 1954:259).

In Irian Jaya (West New Guinea), first the Dutch and later the Indonesians made similar efforts. In the district of Jalémó, for instance, the people learned that "a new kind of stranger who neither spoke nor understood their language would punish any form of violent behavior" (Koch, 1974:223; for a similar policy by the Australians in Papua New Guinea, see, e.g., Reay, 1974:205, 209). During the establishment of the Soviet Union, conflict handled by traditional means among some of the Asian peoples, especially in the northern Caucasus, was treated in much the same fashion, only in this case the settlement of disputes by compensation payments was also viewed as improper by the authorities:

> The history of many peoples shows that usually, over a period of time, the vendetta is gradually replaced by a system of monetary compensation or blood money. The Soviet authorities prevented this natural evolution from taking place by making it a criminal offense to give or receive such compensation. At the same time, they set up procedures for the reconciliation of feuding families. Those who refused to be reconciled were deported (Chalidze, 1977:119).

Repressive pacification occurs in many noncolonial settings as well. Among the Tikopians of Polynesia, for example, the chief of each clan is said to own his group's land, and so is able to repress disputes between his fellow clansmen by threatening to evict them:

> He says to the disputants, "Abandon your fighting that you are carrying on there. Plant food properly for the two of you in my ground." The words "my ground" are not empty of significance. For if the men persist in their quarrel the chief will send a message, "Go the pair of you to your own place wherever that may be; go away from my ground." In fact, they have no ground to resort to; their alternative is the ocean [i.e., suicide], so they capitulate (Firth, 1936:384).

In modern America, the police routinely act as repressive peacemakers when feuds arise between juvenile gangs or between so-called organized crime families, and, for that matter, whenever they encounter fighting or other violence (which is nearly always a mode of conflict management between those involved). Finally, it should be noted that adults such as parents and teachers often relate in this manner to the disputes of children. The fighting itself is defined as offensive and subject to punishment, regardless of why it occurs. From the standpoint of a repressive peacemaker, a conflict between people is not so unlike a conflict between cats or dogs.

MARGINAL ROLES

Although the most general division in our typology of third parties is that between supporters and settlement agents, two of the roles we identify are not totally captured by either of these categories. One of them, that of the negotiator, synthesizes elements of both support and settlement behavior. The other, that of the healer, seems to belong in a class of its own, entirely beyond the rest of the third parties. We close our overview of the typology by examining each of these marginal phenomena in turn.

Negotiators

For present purposes, it is important to distinguish between the concepts of *negotiation* and *negotiator*. Whereas the former refers to a particular *process* of conflict management, the latter refers to a particular *role* that might be performed in such a process. More specifically, negotiation is a process of joint settlement of a dispute (see Gulliver, 1979:5). The person presenting one side's interests may be the principal himself or herself, or a third party acting on his or her behalf. In our typology, the role of negotiator always refers to a third party, to someone who represents a disputant and works out a settlement—negotiates—with the other side (perhaps the other principal, perhaps another negotiator). Since the original parties might negotiate a settlement on their own, however, it should be clear that negotiation does not necessarily involve anyone performing the special role of negotiator (compare, e.g., Gulliver, 1979:3–6).

Negotiators perform a hybrid role, mixing support and settlement behavior. Like advocates or allies, they are partisan, openly taking one side, but, like arbitrators or judges, they intervene in a conflict to resolve it (see Eisenberg, 1976:662–665). They represent only one party, and yet they serve both. In modern society, for example, lawyers often act as negotiators for their clients. In fact, the vast majority of civil complaints and lawsuits in modern America are resolved by a negotiated settlement— worked out by lawyers—rather than by a court judgment, and even criminal cases resulting in conviction usually are settled by negotiation of a guilty plea (known as "plea bargaining") instead of by a trial in court (see, e.g., Newman, 1956, 1966; Buckle and Buckle, 1977; Mather, 1979b). Insurance adjusters are active negotiators as well. They are primarily responsible for successfully negotiating settlements in over 95 percent of all bodily injury claims against insured automobile drivers in the United States (Ross, 1970:24–25, 141).

Negotiators are prominent in many societies, and in some are virtually the only third parties available to handle certain varieties of conflict. Among the Yurok Indians of northern California, for example, negotiators known as *wegô*, or "crossers," apparently handled most of the cases involving different segments of the tribe:

> They were chosen by the parties at issue: two or three, possibly four, to a side. There were always expected to be more than one, since a single man could not properly maintain his case against several opponents. They were however supposed to be impartial enough to be able to reach a fair agreement with the representatives of the other side. . . . They examined the "litigants" and necessary witnesses, then went into conference and rendered a

verdict.... Each wegô received from his client a standard fee of one large dentalium shell. This fee was called we-na'ai, "his moccasin," because it reimbursed the wegô for the walking back and forth he had to do in his commission (Kroeber, 1926:514–515).

The role of the negotiator is also highly developed in the customary law of northern Albania, where each principal in a conflict may, in effect, hire an elder to work out a settlement on his behalf. Each must first deposit a "pledge," such as a gun or watch, with the elder of his choice in order to assure that a proper fee will be paid at the conclusion of the case. (The fee, incidentally, is referred to as "sandals" in one area, along the same lines as the "moccasin" of the Yurok negotiators cited above.) If the principals agree to accept the decision reached by the elders, the fee is paid, the pledge returned, and the case closed (Hasluck, 1954:chap. 13). Settlement by negotiators is prominent in Thailand as well, where each principal commonly relies upon a *phuyai*, or "big person," to work out a resolution with the other side (Engel, 1978:75–77). In tribal Europe, among the early English, Scots, French, Germans, and others, the nego-tiator for a kin group was called a "forspeaker" (see Pound, 1953:70; English translation suggested by Pollock and Maitland, 1968:vol. 1, 215, note 1). As a final example, it might be added that when the duel was a major method of dispute settlement in Europe, the "second," or assistant of each combatant, would often serve as a negotiator to end the conflict before blood was spilled. One early commentator even claimed that "there is not one cause in fifty where discreet seconds might not settle the difference and reconcile the parties before they came into the field." In the same vein, a famous fencing master is remembered for his observation that "it is not the sword or the pistol that kills, but the seconds" (both quotes from Baldick, 1965:38).

Healers

To close our overview, we turn now to an unusual species of third party that manages to intervene in human conflict without seeming to do so at all. This is the healer or, in modern language, the therapist. In some societies this role may be performed by an exorcist or sorcerer, in others by a psychiatrist or medical practitioner. Regardless of the particular form taken, however, all healers share a distinctive approach toward people who have grievances against one another.

Perhaps the most significant characteristic of healers is that they generally proceed without any explicit recognition that a conflict is the occasion for their intervention. On the contrary, their involvement is al-ways understood as a kind of help, a treatment for someone who is suffer-ing from an affliction beyond his or her control. The problem for the healer is to restore the afflicted individual to normality rather than—as in the other forms of intervention discussed above—to contribute to justice (see Black, 1976:4–6). Even though this definition of the situation prevails, healers are actively involved in the enforcement of normative standards, in nurturing conformity in deviants, and in fostering amity between estranged persons. Insofar as the affliction requiring their attention is a pattern of conduct viewed as undesirable, healers act on behalf of a complainant, an alleged offender, or both. To this degree they are properly understood as third parties, and as specialists in the field of social control (see, e.g., Goffman, 1969; Black, 1976:4–6, 118–121; Horwitz, 1982). In calling upon the services of a healer, even for help with their own affliction, people may be dramatizing grievances, enlisting support, or possibly seeking to embarrass someone who has offended them (see Lewis, 1966; Baumgartner, 1981:chap. 2).

Many examples of healers can be found in the ranks of supernaturally skilled persons around the world. For instance, in Somalia (see Lewis, 1966), among the Tonga of Zambia (see Colson, 1969), in medieval Europe (see Cohn, 1975), and in numerous other settings, people behaving in culturally inappropriate ways may be considered to be possessed by spirits and to need curative rituals staged by specialists. Typically, the object is to propitiate, expel, or master the offending supernatural spirit. Such a process is illustrated by the handling of a case in a Swahili tribe of East Africa:

> At that time Chuma had had an episode of mental disturbance. He became irrational and violent and, as his brother described it, would throw men about with the strength of an ox. . . . Chuma's brothers went to Tawalini and found out through divination that his trouble was caused by a *shetani* [spirit] that had been sent to annoy him by the outraged husband of a woman to whom he had been paying attention. . . . The deranged man was exorcised by [a religious specialist]. Seven loaves of bread and seven coconuts were arranged on a table which was held over Chuma's head by his brothers, their hands joining to form a circle around him. A cock was slaughtered . . . and the blood applied to the patient. Then parts of the Koran with special mystical meanings were read aloud. The rite accomplished its purpose; Chuma recovered completely and went back to his occupation of fishing (Gray, 1969:182).

Similarly, throughout Latin America, religious specialists treat unacceptable behavior in their clients by staging rituals to retrieve their souls, which are believed to be lost (see, e.g., Gillin, 1948, 1956).

Also examples of healers in our sense are medical specialists who attribute behavioral abnormality to organic causes and treat it accordingly. Thus, in ancient Egypt and Greece, as well as in later civilizations influenced by them, much unacceptable conduct in women was attributed to a wandering uterus or other reproductive disorder (see Veith, 1965). In this vein, a 16th-century French surgeon, Ambroise Paré, made the following observations:

> For som accidents com by suppression of the [menses], others com by corruption of the seed, but if the matter bee cold, it bringeth a drousiness . . . whereby the woman sinketh down as if shee were astonished, and lieth with-

out motion. . . . If it be more gross, it conferreth a convulsion; if it participate of the nature of a gross melancholik humor, it bringeth such heaviness, fear, and sorrowfulness, that the party that is vexed therewith shall think that hee shall die presently, and cannot bee brought out of his minde by anie means or reason; if of a cholerick humor, it causseth the madness called *furor uterinus*, and such a pratling, that they speak all things that are to bee concealed; and a giddiness of the head, by reason that the animal spirit is suddenly shaken by the admixture of a putrefied vapour and hot spirit; but nothing is more admirable, then that diseas taketh the patient sometimes with laughing, and sometimes with weeping, for som at the first will weep and then laugh in the same diseas and state thereof (quoted in Veith, 1965:114).

Physical remedies were accordingly prescribed for the organic disturbances responsible for these symptoms; fumigations of the uterus, ingestion of herbs and other substances, and applications of ointments were all used in various countries (Veith, 1965). In the modern era, biologically oriented people are more likely to attribute aberrant conduct to disorders of the brain than to disorders of the uterus, and to pursue treatment through the use of drugs that affect neurochemistry.

Contemporary healers are often psychiatrists or psychologists. Unusual behavior, from their perspective, is generally seen as the outcome of underlying emotional disturbances, which can be cured or manipulated through a variety of psychotherapeutic techniques. In the pursuit of a cure, psychotherapists may encourage their patients to discuss their problems at length, may analyze their dreams, and may probe into details of their personal lives. They may orchestrate group encounters or may recommend changes in a person's routine (including commitment to a mental hospital). Some may plan behavior-modification strategies to help people overcome opiate or alcohol "addiction," cigarette smoking, "over"-eating, or violent propensities. Common to all of these strategies is the underlying aim of changing or reordering an individual's personality until it accords with the "normality" of others.

In its own way, the role of healer combines elements of support and of settlement. Healers serve as friends to their patients, doing everything on their behalf. At the same time, they speak with some authority about what, if anything, is "wrong" with a given person and what is necessary to achieve a "cure" or a proper "adjustment." Healers, like negotiators, therefore occupy a composite role. Unlike negotiators, however, or any other third parties in our scheme, they are not identified with human conflict at all. For this reason, in our typology the healer is placed entirely beyond the boundaries within which third parties usually are found.

A NOTE ON LEGAL OFFICIALS

Before concluding, it might be noted that in the foregoing pages we have not given special attention to third parties who intervene in the name of the state, or legal officials. Instead, we have endeavored to show that each mode of intervention occurs in a wide range of social settings, informal as well as formal, and that it would be inaccurate to identify any single species of third party exclusively with law. It should be added, moreover, that the opposite applies as well. Though none of the roles in our typology is performed by legal officials all of the time, all are performed by legal officials some of the time.

In a modern society such as the United States, for example, legal officials as a group perform virtually every one of the 12 roles in our classification from time to time. Police officers often simply give information or advice, prosecutors act as judges when they dismiss cases, judges mediate and arbitrate, and so on. Indeed, it would seem that police officers by themselves perform every role in the typology, shifting from one to another as they move from encounter to encounter (see Cumming, Cumming, and Edell, 1965; Bittner, 1967; Rubinstein, 1973; Bard and Zacker, 1976; Black, 1980:chap. 5). Their role even changes as a single case moves through stages of the criminal process, so that an officer might begin to handle a case in the field as, say, a healer or a friendly peacemaker, resolve it by arrest—in most instances a kind of adjudication—only to find himself or herself merely a witness—an ally of the prosecution—when the case is heard in court. Complainants undergo a similar transformation, since a legal official, the prosecutor, steps forth as their surrogate to pursue their grievance in court (compare Christie, 1977), while still another official of the state, a judge, decides who is right. Similar dynamics are found in conflict management of all kinds. Conflict itself constantly fluctuates, and any classification of its structure should be viewed as provisional, valid only until a new episode begins (see Mather and Yngvesson, 1981).

CONCLUSION

From one standpoint, our typology offers a preliminary vocabulary with which the many species and varieties of third parties may be classified. It thereby serves a purpose similar to that which a handbook or field guide might serve a butterfly collector or a birdwatcher. Beyond this, however, the typology—like other classifications of empirical phenomena—describes a universe of its own, a range of variation. In so doing, it invites inquiry into why such variation occurs.

Our typology thus provides a focus for a sociological theory of the third party: Why do third parties intervene in conflicts in so many different ways? Why does one conflict result in, say, mediation or arbitration while another is adjudicated or repressed? Why does one person intervene as an advocate or ally while another is willing only to give information or advice? The typology challenges us to understand differences in conflict management across communities and societies and, for that matter, across social settings of all kinds. It challenges us to predict and explain the role of third parties from one case to the next. Perhaps in closing we should mention briefly several of the patterns we have so far discovered in the course of our investigations of the third party, considering in particular the social conditions associated with settlement behavior— friendly pacification, mediation, arbitration, adjudication, and repressive pacification. We leave aside for now the social characteristics of the parties in conflict—a topic that has already been explored in some detail as a factor in legal behavior such as adjudication (see Black, 1976)—and turn instead to the characteristics of the third parties themselves.

Our review of the empirical literature on conflict management suggests, for example, that the role of settlement agents is closely associated with their social status in relation to that of the parties in conflict, i.e., their relative status (for further details on the concept of status as used here, see generally Black, 1976:chaps. 2–6). All else being the same, rarely is a settlement agent's status lower than that of the parties in conflict; more often it is about equal, but usually it is higher. What is more, it appears that *the higher the settlement agent's relative status, the more often authoritative intervention occurs.* Recalling the rank order of the five settlement roles by their degree of intervention (see Figure 4-1), this implies that—all else being constant—the status distance between a third party and the principals will be least in friendly pacification, somewhat greater in mediation, greater still in arbitration, then greater in adjudication, and greatest in settings where repressive pacification occurs. Since our purpose here is merely to illustrate the nature of the theory of the third party, we shall not attempt to review the empirical evidence relating to this formulation, but turn instead to a second example.

Another variable that appears to be related to settlement behavior is the degree of relational distance, or intimacy, between the third party and the principals (see Black, 1976:40–41, for an explication of relational distance as a social variable). Settlement agents might be extremely intimate with both principals—as when an entire conflict begins and ends within a single household—or they might be somewhat removed from both, or they might be complete strangers. Generally, the intimacy between the agent and each of the principals is about equal, so that the three parties together form an isosceles triangle of relational distance (see Simmel, 1960:149–153), but the actual distances involved vary considerably. Furthermore, it appears that *the greater the relational distance between the settlement agent and the principals, the more often authoritative intervention occurs.* Friendly pacification thus seems to be most likely to occur where settlement agents are highly intimate with the parties in conflict, mediation would be expected where there is a bit less intimacy, and arbitration in situations where there is less still. Adjudication seems to occur where there is even more distance between the parties—they typically share only the same community or region—whereas repressive pacification appears to be found where settlement agents are the most distant from those whose conflicts they handle and find so offensive. It seems, incidentally, that what applies to intimacy also applies to cultural homogeneity, so that the greater the cultural distance between the settlement agent and the principals, the more often authoritative intervention occurs. In any event, we again leave the empirical evidence aside, hoping that these formulations illustrate the kind of theory our typology anticipates. It should be understood, moreover, that support, as well as settlement behavior, is ultimately subject to this theoretical strategy. It is possible, in principle, to predict and explain each degree of partisan involvement—from the giving of information and advice to advocacy, alliance, and surrogation—with such characteristics of third parties as their relative status, their intimacy with those in conflict, and their cultural identity. It should also be possible to specify how the nature of support predicts and explains aspects of settlement behavior, and vice versa, and to specify conditions under which a negotiator, a healer, or whatever, might appear. The theory of the third party contemplates all of this and more.

Finally, it might be noted that a theory of the third party may prove to have practical as well as scientific interest. Since the theory is intended, among other things, to specify how conflict management varies with the social characteristics of those involved as third parties, its formulations might be used to advantage by particular segments of society or, on a case-by-case basis, by one side or the other in a conflict. Modern courts, for example, are readily subject to manipulation of this kind. Thus, a theory of the third party will ultimately be able to specify precisely how the social composition of the judiciary relates to its behavior. What, for instance, would result from a greater degree of social heterogeneity in the largely homogeneous judiciary of modern America? What would result from an increase in the number of judges who are black, Hispanic, Asian-American, female, working-class, or who have other characteristics that have traditionally been excluded? If such characteristics are indeed associated with specifiable patterns of adjudication—such as lesser severity or a greater tendency to make compromise decisions—surely this knowledge would be relevant to legal policymakers and reformers, not to mention practicing attorneys and their clients. Similar questions might be raised about the social characteristics of juries, police officers, and all the other third parties in the legal process. For present purposes, however, suffice it to say that a theory of the third party such we envisage will present countless opportunities for legal engineering. It may also pose a challenge to conventional conceptions of justice.

Part II

Understanding the Work
That Courts Do

5

The Radiating Effects of Courts

Marc Galanter

The flow of cases into the courts has figured prominently in many recent discussions. Fear that courts may be overwhelmed by swollen case loads (made up in part of matters better handled elsewhere) (see, e.g., the papers from the Pound Conference, 1976) is accompanied by distress at disputants' readiness to resort to the judicial process (e.g., Rosenberg, 1972; Barton, 1975). On the other hand, there is concern to provide "access" to groups and interests that have found it difficult to obtain a judicial hearing (see Cappelletti and Garth, 1978). Notwithstanding their sharp differences about which cases should be in the courts, both sets of critics share a focus on the centripetal movement of cases into the courts and a tendency to define the problem as one of matching cases and forums. Courts should get the number and kind of cases they can handle; cases should find appropriate forums in which they can be resolved.

Author's Note: Preparation of this report was supported by National Institute of Law Enforcement and Criminal Justice Grant No. 78-NI-AX-0137 ("The Development of Empirical Theories of Courts"). The content of this report is the responsibility of the author alone and does not represent the view of the Institute or of the other investigators on this grant.

Parts of this paper were included in reports to the Colloquium on "Access to Justice After the Publication of the Florence Project Series: Prospects for Future Action" in Florence, October 15–18, 1979, and at a symposium on "The Educational Role of Law and Public Participation in the Legal Process" at the Institute of State and Law in Moscow, December 10–12, 1979. The former has been published as "Justice in Many Rooms," in M. Cappelletti, ed., *Access to Justice in the Welfare State* (Alphen aan den Rijn: Sithoff; Stuttgart: Klett-Cotta; Bruxelles: Bruylant; Firenze: LeMonnier, 1981). An enlarged version may be found in the *Journal of Legal Pluralism* No. 19 (1981) entitled "Justice in Many Rooms: Courts, Private Ordering and Indigenous Law."

I am grateful to Murray Edelman, John Griffiths, Tom Heller, Richard Lempert, Steward Macaulay, and David Trubek for helpful responses to an earlier draft of this paper. I would also like to thank Joan E. T. Stearns and Laura Woliver for their capable assistance.

In this chapter I propose to look through the other end of the telescope. Instead of the centripetal movement of cases into courts, I want to look at the flow of influence outward from courts to the wider world of disputing and regulating. I shall argue that understanding the courts and their work requires that we assess this centrifugal flow of influence. I argue further that such influence cannot be ascertained by attending only to the messages propounded by the courts. It depends on the resources and capacities of their various audiences and on the normative orderings indigenous to the various social locations where messages from the courts impinge.

THE CENTRIFUGAL VIEW OF COURTS

Examination of the centrifugal flow of influence from courts is not an enterprise without precedent. Indeed this outward flow is the subject of much professional discourse about legal doctrine, often proceeding on the unstated assumption that the authoritative pronouncements of the highest courts penetrate automatically—swiftly, costlessly, without distortion—to all corners of the legal world. This assumption of automatic penetration has been challenged by several generations of studies of "the limits of effective legal action" (Pound, 1917; Jones, 1969). This includes a tradition of "impact studies," which has demonstrated that the penetration of rules is variable and uneven, and that the rules undergo significant transformation in the process (Grossman, 1970:545 ff.; Wasby, 1970; Levine, 1970:599 ff.; cf. Feeley, 1976:498 ff.). The outward flow of legal influence is also the subject of a tradition of research on deterrence and other effects of sanctioning (Gibbs, 1975), which alert us to the complexity of the interaction between legal and other influences.

We begin our examination of the centrifugal flow with a crude map of the landscape of dispute processing, drawn from several decades of social research on law. Most disputes that, under current rules, could be brought to a court are, in fact, never placed on the agenda of any court. Many of these disputes are "resolved" by resignation, "lumping it," "avoidance," "exit," or "self-help" by one party (Hirschman, 1970; Felstiner, 1974; Merry, 1979).

Of those disputes pursued, a large portion are resolved by negotiation between the parties (Miller and Sarat 1981) or by resort to some "forum" that is part of (and embedded within) the social setting within which the dispute arose, including the school principal, the shop steward, the administrator, and so on. Negotiation ranges from that which is indistinguishable from the everyday adjustments that constitute the relationship to that which is "bracketed" as a disruption or emergency. Similarly, embedded forums range from those which are hardly distinguishable from the everyday decision making within an institution to those which are specially constituted to handle disputes that cannot be resolved by everyday processes.

Of those disputes taken to a court (official forum), the vast majority end (by abandonment, withdrawal, or settlement) without full-blown adjudication, and often without any authoritative disposition by the court. Of those cases that do reach full authoritative adjudication by a court, a large portion do not involve a contest. They are uncontested either because the dispute has already been resolved (as often in divorce) or because only one party appears (Friedman and Percival, 1976; Cavanagh and Sarat, 1980).

We should not assume that courts are places where cases enter and (subject to attrition) proceed normally and typically to a trial, with genuine adversary contest and a decision according to formal rules. Instead, we should see courts as arenas in which various kinds of dispute (and non-dispute) processing takes place (cf. Mohr, 1976). Courts are the site of administrative processing, record-keeping, ceremonial changes of status, settlement negotiations, mediation, arbitration, and "warfare" (the threatening, overpowering, and disabling of opponents) as well as adjudication. Indeed, in most courts, most moves into the formal adjudicatory mode are for purposes other than securing an adjudicated outcome. The principal determinants of these processes must be sought in the goals, resources, and strategies of the parties (including, for this purpose, the court personnel). The "law" and the courts, as institutions, are not therefore unimportant, for the parties' strategic options and resources and even goals are to some extent supplied by the law and the institutions that "apply" it.

To summarize, courts resolve by authoritative disposition only a small fraction of all disputes that are brought to their attention. These are only a small fraction of the disputes that might conceivably be brought to court and an even smaller fraction of the whole universe of disputes.

What are we to make of this profile? Should we regard it as exposure of scandalous deficiencies? Do we wish to have more disputes enter the official system and proceed further toward definitive resolution? Is our utopia a condition in which *all* disputes are fully adjudicated? Surely not, for we know enough of the costs (financial, relational, psychic) of litigation to suspect that (in American society at least) such a condition would be monstrous. But is cost the only problem? Suppose we could eliminate most of it by a system of publicity and anticipatory compliance? Are the benefits so appealing to us? Do we seek a world in which there is perfect penetration of norms downward through the pyramid so that all disputes are resolved by application of the authoritative norms propounded by the courts? We know enough about the work of American courts to suspect that such a condition would be equally unattractive.

Two recent works dramatize this point forcefully. Noonan (1976) shows how our most esteemed courts and judges failed to be responsive to personal needs or social interests when they allowed "masks" (i.e., formal classificatory concepts) to conceal the complex human and social realities in the cases before them. Analyzing some well-known contracts cases, Danzig (1978) traces the implications of the inevitable shortages of resources, limitations of skill and knowledge, and infirmities in the process of capturing the facts that attend adjudication, even at its best. He depicts even craftsman-like and thoughtful judges making decisions that fall far short of either the satisfactory resolution of the controversy at hand or the establishment of viable controls over the area of social life in which it arose. These accounts imply that this imperfect joinder between appellate judging and social setting afflicts not only the hide-bound or the unimaginative, but also the heirs (even the patron saints) of a more expansive style of judging.

In many dispute situations, the participants can devise more satisfactory solutions to their disputes than can professionals who are constrained to apply general rules on the basis of limited knowledge of the dispute (cf. Enker, 1967; Dunlop, 1975; Eisenberg, 1976:658 ff.; Mnookin and Kornhauser, 1979:956 ff.). The variability of preferences and of situations, compared to the small number of things that can be taken into account by formal rules (cf. Kennedy, 1973) and the loss of meaning in transforming the dispute into professional categories, suggest limits on the desirability of conforming outcomes to authoritative rules.

Apart from these practical objections, the ideal of perfect penetration of official norms is subject to the even more fundamental objection that it is a mirage, a chimera, for it attributes to rules propounded in the lofty setting of the legislature or the appellate court a single determinate meaning when "applied" in a host of particular settings (Feeley, 1976:500; cf. Damaska, 1975:528). But most authoritative norms are ambiguous; variant readings are possible in any complex system of general rules. Uniformity of meaning across time and space is an achievement purchased at substantial cost.

A program of subordinating all variation of the law in action to the uniformity of formal law is like a program to make all spoken language an exact replica of written language. No one would deny the utility or importance of written language, but it does not necessarily offer the best guidance about how to speak. We should be cautioned by the way our tendency to visualize the "law in action" as a deviant or debased version of the higher law, the "law on the books," parallels folk beliefs about language usage. Ferguson (1971:222 ff.) observes that

> ... writing almost never reflects speech in an exact way, written language frequently develops characteristics not found in the corresponding spoken language. . . . *[T]he use of writing leads to the folk belief that the written language is the 'real' language and speech a corruption of it.* This attitude seems to be nearly universal in communities which have attained the regular use of writing.

The incommensurability of law in action with the law on the books should not be taken as a commendation of the *status quo*. Nor should the observation of the limited role of courts in resolving disputes be taken as an assertion that courts are unimportant in disputing.

Bargaining Endowments and Regulatory Endowments

The contribution of courts to resolving disputes cannot be equated with their resolution of those disputes that are fully adjudicated.[1] The principal contribution of courts to dispute resolution is the provision of a background of norms and procedures, against which negotiations and regulation in both private and governmental settings takes place. This contribution includes, but is not exhausted by, communication to prospective litigants of what might transpire if one of them sought a judicial resolution. Courts communicate not only the rules that would govern adjudication of the dispute but also possible remedies and estimates of the difficulty, certainty, and costs of securing particular outcomes.

The courts (and the law they apply) may thus be said to confer on the parties what Robert Mnookin and Lewis Kornhauser call a "bargaining endowment," e.g., a set of "counters" to be used in bargaining between disputants. In the case of divorce, for example,

> . . . [t]he legal rules governing alimony, child support, marital property and custody give each parent certain claims based on what each would get if the case went to trial. In other words, the outcome that the law would impose if no agreement is reached gives each parent certain bargaining chips—an endowment of sorts. (1979:968)

Similarly, the rules of tort law provide bargaining counters that are used in a process of negotiating settlements (Ross, 1970). The gravitation to negotiated outcomes in criminal cases is well known. One astute observer concludes that "the actual significance of the sophisticated adversary process before the jury" in American criminal cases is "to set a framework for party negotiations, providing 'bargaining chips.'" (Damaska, 1978:240) The negotiating dimension is found in the most complex and in the most routine cases. Thus in "extended impact" cases the involvement of the courts supplies standards and the setting for negotiations among the parties (Diver, 1979; Cavanagh and Sarat, 1980).

Bargaining may be tacit rather than explicit. The terms of trade may be fixed rather than established *ad hoc* (Feeley, 1979a:462). The bargaining endowment courts bestow on the parties includes not only the substantive entitlements conferred by legal rules, but also rules that enable those entitlements to be vindicated—for example, a rule excluding evidence favorable to the other party or jeopardizing the claim of the other party (e.g., contributory negligence).[2] However, rules are only one part of the endowment conferred by the forum. The delay, cost, and uncer-

tainty of eliciting a favorable determination also confer bargaining counters on the disputants. The meaning of this endowment, of course, is not
fixed and invariable, but depends on the characteristics of the disputants:
their preferences,[3] negotiating skill, risk aversiveness, ability to bear costs
and delay, and so on. A different mix of disputant capabilities may make a
given endowment take on very different significance.

Mnookin and Kornhauser (1979) refer to the bargaining between the
parties as occurring "in the shadow of the law," but this is not the only
kind of "private ordering" that takes place in the law's capacious shadow.
We can extend the notion of the bargaining endowment to imagine the
courts conferring on disputants a "regulatory endowment." That is, what
the courts might do (and the difficulty of getting them to do it) clothes
with authorizations and immunities the regulatory activities of the school
principal, the union officer, the arbitrator, the Commissioner of Baseball,
and a host of others.

The distinction between negotiation and regulation is a relative one.
The continuity between them is displayed, for example, in the continuing
relation between a university and its food service contractor, in which the
process of monitoring performance and negotiating adjustments partakes
of (or may be interpreted as) both (Goldberg, 1976). Plea bargaining
strikes me as another example of the overlapping of bargaining and regulation. And of course, regulation may involve an important element of
bargaining—as in agency "notice and comment" rule making or in the
relations of guards to prisoners, described by Sykes (1958). Perhaps we
should think of bargaining and regulation as the ends of a spectrum, along
the length of which we can find many intermediate (and alternating)
instances.

Courts bestow a regulatory endowment in many ways. First, the
courts provide models (norms, procedures, structures, rationalizations)
for such regulatory activity. Second, there are explicit authorizations and
immunities conferred by the courts (and the law) on an immense variety
of regulatory settings—the school teacher and principal, the prison war-
den, the agricultural cooperative, the baseball league, the union leader.
Such authorizations may be explicit rulings about the regulatory activity—
as in judicial doctrine about the authority of arbitrators, school officials
and church bodies—or they may be implicit in rules of jurisdiction, standing, and other procedural doctrines that deny admittance to cases involving certain kinds of regulatory activity.

Finally, there are the implicit authorizations and immunities that flow
from the general conditions of overcommitment and passivity. Courts are
reactive; they do not acquire cases of their own motion, but only upon the
initiative of one of the disputants. Thus, there is delegation of responsibility to the disputants to invoke the intervention of a court. The expense,
delay, and cumbersomeness of securing such intervention insulates all
regulators by raising barriers against challenging them in the courts.

Public agencies that might monitor such regulatory activity are typically overcommitted. That is, they have more enforcement responsibilities than resources with which to carry them out. So, they typically tend to be reactive, responding only to complaints. In deploying their scarce resources they understandably tend to be most responsive to the more organized and attentive of their constituents. Thus, the regulation exercised by hospitals on patients and their families, by landlords on their tenants, by universities on their students, by unions on their members, or by manufacturers on their customers is rarely subject to challenge by public agencies or in public forums. By a kind of legal alchemy, the expense and remoteness of the courts and the overload and lethargy of other agencies are transformed into regulatory authority, which can be exercised (sometimes through adjudicatory forms) by a host of institutions. Thus, the reactivity and overcommitment of the official legal system maintains and nourishes various kinds of ordering outside its precincts (discussed below under the rubric of indigenous law.)

The disputes that courts process originate elsewhere and may undergo considerable change in the course of entering and proceeding through the courts. Disputes must be reformulated into applicable legal categories. Such reformulation may entail restriction of their scope. Diffuse disputes may become more focussed in time and space, narrowed down to a set of discrete incidents involving specified individuals, or, conversely, the original dispute may grow, becoming the vehicle for consideration of a larger set of events or relationships. The range of normative claims may be narrowed or expanded; the remedy sought may change. The dispute that emerges in the court process may differ significantly from the dispute that arrived there, and may differ as well from disputes in other settings (Engel, 1980:434; Felstiner, Abel, and Sarat, 1981; Mather and Ynvgesson, 1981).

The relation of courts (official forums) to disputes is multidimensional. Decisive resolution, while important, is not the only (nor, I submit, the principal) link between courts and disputes. Disputes may be prevented by what courts do (e.g., by enabling planning to avoid disputes or by normatively disarming a potential disputant). Also, courts may foment and mobilize disputes, as when their declaration of a right arouses and legitimizes expectations about the propriety of pursuing a claim, or when changes in rules of standing suggest the possibility of pursuing a claim successfully. Further, courts may displace disputes into various forums and endow these forums with regulatory power. Finally, courts may transform disputes so that the issues addressed are broader or narrower or different from those initially raised by the disputants. Thus, courts not only resolve disputes, they prevent them, mobilize them, displace them, and transform them.

Thus, the effects of a court (or any forum) cannot be equated with the dispositions in the cases that come before it. There are a host of other effects that flow from the activity of a court—eliciting anticipatory compliance or evasive maneuvers, stigmatizing or legitimizing a line of conduct, encouraging or suppressing the making of a claim, lowering or heightening estimation of conduct or of its regulators.

Special Effects and General Effects

Here we put aside our discussion of courts as sources of endowments to take up another way of looking at these radiating effects of judicial action (or inaction). I begin by introducing a distinction between "special effects" and "general effects." Special effects are the effects produced by the impact of the forum's action on the parties before it. General effects are effects of the communication of information by or about the forum's action and of the response to that information.[4]

To elaborate, by special effects I mean changes in the behavior of the specific actors who are the subjects (or targets) of the application or enforcement of the law—the drunk driver who is arrested, the thief who is convicted, the businessman sued for breach of contract. We can isolate (in theory at least) various kinds of effects on the subsequent activity of these actors. For example, I may rob stores less frequently because I am imprisoned and stores are therefore hard to reach. This is *incapacitation*. On the other hand, I may be placed on probation, and as a result subjected to increased *surveillance* by the police, which makes it difficult to rob stores. My chances for breaching contracts may be reduced by the wariness of those who deal with me, wariness that stems from an earlier suit against me. Their reluctance may reflect the stigmatizing effect of sanctions imposed on me by the court, but it may also flow from the ancillary impact of court proceedings on my credit rating, insurability, licensing, business reputation, standing in other forums, and so forth (see Engel and Steele, 1979:316). Also, of course, such ancillary effects may be produced not only by the substantive decision of the court but also by the costs (including benefits forfeited) and timing of that decision (or its absence). This example involves elements of surveillance and incapacitation. I might also refrain from robbing stores or breaking contracts because I am fearful of being caught and punished again. This is *special deterrence*. Finally, the experience of being exposed to the law may change my view that it is right to rob stores or break contracts. This is *reformation*.

In addition to (or instead of) changing disposition toward the underlying transaction (the theft or the business deal), the experience may change my perceptions and evaluations of the activity of disputing about it, the institutions in which disputes are processed, and myself as a disputant. Thus, debtors who lose collection cases may emerge from the experience with an enhanced sense of political efficacy (Jacob, 1969b), but women who win anti-discrimination cases may be disillusioned with the forum and despair of vindicating their rights (Crowe, 1978). Pending more refined analysis, we might label these effects as *claim encouragement* and *claim discouragement*.

In addition to these special effects of the application of law, we may observe what might be called general effects. The work of courts affects not only those immediately subject to it but others as well. Some of the effects of courts result from the communication of information about what was (or could be) done by courts. Thus, if I am punished for theft or have to pay damages for breaching a contract, others may reassess the risks and advantages of similar activity. This is *general deterrence*. It neither presumes nor requires any change in their moral evaluation of stealing or breaking contracts, nor does it involve any change in their opportunities to commit these infractions. It stipulates that behavior will be affected by acquisition of more information about the costs and benefits that are likely to attach to the act—information about the certainty, celerity, and severity of punishment, for example. The actor can hold to Hart's (1961) "external point of view" treating law as a fact to be taken into account rather than as a normative framework that he is committed to uphold or be guided by. The information that induces the changed estimation of costs and benefits need not be accurate. What the court has done may be inaccurately perceived; indeed, the court itself may have inaccurately depicted what it has done.

On the other hand, communication of the existence of a law or its application by a court may change the moral evaluation by others of a specific item of conduct. To the extent that this involves not the calculation of the probability of being visited by certain costs and benefits but only a change in moral estimation, we may call this general effect *enculturation*. There is suggestive evidence to indicate that at least some segments of the population are subject to such effects (Berkowitz and Walker, 1967; Colombatos, 1969). Other studies provide suggestive but contrasting hypotheses about the conditions under which such enculturation takes place and its relation to the coercive aspects of the law.[5] Less dramatically, perceiving the application of law may maintain or intensify existing evaluations of conduct. Gibbs (1975) calls this *normative validation*.

These do not exhaust the general effects of legal action. Legal applications may be taken neither as facts to be adapted to nor norms to be adhered to, but as recipes to be followed. Using the law as a cookbook, we can learn how to bring about desired results—disposing of property, forming a partnership, securing a subsidy. We may call this effect *facilitation*.

Courts produce effects of the level of disputing behavior as well as at the level of the underlying transaction or relationship. Thus, litigation may have powerful mobilizational or demobilizational effects. It may encourage claimants and lawyers to invest in claims of a given type. It may provide symbols for rallying a group, broadcasting awareness of grievance and dramatizing challenge to the *status quo*. On the other hand, grievances may lose legitimacy, claims may be discouraged, and organizational capacity dissipated. These effects may be labeled *mobilization* and *demobilization*.

Of these various effects of judicial action, a number work through the transmission and reception of information rather than by concrete imposition of controls.[6] Some involve the transmission of information to the actor himself (special deterrence, reformation, claim encouragement, claim discouragement); others involve transmission of information about the actor to specifiable others (surveillance); others involve wider broadcasting of more general information (general deterrance, enculturation, facilitation, mobilization, demobilization). In the real world, these effects do not exist in isolation. A single judicial action may radiate different messages to different audiences.

Of course, these radiating effects need not be intended (or perceived) by the forum (or the disputants). On the other hand, some radiating effects are specifically intended. The forum may attempt to enhance certain of its effects by cultivating a public image (e.g., of implacable severity or sage deliberation), or by deliberately projecting an image of its general patterns of response. Of course, no matter what it tries to project, transmission by the forum is only part of the process. Effects will also depend on the reception side: Who gets which messages? Who can evaluate and process them? Who can use the information?

Thus, the impact of courts on disputes is accomplished largely by the dissemination of information. Courts produce not only decisions, but messages. These messages are resources that parties use in envisioning, devising, pursuing, negotiating, and vindicating claims (and in avoiding, defending, and defeating them). Similarly, courts distribute resources by which some parties regulate others (or resist such regulation). The broad pattern of effects of courts will depend on the way these resources are used.

Just how potential disputants and regulators will draw on these resources is powerfully affected by their culture, their capabilities, and their relations with one another. For example, we would expect that a bargaining endowment would be used differently in dealings among strangers with no prospect of continuing relations (e.g., the typical automobile injury claim) than among parties to a long-term relationship; we would expect it to be used differently when disputants share a normative consensus or when some formidable sanctions are built into the relationship (Macaulay, 1963). We would expect it to be used differently when one disputant is dependent on the other. Similarly, we would expect that a regulatory endowment would be used differently in a continuing than in an episodic relationship.

Like other legal institutions, courts have far more commitments than resources to carry them out. Enforcement agencies cannot possibly enforce all the law, nor can individuals enforce all their rights. In form, courts are open for full adjudicatory hearing of all cases, but, in practice, their capacity to conduct full-blown adjudications is limited to a fraction of the potential cases. Law is more capacious as a system of cultural and symbolic meanings than as a set of operative controls. It affects us primarily through communication of symbols—by providing threats, promises, models, persuasion, legitimacy, stigma, and so on.

If the nature of the courts is to "kiss and tell," in the nature of things they can do more telling than kissing. Their product is double: what they do and what they say about what they do. Messages about both are communicated through various channels to different audiences with different capacities to receive and evaluate these messages (Sarat, 1977b; Macaulay, 1979). Audiences may differ, for example, in their abilities to make a sophisticated assessment of what a court really does (i.e., what their bargaining chips really are) (cf. Ross, 1970; Feeley, 1979a:464–65). Similarly, it has been suggested that the effectiveness of deterrence systems varies with the capabilities of the recipients. Whereas naive amateurs may generalize the high risk of punishment from one type of crime to another, sophisticated professionals who "make relevant distinctions and...put the message into a refined context" will be able to extract more specific and accurate information from the deterrence message (Geerken and Gove, 1975:507). Where control is exerted through communication, the system will be powerfully influenced by the information processing capacities of the recipients, and by the differences in their capacities.[7]

Endowments and Effects

We have used two idioms to discuss the centrifugal flow from the courts: endowments and effects. When we discuss courts as sources of bargaining (and regulatory) endowments, the point of view is that of the disputants. In talking of general effects our stance is more detached. The time frame shifts from the strategic present to the retrospective or predictive. Calculations are probabilistic rather than prudential. Judgments are aggregate rather than distributive. The point of view is that of the detached observer or the remote manager of the system, not of a participant interested in specific transactions. What these viewpoints share is a vision of legal action as a centrifugal flow of symbols, radiating beyond the parties immediately involved. Both lead us to focus on the disputants as receivers of this symbolic radiation. The endowments that courts confer depend on the capabilities of actors to receive, store, and use them, capabilities that reflect their skills, resources, and opportunities. The patterns of general effects that we attribute to the courts depend on the endowments that actors extract from the messages radiating from the courts.

I do not mean to portray these capabilities as immutable qualities intrinsic to the actors, marking the irreducible end-points of analysis. Disputant capabilities derive from, and are relative to, structures of communication and structures for organizing action. Capabilities depend, for example, on location in a network that carries information about rights and remedies and on proximity to "remedy" institutions or "exit" alternatives. The process of distributing and extracting endowments is framed by the larger structures of social life. As these structures undergo change, the character of the centrifugal flow of effects from the courts will change too. For example, changes in political structures and communication systems may bring in their train a shift from reliance on special effects (impinging directly on disputants) to emphasis on general effects (worked by communication about such impingements). Thus Abel (1979:193) suggests that, compared to litigation in the tribal setting, modern litigation in Africa involves fewer courts with larger jurisdictions, prosecution of a smaller proportion of wrongs, and imposition of sterner punishments, shifting from the earlier reliance on special deterrence to reliance on general deterrence. Again, what Friedman and Percival (1976) label the declining role of two California courts in dispute settlement is interpreted by Lempert (1978) as a decline in direct impositions of resolutions on the parties before them. This is compatible with an increase in judicial contribution to dispute settlement by other means, both direct and indirect.

We might expect the mix and the relative prominence of these radiating effects to vary across space as well as over time. For example, the role of general effects of court action, compared with direct effects on the disputants, may be relatively greater in the United States, which maintains a relatively small judicial plant (Johnson and Drew, 1978) but a very large private legal profession, compared to other industrial countries. More than in many places, law in the United States is a private-sector business and private ordering is a prominent part of the legal universe (cf. Selznick, Nonet, and Vollmer, 1969:229).

CENTRIFUGAL MOVEMENT IN A SETTING OF INDIGENOUS ORDERING

We have shifted from seeing courts as resolvers of those disputes which come before them to seeing courts as one component of a complex system of indirect control over the whole system of disputing and regulation. Of course, courts (and other official institutions) are not the only sources of normative messages, just as they are not the only arenas in which controls are directly applied. We must examine the courts in the context of their rivals and companions. To do so we must put aside our habitual perspective of "legal centralism," a picture in which state agencies (and their learning) occupy the center of legal life and stand in a relation of hierarchic control (cf. Mayhew 1971:208) to other, lesser normative orderings such as the family, the corporation, the business network.[8]

People experience disputes and controls not only (or usually) in courts (or other forums sponsored by the state) but at the primary institutional locations of their activities—home, neighborhood, workplace, business deal, and so on—(including a variety of specialized remedial settings embedded in these locations). The enunciation of norms and application of sanctions in these settings may be more or less organized, more or less self-conscious, more or less consensual, and so forth. For convenience I shall use the terms "indigenous ordering" and "indigenous law" to refer to social ordering that is indigenous, i.e., familiar to and applied by the participants in the everyday activity that is being regulated.[9] By indigenous law I refer not to some diffuse folk consciousness but to concrete patterns of social ordering to be found in a variety of institutional settings in American society—in universities, sports leagues, housing developments, hospitals and so on. "Legal centralism" has impaired our consciousness of "indigenous law."

Social life is a vast web of overlapping and reinforcing regulation. How then can we distinguish "indigenous law" from social life generally? Consider, for example, the kinds of regulatory order that are involved in dating, the exchange of Christmas gifts, and behavior in elevators and in classrooms. In each there are shared norms and expectations about proper behavior; violations are visited with sanctions ranging from raised eyebrows to avoidance to assaults, reputational or physical. Clearly there is some sort of regulation going on here. In spite of the continuities, it may be useful to have a cut-off point further "up" the scale to demarcate what we want to describe as "law" of any sort, indigenous or otherwise. (Even though, as Nadel (1953) points out, the operative controls at any point on the scale are likely to be the internalization and reciprocities that characterize the less organized end of the scale.) The scale that I visualize is one of the organization and differentiation of norms and sanctions. As we move up, we get standards that are more explicit and more deliberation about their application that can be distinguished from the ordinary flow of activity in the field. This procedural separation may range from barely distinguishable bracketing of activity to elaborated provision for tribunals, which are separate in time, place, personnel, and formality from the ongoing activity (cf. Abel, 1974). This separation is associated with the appearance of "extrinsic" controls (i.e., the presence of rewards and punishments apart from those intrinsic to the primary activity) (cf. Spiro, 1961). The differentium is the introduction of a second layer of control—of norms about application of norms—along the lines of Hart's (1961) identification of law with the union of primary and secondary rules and Bohannon's (1965) identification of law with the reinstitutionalization of norms. (The present view departs from Bohannon by including as law secondary controls that appear without removal to a separate institutional location.) Although the principle seems to me a coherent one, it does not lead to a specification of what "is" and what "is not" law, for the features that we refer to exist across a whole spectrum of intermediate cases, like the transition from blue to purple. Just where to draw the line depends on the particular purpose at hand. Because the point in this section is the pervasive presence of formidable controls located within the activity being regulated by the official law, I have used the term indigenous law in a more sweeping fashion than would be appropriate for other purposes.

One of the striking features of the modern world has been the emergence of those institutional-intellectual complexes that we identify as national legal systems. Such a system consists of institutions, connected to the state, guided by and propounding a body of normative learning, purporting to encompass and control all the other institutions in the society and to subject them to a regime of general rules (Galanter 1966). These complexes consolidated and displaced the earlier diverse array of normative orderings in society, reducing them to a subordinate and interstitial status (cf. Weber, 1954:140 ff.).

Of course, these other orderings continue to exist. Counterparts or analogs to the institutions, processes, and intellectual activities that are located in national legal systems are to be found at many other locations in society. Some of these lesser legal orders are relatively independent, institutionally and intellectually, of the national legal system; others are dependent in various ways. That is, societies contain a multitude of partially self-regulating spheres or sectors organized along spatial, transactional, or ethnic-familial lines, ranging from primary groups in which relations are direct, immediate, and diffuse to settings (e.g., business networks) in which relations are indirect, mediated, and specialized.

The mainstream of legal scholarship has tended to look out from within the official legal order, abetting the pretensions of the official law to stand in a relationship of hierarchic control to other normative orderings in society. Social research on law has been characterized by a repeated rediscovery of this other hemisphere of the legal world.[10] This has entailed recurrent rediscovery that law in modern society is plural rather than monolithic, that it is private as well as public in character, and that the national (public, official) legal system is often a secondary rather than a primary locus of regulation. The relations between the big (public, national, official) legal system and the lesser normative orderings in society that I have called "indigenous law" are obscured by the portrayal of the big system as all-encompassing, exclusive, and controlling. However, this notion of official law as a comprehensive monolith—and indeed as a "system"—is not descriptive of it but rather part of its historic ideology. Legal regulation in modern societies, as in others, has a more uneven, patchwork character (cf. Tanner, 1970).

The survival and proliferation of indigenous law in the contemporary United States is attested by a literature that contains reports on various social settings. These reports display the immense profusion and variety of these "semi-autonomous social fields" existing in a single society.[11] Indigenous law in the contemporary United States remains concealed from those who are looking for an inclusive and self-contained *gemeinschaft*, unsullied by formal organization, which enfolds individuals and integrates their whole life experience. What we find instead is a multitude of more fragmentary and less inclusive associations and networks, overlapping and interpenetrating. For the most part they are, as Danzig and Lowy observe (1975:681) "socio-economic networks rather than bounded groups." Such partial communities, linked by informal communications (and sometimes by formal communication devices as well) provide much of the texture of our lives in family and kinship, at work and in business dealings, in neighborhood, sports, religion, and politics. There are varying degrees of self-conscious regulation, varying degrees of congruity with the official law, varying degrees of reliance on the support provided by official institutions (see the discussion of regulatory endowments above). This is a realm of interdependence, regulated by tacit norms of reciprocity and sometimes by more explicit codes. The range of shared meanings is limited but the cost of exit is substantial. If we have lost the experience of an all-encompassing inclusive community, it is not to a world of arms-length dealings with strangers but, in large measure, to a world of loosely joined and partly overlapping partial or fragmentary communities. In this sense, our exposure to indigenous law has increased at the same time that official regulation has multiplied.

Mnookin and Kornhauser's analysis of "bargaining in the shadow of the law" in divorce cases helps us to put aside the centripetal view and to focus on the movement of law out from the forum into realms of private ordering. The policy lesson they draw is that the "primary function of the legal system should be to facilitate private ordering and dispute resolution" (1979:986). The divorce example, however, imparts a highly individualistic coloring to the analysis; private ordering is equated with the parties "making law for themselves" in the light of their "preferences" and "the law." Our discussion of indigenous law suggests that private ordering may involve more than disputants devising an *ad hoc* legal regime for themselves. The parties may not constitute an isolated dyad, but may be embedded in (or adhere to) a group or network with its own rules and standards. Making claims on the basis of what is acceptable quality in a trade, invoking "academic freedom," or submitting a dispute to an arbitrator cannot be comfortably subsumed under the notion of "making law for themselves." Each of these is as much an act of affiliation as of legislation; it is a reference to some existing normative structure, not a proposal to erect a new one. Working out a *corpus juris* and constituting a legal establishment are relatively infrequent kinds of behavior (and rarely begin from scratch); most of our justice-seeking is by adhesion.

Where bargaining and regulating take place in the settings of patterned norms and sanctions that we have called "indigenous law," we may be inclined to characterize the whole system somewhat differently. Mnookin's image of "bargaining in the shadow of the law" suggests that the law is *there* and the disputants meet in a landscape naked of normative habitation (or in which such structures are subsumed into their "preferences"). Instead, I visualize a landscape populated by an uneven tangle of indigenous law. In many settings the norms and controls of indigenous ordering are palpably *there*—the official law is remote and its intervention is problematic and transitory. Consider, for example, the businessmen described by Macaulay (1963) or a typical dispute within a university. In such settings the relation might be better depicted as "law in the shadow of indigenous regulatory activity."[12]

The relation of official law to indigenous ordering is not invariably a matter of mutual exclusion (where the former ousts the latter), nor one of hierarchic control (where the latter is conformed to or aligned with the former). Judicial intervention to apply official standards does not necessarily weaken indigenous controls. For example, Zald and Hair (1972:66) suggest that the judicial erosion of the doctrine of charitable immunity and the exposure of hospitals to liability for negligence provided enlarged "incentives and sanctions . . . to governmental and private standard-setting bodies such as the Joint Commission [of Accreditation of Hospitals] to induce compliance with standards on the part of hospitals." Similarly, Macaulay (1966) shows that official intervention in the relation between automobile manufacturers and their dealers led to a growth of internal regulation rather than its attenuation. Randall's (1968) study of movie censorship reveals how the elaboration of internal controls within the movie industry was a reflex of actual (and potential) control by the official law. Just as the character of indigenous regulation is affected in unanticipated ways by developments in the official law, so the presence of indigenous regulation may transform the meaning and effect of the official law.

The effects of indigenous tribunals, like those of official courts, are not confined to direct participation in cases. The work of these tribunals may radiate norms, symbols, models, threats, and so forth. In indigenous law, too, the shadow reaches further than its source. The kinds of bargaining and regulatory endowments that actors extract from the messages depend on their capabilities. Community standing, seniority, reputation for integrity, or formidability may confer capability in the indigenous setting, which would not translate into capability in official tribunals. (Indeed, indigenous law may be insulated from external controls by its constituents' lack of capability to use official remedies (cf. Doo, 1973)). Acquisition of capability to use official courts may lead to erosion of indigenous tribunals (cf. Galanter, 1968). On the other hand, an equalizing of capabilities in official forums may lead to their abandonment and development of indigenous tribunals, as in the labor-management field.)

I do not mean to idealize indigenous law as either more virtuous or more efficient than official law. Although by definition indigenous law may have the virtues of being familiar, understandable, and independent of professionals, it is not always the expression of harmonious egalitarianism. Indigenous law often reflects narrow and parochial concerns; it is often based on relations of domination; its coerciveness may be harsh and indiscriminate; protections that are available in public forums may be absent.

Indigenous law, like other law, has the problem of connecting effective sanctions to its determinations. The indigenous tribunal faces the problem of obtaining leverage over those who are impervious to community opinion, getting them to submit to its jurisdiction or to comply with its decisions. This is compounded where the setting is culturally heterogeneous. Those who share a common location or common interests (e.g., as workers or students) may not share a common culture. Ideas about deference, noise, work performance, child rearing, and so forth may differ among those who interact frequently. The thrust of community law is limited when moral communities are plural and cross-cutting, not self-contained and reinforcing. The most crucial disputes may not be within the community but with entities that are separated not merely by pluralism but also by difference in form and scale. The most significant transactions may be with corporate entities—government departments, corporations—that are not amenable to community persuasion or sanction. Indeed, a defining characteristic of our age is the extent to which transactions and disputes are between units of different scale.[13]

EXPLORING THE SHADOWS: TOWARD A NEW RESEARCH AGENDA

The juxtaposition of the centrifugal view with an appreciation of the persistance of indigenous law points to an agenda for inquiry. The emphasis on indigenous law reflects my conviction that any major advance in our understanding of how official legal regulation works depends on knowing more about indigenous law.

Every legal system has to address the problem of the autonomy and authority of the various other sorts of normative ordering with which it coexists in society. The big legal system faces the question of how to recognize or supervise or suppress the little systems. The lesser orders face the question of how to maintain themselves and promote their concerns in the gravitational pull of the big system. Styles and theories of coexistence vary. Legal centralism is one style of response to this generic question of legal ordering, but it does not necessarily provide an adequate guide to the complexities we encounter in our own society (cf. Griffiths, 1981). Historical and comparative study can help us to visualize the phenomena in which we are embroiled, but the insights derived there from have to be linked to an enlarged understanding of the workings of indigenous regulation in contemporary American society. Systematic exploration of "indigenous" law would require that we seek the conditions and locations in which self-regulation emerges and the features it displays. For example, is there explication of norms, formality of procedure, broad or narrow participation? The social settings in which such regulation takes place are not independent self-contained units; they interact with a larger complex legal order. How then is indigenous regulation related to the regulation projected by the big legal system? What is the relationship between official law and indigenous regulatory activity? Does the latter rely on or borrow from the norms, sanctions, and style of the official law?

Study of the spheres of indigenous ordering leads to exploration of their interface with official forums. How do courts (and other official agencies) supervise and control bargaining and regulation in various social settings? They do so not only by promulgating doctrines and imposing decrees, but also by mediating and fostering negotiation, and by generating messages about their various modes of intervention.[14]

We may envision a kind of "impact" research that would depart from the earlier generation of impact research in several important ways. The older impact research started from the doctrinal pronouncements of appellate courts and asked questions about congruence between that doctrine and practices of other agencies (lower courts, school boards, police, etc.). We are interested in the effects not only of doctrinal pronouncements but of costs, remedies, delay, uncertainty, legitimation, stigma, and all the other components of the total message transmitted by the courts, including trial courts as well as appellate courts, and informal mediation and private bargaining as well as adjudication. The product of the court is not doctrine with a mix of impurities but, instead, a whole set of messages that can be used as resources in making (or contesting) claims, bargaining (or refusing to bargain), and regulating (or resisting regulation). Such impact research would make it possible for courts to educate themselves about the consequences of their patterns—of discovery, settlement, cost, remedies, as well as their doctrinal production. What are the general effects of court routines as well as of the occasional dramatic ruling?

The centrifugal perspective also suggests that if we are interested in courts as sources of messages about entitlements and vindication, then we have to consider not only changes in the messages transmitted but changes in the basic structures for transmission, e.g., the separation of appellate from trial courts. The agenda for research might include experimental alteration of court structures or of transmission practices (e.g., televising court proceedings).

While awaiting the results of research and experimentation, the centrifugal perspective can yield some cautions. For example, it suggests that the financial cost of particular kinds of litigation is an insufficient guide for policy, since it tells us little about the benefits produced by that litigation. These might include not only benefits to the winning party (compensation, vindication, etc.), but to the loser (his "day in court"), to others who might have been victimized by the loser (through incapacitation, rehabilitation, special deterrence), as well as effects on wider audiences (general deterrence, moral validation, channeling, habituation, etc.) that perhaps were mediated through effects on indigenous regulatory activity. Again, the centrifugal perspective suggests that in deciding how the existing supply of courts should be allocated, the distinctive competence of courts as institutions offers only a partial guide. If most of the courts' effects are remote and indirect, it is entirely possible that courts may confer more social benefits when doing what they do less ably, than when doing what they do best.

CONCLUSION

Through the wrong end of the telescope, the work of courts is seen not primarily as the resolution of disputes in official settings but as the projection of bargaining and regulatory endowments into a world unevenly occupied by indigenous regulation, a world in which the influences that emanate from courts mingle with those from other sources. This picture might be thought to imply a new centrifugal variant of the picture of courts as agencies of hierarchic control, securing the penetration of official norms and the corresponding alignment of social activity. This new centrifugal variant emphasizes the dissemination of messages rather than the pronouncement of authoritative decisions and application of sanctions. Such a picture might seem to invite a strategy of control by management of images rather than by determination of cases. From appreciation of the "Potemkin village" aspect of the law it is a short step to devise ways to build more imposing and convincing facades. More modestly, explicit attention to the indirect "educative" effects of courts might make them more efficient agents of legal control.

For several reasons, this model of courts as engineers of control through deliberately projected images is as illusory and partial as the model of courts as authoritative resolvers of disputes. Put differently, there are inherent limits on the educative effects of the judicial process. First, the contours of interaction between the different sorts of educative effects that we have identified remain to be mapped. We might imagine them often to be reinforcing and cumulative, but to some extent they may undercut and undo one another. For example the curtailment of capacity to offend, flowing from incapacitation and surveillance, may reduce occasions for reformation. Again, the coerciveness that promotes deterrence may be incompatible with the sense of volition that promotes internalization (cf. Muir, 1967).

More generally, the messages disseminated by courts do not carry endowments or produce effects except as they are received, interpreted, and used by (potential) actors. Therefore, the meaning of judicial signals is dependent on the information, experience, skill, and resources that disputants bring to them. The ability of courts to calibrate the endowments they distribute or the effects they produce is limited by their ability to predict the distribution of capabilities among actual and potential disputants. These capabilities may change due to factors remote from the courts and in ways not readily knowable by courts. For example, those who become sophisticated about crime may read judicial deterrence messages differently or claimants who become organized may find elaborate procedure and the need for expensive experts transformed from liabilities to assets, and so forth.

The indeterminacy of the courts' educative effects is compounded by the fact that the courts (and the official law generally) are not the only source of such messages. All of the lesser normative orderings (family, work group, church, and associations and networks of various sorts) disseminate messages about norms, infractions, remedies, and so on. The messages of the courts may be amplified, cancelled, or transformed by the presence of these indigenous norms and controls in ways that are beyond anticipation or control by the courts.

The variability introduced by disputant capabilities and by indigenous ordering is augmented by some of the characteristics of the American legal setting. The messages broadcast by the courts do not impinge on potential users by traversing some transparent neutral medium. Typically, disputants do not encounter these messages floating freely, but rather in the context of a local legal culture (Wilson, 1968; Jacob, 1969a; Levin, 1977; Church et al, 1978a). By this I refer to the complex of enduring understandings, concerns, and priorities shared by the community of legal actors (and significant audiences) in a given locality. This "culture" prescribes the appropriate content and style of various legal roles and processes; it defines the uses of the preliminary hearing and the pre-trial conference, the role of the judge in plea bargaining and settlement negotiations, the proclivity to resort to the courts and to invoke various procedural rights, the pace of litigation, appropriate dispositions for particular offenses by particular sorts of offenders, and so on. Judicial messages are reworked and combined with a whole set of understandings and concerns. The meanings of what courts do and the kinds of endowments that disputants can extract from them vary with these cultures.

Local variation is reinforced by the chronic overcommitment of law in the American setting. All legal agencies have more authoritative commitments to do things than resources to carry them out. This overload of commitments results in a massive, covert delegation of power from peak agencies (e.g., legislatures and appellate courts) to agencies and groups below, which decide which commitments should be fulfilled and how much to fulfill them. "Selective enforcement" is chronic and pervasive. The abundance of unfilled commitments forms a great reserve pool of claims that could be mobilized. Incumbents, responding to their own evaluations and to their agencies' "system maintainance" requirements, develop priorities that may diverge from the estimations of concerned (or potentially concerned) publics (cf. Becker, 1963:161). Changing conditions and new awareness produce new potential demands. Interest groups, media, and individual crusaders may challenge existing patterns of enforcement and interpretation, bringing about new understandings of the meaning of the law promulgated by courts and legislators (Galanter, Palen, and Thomas, 1979).

The differing effects of local culture and disputant capabilities are amplified by the scale and complexity of the legal system. In a large, complex legal system like that of the contemporary United States, the messages broadcast by (and to) courts are less determinate and precise than may at first appear to be the case. There is a lot of law (in the sense of authoritative normative learning), more than can be encompassed by any single intelligence, no matter how capacious. New law pours forth from legislatures and even more is promulgated by an ever-increasing array of agencies, stimulated by a general climate of regulatory interventionism. The multiplicity of norms of varying levels of authority and of generality, the inevitable ambiguities, overlaps and conflicts among them, the fragmentation of law making and regulatory powers among myriad agencies with overlapping mandates and jurisdictions, the dispersion of powers of innovation and interpretation among weakly coordinated agencies with little hierarchic supervision—all of these combine to render the messages of legal authorities indeterminate, often obscure, and sometimes malleable. If the stakes warrant and the pocketbook permits, the indeterminate, malleable quality can be enhanced by an investment of skill and resources. (As a recent study of lawyers puts it: "the discovery of a unique issue is likely to be a function of the amount of time that lawyers devote to a case and thus of the amount of money that the client spends on lawyers" [Heinz and Laumann, 1978:1117]).

The notion of comprehensive judicial control through calculated projection of symbols is an idle conceit, as is the notion of judicial control by coercive imposition. Nevertheless, the centrifugal view suggests that advances in our understanding of the radiating effects of courts may provide the cognitive underpinnings for a deeper, more responsible consequentialism, in which courts are supplied with an enhanced capacity for systematic monitoring of the impact of their actions.[15] Presumably, there is some point beyond which such self-regarding would be debilitating to courts, but I know of no reason to believe that point has even been approached.

The centrifugal view portrays courts as our teachers as well as our counselors and provisioners. Our preliminary sketch of the centrifugal flow and its setting suggests that this teaching activity should be interpreted in a way that is both more modest and more penetrating than that suggested by "legal centralism." Like others who proffer advice and ordnance, courts relinquish control over what is bestowed. As educators, too, courts have only partial control. We filter their messages through our interests and biases. We learn from many other teachers, too. What we learn from the courts may be more than they undertake to teach us. They purport to display to us the obligations implied by our shared values and commitments. At the same time, they expose the flawed and halting realization of these commitments. We may learn from courts about the ambivalence of the law's incontrovertible pronouncements, the flaccidity of its inexorable controls, the arbitrariness and indeterminacy of its commands. Courts may teach us to be their critics rather than their followers, creative users rather than passive subjects of the law.

NOTES

1. Lempert (1978:99–100) usefully distinguishes various ways in which courts contribute to dispute settlement:
   (1) courts define norms that influence or control the private settlement of disputes; (2) courts ratify private settlements, providing guarantees of compliance without which one or both parties might have been unwilling to reach a private settlement; (3) courts enable parties to legitimately escalate the costs of disputing, thereby increasing the likelihood of private dispute settlement; (4) courts provide devices that enable parties to learn about each other's cases, thus increasing the likelihood of private dispute settlement by decreasing mutual uncertainty; (5) court personnel act as mediators to encourage the consensual settlement of disputes; (6) courts resolve certain issues in the case, leading the parties to agree on others, and (7) courts authoritatively resolve disputes where parties cannot agree on a settlement.
2. Of course this is in addition to the other functions of rules—to guide courts in adjudicating cases and to guide parties in planning, in defining their expectations, and so on. Qualities that commend a rule for one purpose may make it a disaster for another. Mnookin and Kornhauser (1979:980) give the example of joint custody as a rule that "may have good·characteristics as a background rule for private ordering but may nevertheless be unacceptable as a standard for adjudicating disputed cases."
3. Mnookin and Kornhauser's suggestive analysis is both illuminated and limited by the special characteristics of divorce disputes. For the most

part, the disputants display a lack of interest in general effects, such as precedents, new rules, and so on. So, the "preferences" of the parties lack a dimension that is present in other kinds of disputing by parties who anticipate and plan for a series of comparable disputes over time (see Galanter, 1974b).

4. This notion of "general effects" takes off from the very helpful discussion of general preventive effects of punishment by Gibbs (1975:chap. 3) as usefully elaborated by Feeley (1976:517 ff.). It is simply a generalization from the illuminating and now familiar (if not entirely serviceable, as Gibbs points out) distinction between special deterrence and general deterrence introduced by Andenaes (1966). Theory about these general effects is still inchoate. In a review of the now sizable literature on deterrence, Gibbs (forthcoming:45) observes that since deterrence research has proceeded without controls for other general effects, "all previous reported tests of the deterrence doctrine . . . were really tests of an implicit theory of general preventive effects; and that will remain the case as long as nondeterrent mechanisms are left uncontrolled." Some of the labels for the various effects here are inspired by, but disloyal to, those carefully discussed by Gibbs (1975:chap. 3).

5. Thus, Muir (1967) and Dolbeare and Hammond (1971) both examine the reaction of local school boards to decisions of the U.S. Supreme Court banning officially sponsored prayer in classrooms. Muir finds substantial compliance and substantial enculturation associated with low perceived coerciveness of the legal setting; Dolbeare and Hammond, finding little compliance, attribute the dissociation of practice from legal doctrine to the absence of coercive pressure.

6. Those effects that work through transmission of information rather than by direct imposition of physical controls include many that were classified above as "special," as well as all those labeled as "general." Thus, the category of radiating effects is wider than that of "general effects." Radiating effects enable the law to be "educative" even where there is no direct participation. Indeed, there is evidence that in at least some settings participation may have educative effects that undercut the education supplied by radiation of symbols from remote stations. Compare the disillusionment imparted by experience with courts, discussed by, among others, Sarat (1977b:439,441), Yankelovich, Skelly & White (1978:11,18), and Curran (1977:236) in American settings, and by Kidder (1973:134) and Kurczewski and Frieske (1978:328) in Indian and Polish settings, respectively.

7. Without some knowledge of the (presumably differentiated) reception process, one cannot specify the policy implications of the insight that courts are important symbolic transmitters. For example, Ball (1975) calls for cultivating and cherishing the theatrical "live performance" of courts—as dramatic embodiments or presentations of a normative image of legitimate society—dramatizing the seriousness, importance, dignity, rights, and duties of citizens, surrounding them with ceremonious deference. But he neglects to say who these messages are communicated to— do they really get to a wider audience? Does it matter that we have more or fewer trials? Juries? Newspaper coverage? TV in courtrooms? Does it differ by size of locality, etc.?

8. An attempt to explicate the "paradigm" that is here labeled legal centralism is found in Galanter (1974a) and Trubek and Galanter (1974). This label is borrowed from John Griffiths, who suggests that the state-centered view of legal phenomena is a kind of legal Ptolmaism. Our habit of describing all legal phenomena in relation to the state Griffiths (1981) finds "essentially arbitrary . . . the state has no more empirical claim to being the center of the universe of legal phenomena than any other element of that whole system does. . . ."

9. The notion of "indigenous" law as regulation by the participants engaged in an activity invites comparison with a whole battery of kindred notions. Its ancestor is Ehrlich's (1936:38 and *passim*) "inner order of the associations." I found suggestive Robert Kidder's (1978) contrast of "external" and "internal" law in India, drawing on Victor Li's (1971) distinction of external and internal models of law in modern China.

Social research on law contains a number of conceptual formulations that contribute to our ability to visualize the relationship between the public official legal system and the lesser, partially self-regulating orderings. We distinguish law and morals, public and private spheres, formal and informal processes. Each of these formulations illuminates something of this relationship; none is entirely serviceable. The distinction of law from custom or morality carries in its train a history of conceptual struggles over the meaning of law. Discussions of private, as opposed to public, legal systems (Evan, 1962; Selznick, Nonet, and Vollmer, 1969) contain valuable insights, but the public–private distinction invites us to categorize where we need to measure variation. Much of the same may be said of the often invoked and rarely defined distinction between formal and informal, which collapses into an amorphous mass a vast and changing array of process and structural characteristics.

Moore (1973:720) uses the term "semi-autonomous social field," to refer to an area of social life that

can generate rules and customs and systems internally, but that . . . [are] also vulnerable to rules and decisions and other forces emanating from the larger world by which it is surrounded. The semi-autonomous social field has rule-making capacities, and the means to induce compliance; but it is simultaneously set in a larger matrix which can, and does, affect and invade it, sometimes at the invitation of persons inside it, sometimes at its own instance.

This formulation usefully points to the study of the lesser normative orderings, not as isolated and independent units but as parts of a larger, complex legal order, with which they interact (cf. Fuller's (1969) observation that the working of state legal institutions is permeated by "customary law").

The term "indigenous" as used here is a relative one. Since indigenous systems frequently incorporate cultural elements from the official law, and since their sanctioning systems are often entwined with the official ones, no dichotomous distinction can be made.

10. This rediscovery is often associated with Eugen Ehrlich, (1936). See also Weber (1954:16–20, 140–149).

11. The existing literature includes reports on self-regulation in a variety of business settings, such as shopping centers (MacCollum, 1967); trade associations (Mentschikoff, 1961); heavy manufacturing (Macaulay, 1963); textiles (Bonn, 1972a,b); the garment industry (Moore, 1973); movie distribution and exhibition (Randall, 1968); auto dealers' relations with manufacturers (Macaulay, 1966) and with customers (Whitford, 1968). In addition, there are reports on self-regulation within religious groups (e.g., *Columbia Journal of Law and Social Problems*, 1970) and ethnic communities (e.g., Doo, 1973); intentional communities (e.g., Zablocki, 1971); professional associations (e.g., Akers, 1968); athletics (e.g., Cross, 1973); and work places (e.g., Blau, 1963).

12. This indigenous regulatory activity in turn may be a derivative of bargaining. Getman (1979:917) observes that "collective bargaining shapes labor arbitration and gives it power . . . It is only when unions are powerful, well established and responsive to the needs of their members that labor arbitration works successfully." In this setting, we get "law in the shadow of [collective] bargaining."

13. See Coleman (1974); compare Moore (1978:chap. 3). On the dominance of official dispute institutions by cases between units of different scale, see Galanter (1975) and Wanner (1974); on the effects of this disparity on disputing, see Galanter (1974b, 1975).

14. The relation of courts to negotiation among disputants may be an especially promising place to initiate exploration of the linkage of courts to indigenous ordering. How do formally supervised settlements and mediated ones compare with bilateral settlements and with adjudicated outcomes? Are the norms that govern adjudication given expression in negotiated settlements? Students of dispute processing differ in their readings of the relation between negotiated outcomes and adjudicated ones. The modal view among students of law and society posits a sharp disjunction between norm-governed adjudication on the one hand and bargaining–negotiation on the other. This dualistic view, put forth by Aubert (1963) and by Gulliver (1973), is questioned from two quite different directions by proponents of greater continuity between dispute processes. On the one hand, Kidder (1974) argues that adjudication is best understood as an extension of negotiation–bargaining, providing an arena in which resources and tactics can be arrayed and in which norms are just one more resource. On the other hand, Eisenberg (1976) finds that dispute negotiation is principled or norm-governed, even more so than formal adjudication, in that actors may respond to a wider range of normative commitments than are taken into account in formal adjudication. However, compare Caplovitz' (1974:245) finding that only about half of consumer debtors who settled out of court considered the terms of the settlement fair.

15. A fascinating example of an attempt at such self-observation is found in Renfrew *et al.* (1977). A federal judge, attuned to the primacy of maximizing communication of anti-trust norms to other businessmen, sentenced anti-trust violators to a regimen of giving speeches about their offenses to audiences of their peers. The judge then conducted a survey to gauge the effects. Of course, such judicial messages are only part of

the whole complex of messages radiating from official (and other) sources, and the context may impart to a judicial message a meaning different from that it appears to carry when considered in isolation. Compare McCormack's (1977) argument that token enforcement and non-stigmatizing sanctioning of anti-trust violations have neutralized public reaction against these violations and thus helped legitimize "prohibited" business practices.

6

The Etiology of Claims: Sketches for a Theoretical Mapping of the Claim-Definition Process

Keith O. Boyum

The etiology of claims, as precursors to disputes and to court cases, is not literally *terra incognita*. Anthropological studies in particular offer some perspective; varieties of claims and disputes, and varieties of dispute processing have been charted (see, e.g., Nader and Todd, 1978). However, sociologists of law and scholars of judicial processes have typically taken court cases as given, focusing on processes, outcomes, and consequences rather than on antecedents. On the other hand the number of exceptions to that rule is increasing.[1] As sociological studies of disputing have shifted their attention in the last two decades or so from appellate courts to legal institutions less remote from everyday social life, the connection between disputes just before they enter trial courts and disputes that have become formal court cases has been a focus. Interest in schemes for diverting cases away from courts to other forums is sited there (Johnson, Kantor, and Schwartz, 1977). Sited there also have been analyses of the incidence

Author's Note: This chapter is revised from a paper originally delivered at the 1980 Annual Meeting of the Law and Society Association and the ISA Research Committee on Sociology of Law, Madison, Wisconsin. The research for this paper was supported by Grant Number 78-NI-AX-0139, awarded to the California State University, Fullertion Foundation by the National Institute of Justice, Law Enforcement Assistance Administration, U.S. Department of Justice, under the Omnibus Crime Control and Safe Streets Act of 1968, as amended. Points of view or opinions stated in this Chapter are those of the author and do not necessarily represent the position or policies of the U.S. Department of Justice The research assistance of Karen Adams is gratefully acknowledged.

of legal "needs" in various populations (Abel-Smith, Zander, and Brook, 1973; Blankenburg, 1975; Curran, 1977; Sykes, 1969). The issue *not* tackled has been the generation and discovery in the first instance of cases (that may be ripe for diversion) or of the generation and discovery of legal needs. Thus, Engel and Steele could arrive at the conclusion indicated here, that "there has been little concern with questions of etiology in civil cases" (1979:303)[2]. The task of this essay is to take up that concern.

The etiology of claims (as precursors to disputes and ultimately to court cases) is a topic for empirical theories about courts for reasons beyond the simple fact that there has been little previous work on it among sociologists of law. First, theoretical interest often and appropriately follows policy interest. Concerns about overload and overwork in courts are current (cf. Friedman, chapter 2 and the references there). Understanding how claims are generated may provide perspective on how workloads are generated. Second, there are implications in this for understanding courts as institutions and law as a social phenomenon. Claims have implications for what courts do, both claims made and claims unmade. If an observer defines courts to any extent in terms of what courts do, the claim-defining process has implications for a court-defining process (cf. Krislov, chapter 7). As Galanter (chapter 5) has emphasized the indigenous siting of the effects and radiate from courts, so claims are sited at home, defined at home, and given birth in simple everyday situations.

As I write, my glance strays to a parking lot clearly visible from my office window. The lot is full, but on the lot drivers wait in their cars. An informal queue for available spaces has sprung up, but a recently available space has been taken not by the driver at the head of the queue but by a recent arrival. Let us label the two drivers "Head of Queue" and "Space Stealer." In the next scene, Head of Queue approaches Space Stealer. There is a short conversation. Space Stealer drives away and Head of Queue parks in the space.

Though not a party to the transaction just described, and although I have not interviewed the drivers, I believe that I know something about what happened. The challenge is to fully describe the process. One might casually say that Head of Queue presented a claim to the space and that Space Stealer accepted Head of Queue's claim, a dispute thereby being averted. The harder question is why Head of Queue brought the claim at all. Describing the situation more elementally, we might see, first, that Head of Queue noticed that his or her *circumstance* did not include possession of a parking place. (Conceivably, Head of Queue could have failed to recognize this fact, could, for example, have stayed home today and never thought about parking.) Second, Head of Queue recognized that his or her circumstance *could* have included a parking space, for one had, after all, opened up. Third, Head of Queue *judged* that his or her circumstance *should* have included a parking space. (Head of Queue might have reached a different judgment: suppose that the space opening up were reserved for handicapped persons, official university vehicles, or for designated high administrative officials.) Distinguishing or defining a circumstance, the estimate of a circumstance, and the judgment about a circumstance—we shall take up these elements in turn as we consider the decision to bring a claim.

DEFINING CIRCUMSTANCES

One's circumstances can be afforded a variety of definitions—perhaps, literally, an endless variety. I might say that my circumstance is that I am some particular height, hair color, eyesight acuity; my circumstance is that I have a typewriter at my disposal, own some books; my circumstance is that I do *not* own a sports car, or a rocket ship. Out of what is surely a welter of possible definitions of my circumstance, I must define one or a few on which to focus before taking any action with respect to it (or them). We may be explicit about the philosophical position this implies. We would view circumstances as objective phenomena, existing independently of definition or perception, yet the importance of circumstance for us begins only with its definition. There is thus a substantial subjective component to circumstance. Circumstances must be defined, not merely recognized.

If we consider an ordinary motor vehicle accident claim by way of example, some of the processes involved in defining circumstances may be clearly set out. Prior to such a claim being brought, an event must have occurred. The appearance or configuration of at least one car has been abruptly altered as a consequence of coming into contact with another car. We may suppose that the driver who suffered damages to his or her car had no particular focus on his or her circumstances with respect to the state of, say, the front fender prior to the event of the collision. We might suppose that the *event* stimulated the definition of circumstance. We may note, too, that the claim is about the circumstance (of a crumpled fender) and not about the event (the contact or collision) in this hypothetical case. Events, then, are in the class of agents that provide focus and that stimulate definition of circumstances. Events may be known by changes in circumstances. Events are active happenings, in this view, restricted to definable points in time.

The key here is that a change in circumstances brings about a focus—a definition—of circumstance. Events are abrupt changes, but, logically, changes may be gradual, too. We would propose what may be obvious: the probability that a change in circumstance will provoke a definition of and focus on that circumstance varies directly with the *rate* of change.

We may move at least a modest distance beyond rate. Two other qualities of a change in circumstances will also affect the probability of such circumstances being defined and attracting focus: the magnitude of change and the scope of change. (On these terms, cf. Grossman and Grossman, 1971.) By *magnitude* we mean amount—whether the change is substantial or incremental, whether in our hypothetical motor vehicle claim a fender was crumpled or the paint on it slightly scratched. By *scope* we mean the number of domains affected by a change. A rise in the cost of energy could affect the choice of where one lives (close or far from work), the house in which one lives (small and energy-efficient versus large and open), the cost of one's food (which must be transported, after all), the choice of one's entertainment (near activities versus far activities), and more. By contrast, a college freshman who receives a course grade would probably experience a change in circumstance largely restricted to one domain (though we could imagine occasions where more than one domain would be affected). In parallel with our proposition about rate, we may say that the probability that a change in circumstance will provoke a definition of and focus on that circumstance varies directly with the scope and with the magnitude of change.

Change in circumstance, then, can provoke definition and focus on particular circumstances. Without a defined circumstance and a focus on it, claims will not arise. The rate, scope, and magnitude of change are directly related to the probability that definition and focus will occur. With this said, we may proceed to some consideration as to how rate, scope, and magnitude interact, and in providing some examples we may provide some intuitive grounding for our construct.

Figure 6-1 sets out eight combinations, which can be found in cumulating three dichotomized variables. (We dichotomize obviously continuous variables in Figure 6–1 for ease of presentation.) *Rate* may be fast or slow; *magnitude* may be small or great; *scope* may be broad or narrow. Our categories run from fast-great-broad in the upper left cell to slow-small-narrow in the lower right cell. It seems apparent that fast-great-broad changes circumstances (and in that they are fast changes, we would think of these as "events" in everyday parlance) would have the highest probability of bringing about a definition and focus on particular circumstance. Conversely, changes in circumstances that were slow-small-narrow could easily go unrecognized. Subtract recognition and a focus on that circumstance could not take place; subtract focus, and estimates and judgments about that circumstance would not occur; thus, claims and disputes would not arise.

More challenging is a further sorting out of the effects of these variables. With respect to definition and focus on circumstances, which of the three is most important?

Largely on the basis of intuition we propose that *rate* of change in circumstance is the most important key to defining and focusing on circumstance. A review of the cells in Figure 6-1 in which a slow rate is

FIGURE 6-1   The Effect of Three Variables on Circumstance-Definition

Scope of change	*Rate of change of circumstance*			
	Fast		*Slow*	
	Magnitude of change		*Magnitude of change*	
	Great	*Small*	*Great*	*Small*
Broad	Individual is fired from job.	Individual receives pay raise of less than cost-of-living.	Individual's job gradually loses substantial status.	Individual's job loses a little status over time.
Narrow	Employer loses 1 valued employee to another job.	Employee fractures finger, slightly hindering production.	Employer experiences gradual decline in worth of a key employee.	Employee morale increases slightly as 2 workers become friends.

operative suggests that changes simply could be missed if they were not abrupt. This is true even when a change of great magnitude is involved (i.e., a change in virtually *all* of something), and even when a change of broad scope is involved (i.e., a change which encompasses many domains, not just a few). Even in a life-or-death circumstance, slow change may be unrecognized, at least at first.

We propose that *magnitude* of change in circumstance is second to rate with respect to provoking definition and focus on circumstance. To lose virtually all of something, for example, would seem to provoke notice more than the loss of a small amount of something—and this would be true even when the small amount crosses many domains. Because of that, we propose that scope plays no part in defining and focusing on circumstance. I am as likely to recognize (define and focus on) a torn fingernail as I am to recognize substantial damage to my hand or arm. Of course, the latter would be more likely to provoke a claim, and even though we reserve until later an extended discussion of claim-bringing, some contrast between circumstance-definition and claim-bringing may make our current observations clearer.

For the explanation of claim-bringing, *rate* of change in circumstance is of virtually no consequence except (and it is a substantial exception) as far as circumstance-definition is a necessary precursor to claim-bringing. For claim-bringing, the size of change in circumstance (of a loss, ordinarily) has been often recognized as an important key. "Size" of change in circumstance is in the present terms some combination of magnitude (amount of change) and scope (breadth across domains). We will argue later that magnitude and scope act in combination (with duration) to affect probabilities of claim-bringing.

For circumstance-definition, however, we can usefully distinguish the relative importance of rate and magnitude. Magnitude, we have said, is secondary to rate. Using the dichotomies offered in Figure 6-1, we can distinguish four situations, ordered from most likely to provoke definition and focus on circumstance to least likely to provoke such definition and focus. These are offered in Table 6-1.

TABLE 6-1 Changes in Circumstance Most to Least Likely to Provoke Definition and Focus in Circumstance, by Rate and Magnitude of Change

Likelihood of Circumstance Definition	*Characteristics of Change*	
	Rate	*Magnitude*
Most likely	Fast	Great
	Fast	Small
	Slow	Great
Least likely	Slow	Small

As already noted, the basis of Table 6-1 is intuition in large part, and one could reasonably suggest that proposing that fast and great changes are noticed more frequently than are slow and small changes is self-evident. The merit of this analysis would be found, then, first in the very fact we are in good accord with "common sense"; second, in our proposition that fast but small changes are likely to provoke definition and focus on circumstance than are slow but great changes (perhaps not quite as self-evident and therefore more theoretically interesting); third, in our proposition that scope plays no role in circumstance-definition; and fourth (and most generally), in our insistence circumstance-definition, as such, as a necessary precondition to further activity, including claim-bringing.

ESTIMATING CIRCUMSTANCES

We may now observe that one cannot notice a change in circumstance without making a comparison, even if implicitly, to what has gone before. With this we can propose that some comparisons are more likely to be accurate than are others. Given the suggested significance of rate of change, it would seem that when change in circumstance takes place at a fast rate, the individual has had little time to forget the dimensions of past circumstance. By contrast, we can easily imagine misperceptions of past job status in which changes in that circumstance have taken place slowly (as in Figure 6-1). The same would be true for slow changes in climate, slow changes in the worth of an employee, and so forth. Given the passage of time, which we introduce by stipulating a slow rate of change, individuals can forget. Again, from this vantage, rate of change seems particularly significant for defining and for engendering focus on circumstance.

Taking this idea of comparison a step further, we can consider comparisons of circumstance not only with past circumstance, but also with possible future circumstance. Comparisons of the present with the past are very probably easier to make in most instances than are comparisons with possible future circumstance. Whereas (at least in a limited sense) one's past has an objective reality, comparing one's present circumstance against a standard of possible future circumstance carries with it the problem of defining a particular future circumstance. At least some images of possible future circumstance may be religious or mystical or utopian in origin. More ordinarily and more frequently, however, images of possible future circumstance would be rooted in comparisons of one's lot in life with the circumstances of other individuals or groups.

We may sum up in this way. Our first step in a process eventually leading to claim-bringing is a definition of and focus on circumstance. We have said that change in circumstance is an important key to definition and focus, and that change, in its nature, implies a comparison with past circumstance. Comparison with future circumstance is a second option; this frequently involves reference groups, and such reference groups can change. Happenings in the larger world can bring this about, as when technologically advanced persons or groups arrive on the scene of technologically less advanced groups for the first time. Beyond this, however, change in criterion groups can be urged upon an individual with an explicit goal of bringing about a change in that individual's evaluation of his or her own circumstance. As an example, groups like the American Cancer Society do so in urging people to give up smoking to avoid the heart disease, cancer, and so forth experienced by a large proportion of heavy smokers.

We notice, too, that in some of these instances circumstances are not easily defined, and thus significant effort that may amount to evangelizing is required to achieve circumstance definition. The American Cancer Society acts in this way in carrying its message to smokers. We can understand why such an effort should be required by reference to our earlier argument about rate of change. We said that rate of change is an important key in winning circumstance definition, yet smokers experience virtually no change in circumstance in the short run, at least in the subjective experience of smoking.

EVALUATING CIRCUMSTANCES

The evaluation of differences in circumstances is the next analytically distinct stage. One evaluates by reference to social norms. Such norms tell us whether our circumstances are what they should be, are due us in some sense, or are "undue." Clearly, this can be idiosyncratic. Clearly, a facet of many disputes is contention about which of two or more apparently competing social norms should govern. Even in the face of this, however, we may propose a modest structuring of three different and broad categories of social norms, which is useful for our thinking about the very early stages of dispute generation.[3]

The most fundamental social norms, and thus the most widely understood and accepted (and thus to some extent the simplest to invoke when evaluating circumstances), may be those dealing with exchange and reciprocity in social relations. Norms that support a balance in social exchanges and that demand the requiting of benefits or injuries are familiar to nearly all persons in nearly all places at nearly all times.

Norms that require similar people to be treated similarly may be harder to know and use in evaluating circumstances. The central problem is the basis on which essential similarity is judged. Persons who are essentially similar in one dimension may be very dissimilar in another, and whether they should be treated similarly in a given allocation is therefore open to argument. At least in practice, then, and perhaps even at the level of an abstraction, equality of treatment norms would enjoy less acceptance than norms supporting balance in social exchanges or the requiting of benefits or injuries.

More difficult, and third in this ordering, are norms that require the provision of similar circumstances to similar persons. This is equality of result as opposed to equality of allocation. Norms commanding equality of result would require allocating more to A than to B if A's circumstances presently include less of the value being distributed than B's circumstances presently include. As with equality of treatment, a problem here is to define essential similarity, but beyond that, equality of result may directly conflict with equality of application. We propose that norms in this third category would enjoy less acceptance and use than would either of the first two.

CLAIM-BRINGING

From what we have said thus far, in arriving at the point of decision on making a claim an individual must first define and focus on a circumstance, must note a difference in circumstance, and must evaluate the difference as being undue him or her. The highest probability of arriving at the point of decision (to make a claim) is if a change in circumstance has occurred rapidly, prompting a comparison with one's own past circumstance, and if a decision as to whether the circumstance is due or undue can be made by reference to norms in the families of balance in social exchange, or reciprocity. In contrast, the lowest probability of arriving at the point of deciding whether or not to bring a claim is defined by the opposite characteristics: no change in circumstance or very slow change; comparison of circumstance with an image of possible future circumstance; judgment of circumstance as undue by a social norm difficult to understand or to accept. On the one hand, two cars may collide (rapid change in circumstance, comparison with past, ordinary or easy-to-use social norms invoked). On the other hand, consider the hard task of community organizers (cf. Alinsky, 1969). The circumstances of the people with whom the organizers work may not have changed (although when they have, as in a labor dispute, the organizer's task may be easier). The organizer must, without a change in circumstance, stir people to achieve circumstance definition and focus. Then the organizer must invoke a new reference group. The organizer then must win support for the notion that circumstances are undue, as judged by a standard more difficult to understand and use than simple reciprocity or balance in social exchanges.

All possible claims are not brought, of course, even from among the set of those that have surmounted the circumstance definition, comparison, and judgment hurdles. Some explanations for this depend on differential abilities to carry forward disputes, including differential abilities to define, compare, and judge circumstances. (These are treated in a little detail below.) Beyond these factors, the common-sense observation that some claims may simply not be "worth" bringing, may not be "big enough," finds predictable echoes in the scholarly literature (cf. Hunting and Neuwirth, 1962). We may briefly pursue the idea of *size* of undue circumstance in relationship to claim-bringing, in a way analogous to our discussion of circumstance-definition.

In Figure 6-1 we proposed three variables by which to characterize circumstance-definition: rate, scope, and magnitude. Of these, rate was proposed as especially consequential for circumstance-definition, and scope was thought not consequential. Now, for a claim-bringing decision, magnitude will obviously play a role, even as it played a role in circumstance-definition. (By magnitude we mean great or small, a lot or a little of some value.) However, magnitude is not all that one can or should say about "size." To parallel the discussion accompanying Figure 6–1, we would argue that scope is an element of size: the number of domains across which the circumstance extends implies greater or smaller size. In Figure 6-1 and the discussion accompanying it we also had a variable for a time dimension—rate. Surely rate of change in circumstance has little to do with the size of a circumstance, even though it may be important in winning notice of some change in circumstance. Our variable for the time dimension here, in considering size, is *duration* of the circumstance. This accords well with ordinary language and ordinary practice. If pain is inflicted on me, it makes a substantial difference as to whether the pain is brief or whether it lasts for years. The effects of an amputated foot last longer than the effects of a broken foot, which in turn last longer than the effects of a mild sprain, which in turn last longer than the effects of a mild bruise, and so on.

We propose, then, that decisions about claim-bringing are a partial function of size of a circumstance (which has been judged undue), and that size may be understood in terms of three variables, magnitude, scope, and duration. Beyond this we may offer a conjecture as to how these three variables combine. We would argue that they are multiplicative: magnitude $\times$ scope $\times$ duration. Unknown are the coefficients for these variables, and their relative weight might be something other than (1) each. (They might, for example, be properly weighted as magnitude (4) $\times$ scope (2) $\times$ duration (1), or anything else.) Nevertheless, it follows that the same sizes of claims can be achieved through different combinations of the three variables.

A little speculatively, it may be that duration should, in fact, be assigned a lower weight than magnitude and scope when assessing size. Duration, after all, involves a prediction of the future in instances in which claims are brought on the basis of anticipated duration (instead of actual happenings over time). Moreover, even when duration refers to time that has already passed, memory must be invoked, and memories can grow dim over time. Thus, duration may be weighted least of these variables, considering that memories may be especially dim when circumstances of small scope and small magnitude are involved.

It remains for all of this to be scrutinized in the light of experience. Although we have no independently collected data for the purpose, a handful of the best surveys of "legal needs" can be usefully reviewed. In doing so we may be able to pose the prior questions not posed by those who have taken needs for advice or the existence of problems or the existence of legal needs as givens (rather than as phenomena to be explained). In making this review, we may assert the usefulness of constructs such as we have proposed here. Moreover, there are data (though they are limited and few) from these surveys which at least suggest that processes similar to those we have proposed are at work. In a way, then, we will be taking this literature largely on something other than its own terms. The intention in doing this is to be heuristic, and not to inappropriately criticize previous work for not being something other than what it is.

RE-EXAMINATION OF "LEGAL NEEDS"

Four studies of legal needs (and related phenomena) are of particular interest, on grounds of being relatively recent, well done, and suggestive. Three of these (Sykes, 1969; Levine and Preston, 1970; Abel-Smith, Zander, and Brooke, 1973) seek to discover the incidence of needs for advice, problems, or legal needs among groups of poor persons (in London, Wisconsin, and Denver, respectively). Curran (1977), by contrast, reviews the incidence of legal needs across income groups in a survey of the adult population of the United States.[4]

In their study in three London boroughs, Abel-Smith, Zander, and Brooke sought to "define the extent of unmet need (i.e., need for advice about legal problems)" (1973:110) and did not explicitly focus on how problems were generated. Rather, they "simply (asked) respondents whether they had particular problems" (1973:110) at any time within the previous seven years, using for this purpose a questionnaire that covered seventeen ordinary situations. After probing for some details about the situation or problem, the study team made intentionally conservative judgments about the number of respondents who were in need of advice about the problem they reported having had. From there the study team was able to ascertain the proportion of those needing advice who had in fact received advice, by problem type. For the present purposes we may compare the four problem types for which needed advice was least frequently obtained with the four problem types for which needed advice was most frequently obtained (1973:154) in Table 6-2.

TABLE 6-2   Patterns of Advice-Taking in Three
London Boroughs

Problem	% of Cases When Advice Was Needed but Not Taken
Defective goods	92
Installment arrears	90
Social security benefits	81
Debtor would not pay	72
Accidents	42
Taken to court for debt	42
Attempted eviction	31
Buying a house	0

If these data are pertinent to the constructs we have proposed, it would be at a claim-bringing stage, where we argued that size of a claim (understood as scope × magnitude × duration) is important. Both "common sense" and somewhat more exact formulations (such as ours about size) suggest that people will recognize the importance of buying a house.[5] Defective goods clearly present a smaller size of circumstance (or potential claim).

It is also suggestive (but only that) that changes in circumstance are more abrupt in accident situations in which one is taken to court, in which eviction is attempted, and in which one buys a house, than is true for a purchase in which a defect may not be apparent until some time elapses.

Some time may be required before concluding that a debtor will not pay, and there may have been no change in circumstance at all in instances of social security benefits not received. We might think that Table 6–2 thus shows a pattern consistent with our argument that abrupt changes in circumstance lead to definition and focus, the first requisite for eventual claim-bringing. Simply on the basis of these numbers, however, we can say nothing stronger, for the study team asked only about situations that had, in fact, been noticed.

We are left only with the possibility of arguing plausibility, but let us try. We want to know whether there were situations in which (a) some changes in circumstances could have been slow and gone unnoticed; (b) some circumstances were not evaluated by reference to a possible future condition even though they might have been; or (c) respondents may have failed to judge their situations undue because of an inability to employ a "difficult" social norm necessary to reach such a judgment. We may look again at the categories of problems, in Table 6-2, this time with regard to the frequency of their occurrence in the population surveyed (see Abel-Smith, Zander, and Brooke, 1973:146–153).

TABLE 6-3   Frequency of Problems in Three London Boroughs

Type of Problem	% Reporting Such a Problem Within Past 7 years
Defective goods (worth more than £ 5)	16.4
Installment arrears	4.3
Social security benefits	5.5
Debtor would not pay	7.5
Repairs undone (tenants only)	22.6
Accidents	14.7
Taken to court for debt	2.0
Attempted eviction	1.9
Buying a house	4.5

On the list of nine problems in Table 6-3 (repairs undone has been added to the list from Table 6-2), we would propose that six problem types are associated with a wholly plausible frequency of occurrence for this population. "Events" these are (save one), with changes in circumstances happening quickly; only "debtor would not pay" might take time to be noticed. (Even there, however, poor people—whose circumstances would rather frequently be defined in terms of lack of money—would usually notice a debt not repaid.)

Problems with "social security benefits" might never be perceived, and we can speculate that there were others in this sample who, in the absence of a change in their circumstances, never focused on payments when frequency and amount of payments did not change. Moreover, except when payments are reduced, circumstances must be evaluated against a possible future condition; beyond that, the standard for judgment might necessarily be the difficult-to-use criterion of equal result. With respect to "repairs undone" and to "defective goods," we would make similar observations. Housing can fail to meet reasonable standards, but without some change (like broken plumbing), circumstance-definition is less likely. Without some change, an evaluative criterion focusing on the future would be required, and "difficult" social norms would be needed for judging such a circumstance as undue. The same may be said of defective goods.

The point to this, as we said, is to assert the usefulness of taking legal needs not as givens but instead as phenomena to be explained. Using the London study data as a reference point, we have posed different questions. Beyond this, we would argue from our point of view that circumstances that could be considered "needs" are more frequent than respondents in a sample survey would be expected to report.

An argument, which we construe as supporting this point of view, emerges from an analysis of a survey of low-income groups in a "middle-size urban community" (Levine and Preston, 1970:81). Respondents were queried about their problems, both "concrete" (i.e., actually experienced) and hypothetical (in which respondents were asked to report what they *would* do about such problems if they had them). In their conclusion Levine & Preston report that (1970:109)

> [a] recurrent theme throughout the findings was that people were not aware of many of their rights. . . . Subjects' responses to the most crucial poverty problems—welfare, consumer, and landlord-tenant difficulties—indicated that in these areas they were less knowledgeable about available rights and remedies. . . . Undoubtedly knowledge about rights crucially affected response style to problems.

Respondents, in short, had more problems than they were aware of. These authors' remarks about knowledge of legal rights are to the point, yet we would argue that a fuller understanding of the phenomenon might be gained by asking the questions suggested by the perspective proposed here. What proportion of the variance is attributable to the absence of definition and focus on the particular circumstance at issue? (In the Levine and Preston study, perhaps little or none is so attributable, in that their survey questions supplied definition and focus.) What proportion of the variance is attributable to the requirement for an evaluation by a standard of possible future circumstance, instead of the "easier" standard of previous circumstance? What proportion of the variance is attributable to a requirement in the situation for employing "difficult" norms when making judgments about circumstances? Rather than guessing at the answers, we argue the utility of the questions.

A study of the legal needs of the poor in Denver (Sykes, 1969) is of particular interest in considering the perception of problems (or needs). Some 402 households in a poor area of Denver were surveyed, and 43% (n = 170) reported having had a legal problem within the previous five years. Another component of the Sykes study was to submit the interview protocols to a panel of attorneys, asking the panel for their "diagnoses" of legal needs. The 120 respondents who in the view of the panel of attorneys had a legal need but who did not perceive such a need themselves draw our attention. Sykes says only that many of these unperceived legal needs involved "administrative" agencies and criminal matters" (1969:267). We are left, therefore, in the position of having to speculate, but it does not seem farfetched to suppose that a change in circumstance was frequently absent among the 120. Further, a claim for increases in benefits received, as an example of an "administrative matter," would probably involve evaluation of present circumstances against a possible future; the judgment of such circumstances as undue would mean use of a social norm of more difficulty than simple reciprocity or exchange.

To Abel-Smith, Zander, and Brooke, a "need for advice" was noted when a perceived, serious problem existed. To Sykes, a "legal need" existed even when it went unperceived. Levine and Preston looked for "problems" in their survey rather than needs for advice or "legal needs," and while largely taking their respondents' own perceptions of problems as marking the existence of such problems, paused nevertheless to consider the issue of problems for which respondents had no response. All three studies surveyed low income populations.

Curran (1977) reports the results of a sample survey of the U.S. population as to legal needs. This study, therefore, goes beyond low-income populations to include respondents at various levels of income, education, and so on. Respondents were asked to report whether they had ever had problems of various types. It is of interest that the mean level of education of those who reported having had a particular problem was higher than those who reported never having had such a problem, in all but three of eleven problem categories. The greatest such difference was in a category of Constitutional problems, including infringement of Constitutional rights with respect to employment, dealings with government agencies, dealings with police; access to or availability of goods, services, or credit, education, and more (1977:121, 126).

Some problems involving Constitutional rights may have no particular change in circumstance associated with them, and may have gone unmentioned in the survey. Many such problems would involve evaluation by a standard of possible future circumstance. Many such problems would require judgment by a standard more difficult to employ than would be suggested by norms of reciprocity or exchange. We would expect that better-educated persons would be more likely to surmount these problems of definition, evaluation, and judgment than would more poorly educated persons; and because Curran's study was not restricted to low-income groups (in which one may presume that educational levels are lower than in the population as a whole), good comparisons are possible. In fact, Curran reports that the mean years of school completed by respondents who reported having had a problem involving infringement of Constitutional rights exceeded 13, whereas the mean level of education of those who reported never having had such a problem was less than a high school diploma (1977:126).

DIFFERENTIAL ABILITIES TO DEFINE, EVALUATE, AND JUDGE CIRCUMSTANCES

We can now turn to a more general consideration of what we have in effect already introduced with our mention of the impact of education on these earliest stages of claim-bringing. The general proposition is that some kinds of persons are more likely than other kinds of persons to achieve definition and focus on particular circumstances; some kinds of persons will find it easier than other kinds to evaluate circumstances against standards other than the *status quo ante*; some will be more able than others to judge circumstances according to norms which are hard to understand or which are not very widely accepted. Given the way we have outlined the early stages of claim-bringing, education (in and of itself, but also standing as a partial surrogate for intelligence—I.Q. or whatever) is an obvious choice.

Psychological variables may also be given consideration. We may readily imagine that some persons are "defensive" about their circumstances—watching, assessing, and guarding them with particular care—whereas other persons are less defensive. Changes in circumstances that are incremental or slow might be noticed and might be focused on by defensive people, whereas less defensive people would fail to notice or to focus. We may suggest further that personal needs for success or achievement would prompt evaluation by a standard involving possible future circumstance. Persons lacking such needs might be less inclined to look to the future when evaluating their circumstances.

We may also mention organization and access to resources. Consider a medium-sized business enterprise. The circumstances of such an organization are well defined and monitored; changes in profits, and even lack of changes in profits, do not go unnoticed. Persons within such an organization are assigned specifically to monitor circumstances, and even to assess circumstances against possible future circumstances (e.g., how profitability might be increased). In fact, such an organization may also include someone who especially attends to a function of understanding norms, by reference to which the organization's activities may be justified (or by reference to which the organization may make a potentially beneficial claim).

We might plausibly argue that other kinds of resources play a part here, too, and that parties with such resources are more likely than parties without them to make their way through the earliest stages of a claim-bringing process. "Party capability" is a reasonably well-explicated concept (cf. Galanter, 1974b, 1975, and chapter 5). We will not, then, offer more treatment of it here, apart from two observations. First, the effects of differential party capability extend, in our view, to stages in a claim-bringing process prior to the actual identification of a claim. Second, at these early stages there may be reason to especially consider differential education or intelligence—cognitive capacity; for if we are right in saying that definition, focus, evaluation, and judgment of circumstances are necessary conditions for bringing a claim, it would follow that *ability* to define, focus, and so on, is essential.[6]

CONCLUSIONS AND IMPLICATIONS

These ideas may help us to understand the genesis of claims and, ultimately, of court cases. Of course, not all claims are brought to courts. Moreover, not all circumstances that are defined, evaluated, and adjudged "undue" result in claims. Thus, it is clear that these ideas are not sufficient for understanding the appearance of court cases, nor even for understanding the appearance of claims. There may be more utility in these concepts for thinking about claims and cases that are *not* brought. Even there, however, it is clear that some claims are not brought due to perceived imbalances in a power situation (e.g., tenant versus landlord and fear of eviction), due to low apparent potential payoffs for claims that are simply not "worth" bringing, or to other similar factors.

However, among the population of claims not brought we would identify some categories for which the explanatory role of these concepts is larger. Torts would not be among these: an event is usually involved in torts, providing definition and focus. Evaluation is typically done with reference to the *status quo ante* in tort claims. Contract claims would similarly not usually be among these. Most ordinary criminal complaints would likewise involve a circumstance-defining event, an evaluation by reference to the *status quo ante*, and a judgment by a familiar normative injunction.

Instead of these items of "standard business," we would concentrate on nonstandard business, on entitlements, which, in addition to being newly provided in many instances, are predicated on propositions drawn from sophisticated understandings of a just social order. Transactions in which the government is involved and perhaps especially transactions in which the government distributes values to specified groups of persons seem to fit neatly in this category of nonstandard business as we have oulined it. This would include Sykes' "administrative matters," which were prominent among the needs which attorneys identified but which survey respondents did not. This would include many welfare, consumer, and at least some of the landlord–tenant difficulties with which the respondents in the Levine and Preston study had difficulty (1970:109). This would include a proportion of the problems Curran categorized as Constitutional, and probably also a proportion of the "consumer" and "governmental" problems (1977:109, 115). Our comments about these kinds of business have already been outlined.

Beyond this, finally, it would seem from this perspective that simply extending access to means and forums for claim and dispute processing to groups with little education and income would not of itself result in claims being brought that fall outside standard business categories. Indeed, that has been the pattern reported in many schemes sited in many jurisdictions. There was little indication of nonstandard business being brought under the first year of experience with the "Shreveport Plan" (Marks, Hallauer, and Clifton, 1974). "Usual legal services" consumed the "entire time" of Legal Services attorneys in the first years of the Office of Economic Opportunity's Legal Services Program (Levitan, 1969:186); a "Complaint-Mobile" service operating on the streets of San Francisco has handled ordinary business (Hager, 1979); and there are numerous other examples. To go beyond that takes active involvement by reform-minded attorneys or their functional equivalents, for assistance in *generating* claims is needed where nonstandard business is involved, not just assistance in pursuing claims. Political fights over the proper role of American legal services programs demonstrate that reform-minded attorneys can effectively render such assistance, and that there are in effect, claims waiting to be defined out there (cf. Johnson, 1978:ix–xxiii, 192). We are not the first to notice the truth of that. Our intended contribution is to systematize an understanding of it.

NOTES

1. See in particular Felstiner, Abel, and Sarat (1980) and Fitzgerald, Hickman and Dickens (1980).
2. There is, however, a substantial literature on the causes of crime. See, e.g., the bibliographies that are entry numbers 12, 133, 151, 155, 206, 208, 216, and 221 in a bibliography of bibliographies in criminal justice (Klein, Horton, and Kravitz, 1980); and see also the nonbehavioral science perspectives on the etiology of criminality in Brantley & Kravitz, 1979. Throughout the present discussion, civil actions will be the usual refer-

ence and most examples will be civil rather than criminal, but in the author's judgment, the overall scheme would apply with only minor modifications to claims that may result in the filing of criminal complaints.

3. The discussion of social norms that follows may seem culture-bound, and perhaps rightly so, yet it has been seriously argued that social behavior as exchange is fundamental (Homans, 1958). It has been equally seriously argued that a norm of reciprocity is universal across human cultures (Gouldner, 1960, and the references there). Functional analyses are usually advanced in explanation of the apparent universality; that is, a norm of reciprocity contributes to and indeed may be necessary for social system persistence. As to the ubiquity and difficulty of notions of equality, see, generally, Pennock and Chapman (1967).

4. Particular attention to poor people is characteristic of much of the literature on the incidence of legal needs. That is unsurprising in that interest in the topic was spurred by the American "war on poverty" in the 1960s, in the context of which proposals to extend legal services to the poor were taken seriously. A natural part of that was an interest in how much in the way of legal services poor people could use, or needed in some sense.

5. Even more critically, it is a crime in the United Kingdom for anyone other than a lawyer to infringe on the legal profession's state monopoly of conveyancing. I am indebted to Professor Paul Robertshaw of University College, Cardiff, for pointing this out to me.

6. We acknowledge, too, that this essay has been little concerned with social processes of mobilization in bringing claims. For a treatment of aspects of that, see Mather and Yngvesson, 1981.

7

Theoretical Perspectives on Case Load Studies: A Critique and a Beginning

Samuel Krislov

INTRODUCTION: OVERVIEW OF A CRITIQUE

Studies of case loads in courts have to date been disappointing. The promise has seemed great, but even in the context of social science inquiry, where reach perennially exceeds grasp, the results have been meager.

The promise seems clear. Unlike most areas in the study of the judicial process, there are definite outcomes implied. Results from case load studies seem readily determinable and such results, it would seem, should have relatively unambiguous content. The decision to litigate is a simple act, if one that has behind it complex stresses and behavior,[1] yet the sweep of influences upon potential litigants contains the promise of measuring significant relationships through a narrow band of direct observations. With a dependent variable—case loads—readily available for effective hypothesis testing, the area seems ripe for significant progress.

Author's Note: This chapter is revised from a paper originally delivered at the 1980 Annual Meeting of the Law and Society Association and the ISA Research Committee on the Sociology of Law, Madison, Wisconsin. The research for this paper was supported by Grant Number 78-NI-AX-0139, awarded to the California State University, Fullerton Foundation by the National Institute of Justice, Law Enforcement Assistance Administration, U.S. Department of Justice, under the Omnibus Crime Control and Safe Streets Act of 1968, as amended. Points of view or opinions stated in this chapter are those of the author and do not necessarily represent the position or policies of the U.S. Department of Justice. The research assistance of Karen Adams is gratefully acknowledged.

Dominating the area has been a sometimes explicit, sometimes tacit, assumption. Modern society is viewed as involving a progressive, probably geometric, creation of litigation. This notion is an important legacy from Durkheim (1964), whose seminal influence on sociologists of law is comparable to Weber's influence on sociologists of bureaucracy. Durkheim's suggestion that organic solidarity progressively supplants mechanical solidarity provides the foundation for an expectation that litigation will also increase. In addition, a decline in autonomic relationships and the rise of anomic relationships in modern society reduce the inhibitions against appealing to third parties for adjudication. Most briefly put, the thesis is that complexity plus estrangement lead to litigation.

Efforts to confirm Durkheim's thesis have had a curiously unsatisfactory history. Nothing neat has been forthcoming and anomalies abound.[2] In general, the lack of any clear affirmation of Durkheim's thesis has been shrugged off, frequently attributed to imperfect data. Indeed, the data are difficult to work with. As will be noted below, the seeming simplicity of the filing records at closer inspection turns into overall complexity. Great leeway is available to record keepers in matters of definition and counting. Thus there is great potential for mischief due to individual variation over time as definitions change, and in various courts in the same system even at the same date and time. Data problems, however, are not unique to this area. As Oskar Morgenstern so pungently and definitively observed, "all data are bad; there is only good or bad reasoning about them."[3]

It remained for Jose Juan Toharia to place the genuine problem and challenge to Durkheim's hypothesis in perspective. Using Spanish data embracing 63 years, Toharia demonstrated a crucial factor that had been neglected in simple extrapolations: the growth of supplementary and even rival agencies for settling disputes. Thus, while the total of appeals to third-party decision making did apparently increase, the official court system did not reflect this same simple trend. "... [E]xtensive by-passing of the courts has taken place, while, on the contrary, legal activity has increased enormously" (Toharia 1973:40). The very same complexity and inventiveness that created the new and ill-defined relations that Durkheim saw contributed to the establishment of novel and recombinant institutions—arbitration, grievance procedures, insurance structures, advance financial guarantees—which have aided, abetted, and supplanted conflict resolution in courts. At different times these were envied and fought by courts, or were welcomed and encouraged. However, just as predictions that the Post Office would blossom over time ran afoul—not of a mistake in the concept of increased communication but rather of the assurance that even a legal monopoly would necessarily ensure continuation of existing patterns and trends—so it is with courts and the resolution of conflict. Indeed, the Post Office analogy is even more powerful, given its competitors—messengers and couriers, package delivery, telephone, and wire, which in turn trail off into the transmission of whole images and data and to computer interlinkage. In the end, the definition of communication becomes blurred. With court rivals, too, the line of adjudication trails off sharply into negotiation and *ad hoc* contrivances.

The Toharia emphasis also brings the pricing aspect of the judicial system into focus. The discovery of rival enterprises strongly underscores the complexity (and, therefore, non-comparability) of the decision to litigate. The apparent simplicity of the dependent variable—case load—disappears. Case load is not merely a complex function of social interactions and of limits, mechanisms, and "prices" (that is, costs attendant upon the prescribed course of litigation) as set by the authorities, but also of the limits, mechanisms and costs attached to the non-official means of resolution. The data problems we have only hinted at and the theoretical–empirical relationships that have been uncovered go a long way toward explaining the unrealized nature of this sector of research.

For all of this, our argument is that these obstacles, formidable as they are, would be overcome, or at least seriously attacked, if it were, in fact, case loads that interested researchers. As we shall try to show, however, case loads are to inquirers (other than court planners) a means and not an end. Court case loads are surrogates for researchers' real (and diverse) objectives. Thus, researchers have scurried away as the complexity of the issues emerged, because case loads *per se* simply didn't interest them. Scholars have largely abandoned any pursuit of rigorous understanding of case loads, pursuing other research modes instead. We shall argue here for a return to the "case load model," attempting to identify the schools and objectives once explored through the approach. We shall also suggest better surrogates for pursuing the real goals. The argument is essentially for restoring continuity in research.

FOUR APPROACHES TO EXPLAINING CASE LOADS

Nominalist v. Essentialist Definitions of "Court"

The dichotomous impulse that Gilbert and Sullivan saw as contriving that every child was born a liberal or a conservative has come to an end in British politics, but it persists in the form of approaches to definitions. Nominalists and essentialists have been in fearsome debate at least since the late medieval period, and the forms of disagreement are continuously renewed in different guises and spheres—even in areas like physics where presumably the issues had been settled. The basic positions are relevant to the analysis of courts and legal systems as well. Thus Lawrence Friedman has informally suggested that courts should not be viewed as having functionalist integrity but be studied as pragmatic histories, like that of the drugstore. Drugstores evolved from Ye Olde Apothecary Shoppes, not by any inner logic, but because of American Sunday-closing laws, which permitted them exemption that led them to carry items people were likely to want to purchase on the sabbath and which legislatures had not had the foresight to outlaw in specific terms. Therefore, to understand or describe the "drugstore," neither its name or its basic purpose would be helpful. Either an evolutionary history or a specific inventory would be necessary to delineate its operations.

Since courts deal, even in our society, with a multitude of types of issues and in quite different formats, Friedman argued, it is best to approach them in this anthropological agnosticism, much as one should with the drugstore. Presumably, this prescription for clear-sightednesses has allowed Friedman himself to demonstrate the remarkable extent to which courts are non-adjudicatory, serving instead as ratifiers or even a mere registrars of agreements reached between the contesting parties (cf. Friedman and Percival, 1976). In this view, structures analogous to courts such as mediation services, marriage counselors, arbitrators, ombudsmen, and media complaint settlers may be understood vis-á-vis courts much as the variety store, the dime store, and the hardware shop are understood in relation to drugstores—as rivals who have evolved their own particular and probably accidental mix of wares or services. In this nominalist approach courts are what courts do, as is the case with other social structures. Empirical observation will supplement the nominal definition with descriptive content.

Martin Shapiro outlines an essentialist position in his fascinating treatment of "courts" in *The Handbook of Political Science* (1975). In a sense, Shapiro begins with some of the observations Friedman has impressed upon students of court behavior, together with mordant generalizations of his own. Taking as the standard model of the judicial process a single judge (with or without a jury) sitting in deliberation as adversaries make their case, Shapiro notes that even in the American court system this model is less than ubiquitous, and in other systems may be nonexistent. Appeals proceedings in American courts are seldom before a single judge, and in some systems the standard court is a three-judge affair. *Ex parte* (one-sided) proceedings take place on many matters in American courts, and substantially, *ex parte* deliberation remains the rule for whole domains of proceedings (such as mental commitments). Orders may be written, signed, and delivered wholly without adversary proceedings. Non-adversary administrative events routinely take place in courts. In other systems, "judges" are activist legislative-administrative officials, like the Mexican judge described by Laura Nader (1969a) who unilaterally ended a grain monopoly under near-famine conditions.

In noting these departures from it, Shapiro suggests that the "standard" adjudicatory model is, in fact, not the most appropriate one for courts. Rather, he postulates a family of models, the core of which is mediation. Here he locates the true function of courts, and suggests that the adjudicatory model develops in part for convenience of the functionaries. In true mediation both enforcement and the very fabric of law in which the question is to be negotiated are themselves part of the process. The judges seek an external standing law and enforcement power because of the internal advantages offered by such features. However, Shapiro suggests that formalization of law, for all of its apparent advantages, threatens the essence of the process, the very mediational aspect that is ultimately vital to judging itself.

Of course, Shapiro's is just one of many formulations that attempt to define the essence (or even *an* essence) of courts of law. His essentials are quite different in content and even purpose from, say, Lon Fuller's (1964:39). While all essentialists recognize that courts in practice take on side functions, or even fail in their allegedly prime purpose, they still put forward some core as being necessarily there—or failure as an institution presumably is total.

On the other hand, even "nominalists" exclude from the family of courts institutions that meet some implicit or explicit definitions of "courts" (i.e., meet some essentials). Certainly, the word "court" is not a sufficient clue as to what to include, for it can be used by a private organization (such as the "Science Court") or even by an apartment house (e.g., "Croydon Court"). Indeed, the original court was that of the king, and was non-judicial. One is reminded of the Parisian chain of restaurants with high prices and (largely) tourist goods called "le drugstore," which sell no drugs at all. Would one attempt a definition of drugstore centered around these? And if not, why not?

For proper discussion of case load, the significance of the debate lies both in clarity of thought and in the dirty work of measurement. As we shall show, dispute resolution is so ubiquitous a phenomenon as to overwhelm us. Boundary definitions are needed to guide our collection and treatment of data. Without some understanding of what is being appraised, the meaning of propositions tested has varied from scholar to scholar, or worse yet, has remained murky and shifting even within the work of an individual.

Bearing in mind the weightiness and persistence of these antinomies, the approach taken here is a modified essentialist one. It assumes a core of meaning must exist to permit even ostentatious definition. At the same time it recognizes that the functionalist approach implicit in any strict essentialist definition has failed to demonstrate that social success is possible only with satisfaction of the need defined—for "le drugstore" exists without the sale of prescriptions, and "Joe's Pharmacy" may successfully become "Joe's ice cream parlor and luncheonette." Neither do we have any demonstration that a special social function must be performed only in a particular, well-defined structure. Thus, Joe's Pharmacy may sell bus tickets, be a shipping center for packages, handle liquor, and clear its profit on illegal "numbers" sales, and yet be a drugstore, while the

"Grand Giant" has a large over-the-counter drug business that turns a huge profit, but for most purposes is not accounted a drugstore but a "supermarket."

This is, admittedly, a coward's way out. The definition attempted may be fatal to all work in the area. It may be that to assess *any* approach we must account for total litigation, wherever it takes place. The immense difficulties such a conclusion would entail justify reaching that conclusion later rather than earlier. Further, theories are not presently available that would permit a more inclusive and more essentialist definition, but the possibility that the focus is misguided cannot be dismissed.

The problem of applying this approach to courts, then, is to define the core of meaning attendant upon them. To find any mediation or decision making at all as sufficient to define that core would be (as lawyers occasionally seem to wish) to judicialize the whole world. Anthropologists and sociologists therefore usually require a structure separate from kinship arrangements before they will speak of "mediation" or "adjudication." Third-party intervention, with some degree of acceptance of the decision by the two original parties, in a patterned and socially accepted way are necessary before they speak of adjudication. Courts are generally understood in modern societies to be part of the coercive power of the state machinery. We distinguish them from arbitration structures (privately constituted units whose decisions may be enforced ultimately by courts) or from regulatory agencies by the fact that these latter two structures, otherwise often more court-like than any real court, must exercise their authority through recourse to processes of their twins and rivals.

Within this family of institutions, there are many different types of structures and numerous explanatory schemes for their growth and development. We shall attempt to delineate them in terms of differing approaches.

Functional-Need Theories

The mediational function is so ubiquitous that it is often taken for granted. Whether it is called arbitration or dispute-resolution or trouble-shooting or marriage counseling, it permeates social existence. In most primitive societies, kin and elders perform this service invisibly, but in all societies the function is necessary. Good dispute-settlers perform not one but many functions:

1. They directly resolve or help resolve matters.
2. They restate the issues in new perspective, permitting symbolic or minor victories for both, or in other ways "cool the mark off."
3. They develop rules and procedures for handling trouble-cases.
4. They establish factors or resolve ambiguous data, which help not only in the resolution of present conflict but also in later conflicts.

5. They may develop new perspectives, which transform a dispute from a zero-sum game into one in which both parties may win something.

In one sense, all theories about courts are functionalist, much as we all speak prose. The question is the degree to which the theorist regards the relationship of court to social need as highly dynamic or as relatively static. Those who place primary emphasis on functional theory look to social developments—industrial growth, urbanization, and so on—for primary explanations for the appearance of cases and, indeed, of courts themselves. Others see social need as the matrix or primary cause of courts and cases only at threshold levels or initial stages, but see autonomous development occurring around the structures created to process cases. Some explanations for cases thus center upon the people performing "law jobs." Courts can be viewed as bureaucratic agencies that require cases; lawyers may create cases in order to win rewards for doing so; the structure of contesting agencies can engender cases; or even the psychological spirit of the society can encourage case-bringing. "True" functionalists do not necessarily discard these factors, but tend to find them epiphenomenal or marginal in their impacts.

The Purest of the Functional Theories: Utilitarian or Economic

Functional theories associate the appearance of courts and cases with societal needs. The utility maximization hypothesis does this with almost surgical exactness, particularly when prices are represented by one uniform measure (such as dollars or some other currency). From this standpoint, one would understand the development of courts as the most price-efficient agency for performing specific social services. As they do this, courts prosper or falter. Rivals develop or, indeed, may antedate official courts. While official courts have certain sanctioning and enforcement advantages, they also have certain hidden costs. Of these, the most important is their accessibility or lack of it. Almost every society has some notion that its public dispute mechanism should be easily available to all with general grievances; full costs are therefore not usually transferred to the parties. At the same time, there is a subterranean recognition that the number of potential disputes in society is very large. Generally, some costs are therefore overtly associated with resolution to ensure a threshold minimum of seriousness of the issue complained of. In point of fact, most societies prefer a somewhat hypocritical or less demythologized approach. The costs of litigation are hidden or problematic. Capacity is provided, but with hidden restraints or values attached. Thus, courts may be nearby or hundreds of miles away, in session at convenient hours or severely limited. Decisions may be easily arrived at, or the process may be convoluted. Delay may be, and indeed usually is, a major part of the rationing a non-free public good.

The basic price mechanism for access to courts has proven to be queueing (which implies waiting time). This has the effect of removing cases from public processes through atrophy, settlement, or creation of quicker dispute resolution alternatives such as private arbitrators. Expansion of public capacity lowers costs and brings on more cases; contraction tends to deflate the number of cases. The result is an equilibrium at various levels, with backlog a poor indicator (if any) of whether too much or too little in a society is judicialized. This picture of courts as resembling an equilibrium number of cars on the public roads (in which the numbers of cars expand to congest any given level of roads) leads to a paradoxical result from the standpoint of our concern.

Given strong economic motivation of private parties to seek use of a subsidized good, the determinant of actual usage is the government. The value of the public subsidy is that of the service minus court fees, discounted by the costs of delay or the difference in costs as between courts and other modes of dispute resolution.[4] Cases heard by alternative means will usually be ones in which both parties have an interest in prompt decision. The run of cases that go to trial includes an undetermined number in which a party has a vested interest in non-decision, and gains by delay; the costs there include the gains and losses of fighting for and averting delay, respectively. The verdicts will not yield good approximations of the parties' calculations. A better measure than "payoffs" in a narrow sense here is prior knowledge of the parties' thinking (or some construction of it from "objective facts"). Decisions that otherwise would appear irrational will become more explicable, but we know of no effort to distinguish between those two situations—that is, between the situation in which payoffs from litigation will indicate litigants' calculations and the situation in which outside information is needed to reconstruct the calculus.

Presumably, the best measure of public need would be some total or ratio of non-public and public resolution. Even that would be problematic since there is no inherent reason that public decision making should constitute any specified segment of the totality. Indeed, as is inevitable, some purists of the Chicago school have suggested that private arbitration and full-cost sharing by the parties should be totally substituted for present arrangements (see, e.g., Becker and Stigler, 1974; Landes and Posner, 1975).

If the pure economics of law contains a remarkable understanding of backlog, the looser functionalists more cogently outline the need for public purpose in courts. Weber's account of bureaucratic need for centralization and strict accountability provides a strong departure point, and his cycle between *Kadi* justice (personalistic and true to the parties) and bureaucratized or universalized justice provides the perimeters. Privately arrived-at justice has severe and crippling weaknesses, including at least these:

1. Pricing and paying create suspicion that the content of decision can be purchased as well as the process.
2. Enforcement at the ultimate point of defiance would be lacking, and would be known by the parties to be lacking in many instances.
3. The law to be applied and the process employed alike may be open to bargaining, and under such volunteerism stronger parties may extract advantages unwarranted by the fact situation.

To be sure, these aspects are still present in public courts, but they are at minimum there and they do not constitute a special or more serious objection to private decision making within a publicly created legal order, precisely because that order has behind it the constraints and supports, limits and reinforcements, of the public system.

Critiquing the Functional Approaches

Beyond these strong, essential truths that are moderately obvious, functional approaches tell us little indeed. Societies must have agencies of reconciliation and decision and enforcement, to be sure, but these may take different forms, even *within* the public sector. Little or no specification of individual behavior can be found in functional theories, since the impact of gross societal changes on any one individual's lifetime behavior pattern (never mind one conflict) seldom tests any boundaries of social necessity. Parsons (1949:89–94) himself notes the dilemma in discussing the Hobbesian justification for obedience: if the risk of collapse of authority is the sole justification for compliance, an individual on the deathbed (or nearly so) has no strong stake in social tranquility and might be expected to run amok. Parsonian and other structuralists therefore posit more complex motivations at the individual level, and avoid that type of dilemma.

The requisites of a social system are thus achieved by a combination of utilitarian calculation and strong social protective processes, including socialization, and are therefore based upon some strong human needs that transcend rationalism. Furthermore, the functionalist notes that not all attempted social systems even develop, let alone endure. In taking this realistic, complex, and unmeasurable view of institutions, however, one sacrifices pre-vision—let alone tight prediction—for a system that cannot fail to account for all events when called upon to post-dict. In essence, the problem is analogous to the problem of explaining the emergence of the family. A powerful explanation of parent behavior seems to inhere in the helplessness of the infant over a long period of time, but close examination demonstrates that *need* cannot create the responsible behavior. Rather, one must develop notions that selection of a species with strong mothering and fathering instincts together with regularized sexual habits has apparently taken place. The "powerful" single hypothesis dissipates into vague (though almost certainly accurate) probabalistic statements of tendencies that we can without difficulty heap about with counter examples.

Beyond lacking much explanatory power at the individual level, functionalism here as elsewhere has no measure, nor even a promising approach to a measure, of adequate levels of a function (here the mediational function). In any society some issues rage on, and not necessarily in court. Two "families" of the "Cosa Nostra" have been killing each other for some years as this is written, without apparent collapse in the Cosa Nostra and no discernible basic consequences for the United States. To be sure, if over time more members are killed than replaced, the "families" will disappear, but one need not know arithmetic, let alone functionalism, to have that exoteric "insight."

Concretely, then, functionalism suggests neither how litigants, judges, lawyers, and the rest, are likely to conduct their affairs, nor how much litigation will actually be resolved or handled in any particular pattern, nor indeed does functionalism suggest much about dispute resolution other than that some of it *be* there. That seems to be sufficient justification, so long as things are smooth. Upon collapse of a system, it will presumably be sufficient to announce a total failure to resolve matters. These are meager rewards for so much effort. Success in survival, and failure in collapse, can be direct tautologies and do not require longer versions to be unhelpful.

Organizational, Hierarchical, and System Theories

A second family of explanation arises from the internal needs and relationships of the court system itself. These explanations, of course, recognize the need to accommodate external needs and pressures for social use of courts. However, they tend to find the potential for court action for most purposes practically unlimited, so that the actual mechanism having real consequence is the judicial system itself.

A first question is necessarily the degree to which any of the theories of systems or hierarchies is, in fact, applicable to courts. Certainly, those with rigorous notions of organizational homogeneity or maximization would not easily fit judicial systems at all. As critics of such approaches and terminology quickly point out, the "justice system" includes separate structures organized antithetically, as well as others that are simply independent. Judges are chosen, and in many significant ways protected, in order to encourage their independence. Police and prosecutors are in open opposition to the defense bar (and lawyers generally), though they adopt adversary roles more loosely as against general corporation and labor lawyers.

Most "system" or "organization" theories, however, recognize the permeability of boundaries and the diversity of objectives of the participants. The older street hierarchical models generally presupposed clear goals and were, in fact, largely indistinguishable from functional–utilitarian modes of analysis. Some pure command theories were independent of such rationalism. Indeed, because goals were seen as existential, command was postulated as the only feasible resolution. But these have been regarded as archaic or non-theoretical in modern discussions in which consent and motivation are viewed as the heart of what is sought. In sociological and psychological circles, indeed, simple organizational goals and loyalties are seen as simplifications that badly distort.

In these views, most clearly exemplified by Herbert Simon (1957) and others like James March (March and Simon, 1958), organizations are conglomerates with distant connections and loose bonds. Within the organization there are multiple purposes being pursued, and management is the art of cajoling coordination among diversity. The range of interests is such that this school of analysis includes consumers as part of the organization and pricing as part of the organizational system of exchange and coordination. Barnard (1938) was the Adam Smith of this approach, but, depending on taste, Herbert Simon or George Homans (1950) or perhaps Peter Blau (1956, 1963) emerges as its Ricardo. From their efforts, we have in front of us a concerted approach in which "simple," "maximizing" organizations like industrial and manufacturing enterprises emerge as conceptually complex as the Department of Defense or the United Nations.

So the justice system emerges as no less—but surely no more—analyzable than other structures. If the courtroom is characterizable, as a leading scholar put it at a conference, by the fact that the major participants—defendant, lawyers, even the judge—would just as soon be elsewhere, that is a perfectly good description of a wartime army unit, an operating theatre at a hospital, and most classrooms. In short, for purposes of applying most organization theories, the justice system will suffice.

Internal aspects of the system obviously have considerable influence upon expectations and outcomes. In courts, as in a variety of other organizations, the very output measures used are internally controlled. Certainly that applies to the number of cases.[5] Subtle changes are also under control of individual judges and may well escape the attention of researchers, but nevertheless erode comparability. As the system defines or redefines expected standards or goals, judges and their employees may consciously or unconsciously effect changes in the calculation of whatever is being measured. Certainly in this respect their behavior is similar to that of others in an organizational and performance context.[6]

More significantly, rule changes and substantive decisions can drastically affect the ability of parties to employ the legal order. Although judges are unique among decision makers in that they are compelled to make a timely decision on a matter properly before them, they can alter the circumstances and definitions of what it is that is before them. These powers are multi-dimensional. Judges can bring about changes that alter:

1. What is cognizable before specific courts or courts in general, the most representative of which would be rules about standing and justiciability.
2. The motivations and expected payoffs of one or more litigants or potential litigants.
3. The supply or motivations of attorneys, prosecutors or other legal representatives.

In a certain sense, of course, all these questions are arbitrary. Boundary questions will always arise and courts will have freedom to expand and contract their domain. One consideration they can, if they wish, include in that decision is workload.[7]

It might appear, moreover, that such matters are readily resolvable. Jurisdictions change or they don't. In point of fact, the issue is difficult to deal with because the flow of cases shifts with social changes, and the social function involved in dealing with them has altered in meaning over time. Minimum amounts required for a court to hear a case may, of course, be interpreted in light of some constant dollars or other coinage, but that reflects, at best, purchasing power, and conundrums remain. What, for example, was the cost of buying a television set in 1850? Beyond such not-really-trivial questions is the fact that for most purposes we are interested not in the buying power function of the amount but in its social frequency or situational applicability. For this, purchasing power is at best a poor surrogate if one compares over any long period of time. Changes in jurisdiction occur no matter what one asserts or does. Studies over time such as the pathfinding effort by Friedman and Percival (1976) together with replications such as McIntosh's (1978) analysis of St. Louis courts over two centuries are unable to easily distinguish between the changes of the surrounding environment and those consciously created by judges and others. The decline of cases involving fur pelts in St. Louis no doubt is mostly due to the virtual disappearance of the fur industry. Even there, however, is not the decline of the industry also a reason for judges to downgrade cases involving pelts? This downgrading often takes place in terms of informal practices on priorities, time and attention on cases, burdens of proof, and a variety of possibilities well understood or sufficiently intuited by the local bar, but difficult to detect by crude reconstruction after decades have elapsed.

The crucial point here is that courts may shape their own functioning, rather than the reverse. This is well captured by the important shaping work by Kagan et al. on state supreme courts (1977, 1978). They show how these courts have been evolving from simple courts of review available on call to third-tier policy-creators that give selective treatment to cases at their own discretion. This parallels the development of the U.S. Supreme Court, which was achieved with the full authorization of Congress in the Judges Bill of 1925 (43 *Stat.* 936), largely at the initiative of Chief Justice Taft. At the state level, a good deal of the change has followed the federal pattern, which involved considerable judicial lobbying, but a surprising amount has been the result of unilateral action of the judges themselves. Furthermore, the change has not only been to allow the judges to deal with "important" and "precedent-making" cases, but also has involved more basic changes in the types of cases heard. We have seen a diminution of commercial cases and a greater concentration upon cases involving social policy and personal rights.

To be sure, this latter matter concerns the distribution of hearings by types of cases within the judicial system rather than the total exclusion of some types from all courts, yet reducing or enhancing chances of appeal to the highest court profoundly changes calculations by the parties (including expected costs and probabilities of winning), which can have important consequences even at the level of initial entry.

Courts can indicate encouragement of causes by their narrow or broad understanding of who may litigate. For example, the growth over the past four decades of the concept of "class action" has permitted federal courts to deal with many matters formerly closed to their purview. How courts interpret Congressional authorizations for standing is also highly determinative, since Congress is difficult to stir even in reaction to an incorrect interpretation. Much the same is true of substantive decisions. When we reach decisions on the merits, courts not only make a ruling on the instant case but give some cues as to the probable flow of future ones as well. Certain cases are thus encouraged, other discouraged. This is particularly true when there has been development in analogous fields, allowing lawyers to simply adapt arguments with a high likelihood of prevailing. Women's groups have recently used equal protection arguments from precedents dealing with blacks, and from cases involving welfare and other bureaucratic precedents, to harmonize their rights with gains made by other groups during the Warren court era. The Burger court became, almost by accident, the vehicle both for a large number of cases and the authors of progressive precedents. They could not easily have decided differently. This has, in turn, encouraged other and more really *avant garde* claims at lower court levels.

Activity may also be created by rewards to lawyers. Courts have considerable control over such matters, of course. Personal injury suits are handled in the United States generally through a contingency fee of one-third to one-half for the attorney if successful, but no return if no award results. This arrangement—officially frowned on in many countries as encouraging ambulance chasing—is largely a product of court rules and policing. In general, courts do provide considerable control over fees. Even when legislatures provide for recovery of reasonable fees, as in cases brought under the National Environmental Policy Act (83 *Stat.* 852, 42 U.S.C.4321-47), courts interpret the law as to when fees can be paid and what is an appropriate fee. A very considerable proportion of public interest law is built on the expectation of such funds becoming available in a reasonable number of cases, permitting private funds to cover cases that are lost.

Courts also have direct control over the supply of lawyers. The move to the integrated bar was in many states simply court-ordered, and this compelled lawyers to join bar associations, with ancillary requirements such as participation in health insurance and pension plans. Several state supreme courts have imposed continuing education requirements on lawyers in service. Admission and disbarment is done under court supervision. This power has not often been used to directly control numbers of lawyers, though some out-of-state lawyers have, at times, found obstacles to practice reminiscent of guild arrangements. Actual diminution of the supply of lawyers, however, is sufficiently controversial that the courts have preferred to be a silent partner backing bar groups rather than acting on their own. In recent years, in any event, these matters have increasingly become legislative concerns.

All of this indicates rather strongly that courts are in a position to modify their environment and can operate autonomously, and in a number of different ways they do so. It does not indicate that, in fact, system theory is a useful or desirable way to analyze whole court systems. Indeed, it is not at all difficult to further disaggregate, to speak of individual courts or judges on the one hand, and the parties, attorneys, and court personnel on the other. This question of appropriate units or modes of analysis is hardly unique to courts, and is analogous, almost isomorphic, with Graham Allison's (1971) vaunted analysis of foreign policy decision making; only the names need be changed to inform the innocent. His division is essentially rational decision making ("classical" model), decision-process analysis (organizational model), and interaction of forces (bureaucratic politics model).

The notion of autonomy of decisions by individual units is, in fact, much stronger for courts than for bureaucracies, and the case there is imposing. Certainly, as with bureaucracies, day-to-day control lies with the courts and it is their own interactions and problems that constitute their living space and environment. More than that, the courts are assumed to have a monopoly over the matters before them. In actual fact, the situation is more complex and there are interpositions from various sectors on that control. Still, unlike a foreign policy or atomic energy issue, it is not simply expertise that gives lawyers primacy on the case in hand. There is a myth of neutrality, an insistence on legitimacy, and even a connotation (and in some aspects a statutory reality) of illegality on the part of those who stray into attempts to influence judicial decisions. The structure of the legal system is intended to make it more effective through the distillation of insularity. Rules therefore try to define and control a well-regulated system. At least two social groupings within that system—judges and police—report that that even carries over to insularity of social contacts and the difficulties of maintaining old friendships or the forging of new ones outside the ranks of those groups.

The emphasis on bureaucratic processing has uncovered some truths about the nature of proceedings in courts and has forced new attitudes and questions as well. The issues adumbrated in Herbert Packer's (1968) famous "crime control" versus "due process" model were brought into clearer and wider focus with Blumberg's arguments on bureaucratic convenience (1967a, b, 1970) and Sudnow's (1965) parallel discussion of legal defenders as entering more fully into administrative partnerships with judge and prosecutors. While research has indicated the latter two are simply not very accurate descriptions, they have helped focus attention on the realities of plea bargaining over trials. These realities have been noted in the better research efforts at least since the Moley (1929) studies (including crime surveys in Illinois, Missouri, and Cleveland). In spite of this, criminal law had been taught and discussed as though trial was the norm and bargaining the exception. As the school of "law in action" gained dominance, acceptance of empirical discovery was finally complete, even in popular discussion. It was recognized that a subsidiary "trial" was involved as a regular administrative process. This in turn generated extensive debate on the appropriateness of plea bargaining, a debate at long last about realities as opposed to idealized views of criminal law.

These insights into the realities of criminal proceedings had carryover effects into the civil area. Again, it was found that trial was only one way that courts deal with problems, and that back-door negotiating or encouragement was a normal part of judging. On close view, courts do more (or less) than decide or ratify in civil matters, too. On some matters they are overt registrars. Friedman's work argues (and Sarat and Grossman (1975) highlight) that courts increasingly do the non-judicial things, becoming even less trial-like in their daily operations. This approach sees such trends as being a result of the judges' motivation to avoid the cost of decisions in time and psyche, rather than as a result of any ideological desire to compel a maximum of individualistic self-accommodation. Thus, it accounts for plea bargaining in a different way (but not in a separable or testable way) from the maximization school of thought.

The Influence of the Systems Model

Under the influence of the systems model a number of important reforms have taken place, some of them having opposite and nearly equal effect. First, efforts have been vigorous to achieve better coordination, applying business and planning tools. The judges have been encouraged to deal with prosecutorial structures, to create or strengthen their own administrative capabilities, and to adopt organizational techniques like computer programming. Court administration has emerged as a flourishing profession. In short, the notion that the legal system is a bureaucracy has led it to act like a bureaucracy. The notion that its actors are in some fundamental sense acting in concert has led to external pressures and inducements to make them act in concert. Some of this has clearly been to the good. On many matters, data for the first time in history seem to be reasonably well collected and available. Even on such things as dockets, the various forms of PROMIS (a computer program originally developed for prosecutors—hence the acronym) have emerged as the first readily usable tracking arrangement for cases wending their way through the courts and have proven useful as tools for other system components. In short, the absence of even elementary coordinating tools has given impetus to such steps and has provided the approach with some rather cheap victories and justifications. At the same time, planning and other cooperative ventures cause disquiet as they promote at least the image of those things Blumberg and Sudnow have inveighed against as sordid realities. The fear is that joint staffing and a habit of cooperation will lead to the judicial equivalent of the "cozy triangle" of administrators, legislators, and staff often found in the regular bureaucracy.

Second, the view that "insiders" were dominant without adequate checks also led to a movement to bring civilian perspectives into play. Thus, the influence of the systems model led to reform here, too. Traditionally, the bar associations and the bench were empowered to control lawyer excesses, whereas attorneys were expected to call the attention of other judges to excesses by judges. Extreme cases could be brought to legislatures for impeachment. Such instances were rare and legislators over time have become ever more loath to spend valuable time on such matters. The expectations that judges and lawyers would police each other proved reasonably effective only in very gross abuses, lawyers being particularly unable to cope with judicial courtroom tyranny or incompetence, senility or alcoholism, out of fear of jeopardizing cases before a judge so complained of, or even of other judges rallying to a companion's defense. Similarly, bar committees and judges did not act frequently or in tough fashion with fellow attorneys and were perceived by the public rather correctly as lenient white-washers.

With strong cooperation of leaders of the bar, including such figures as the late Justice Tom Clark, many states have now instituted parallel disciplinary commissions for both judges and lawyers, with public representation supplementing representatives of the bar and bench. By and large, however, the lawyer monopoly over court rules and procedures has persisted even in the face of arguments that justice would best be served by expanding the role of the community in structuring the system.

A third type of by-product from the system approach has been greater sophistication about interconnectedness and the consequences of reform. Lawyers are great tinkerers and expect logical and predictable results from language or other changes. They also tend to be impatient with empirical proof, finding most outcomes obvious and predictable, usually over-extrapolating from their own experience. As a result, the legal order abounds with "experiments" that have failed, but the failure of which is never made known to anyone, or indeed the outlines of which are being implemented elsewhere in the serene assumption that it was a success.

Essentially, the system works the way it does because it represents an equilibrated behavior system. Changes are likely merely to cause adjustments producing in the end much the same equilibrium, or adjustments in directions different from anticipated. So, compulsory long-term sentences for use of a gun in any crime may result (and has) in police not listing the charge in analogous cases, juries returning more innocent verdicts rather than forcing long terms for minor matters, or judges engaging in elaborate hair-splitting over the difference between their discretion to eliminate a charge (permitted) and their right to not sentence for it (forbidden). The original premises of what is now called "presumptive sentencing" were wildly different from the resultant legislation. Early bills would have flooded prisons in the name of reducing sentencing, though making punishment more certain and more equitable. The early skepticism and resistance allowed closer examination and refinement, but the evidence is that still many unexpected aspects are emerging in different settings.

Characteristic of this type of analysis, as illustrated by the examples cited, is the rather loose articulation between the approach and the conclusions derived therefrom. In fact, this is a two-way matter. On the one hand, the conclusions are consistent with the system approach, but they are not the only conclusions possible. On the other hand, one may understand and appreciate the conclusions cited above and others of this sort without resort to the theory or approach.

The criticism of the system approach and its cognates (an approach given considerable impetus by the Law Enforcement Assistance Administration and other 1970s attempts to provide better legal service) has been that it is an inappropriate, over-centralized, and constricting concept. It is suggested that it leads to inappropriate analysis and over-emphasis on central controls to the detriment of justice. It is difficult to take that line of criticism seriously when the approach leads pretty much wherever one wishes. To be sure, cooperation between the authorities could get too cozy, but that does not appear to be in the cards. In the interim, innocent (or, for that matter, guilty) citizens are not much threatened by small improvements in the mechanics of the courthouse. There is nothing inherently sinister about good facilities or careful planning, and if the authorities coalesce to the point of injustice, it will not be as an intellectual product of a faulty conceptual scheme.

Value Systems

The nature of judicial systems makes values a prominent feature in what looms as the cathedral of decision or the "Temple of Justice." Resting as it does on moral suasion, the legal order finds it necessary, not merely useful, to emphasize its basically normative character. The concept of norms can be studied in a number of ways and it is by no means excluded from empirical or even rigorously scientific examination. Thus, scientific examination of conditions leading to new norms, or a theory of a cycle of normative evolution— to cite a few relevant notions—could easily be a concern of empiricism.

One approach suggests the dominant force in litigation is inherent in its symbolic content, the playing out of a rule finding meaning. Simply put, the agenda of courts is seen as altered by new rules that demand boundaries. Whether generated by new legislation or a new precedent, or a breakthrough in jurisprudential thinking, doubts about a doctrine come to the fore and creative lawyers seize upon the opportunity to link their cases with the rule-logic suggested by the doctrine. In so doing, they may hasten or retard the unfolding of the rule, of course, but it is the natural evolution of the concept that is seen as central. At times, the impetus will be new social conditions that challenge the overt interpretation and in that sense could be considered primary, but even that manifestation can also be interpreted as the playing-out of imminent meaning, even if not recognized in the original concept.

An important exponent of this approach was Lon Fuller. A small but sharp example of his reasoning is to be found in his concept of the "bridging case" (1934). To get from one interpretation of a doctrine to a new one is seen as an intellectual Kuhn-like puzzle that may require a conceptual breakthrough. White primaries could not easily be outlawed in the 1930s because political parties were seen as private meetings of a voluntary club, but when ballot box stuffers in a Congressional primary were punished for violation of a federal anti-corrupt practices statute, it was because of the now-acknowledged nexus between primaries and regular elections. Such a ruling made outlawry of white primaries not just possible but virtually mandatory. The conceptual mold had been cast, and it was necessary to stamp its pattern on all appropriate material.

What is not clear is whether this represents a central notion, or an interesting aside. Efforts such as Fuller's or Wechsler's (1959) to furnish organizing notions for sharply distinguishing the judicial process from other political enterprises have not been advanced to further empirical study of the process but to provide normative guidance for practitioners and benchmarks for sideline watchers. Thus, Wechsler's notion that the law should reflect "neutral principles" (or perhaps more accurately than he himself formulated, "principles capable of application without distinction to all parties in similar circumstances") was intended primarily as a critique of the "state action" concept.[8] Interestingly, either Wechsler or the lack of an underlying logic has resulted in a freezing of the doctrine, but nothing like a rollback. In essence, Wechsler to the contrary notwithstanding, the judges have concluded that the state action principle covers unusual and extreme situations that nothing else can handle adequately. That the civil rights movement resulted in some strained interpretations of state action has not resulted in any pronounced rollback.

In one sense, the observation of the unfolding of principles is tautological unless one assumes a categorical imperative (or other rule) that repealed all others. (Even Kant permitted silence and not compulsive truth-saying while absolutely forbidding lies.) In another sense, it suggests an evolution that Levi's justly respected work, *An introduction to Legal Reasoning* (1948) bears out in at least one instance—a natural cycle of *adaptive* concept making. Perhaps because of the circularity of the "need of the time" versus the "adaptive cycle" notions and the difficulty of creating a falsifying circumstance, this, too, has not been a stimulus to empirical study. (In a negative or abortive effort at adaptation, presumably we would dismiss the judges' efforts as uncreative—a euphemism for "dumb").

Fuller (1968) has also suggested that systems may be examined for conformity with agreed-upon principles, that the amount of justice delivered by a system is ascertainable. This has been argued by some as a normative, by others as an empirical, concept. As a normative matter, the mode ostensibly urged by Fuller is primarily a form of what I call "the pirate ship" dilemma. Is a Barbary Coast kingdom of the 1800's a legitimate state? Does one owe the trappings of sovereignty to such an enterprise writ large as Nazi Germany? To bring the matter back to our domain, do divorce statistics even have the same meaning in such a society, in which the grounds for divorce might well be "racial purity?" Fuller and his followers at Berkeley's Law and Society Center—a handful, but an impressive group—essentially say it is not. The empiricists' criticism that they are confounding several difficult quandaries involving differing levels of analysis seems to them to be begging the question, even cowardly. The products of the approach have, to date, been interesting but not of a type contributing to the empirical theorizing discussed in earlier sections, thus providing some credence to the empiricists' arguments.

Another approach involves the tracing of jurisprudence to its fundamental assumption or *grundnorm*. This conceptualization by Kelsen (1945) was conceived as semi-sociological in that fundamental social principles were to be vindicated through litigation. H. L. A. Hart's reformulation (1961) is at once more sociologically and philosophically refined, finding sources of rules rather than a single-rule origin. However, it has been the philosophical thrust that has dominated. If Dworkin is to be regarded as the culmination of Hart's thoughts, it has restored the autonomy of doctrinal resolution, at least insofar as one can follow the postulates of *Taking Rights Seriously* (1977).

Similarly, Rawlsian approaches utilize empirical notions to suggest measurability of normative values as, e.g., in Rawls' (1971) use of optimalization notions to define equity, but they do not turn around to empirically evaluate the *consequences* of norms or other measures of the type here suggested.

Rather, efforts have been much tamer. Packer's (1968) packaging of the "due process model" (a value concept) versus the "crime control model" (a sociological and institutional analytic tool) was the most ambitious effort, and has led to a number of empirical and quasi-empirical studies. The extent to which it could provide guidance for a study of the actual role of the legal order is not clear. To the best of our knowledge, use of norms in operation has not been one of the many dissertation topics spun out of this interesting but overworked dichotomy.

Still, narrower approaches have been attempted in court related processes which could be applicable. Wildhorn et al. (1976) have shown one can evaluate court achievement in terms of carefully delineated performance standards. These standards are somewhat tightly drawn so that the study has some of the aspects of shooting minnows in a pail, and is remarkably uninformative as to any conclusions to be drawn. While courts are like most agencies that seek broad scrutiny but do not really hunger for evaluation, this narrow approach has not drawn imitation or enthusiasm.

A BEGINNING

In essence, then, scholars use case loads for convenience, and as surrogates for quite different things. Essentially, we are arguing that those "quite different measures" should be made explicit. Further, it would appear abandonment of this poor substitute will strengthen rather than weaken the precision of the various approaches. We summarize our argument in Table 7-1.

The *utilitarian* approach in Table 7-1 is perhaps most familiar to us, as the Chicago school has been making such arguments for some time. Litigators pursue advantage. Prosecutors maximize important litigation and manipulate resources to secure the greatest punishment in the most serious cases for the greatest number. Private calculators have an even simpler approach. They maximize expected income, which is a product of their expectation of winning and their expected gain minus anticipated costs.

The process of filing and persisting with a case therefore reveals expectations. Case loads reflect such calculations. If we could obtain pri-

TABLE 7-1 Summary Critique of Theories of Case Loads

Approach	Mode of Analysis	Caseloads as:	Substitute for:
Utilitarian	Price Calculation	Clearing Price	Individual and group utilization
Functional	"Social needs"	"Temperature" of a society	Activity rates and account rates
System	Internal needs	Equilibrium	Capacity and alternative cost
Norm	Logic and implicit	Measure of marginal interpretation or clarity	Concept of norm cycle

mary, direct data on calculations, however, we would be much better off. The decision to file is used to simulate calculations of costs and benefits, and one or both inferences may be quite erroneous.

The *functional* mode in Table 7-1 is almost as familiar. It assumes social conditions predominate and that individual calculations are constant or nearly so. Litigation is a product of social conditions and a regular by-product of social transactions. Increased litigation then reflects some variable within the society. Transactions must be increasing if litigation has grown, or, alternatively, some serious dislocation has taken place in society, changing the propensity to litigate. In one or the other sense, these gauge societal "temperatures." What is sought is really not litigation, but underlying activity and social tendencies.

The *system* approach in Table 7-1 emphasizes considerations normally labeled "bureaucratic." It suggests that pace and outcome are products of available resources and needs within the justice system. Capacity and workload dominate case load. Haley's (1978) discussion of the Japanese restructuring of rules whenever there is a flow of new cases is a good illustration of these notions. This is closest to the use of case load in pristine form, though other costs are still absent from a full calculation of judicial system needs.

While little is made of the *normative evolution* notion (shown as "norm" in Table 7-1) in systematic fashion, it is often alluded to in writing and even more frequently in oral discussion. Case load is assumed to be a reflection of the stage of clarity of rules. Legislation or regulation, when new, opens up litigation. Clarification is needed and parties will find litigation necessary to conduct their affairs; ambiguity is the mother of litigation. While ambiguity is never eliminated, clarification of major problems takes place. Litigation abates until something changes—the statutory base, court decisions in cognate matters, the social relations involved—to cast the matter in a new, ambiguous light. Litigation is therefore a reflection of the cycle of legal certainty. Except for some discussion of the "efficiency" of common law decisions that impinges on this notion, there is no literature that attempts to map or describe this normative evolution except in terms similar to the global discussion attempted here.

In reviewing dominant areas of concern, then, we shall bear in mind this broader view of what scholars have sought in their investigation of case loads. While at times we shall resort to sleight of hand and continue to employ what we have available, it will also be modified by what we wish we had.

The essential problem is that the approach to case loads has been to get at matters not necessarily easily deduced from case load inquiries even in simple form. Given the complexities discussed, the task has proven to be even more elusive. As we work toward amplification of empirical theory, the next task will be to examine what is masked by case load data and to find less indirect and more satisfactory measures of the diverse aspects of the system.

The effect of current approaches is not precisely on "all fours" with the fable of the elephants and the wise man. Adherents of different views are quite aware of the impact of other causative factors, but for quite divergent reasons emphasize those aspects that they deem major and subordinate or ignore others.

A system of propositions can be developed from these assertions, however, which can be compacted into a number of *ceteris paribus* statements. These must approximate the following (though no doubt some differences of taste and nuance will develop with different compilers):

1. Litigation is a by-product of transactions. While types of transactions have differing rates of "trouble-cases," these rates are fairly constant. Thus, an increase in social transactions will produce a proportionate increase in litigation.
2. Litigation is the product of social propensities to litigate and the occurrence of trouble-cases is not automatically determined by base-facts in dispute. Rather, ability and willingness to litigate vary. One may increase propensity without altering transactions.
3. Opportunity to litigate can be altered (1) by changes in decision system, limiting or expanding opportunities, or raising or lowering costs; and (2) by outside alternative opportunity. Other efforts will develop some of this thinking, but some caveats and enlargement of each is in order.

Neither objective rates for any type transaction nor transaction frequency have been successfully arrived at for any legal system very convincingly. While projections have been reasonably made (usually, simple linear projections of case load trends have been as accurate as anything), they are in effect projections of some vector of *both* rate of transaction and rate of litigation, and not finely tuned to their aspect and/or its growth. That is, the "pure" projection of transactions is seldom possible because neither of the other two dimensions is kept constant to any appreciable extent by societies (which may manage conflict first and measure or anticipate it only second).

Actual litigation rates clearly reflect costs and ability to pay versus opportunities to succeed and what will be gained. Such assessments must be made in the absence of clean information and usually without good measures of either factor.

One dimension here is the actual demonstrable cost. A second area is the *perceived* costs and advantages. Yet a third is psychological costs and advantages. The first requires no great elaboration. Court fees specified in advance are clear examples. Guesses about lawyers' fees and investigation charges are colored by an individual's information, imagination, and daring. These in turn may be affected by proximity to lawyers whose conservatism may promote realism about the process or romanticism about payoffs, or both. Finally, how one approaches litigation may be psychological. In a small community, destroying the social fabric through litigation may be a burden that reduces litigation. It has been suggested that there is something called "claims consciousness," and Zeisel, Kalren and Buchhloz (1959:236) have certainly shown that large cities have larger litigation rates, well beyond simple explanation on frequency grounds. Silberman (1978) has shown different age cohorts do verbalize quite different propensities to litigate, though he has not shown this leads to litigation behavior, nor does he dispose of the possibility that propensity to sue is related to age rather than to difference in the zeitgeist. Furthermore, while the emphasis of such research as it exists has been on plaintiff behavior, litigation is a "takes-two-to-tango" proposition. Resistance to easy-going accommodation is an obvious counter-hypothesis to the more facile propensity-to-sue argument. It is proposed, for example in the Zeisel et al. illustration that individuals in small towns may settle cases for fear their reputations would suffer. Some businessmen are notorious for paying their bills on the courthouse steps, as it were, making a profit on the money during the extra time. These hard-headed, and even ruthless, attitudes may also vary from place to place and time to time. Table 7-2 illustrates the point.

The notion that litigation is not merely a product of the plaintiffs' attitudes is *not* a trivial or semi-serious proposition. There is a tendency in current discussions to suggest a one-sided propensity to sue as the sole cause of "litigation explosions," or indeed of simple increases in the number of cases filed in courts. As Table 7-2 suggests, obdurate possessors of goods, landlords, and officials who control rights may create conditions driving even those most reluctant to sue into court. As Table 7-2 suggests those two parties are not interchangeable. Claims callousness is not, in our view, as generative of litigation as is claims consciousness. Hard-hearted defendants serve notice that the costs of suing are high. At the

TABLE 7-2 Level of Cases as a Reflection of Attitude Types*

	Claims Callousness	
Claims Consciousness	*High*	*Low*
High	Many cases	Some cases
Low	Few cases	Few cases

* A quasi-serious typology based on a semi-serious suggestion by Lawrence Friedman and Marc Galanter.

same time we emphasize the often-neglected role of the unreasonable defendant in an era in which only plaintiffs are seen as creating social costs.

In a sense, opportunity is a reciprocal of cost or gain, but the degree to which this aspect of litigation is under the control of others makes it a different dimension. Without totally repeating our earlier discussion, it still does seem appropriate to note a consistent adjustment by authorities to demand, and further, that adjustment may be to *constrict* capacity when demand exceeds supply and (although this is a somewhat rarer paradox) to ease rules when the resources are underutilized. That is to say, when courts become congested, the appropriate rule makers (sometimes the judges) may add to capacity, or they may make it harder to litigate. On close inspection, both appear logical and rational solutions. Conversely, we have postulated a tendency by litigants to absorb capacity, analogous to the increase in traffic to fill roads, since costs of litigation are seldom true or unsubsidized costs with queueing the real rationer. When this does not spontaneously occur, it is easy for most judicial systems to simulate working at capacity, but in rare instances new rules may develop.

The school known as reflecting an "economics of law" has made a contribution to our understanding of the process by emphasizing the availability of substitutes for formal litigation available in a society, and we have tried to emphasize that availability. Whereas their discussion has centered upon substitutability of arbitration and similar decison processes, judge-like in real life, the actual substitutes trial into invisible competition. We have already suggested the Post Office and computer conversation as rivals, and yet not clearly rivals. Similarly, good legal advice from a dispassionate, competent predictor is potentially both a substitute or a prelude to adjudication, and it would take a Solomon-like accountant—equally wise and arbitrary—to assign the share of legal costs that involves one or the other.

It seems obvious even from this skeletal discussion that case load writers have assumed that each of the types of variables operate independently of the other. Even when interactive effects are noted, it is assumed that they could be disentangled. That is to say, most sophisticated court load analysts are aware that availability of court remedies affects frequency of suits, which relates to profitability of legal practice, which affects supply of lawyers, which in turn might affect availability of remedies. Each of these effects, even if they are interactive, is seen as measurable in principle by quite simple means, even if empirically they have been difficult to tease out. Let these factors be linked not in simple cause–effect relations but in some synergistic ways. This possibility, that social attitudes toward litigation plus availability of lawyers and new court rules is not of the form (a + b) but rather of (a × b), deserves serious attention as well.

In sum, then,

1. The next phase of studies needs fewer ideological commitments and expectations that certain *types* of variables will predominate. More creative variables are always welcome, but attention solely to psychological or utilitarian or institutional variables (as the case may be) seems to belie the interactive aspects of the process. This is, then, in part a call for eclecticism in the selection of variables, given our observation that different approaches or theories about case loads have quite different strengths and weaknesses.

2. However, helter-skelter conglomerates will not do either. Much of the work has been characterized by completely *ad hoc* blending of sometimes diverse strands. These are averaged, or distilled, in very odd ways. Moving in the right direction is not always a virtue. Careful reasoning about what is being attempted *is* always welcome.

3. Careful testing of well thought out specifics is quite within reach. Indeed, we have suggested (in Table 7-1) that, in fact, *direct* testing of many fundamental notions is possible, with case load as a corrective.

4. When surrogates are utilized, a precise understanding of what is gained or lost by the measure is needed, and such recognition will help in overcoming the Scylla–Charybdis of the preceding two points.

5. The unconscious assumption that differently identified factors operate additively should be avoided. It is possible that they are synergistic, or cancelling, or that they interact differentially at different levels. Complex relationships in complex situations are to be expected. Simple models should be tested first, but awareness of other possible relationships should be on our minds. The studies attempting to "explain" litigation have so far been unable to do so, but almost universally they are tests of this simple notion. Successful explanations of this sort are not ruled out, but they seem less likely in light of experience. Studies showing lack of expected relationships should in the future also test more complex possibilities.

6. The notion of alternative resolution should be explored in at least some of the investigations so that we might distinguish between unresolved matters and those handled more cheaply. (The Wisconsin litigation project should shed some light here.) However the "invisible seam" argument developed above may make this a will-o'-the-wisp inquiry and we should be prepared for possible disappointment. It simply may not be feasible in more than the most nominal sense to distinguish between court and non-court dispute resolution, so that any scientific quest "explaining" their domains is thereby rendered futile.

NOTES

1. The responses (i.e., decisions) of judges have generally been studied as complex responses to simple stimuli, in contrast to the view of individual decisions to litigate. This view of judicial decisions may be partially responsible for the fact that studies of this type have been infrequent in recent years, but the fact remains that in a brief period of creativity, the study of judicial decision making far outstripped in results anything that case load studies have yet produced. See generally Schubert (1959, 1964, 1974a,b) and Rohde and Spaeth (1976) for a sample of studies of judicial decision making.

2. This lack of clean findings may explain a troublesome phenomenon that characterizes case load efforts: typically, researchers have undertaken only one study and then have abandoned the area.

3. The exact quote may be apocryphal, but Morgenstern seems to have made the point (if not quite that pungently) in print. A general reference is Morgenstern (1963).

4. It is assumed here—probably somewhat inaccurately—that lawyer's and investigator's costs will be constant with alternative modes of decision).

5. So, for example, a recent decision of the Federal Judicial Conference (Judicial Conference of the United States, 1976:193) to count as separate cases single decisions that deal with one tract and issue but that involve separate landowners meant that the number of such cases not only was increased but also could vary much more dramatically from year to year. Again, a decision in 1916 (American Law Institute, 1934:37) to cleanse the doctuts of the federal courts, involving the dismissal of all cases in the backlog and requiring re-filing of any that sought further consideration, illustrates internal control of output measures. Inevitably, there are dead cases, involving parties departed or unwilling to take yet another step; therefore, the reported backlog figures were dramatically reduced.

6. So, in California when Governor Edmund G. Brown, Jr., criticized the judges because certain measures showed them to be spending about four hours per day on case-related matters, a new measure including all judicially related time was developed. Governor Brown promptly announced it was his criticism that caused the judges to work hours more per day. (In point of fact, nothing had really changed at all.)

7. It is argued by John Haley (1978) that Japan's vaunted low litigation rate reflects not, as is usually argued, a reluctance of Orientals to appear before third party decision makers, but rather a determined effort by judges and other decision makers to keep the courts at a low volume. The standard explanation of lack of cases has been that there is a loss of face in Chinese and Japanese societies when individual or family resources fail to mediate a dispute, and that case-bringers acquire the stigma of a disrupter. Haley argues, however, that what has happened is that any increase in litigation has provoked changes in jurisdiction that keep the number of cases at close to a steady-state level.

8. Since the Fourteenth and Fifteenth Amendments prohibit only state denial of life, liberty, property, or the vote, private discrimination had been historicaly free from Constitutional restriction, but beginning with *Marsh v. Alabama* (326 U.S. 504, 1946) the federal courts began to take a broad view of what constituted "state action." In *Shelley v. Kraemer* (334 U.S. 1, 1948), use of the courts by private persons was held to involve state action (for courts are provided by states), and this was therefore controlled by the Fourteenth Amendment. When federal and state civil rights legislation began to regulate civil matters, the courts apparently found less need to stretch the doctrine. As critics point out, ultimately, all human interactions could be held to rest upon legal approval and enforcement.

Part III

Understanding How Courts Do Their Work

8

Courts as Organizations

Herbert Jacob

Many people express some surprise when it is suggested that courts are organizations. When they think of organizations, they picture large corporations and public bureaucracies. Courts, by contrast, are typically small and not visibly bureaucratic, yet it is commonplace to think of courts as institutions. Moreover, they are complicated bodies that encompass large numbers of people occupying specialized role positions. Courts also have peculiar ways of accomplishing their tasks that require mastery of arcane rules and procedures. Most importantly, courts are task-oriented institutions devoted to performing specific functions, which are allotted to them by a polity's constitution. Thus, courts are groups of people engaged in a common task, interacting on a regular basis, performing specialized roles, utilizing specialized knowledge, and responding to some direction and supervision from others.

However, if we attempt to become more concrete in our description of courts, we falter on the large number of variations that exist in the United States (cf. Ryan et al., 1980). Some courts encompass more than 100 judges working in as many courtrooms scattered over many buildings; others have but a single judge. Some have jurisdiction over an entire state or metropolitan area; others cover only a small portion of either. Some can handle any matter arising out of the legal system; others are limited in their scope to petty or major criminal cases, to personal injury cases or to divorces, to the probate of wills, or to some other specialty. Some courts operate with a full panoply of aides including bailiffs, clerks, court report-

Author's Note: This chapter was prepared under Grant 78 NI-AX-1037 from the National Institute of Justice, United States Department of Justice. All opinions and conclusions are those of the author alone; the points of view and opinions stated in this chapter are those of the author and do not necessarily represent the position or policies of U.S. Department of Justice. The author wishes to acknowledge the helpful comments of the editors, of Lawrence M. Friedman, and of Lawrence B. Mohr.

ers, law clerks, court reporters, and secretaries; others have only a single assistant who provides all these services. Some have elaborate administrative structures to assign cases, rotate judges, provide clerical assistance, and monitor judicial performance; others have none of this. Thus, the generic term—courts—includes a great variety of empirical phenomena even when we restrict our attention to the United States. They have in common certain functions and operating characteristics, but they differ considerably in structure, work load, and working style.

Organizational studies have rarely considered courts within their domain.[1] They have more typically focused on business organizations and public executive agencies. However, an increasing number of court studies use an organizational framework (Blumberg, 1967a; Carter, 1974; Eisenstein and Jacob, 1977; Nardulli, 1978) or discuss the organizational framework as a fruitful research approach (Mohr, 1976; Henderson, Guynes, and Baar, 1980; Clynch and Neubauer, 1981). Nevertheless, as we shall demonstrate, much can be learned about courts when one examines them in an organizational framework.

Just as courts differ markedly among themselves, organizational studies also do not come from a single mold. There is no over-arching theory of organizations; instead, there are many overlapping perspectives on the study of organizations. Some concentrate on the distribution of power within organizations; others focus on the patterning of communications within them. Some concern themselves principally with the impact of technology on work tasks and performance, whereas others concern themselves more with the adoption of innovations. Some place their emphasis on decision making, problem solving, and organizational intelligence. For other studies, the principal focus is on the recruitment and socialization of personnel. Another perspective focuses on the exchanges that take place between organizations and their immediate or more distant environments. Each of these perspectives offers some considerable insight into the operation of American courts, although not all are equally pertinent.

We may attempt to build toward an empirical theory of courts by utilizing this literature. While it does not provide a completely cohesive set of hypotheses, it serves as a heuristic device to sensitize us to aspects of judicial processes which otherwise go unnoticed or unlinked to each other. It often demands the skills of an anthropologist to collect data through observation. It allows us to sythesize the materials collected by historians. It subsumes many of the concerns of the political scientist, who is often interested in coordination of agencies, in decision making, or in the impact of judicial decisions.

My argument in the following pages is that organizational studies promise considerable insight into the manner in which courts work. They can profitably guide both research and reform. I will not argue that the organizational perspective is the only useful framework for studying courts, nor will I deny that this perspective does not blind us to concerns that are sometimes significant. I will proceed by reviewing the conceptual foci of organizational studies with occasional references to their applications to courts. I will then examine several explicit applications of organizational concepts to courts and critique a number of other studies that might profitably have utilized the organizational framework but did not. I shall conclude with a review of issues that are not addressed by the organizational approach.

THE DISTRIBUTION OF POWER

One of the most enduring concerns of organizational studies has been the distribution of power. Indeed, for some, a defining characteristic of organizations is the presence of a hierarchy (cf. Weber, 1958:197). Those at the top of the hierarchy have authority to supervise and direct those on lower rungs. The most encompassing decisions are made by those at the top. They are supposed to enjoy the greatest discretion, whereas those in lower positions make decisions that affect fewer persons and are more constrained, especially by the guidelines promulgated from the top.

Not all organizations have a strong hierarchical structure. University faculties are notoriously loosely coupled into larger groupings. Research laboratories similarly sometimes lack a strong hierarchy of authority. Most organizations, however, exhibit hierarchy in some aspect of their structure. Where it is present we are led to expect a higher degree of central coordination and control than where it is absent. Its existence in some elements of an organization is likely to spill over to others and guide the behavior of organization members.

American courts have several hierarchical characteristics. A weak hierarchy exists between so-called upper and lower courts, by which we generally mean appellate and trial courts. Appellate courts are usually not true hierarchical superiors to trial courts, but they may overrule trial court decisions. Their review of trial court decisions, however, is initiated by litigants. It is not motivated by a policy focus of the higher court, nor does it constitute a systematic quality control of the work of trial courts (Davies, 1980). Supreme courts often promulgate procedural rules that govern trial courts, but they exercise no continuous supervision over day-to-day trial work and almost none over the flow of cases that trial courts process. They almost never hire, transfer, or fire trial judges or other trial courtroom personnel. They have little or no influence over trial court budgets.

Another kind of hierarchical structure had developed among American courts in recent years. Most states have developed an office for court administration, which often works under the nominal supervision of the state's supreme court or under a collegial body representing all judges

(Berkson and Carbon, 1978). These offices collect information about the flow of court business and, in some instances, have the authority to transfer judges temporarily to alleviate disproportionately heavy work loads in some courts. Moreover, within large city courts, a small hierarchy has often been developed with a chief judge, a local court administrator, and assistants who do for their trial courts some of the same work as the state court administrator. All of these hierarchical accretions to the basic court structure, however, do not provide the degree of hierarchical supervision that is found in many other organizations.

Most important of all, perhaps, is the fact that the basic work unit—the courtroom—is not organized in a strong hierarchical fashion. Judges are the nominal and formal superior of all others in the courtroom work group, but in fact, judges share their power with the attorneys who work there. The degree of sharing varies, but it is rare to find a judge who operates as a true hierarchical superior to all others in the courtroom. Trial judges almost never control the assignment of other personnel and often do not control the appointment of such ancillary staff as clerks and bailiffs. They also exert only a variable influence over procedure and flow of cases.

The weakness of hierarchy in courts contrasts sharply with that of most structures studied by organizational theorists. Formal organization in courts is not primary but secondary. Relationships are most significantly structured by informal patterns of organization. Therefore, to understand distribution of power and influence in courts, one needs to examine their informal organization.

The distinction between formal and informal power has long been an important one in organizational studies. In some instances, those at the top exercise less real power than their exalted position suggests. On the other hand, persons in lower positions exert more power than one would assume from their hierarchical position because they have strong social ties with other members of the organization, because they are key links in the communication flow of the organization, or because they possess special skills or expertise that nominal superiors depend upon. Almost every organization has been found to possess an informal structure that is not entirely consonant with the formal one. In almost every organization, some of those who are nominal inferiors exert influence and power over their nominal superiors. (For a summary of the organizational literature on this point see Blau and Scott, 1962:143–144; Mintzberg, 1979:10–11, 37, 46).

This phenomenon has been well documented for American courts at every level. On the U.S. Supreme Court, for instance, Danelski (1961) noted the difference between task leadership and social leadership. On some occasions, a chief justice exercised both, but often one or both functions were performed by another justice on the court. Murphy (1964) showed the same phenomena using somewhat different sources in examining the strategies used by Supreme Court justices to sustain their policy views through the collegial decision making process that typifies that court. For trial courts, it has almost become a commonplace for researchers to show that judges share their power with attorneys and sometimes with other court personnel. This is especially evident in criminal courts, where prosecutors possess more information than other courtroom personnel and have a disproportionate influence over the docket and disposition of cases. Moreover, prosecutors often have greater influence because they are permanently attached to the courtroom and handle all cases coming to it. Because the prosecutor typically screens cases and may dismiss them, prosecutors also regulate the inflow of cases and can exercise some control over the courtroom's work load. That function—not shared with any other member of the courtroom—gives prosecutors special influence in criminal courtrooms. Defense attorneys and their clients, however, also have some influence, since they may insist on a trial and may make everyone else's work considerably more difficult by filing motions challenging the validity of the prosecutor's evidence. (See Blumberg, 1967a; Cole, 1971; Eisenstein and Jacob, 1977).

These considerations lead us to expect a quite different informal structure in courtrooms handling civil matters. No one in a civil courtroom occupies a position analogous to the prosecutor's. The only regular among the professionals is the judge, as a wide variety of attorneys moves in and out of the courtroom to process cases. Hence, we would expect the judge in civil courtrooms to be much more influential in directing the disposition of cases. Moreover, we expect less well-developed informal routines because the informal structure is less stable than it is in criminal courts. Informal structures in civil courts are also likely to be less well articulated. However, the more specialized the courtroom, and the more a regular set of attorneys works in it, the more it will resemble criminal courtrooms in informal structure. Thus, a small set of defense or plaintiff's attorneys may exercise considerable influence in courts specializing in personal injury cases (Ross, 1970; Rosenthal, 1974) or housing cases (Mansfield, 1978). In contrast, judges often exert the most influence in general jurisdiction civil courtrooms because no attorney controls a large portion of the docket. Nevertheless, attorneys shape the issues and make many procedural choices that affect the outcome of a case.

Thus, the informal structure of courts consists of very complicated and varying relationships. These informal patterns reveal more of the power structure of courts than does the formal pre-eminence of the judge.

Another element of organizational structure is the work group. It exists at both higher and lower levels of a hierarchy. It consists of those persons immediately engaged together in a set of tasks. In courts these work groups usually develop informally and are given little or no official recognition. At the appellate level, they include the judges and their legal staffs. For instance, on the U.S. Supreme Court, a work group consisting of law clerks clusters around each justice; it is as significant (although not as powerful) as the work group consisting solely of the nine justices assembled in their conference room. In trial courts, the work groups consist of attorneys and the judge clustered in a particular courtroom.

A significant amount of attention has been devoted to work group characteristics in the organizational literature. The cohesiveness of the work group has been recognized as a key characteristic. March and Simon (1958:69) and Blau and Scott (1962:109) hypothesize that greater homogeneity of backgrounds of members is related to greater perceived goal sharing. Further, the degree of goal sharing is related to identification with the group (March and Simon, 1958:66), as is the frequency of interaction (Ibid.; Blau and Scott, 1962:112) Likewise, the more uniform the opinion of group members, the more cohesive is the group. The more cohesive the group, the greater is its control over its members (March and Simon, 1958:60). Group cohesion has been found to raise worker satisfaction and to lower turnover (Mayo and Lombard, 1944), to promote productivity in one study (Kahn and Katz 1952) but to have no effect in several others (Schacter et al, 1953; Seashore, 1954). Productivity may be affected by intervening variables such as value orientations of the group (Blau and Scott, 1962:95–96). Finally, Etzioni (1975:235) suggests that the amount of consensus in work groups is affected by how they are legitimized. Work groups whose legitimacy rests on ethical values tend to have a higher degree of cohesion than do groups based on material goals or on coercion.

Research on courts, particularly at the trial level, has recently begun to take note of work groups, expecially with regard to their impact on criminal proceedings at the trial level (Eisenstein and Jacob, 1977). The key characteristics so far examined have been courtroom work group stability, with less attention paid to cohesion, normative consensus, or productivity, However, unlike work groups in industrial or bureaucratic settings, courtroom work groups operate without a hierarchical supervisor. They are part of the informal rather than of the formal organizational structure. Thus, the findings of organizational research in more traditional settings may not be fully applicable to courts.

Another important characteristic of court work groups is that they usually are only loosely coupled to one another. Just as the formal court organizations are not linked together in a closely knit hierarchical pattern, so these informal work groups lack hierarchical linkages to one another. The work groups Eisenstein and Jacob (1977) describe possess tangential links to one another through associations that their members have with members of other work groups in their sponsoring organizations. The loose coupling of the work groups reinforces the formal lack of hierarchy in the courts.

Thus, the organizational framework focuses attention on the presence or absence of hierarchy. The presence of hierarchy encourages central coordination and control; its absence discourages it. Where formal hierarchy is absent, it may be replaced in part by an informal hierarchy. Moreover, the work group merits particular attention both for the way it is organized and for the manner in which it is connected to other work groups and the larger organization.

Organizational analysts have also distinguished between different bases of power for those at the top. Max Weber distinguished between those who exercised power on the basis of traditional, charismatic, or legalistic conceptions of legitimacy. Power based on tradition rests on past obligations and ties; it is often inherited power. Charismatic power is based on the psychological appeal of the leader to his subordinates. Power based on legality is delegated to the leader on the basis of formal characteristics that he or she fulfills. Power in organizations is usually based on legality, although those who wield informal power often do so on the basis of charisma or tradition even though someone else holds the formal leadership position based on legality. A somewhat different analysis by Etzioni suggests that power may be based on coercion, remuneration, or norms. Coercive power is typical of an army or prison; people obey men at the top because they are forced to obey. Remunerative power is typical of business organizations; people are motivated to obey by the promise of pay. Churches, universities, and courts may be examples of organizations driven by normatively based power; people obey superiors because they think it right to do so. Etzioni recognizes that organizations may utilize several power bases sequentially. At one point an army general may win compliance by threat of force; at other times, he may win compliance by recourse to patriotic appeal, a normative base.

Little research has been done on the basis of power in courts. With respect to the courts' formal leadership, it has generally been assumed that judges exert their power because of their legitimate claim to it and that claim is rooted in what Etzioni calls a normative base—the sense that justice will be done when it is dispensed by a judge. On the other hand, it is also clear that courts exert their power over litigants on the basis of the threat of coercion. That is as true for civil courts as for criminal courts. Finally, we know that many courtroom personnel are there because of financial inducements; they are payrollers and power over them is exerted by threatening the loss of remuneration. It is even not uncommon for lawyers to respond to this threat by mounting a compelling performance for the gallery so that new clients will seek them out. Thus, it appears that all three bases of power that Etzioni identifies operate in the courtroom context, although to varying degrees for different participants. This may help explain the quite different ways in which courtroom participants respond to the same events. Judges, for instance, may express outrage when a delay is requested because "justice delayed is justice denied," whereas attorneys favor such a delay if it reduces their work or increases their compensation.

BOUNDARIES AND THE ORGANIZATION'S ENVIRONMENT

Closely related to a concern about the distribution of power within organizations is the question of what constitutes the boundaries of an organization. This is important to the distribution of power because those outside the organization's domain are under less control from organization leaders than are those within it. Some influence, however, extends beyond organization boundaries because organizations are not totally autonomous institutions. Organizations are permeable institutions, from which the authority of leaders reaches out to nonmembers and into which the influence of persons in the environment extends to affect internal organizational processes (Thompson, 1967). However, influence is generally greater within an organization than outside it.

In many instances, the boundaries of organizations appear to be clear. It is generally not difficult to tell who is part of General Motors and who is not on the basis of who is employed by it. Religious orders generally have well-defined criteria of membership. There is rarely a question about who is a member of the armed forces and who is not. Yet even in these instances, there are interesting border line cases that may prove troublesome. Are franchised dealers part of General Motors? In what sense are occasional church-goers members of a religious group? And what is the position of irregulars in an army?

Outsiders in the environment are important to an organization because they provide the organization's resources and raw materials for its processing. Business organizations typically face both customers (or clients) and suppliers. The same is true for governmental organizations. In both private and public spheres, customers (or clients) and suppliers are not entirely independent. The perceptions held by one group are likely to affect those of the other.

Both the supply of business and of resources with which to conduct it affect the internal operation of organizations. The amount of business that an organization must transact affects the ways in which it organizes itself. Operating routines during slack periods often are insufficient during peak periods. An organization that can count on the same amount of business coming in at all times may organize itself differently than one which faces drastic fluctuations in its work load. Fluctuations, of course, may occur not only in the amount of business but also in its type. If the same mix of demands comes in all the time, an organization can organize itself differently than when it faces a fluctuation in the mix of demands it must process. Thompson (1967) has considered these problems in considerable depth. He suggests that organizations seek to buffer themselves from such environmental fluctuations by establishing special input or output units, by attempting to smooth out demands that the environment makes on it, and, in the last resort, by rationing its resources among the demands that survive the buffering and screening sheltering the organization's central processes.

These considerations have many apparent applications to studies of courts. As Galanter (chapter 5) and Yngvesson and Mather (chapter 3) point out, courts are only one of many dispute-resolving institutions. Whether a dispute is brought to court depends in part on the disputants and in part on the court. While courts are usually viewed as passive institutions, they do not entirely lack the will or the means to attempt to shape their environment in order to protect themselves (Krislov, chapter 7). Appellate courts, for instance, have resorted to various devices to shelter themselves from excessive demands. These include asserting discretionary jurisdiction and refusing to hear many cases filed with them, establishing technical requirements that allow them to dismiss cases in which they have no discretionary jurisdiction, or relying on associated organizations like the Attorney General's office to screen out cases (Davies, 1980).

At the trial level, one of the most significant differences between criminal and civil courts is the manner in which they attempt to reach out to their environments and control the influx of cases. Criminal courts rely heavily on prosecutors to screen cases and to channel the remaining cases to the most efficient processing routines available (Mcintyre and Lippman, 1970). In civil courts, a variety of other devices are used to attempt control over the docket. Technical filing deadlines weed out some cases; the practical need to have an attorney eliminates a host of other potential cases. The widespread use of mandatory pretrial conferences for settling cases are another such control device to limit the number of trials. No participant in the courtroom, however, exercises the kind of control over these procedures that the prosecutor enjoys in criminal proceedings. Consequently, it is more difficult to hold any single person responsible for controlling the civil courtroom's work load.

Courts, like other organizations, also respond to fluctuations in demand with changes in internal processing routines. When a special kind of case becomes particularly troublesome, courts may establish new routines to accommodate them. For instance, a large influx of criminal appeals in California apparently led the first district appellate court to establish a central legal staff to process "routine" criminal appeals in the name of the court (Federal Judicial Center, 1978; Davies, 1980); Likewise, trial courts often establish special divisions for particular cases, even though their formal jurisdiction is general. That is the case of the Cook County Circuit Court in Chicago. Rationing also occurs in courts (Zeisel, Kalven, and Buchholz, 1959:155–167). Cases are given different priorities and attorneys are allowed to appear in only a limited number of cases. Jurisdictional limits may also be altered to move cases perceived as trivial into other arenas, such as neighborhood justice centers.

Thus, a concern with organizational boundaries and environmental demands lead court researchers to consider the many ways in which courts attempt to reach out to control the demands made upon them. Rather than allowing us to view courts as passive vessels into which society pours its woes, this perspective sees courts as being actively engaged in exchanges with institutions (cf. Feeley and Lazerson, chapter 9) and individuals in other environments. Courts, like other organizations, attempt to shape their environments and to control their impact on them.

COMMUNICATION PATTERNS

Closely associated with the concern for the distribution of power is a focus on communication patterns within organizations. Etzioni (1975:242) distinguishes two kinds of communications: instrumental and expressive. Instrumental communications concern the technical elements of the tasks faced by the organizations. Expressive communications are about the norms and values of the organization. In addition, Etzioni and many others who write about communication nets have tried to outline the several directional patterns characterizing organizations. Much of this work is based on experimental studies with small groups (Bavelas, 1950; Guetzkow and Dill, 1957), although there are also some suggestive studies of actual organizations, particularly one of a research group by Shepard (1954). As summarized by Mintzberg (1979:205), communication nets may take the shape of a wheel in which all communications travel from the periphery to the hub, a "Y," a linear chain, a circle, and an "all channel pattern" in which everyone talks with everyone else. Evidence from experimental studies (Mintzberg, 1979) indicates that the more an organization is differentiated, the more restricted are communications. This has the advantage of affording opportunities for coordination at focal points along the communication net, but it also has the disadvantage of excluding some members of the organization from information that flows along the communication net.

Communication patterns in courts have not been extensively studied. However, communication of information lies at the core of courtroom activities. Indeed, one may conceive of courts as essentially information-processing organizations. Courts receive information about problems or conflicts and, on the basis of that information, they issue commands (i.e., decisions) that permit designated persons to take certain actions. The ways in which courtroom communication patterns affect the contents of the messages conveyed therefore potentially have a very significant effect on the work of courts. In the courtroom itself, most communications resemble the wheel, since they are mostly focused on the judge and/or jury. Jurists have devoted considerable attention to the flow of communications in trials and formal hearings; they are surrounded by complex evidentiary rules. However, much less attention has been paid to the design of information flow for out-of-court settlements. Outside the trial arena, communications are more likely to consist of segregated chains. Thus, the judge talks with his subordinates (his law clerk or secretary); the defense attorney speaks to his client and separately with the prosecutor or attorney for the other party. He and the other attorney also will have conversations with members of their respective office staffs. When a conference occurs between the contending attorneys and the judge in his chambers, the communications resemble a wheel. One consequence of this variety of communication patterns is that it is difficult to identify control points in pretrial bargaining. One suspects that many efforts to reform pretrial proceedings in both criminal and civil cases have faltered on the failure to take into account the actual communication patterns that characterize these proceedings and the functions those communication patterns perform for the organization.

No single directional pattern of communications exists in the court. Rather, there are several patterns, which dominate at different stages of a court's work. That undoubtedly is one of the factors that creates the impression that courts do not fit the usual mold of organizational structure; courts utilize a wide but finite array of communication patterns, which makes them appear to be superficially formless to the observer.

Little systematic research has examined the ways in which courtroom communication patterns affect the outcomes of cases. At the trial court level, Eisenstein and Jacob (1977) speculate that the more informal communications in plea bargaining conferences reduce uncertainty and permit organizational members to exercise better control of the outcome than if information were conveyed through testimony at a trial. Horowitz (1977) argues that formal court proceedings are particularly poor receptors for information about complex issues that involve courts in policy formulation. Many of Horowitz's objections are based on other characteristics of litigation, but some are related to the style of communication within courtrooms—the manner in which testimony is taken.

DECISION MAKING IN ORGANIZATIONS

Those organizational researchers concentrating on decision making have a somewhat different focus; they are less concerned with organizational structure than with the behavior of organizational members. The activities that these researchers concentrate on deal with the making of choices.

Decision making theorists see the problem as one of organizational intelligence and organizational learning. The organization (through its dominant members) has value preferences that it seeks to meet. It generally does not attempt to maximize these values, but only seeks to satisfy them—i.e., do well enough given certain costs and resource constraints

(Simon, 1957; March and Simon, 1958). Two different kinds of decision making may be identified. The first deals with routine activities. The organization devises normal responses to repetitive problems or stimuli. The only decision required from workers is the choice of the appropriate program to respond to the stimulus. That requires training workers to respond appropriately and providing them with pertinent information so they make the right choice. The second type of decision requiries much more complex behavior; it responds to unique stimuli and requires an innovative response. The outcome of this behaviour is often the development of a new program of routine responses.

The ability of an organization to innovate depends upon ability of the organization to detect performance gaps, its possession of slack resources to attend to such problems, its possession of search procedures for identifying new behaviors that will overcome the performance gap or respond to the opportunity, and its ability to implement changes once they have been identified.

Cohen, March, and Olsen (1972) have identified three different search procedures for identifying solutions to nonroutine problems. The first is the analytic method most organizational researchers have presumed. It consists of the rational, systematic search for alternatives and involves the weighing of costs against benefits and choosing the solution which satisfies best. It is most likely to be invoked when problems are well defined, when a well-developed technology exists with which to address the problem, when only a limited number of decision makers are involved, and when they possess the requisite expertise to confront the problem. The second search process invokes different criteria. The most satisfying solution is not the one which has the best cost/benefit ratio but the one which most satisfies people who are influential in the organization. This kind of political process occurs most frequently when the problem is not as well defined as when analytic decision making is used, when the problem solving technology is not as well defined, and when some non-experts participate in the decision making process. Finally, the third kind of problem solving process is called by Cohen, March, and Olsen the "garbage can" model. It is a confluence model in which solutions that are available in the environment seek out problems in organizations. The adopted solution is chosen somewhat by chance; it happened to be available when decision makers needed to come to closure. This process takes place when problems are ill-defined, when no technology offers a reliable result, when many persons drift in and out of the decision process. The decisional outcome is much affected by deadlines, because the alternative chosen is the one that happens to be available at the time the decision has to be made; it is chosen by those who happen to be present at the final moment. Outsiders as well as experts may participate. In this situation, Cohen, March, and Olsen suggest that solutions are searching for problems.

Although decision making lies at the heart of the judicial process, few researchers have applied the insights of organizational studies. Mohr (1976:628–641) suggests that courts move from one to another mode of decision making concomitant with variations in resource constraints, goal compatability, stability of participation, and norms about redistribution of the values that are being contested. He writes (1976:640):

> ...courts are not confused, nor are they volatile, nor exceptions to some rule. They behave in this fashion simply because submodel of choice depends upon context of decision and measures on the contextual dimensions may vary appreciably in such courts from case to case.

Thus, organizational research suggests several lines of inquiry for courts. One is to focus on the distinction between routine and innovative decision making. Routine decisions are those in which standard procedures are invoked. Innovative decisions are those in which previously established routines fail and the organization must respond to a developing performance gap by a creative response. In courts, routine decision making is studied more for its outcomes than for the conditions to which the routines are successfully applied. Routine decision making involves the invocation of standard operating procedures (SOP). Much of the work of court personnel is to place cases into previously defined catagories of SOPs. Thus, courts have SOPs for intake and for chanelling cases to alternative decision processes—negotiation, bench trial, or jury trial. Some research has been devoted to uncovering the informal rules governing these routine decisions (e.g., Mather, 1974). In some courts there are also well-developed formal rules to route cases. Formal decision processes are encompassed in well-developed SOPs. Very little doubt exists about how trials should and most do proceed. On the other hand, informal proceedings such as plea bargaining are less well governed by formal decisional rules. For instance, the choice of a guilty plea, or bench trial over a jury trial, is one that crucially affects a court's work load. Court observers agree that these decisions are made informally, but the SOPs used to channel cases to each of these mechanisms have not often been the subject of systematic research. Even less attention has been directed to input routines that govern the acceptance or rejection of civil cases by courts.

Sometimes, well-established routines—the accepted SOPs—fail. For instance, a new divorce law may stimulate a wave of cases with different characteristics than those formerly brought to court, or a new technology like solar heating may provoke conflicts that are not amenable to proccessing according to established routines. The failure of SOPs to accommodate new situations produces stress within the court and the need to innovate. Courts, however, are not known to be particularly innovative.

Some of the work on innovation in the organizational literature provides some suggestions as to why courts do not often innovate. Zaltman,

Duncan, and Holbek (1973) propose considering innovation as a two-stage process, consisting of initiation and implementation. Characteristics of organizations affect each of these stages in different ways. Initiation results from an awareness of a performance gap or insufficiency within the organization and from a capability to undertake a search for alternatives. More complex and less formal organizations are more likely to initiate innovations because the variety of outlooks encompassed in more complex organizations and the flexibility of less formal organizational structures enhance the capacity to initiate innovations. Courts, as organizations, are not very complex; they are dominated by a single profession. On the other hand, courts often stress formality with procedures that are relatively inflexibly prescribed. With respect to implementation, Zaltman, Duncan and Holbek suggest that centralized organizations do best because they have the ability to supervise the implementation of an innovation. Again, courts lack the crucial trait; they are relatively decentralized and each judge has considerable independence in determining whether to accept a new way of doing things. Given these characteristics, one would not expect much innovation from courts. Moreover, when courts do innovate, one would expect them to do so as the result of a political or garbage can process. This is because neither the problem nor the technology for solving it is usually well defined when courts face the necessity of developing new procedures to overcome performance gaps.

Another line of inquiry suggested by decision making studies focuses on the manner in which courts reach their decisions. This involves consideration of the way in which information and goals intersect. Thompson (1967) notes the importance of the "core technology" of an organization. He delineates three kinds of technology: a long-linked technology typical of mass production factories, a mediating technology that many service industries employ to bring together people with common needs, and an intensive technology that typifies work in a scientific laboratory or in a doctor's office. The last is also the predominant technology employed by courts.[2] It is characterized by an uncertain relationship between the techniques employed to do justice and the end product of the courts. It is also a technology that depends heavily on continuous feedback. It requires allowing those who perform the tasks considerable discretion to apply their expertise because that expertise has not yet been codified in a way that permits the tasks to be performed through close supervision by less professional personnel.

Using an intensive technology, courts try to transform information and public goals into just decisions that at least temporarily resolve conflicts in a manner acceptable to most litigants and to those in the environment who must provide support for the courts. This mode of analysis is uncommon in court studies. One quasi-example is Horowitz's recent study of courts, which, although not grounded in organizational theory, explicitly analyzes the information base and the search processes used by courts for making policy decisions. Horowitz (1977:33–56) argues that several characteristics of courts make it difficult for them to confront policy issues appropriately. According to Horowitz, courts typically focus on narrow issues raised in litigation, and these issues are framed in terms of claimed rights and duties rather than in terms of plausible alternatives, which might lead to desired results. Moreover, litigation is generally piecemeal; all aspects of a policy issue are usually not raised in a single suit, but only those which happen to concern the litigants. The litigants volunteer themselves and do not give notice to other potentially interested parties. Litigation usually takes a two-sided pose, making it difficult to consider other claims and other interests. Thus, the litigation process is peculiarly unrepresentative. The search for appropriate information is hindered in litigation by the requirement for direct testimony and the lack of expertise among judges (not to speak of juries) in the substance of the dispute. Judges are expert only in the application of legal rules; they usually know little about economics, statistics, physics, or other bodies of scientific knowledge. Finally, Horowitz suggests that courts do not have a built-in feedback process by which they can routinely monitor the results of their policy decisions. As long as litigants can live with the results—which may mean going to other policy making arenas for relief—courts will not see further litigation about their decisions. Even though a decision works badly and produces unanticipated and unwanted results, it may go unaltered for lack of further litigation.

Although Horowitz's analysis is not grounded in organizational theory, it taps many of the same concerns. One of the problems implied in Horowitz's analysis is that courts do not have clear organizational goals to pursue. As Eisenstein and Jacob (1977:24–28) indicate in their analysis of criminal courts, such tribunals pursue both expressive and instrumental goals. The former are vaguely stated in terms of "doing justice"; the latter involve maintaining their own organizational integrity by protecting their resources, avoiding criticism from influentials in their task environment, and reducing uncertainty that might hinder decision making. These goals, however, are not necessarily congruent with those of litigants. Litigants go to court to fulfill a wide variety of purposes—to get payment of a debt, to evict a tenant, to obtain compensation for an injury, to build where the zoning board has prohibited construction, to get someone to hire blacks or women, to prevent pollution, or some similar purpose. Litigants often have an interest in getting the best possible decision from a court and they may perceive litigation as a zero-sum game. They will often seek to maximize rather than satisfy, since they do not have to pay the additional costs of moving from a satisfactory solution to a maximal one once a case has gone to trial. In theory, courts incur no costs in devising such maximal solutions because such decisions end a trial just as well as does a satisfying solution. Courtroom personnel, however, do have to pay the costs of these maximal solutions. They may cost more time, require greater preparation, expose the lack of expertise of the judge and attorneys, and increase uncertainty. Hence, courtroom personnel seek to push litigants toward settlements that litigants do not necessarily perceive to be in their best interests (Rosenthal, 1974). This is an unavoidable conflict between the courtroom and the people it serves. It may lead to devices to disguise the courtroom's interests by seeking to convince litigants of the virtue of settling or it may seek to shift the courtrooms' costs to litigants by imposing long waiting periods for those who insist on a trial or by diverting them to other tribunals.

The goals and values pursued by courts are a concern of much judicial research. That body of research has mostly focused on the role that judges' personal values (or ideologies) play in that decision making process (see Schubert, 1965; Rohde and Spaeth, 1976). No effort is made in these studies to compare the effect of personal values with institutional goals; rather, these studies claim that personal values, such as economic liberalism or civil libertarianism, can explain much decision making behavior of Supreme Court justices. It is a telling commentary on the ambiguity of the Court's institutional goals that they are not even considered in this research, largely because they have been poorly articulated. However, the emphasis on individually held values of justices probably underestimates the effect of institutional forces on the Supreme Court. Organization theorists—in addition to noting the distinction between instrumental and expressive goals, mentioned above—have also distinguished between goals that promote the organization's maintenance and those that are oriented to the organization's external environment (Gross, 1968; Mohr, 1973). Most judicial research on goals has considered the latter (which are weakly articulated in courts) to the neglect of the former (which are often thought to be illegitimate with respect to courts).

At the trial court level, other studies have attempted to assess the impact of role orientations (Sarat, 1977a; Gibson, 1977a) and certain kinds of information, especially on the sentencing decision. For instance, numerous researchers have examined the importance of information about defendants' race, social status, prior criminal record, and gender on the judges' sentencing decision (Hagan, 1974; Uhlman and Kritzer, 1976; Uhlman, 1977; Eisenstein and Jacob, 1977). These can best be understood not as studies of idiosyncratic decision making but rather as attempts to delineate the character of the courts' core technology. The debate over whether race or gender affects a sentence is not directed to a single judge but concerns how certain kinds of information will be referenced in a decision making routine.

A logical extension of the concern with individual values and their effects on decisions is an interest in the recruitment and socialization of organization members (Van Maanen, 1976; Wanous, 1977). Workers have to be induced to join the organization. In some instances, those recruited are chosen because they have the skills required by the organization. In most cases, however, the organization teaches the requisite skills. In almost every instance, the organization also indoctrinates new members in its norms and in its operating procedures. The teaching process may be formalized in probationary period and with in-service training at regular intervals during the course of a person's employment. Alternatively, it may be left to informal contacts between novices and experienced workers. The more highly trained and organization's recruits are, the more likely it is that socialization is left to informal processes, but some process must exist whereby new members learn the organization's SOPs.

Courts recruit both highly professional and nonprofessional workers. Attorneys must pass through a long period of professional training and must pass a professional certification examination before practicing law. Judges do not take a special examinations, but they are recruited from the pool of licensed attorneys and usually come from the ranks of those lawyers who have appeared in court for litigation. However, many new judges undergo no special training; they often simply pass from one side of the bench to the other upon their appointment. A few states and the federal judiciary now have formal training sussions for new judges that last a few weeks, but most judges still receive no formal initiation into their new tasks except the informal guidance provided by colleagues (Alpert, 1981). The same is true for attorneys working in courts. Those attorneys working for large offices are often provided an apprentice-like experience in which they are taken under the wing of a more experienced attorney for a short period of time before being left to their own devices. Attorneys working on their own do not have even that kind of training. Heumann (1978) provides a vivid description of the informality of the socialization process for both attorneys and judges in a criminal court.

The nonprofessional workers are the bailiffs, secretaries, clerks, and court reporters. They are not graduates of long professional training programs. Although they sometimes come to the court with special skills, they often must be trained in a particular court's ways after their arrival there. However, even these workers tend to be trained through informal practices rather than in a formal training program.

The effects of this haphazard recruitment and socialization process for the courts have not been systematically considered. Comparing courts to other units studied by organizational theorists suggests that the lack of controlled recruitment and formal socialization helps produce low consensus among court personnel about organizational goals. It also probably accounts for the large variation in court proceedings that one can often find in even a single locale.

ACTUAL AND POTENTIAL APPLICATIONS

Some court researchers have used organizational concepts implicitly or explicitly in recent years. Others have done research on topics that could easily be re-analyzed in the organizational framework. These studies serve not only to illustrate the benefits and potential for the application of organizational theories to court research but also the warn us of its limitations.

The first major study to suggest the organizational paradigm is Abraham Blumberg's *Criminal Justice* (1967a). Blumberg, in his first edition, argues that the criminal court he studied behaved like a bureaucracy and that bureaucratic norms had replaced adversarial norms. That meant, according to Blumberg, that defense attorneys had been coopted by the court and that they often placed organizational maintenance goals above those which supposedly governed the adversarial process. They preferred to plead their clients than to bring them to trial.

Blumberg's formulation was enormously influential; it made evident the systematic erosion or adversarial practices that underlay the widespread use of plea bargaining. Blumberg uses organizational ideas as heuristic devices rather than as a formal model to guide his research. Indeed, he does not refer to organizational theory; he speaks of bureaucracies as if all organizations were bureaucratic. Consequently, Blumberg is insensitive to the tension between the long-linked and mediating technologies used by bureaucratic agencies and the intensive technology used by courts.

Blumberg is quite successful in describing some of the SOPs of his court and the structure of incentives that causes participants to comply with them. He does not, however, test the hypothesis that certain characteristics of the court—especially its work load—led to its straying from adversarial procedures, nor does he examine very fully the SOPs that channelled some cases to trial while others were funnelled into the plea bargaining routine. Because the study is more cross-sectional than longitudinal, Blumberg is unable to relate changes in organizational characteristics with changes in the work load presented to the court and with alterations in other elements of the court's environment.

Eisenstein and Jacob's *Felony Justice* (1977) is in some ways a direct descendant of Blumberg's book. They seek to avoid to avoid Blumberg's error of treating all organizations as bureaucracies. They are self-conscious in their application of selected organizational concepts. They pay particular attention to the structure of work groups and the interplay between the work group and its environment. Their data suggest that differences in work groups produce somewhat different outcomes and that differences in the stability of work groups are associated with differences in the utilization of various processing routines (plea bargaining, bench trials, and jury trials). Their utilization of organizational concepts, however, is quite eclectic. They assert that a variety of goals motivate courtroom participants, but they do not have any data that directly describe those goals. They have little information about the interactions that take place within courtroom work groups, and they provide little description of the SOPs that channel cases to one procedure or another. They do provide rich desciptions of plea bargaining and bench trial routines, and illustrate how these are designed to minimize uncertainty and to satisfy some of the implied goals of the courtroom work group. Their work, like Blumberg's, is more suggestive than dispositive. It indicates the potential for applying organizational concepts but it does not test specific hypotheses from those theories.

Nardulli's *The Courtroom Elite* (1978) supplements data Eisenstein and Jacob used to address some different problems suggested by the organizational framework. Nardulli pays particular attention to the manner in which cases are categorized by courtroom participants—their dispositional value—and the degree to which courtroom participants have been coopted to its norms—their responsiveness. Unfortunately, like Eisenstein and Jacob, Nardulli's work is richer in theory than in empirical data. He, like they, lacks observational data and interview responses to demonstrate the validity of his hypotheses.

The data that Eisenstein and Jacob and Nardulli lack are to be found in Lynn Mather's work. Mather's *Plea Bargaining or Trial?* (1979b) is not written from an organizational perspective; rather, she describes the activities of the Los Angeles Superior Court in terms of a "subculture." Her work, however, can be reinterpreted in the organizational framework with great profit. Almost the entire book concerns a detailed description of SOPs that govern the assignment of cases to attorneys and judges (i.e., to work groups) and to different processing routines (pleas, bench trials, and jury trials). She provides us with a more detailed description of these SOPs than does any other researcher of criminal courts. If we view these norms or rules as SOPs in an organizational framework rather than as norms of a subculture, we are sensitized to some answers to puzzles to which she only alludes. She notes that some public defenders are mavericks in that they take more cases to trial, but she also notes that these are mostly senior public defenders who are assigned more serious cases, which would be expected to go to trial in more instances. Viewed from an organizational perspective, such as assignment makes sense. It gives "mavericks" a task that, while risky because a trial may be lost, is nevertheless more fully bounded by rules and procedures than are many other tasks. One might have pursued this matter further by examining the interactions of these attorneys with other members of the work group to see how well they fit into the organizational structure and to what pressures they were subjected. In addition, one would probably come to a different conclusion about the exclusion of defendants from crucial processing decisions. That practice seems, from the organizational perspective, to serve a maintenance function by which the organization isolates itself from erratic external influences.

Lief Carter's *The Limits of Order* (1974) explicitly utilizes the organizational perspective in a study of a prosecutor's office in California. His setting is apparently quite different from most others studied. Interactions with defense counsel appear to take place mostly in the prosecutor's office rather than in the courtroom. There appears to be little continuous interaction between prosecutors, defense counsel, and judges as a work group. Thus, most nontrial activities seem to be located in the prosecutor's office, where they are subject to the constraints of that organization's structure. Applying Thompson's (1967) ideas, Carter stresses the importance of technological and informational uncertainty. The former refers to the uncertainty between activities that the prosecutor engages in and the results which are thereby produced; the latter concerns the unreliability of the information that he processes. These two characteristics lead to the employment of an intensive technology in which prosecutors pay close attention to idiosyncratic details of each case and are permitted wide latitude in their handling of a case rather than there being an insistence on a standardized method of proceeding. Carter describes few informal SOPs; he contends that variation rather than standardization governed the working of this office. He does not emphasize the linkage between operating procedures and the exchanges that take place between prosecutors, defense, attorneys, and judges, except to indicate that "trusting" relationships were highly valued between prosecutors and defense attorneys because they reduced informational uncertainty (1974:86).

Another element of the court organization's functioning is suggesting by Milton Heumann's *Plea Bargaining* (1978), which examines the socialization process in Connecticut criminal courts. Heumann emphasizes one important feature of court work groups—especially prominent in the Connecticut courts he examines—the informal character of the socialization process. Indeed, he prefers to describe it as adaption rather than socialization because much of it occurs through learning rather than through teaching. However, both take place, as is illustrated by the following exchange between a neophyte public defender and a judge as reported by the attorney:

> ... the judge said: "Well, we'll see you tomorrow and, well, just play along with everyone else. Don't file a lot of motions. Don't mess around like those legal-aid attorneys, filing all their motions. Don't file a lot of motions and don't make a lot of noise." (1978:63).

While Heumann occasionally uses the term "organization," his study is not based on organizational theory premises. As a consequence, Heumann is not led to examine the SOPs that characterize the work groups to which his defense attorneys, prosecutors, and judges are adapting. He does not consider the impact of organizational structure (the prosecutor's office, the public defender's office, the manner in which Connecticut judges are assigned and supervised), variations in the character of the case load, or differences in resource availability. Thus, while Heumann has undoubtedly put his finger on a very important element of the organizational process in criminal courts, he has not systematically linked it to other elements of the court's organizational structure.

Malcolm Feeley's *The Process Is the Punishment* (1979b) also comes close to using organizational concepts. He uses the organizational language at the beginning of the book, where he rejects the notion that courts are bureaucracies, preferring to think of them as "open systems" that lead one to focus on interactions among participants, especially among those constituting the courthouse work group (1979b:19–20). He then discusses in considerable detail the conditions under which judges, prosecutors, and defense counsel are recruited into this work group, and the conditions under which they work. He is not as successful as Mather in outlining the SOPs used to accept cases and to channel them to various processing routines, or the SOPs characterizing the processing routines themselves. However, he notes, as Mather did, that decisions about how to process a case are the result of an evaluation of the "worth" of a case and the character of the defendant. These evaluations are made jointly by defense counsel and prosecutor. In New Haven's lower court, however, defense attorneys play a more aggressive role than in most other courts; the relatively passive posture of prosecutors appears to be an adaptation by them to a case load that is heavier than that of defense counsel. Judges play a passive role, too, because in Connecticut they frequently serve in districts other than their own and thus are often outsiders in the courthouse.

Unfortunately, Feeley's work does not build on Heumann's. Feeley adds considerable detail about the circumstances surrounding the recruitment of judges—details that are lacking in Heumann's account—but Feeley does not tell us how the variations in socialization that Heumann examines affect and SOPs he uncovers or the interactions that the reports. Indeed, no reference to this portion of Heumann's research appears in Feeley's book.

What we have, then, is the core of a paradigm that might go far in filling gaps in individual research efforts. From Lief Carter's study and, to a lesser degree, from Eisenstein and Jacob, we have learned about some of the SOPs used to screen cases that the police bring into court. From Mather and Feeley, we learn about the SOPs used to channel cases to different processing routines; Eisenstein and Jacob, Mather, Feeley, and Heumann describe the procedures entailed in each of these processing routines. Heumann describes the manner by which people in the court organization are socialized into their roles; Feeley presents more evidence about how they are recruited. Organizational theory asserts that all of these characteristics are closely related. The kinds of persons recruited into work groups and the manner in which they are socialized affects the SOPs they use to process cases. On the other hand, screening affects the workload, which in turn affects SOPs. Finally, SOPs effect work group relationships and the structure of the organization. Thus, the SOPs seem to work well in Los Angeles, where there appears to be a rather long period of socialization and work group participation. They work less well in New Haven, where there is much turnover in the lower criminal court that Feeley describes. Whether a judge, prosecutor, or defense attorney plays the leading role in the work group seems to depend upon the resources available to each and their commitment to the work group. Where the commitment is low (Feeley's New Haven judges) or where the work load is extrememly high (Feeley's prosecutors), participants will take a less active role than where the opposite conditions exist. Defendants are considered outsiders to the work group and will be pushed around in various ways—excluded from negotiations whenever possible (Mather's Los Angeles, and Eisenstein and Jacob's Chicago, Detroit, and Baltimore) or pushed aside by gruff mannerisms (Feeley's New Haven). This exclusion of defendants serves to maintain the understandings that work group members have established with each other and to conserve scarce resources, since prosecutors need not take the time to explain procedures and details of cases to every defendant. An element that is lacking from each of these case studies is an examination of how the outputs of these courts (their decisions to fine, imprison, or free defendants) are received by relevant elements of their task environments and how these court organizations adapt themselves to those reactions.

That future research can also be informed by these organizational perspectives is is illustrated by a recent solicitation by the National Institute of Law Enforcement and Criminal Justice (NILECJ (1979a). This solicitation seeks to investigate the impact of state court unification on court performance. It particularly focuses on trial and appellate case disposition on the one hand and on the performance of staff functions for courts on the other. It thus focuses on the nascent elements of hierarchy existing in state courts. It provides an excellent opportunity to examine the effects of various hierarchical arrangements on the recruitment and socialization of judges and other court personnel, their use of SOPs, and the kinds of informal work group structures they develop. There is, of course, the possibility that the amount of hierarchical control in most state court organization is so slight that variations do not cross the threshold to the point where they might have a differential effect. Nevertheless, this is a promising direction for inquiry.

Another NILECJ solicitation (1979b) also utilizes organizational perspectives to address the effects of pretrial processes on the consistency of handling cases and on the reduction of delay. It thus focuses on the informal SOPs that characterize many trial courts. In this solicitation, however, informal structures, norms, and SOPs are treated as if they were extrinsic to the court's organization rather than being an integral (or perhaps even the defining) part of it. On the other hand, it commendably calls for examining incentives within the organization and for understanding its compliance structure. It perceives delay as a product of many factors; it suggests that the imposition of rigid processing deadlines will have unforeseen consequences at other points in the adjudication process.

Much less research has been done on work groups in civil proceedings, and little of that has used an organizational framework. The paucity of research reflects many factors, one of which undoubtedly is the apparent organizational formlessness of civil courtrooms. While many of them specialize in some routine matters that come to court in great volume, many others do not. Even those that specialize have fewer regulars than do their criminal counterparts. However, some of the concepts of organizational studies can illuminate the work of civil courtroom work groups even as they do those of criminal courts.

Marc Galanter's (1974b) observations, for instance, about the relative advantage of repeat players in civil proceedings makes more sense, I believe, in an organizational setting. Repeat players have their advantage because they get to know the SOPs of work groups and can bend them to their advantage Moreover, repeat players are themselves likely to be significant members of the work group. They are "insiders," who can manipulate the process against outsiders in the cause of maintaining the work group's integrity. Repeat players are likely to be coopted by other members of the work group, who in this instance include not only the judge but also clerks and possibly opposing attorneys.

The recent examination of small claims courts by Ruhnks, Weller and Martin (1978) also illustrates how an organizational perspective—had it been used—might have led to more illuminating results. The study examines participants piecemeal—the judge, attorneys, litigants, and other courtroom personnel—rather than examining the patterns of interaction between them. There is little in the report to indicate how these interactions vary in intensity. There is no indication of how the work product differs when work groups exhibit different characteristics. The report stresses the significance of certain attributes for small claims court judges—their need to be more active than other civil judges—but provides little information about how such traits effect the manner in which the court operates as a whole entity. Nor is there much awareness that certain SOPs may have important ancillary consequences, such as providing official assistance to prose litigants through the clerk's office and its consequences on the court's ability to control its case load.

The kind of ethnographic research that so enriches Mather's work still needs to be done in the setting of a civil courtroom. It is likely that such an effort will uncover the same kind of "subculture" or organizational regularities as revealed in criminal courtrooms, although the specific characteristics of these civil court work groups will undoubtedly differ from their criminal court counterparts.

CONCLUSIONS: WHAT ORGANIZATIONAL CONCEPTS CAN AND CANNOT TELL US

The benefits of using organizational concepts for studying courts may be summarized as follows:

1. The organizational paradigm provides the researcher with a checklist of phenomena for which to look. In this case, it is a heuristic device.
2. The organizational paradigm provides the researcher with hypotheses (such as those we have discussed in the sections above) against which to measure the significance of particular characteristics of courts as organizations.
3. The organizational paradigm guides the researcher by suggesting connections among various parts of the court process. As a more specific instance of a systems approach, it militates against viewing related phenomena as if they were separate or isolated.
4. The organizational paradigm particularly calls attention to the role of SOPs in decision making and the manner in which these SOPs develop and are transmitted to members of the organization.
5. The organizational paradigm calls attention to the significance of exchanges between the organization and its task environment. These exchanges are two-way relationships with those in the organization attempting to control the environment, and vice versa.
6. The organizational paradigm makes clearer the obstacles to reform that exist for courts. Innovations are particularly difficult for courts to implement because of their decentralized structure, with little hierarchical control over subordinate units.
7. The organizational paradigm also points out the importance of observational research techniques for understanding court activities. Examination of aggregate statistics or court files will usually not suffice for uncovering the relationships that make a courtroom work group distinctive.
8. Use of the organizational paradigm may enable us eventually to develop a typology of court work groups that is independent of the criminal–civil distinction. That distinction does not illuminate the differences in courtroom operations; rather it blurs fundamental similarities, such as the kinds of SOPs that seek to control case flow and the dependence of the work group on its task environment.

This assessment of the utility of organizational theories is somewhat more sanguine than Mohr's (1976). Like Mohr's, it places little emphasis on hierarchical elements of organizational structure, but more on the decisional processes that are so prominent in the courtroom's work. However, it sees the value of organizational concepts as extending beyond this emphasis on decisional processes to an examination of exchanges with the environment and the impact of recruitment and socialization.

Nevertheless, the organizational paradigm—like all heuristic devices— also blinds the researcher to some aspects of his subject matter. It does not, for instance, permit us to focus very well on the distributional effects of court actions nor on the societal role occurs play in conflict management as Galanter, Friedman, and Yngvesson and Mather emphasize in their chapters in this volume. The organizational paradigm is well suited for a microscopic analysis of courts; it is ill suited for macroscopic analysis of the consequences of legal action for the society in which it takes place. Further, while all organizations incorporate normative biases in their operations, and the organizational paradigm allows the observer to understand their impact, the paradigm does not readily lend itself to a value analysis of the organization itself. In a sense, organizational analysis is introspective. Thus, it is better for telling us what courts are and how they operate than for describing what they do for the society in which they exist.

NOTES

1. Etzioni (1975:65) writes: "There is almost no relevant data on the relationship between lower and higher participants in the hierarchy of judges and court administration."
2. For a dissenting view, see Henderson, Guynes, and Baar (1980).

9

Police-Prosecutor Relationships: An Interorganizational Perspective

Malcolm M. Feeley and Mark H. Lazerson

INTRODUCTION

This essay explores police-prosecutor relations in light of emerging theories of interorganizational and open-systems analysis. This perspective, we will show, illuminates important, but as yet little-explored, features of the criminal justice system. In particular, it suggests the need to consider additional factors in accounting for disposition of cases in criminal courts.

Our point of departure is that vast amount of reformist and scholarly writing that characterizes the criminal justice system as a funnel or as a sieve. This metaphor is employed to portray the attrition, fall-off, drop-out, or loss (of either dismissed cases or reduced charges) of criminal cases as defendants proceed from arrest to conviction. Implicit in the use of these and similar metaphors is the view that arrests are supposed to lead to conviction, excepting those few which are dropped due to faulty police practices and the different standards for decision used by police and courts. Whatever their precise orientation and explanation, such studies of courts tend to regard dropped cases and reduced charges as evidence of goal displacement due to such various concerns as organizational maintenance, self-interest, cooperative and cooptive behavior, the need

Authors' Note: This work was supported by a grant from the National Institute of Justice, and an early version of this chapter was first presented at the Workshop on Empirical Theories of Courts, Stanford, California, November 7–8, 1979. We wish to thank participants in that workshop for their helpful comments.

to allocate scarce resources, and other factors suggested by organizational analysis. While we do not dispute the importance of such factors, we suggest that there is value in viewing the activities of courtroom work groups in a broader context—from an *interorganizational* perspective.

If such an approach is undertaken, the arresting officer is likely to emerge as a central figure, because we believe the importance he attaches to an arrest is often reflected in the eventual disposition of the criminal court. Of course, there is the obvious fact that most prosecutors are passive and reactive agents who depend upon the police to bring cases to them.[1] What we suggest is that it is the arresting officer's method of gathering and presenting evidence and his structuring of the arrest report that determine the outcome of a great many cases. In such situations, the deliberations of the courtroom work group become little more than a ratifying process of the definitions previously established by the officer, rather than an exercise of independent judgment shaped by the work group's own set of concerns.

More generally, we see the need to view arrest and the subsequent disposition of arrests in terms of the interaction of police and prosecutors. The nature of the relationship between these two semi-autonomous institutions should be more carefully scrutinized. If we are correct in our assertion that the police play an important role in affecting the disposition of criminal cases in the courts, then the particular ways in which prosecutors and police relate to one another need to be treated as a central problem. Interorganizational analysis provides a fruitful way to order this enterprise.

Our purpose here is to review the emerging literature in interorganization theory, illustrate its usefulness for examining police–prosecutor relations, and point out some avenues for research that it suggests.

INTERORGANIZATION THEORY

Organization theory traditionally has treated organizations as autonomous units; it has focused upon the organization's effort to remain a self-contained entity within a larger environment. A major concern in each school of organization theory has been how the organization's goals endure in the face of centrifugal forces. Early writers in the *human relations* tradition sought to identify those conditions that affect productivity, morale, effective leadership, the optimal size of the work group, and so on, in order to make institutions more efficient in achieving their formal goals. The *group relations* school has focused on tensions between individual and organizational aims, conflict among members of the organization, and the relationship between the organizational structure and its goals. Similarly, the *institutional school* has focused on organizational goals, but much of its analysis has concerned the departure from an organization's original plans in its struggle for survival and expansion.

None of these traditions has ignored the fact that organizations remain dependent upon the larger environments within which they operate. Indeed, one of their major concerns is how organizations respond to external changes. Still, theories of formal organizations continue to regard organizations as autonomous units, and research concerns focus on internal forces shaping the pursuit of institutional goals. This perspective has informed a great deal of recent research on handling cases in criminal courts, and has, we think, ignored the possibility that outcomes in courts can be shaped in significant ways by actors outside the court organization or courtroom work group. In particular, we suggest a perspective that will link two separate organizational spheres, the police and the courtroom work group. We begin by reviewing the emerging literature in interorganizational analysis and then turn to examine operative norms and perspectives of street-level police work and the courthouse.

It is only recently that organizational theorists have begun to systematically address interorganizational relationships in a systematic way. Here the organization is taken as the unit of analysis and the objective is to understand how organizations with divergent and conflicting goals relate to one another. This new development appears to be part of the trend toward recognition of the importance of the environment in shaping activities within organizations, as well as a merging of organization theory with systems theory. This interest reflects the realization that we live in an increasingly interdependent society, in which important social decisions are the result of joint actions or shared responsibilities by two or more relatively autonomous institutions. This trend is especially pronounced in the study of public policy, in which policies are often the result of legally mandated responsibilities that require cooperation among several organizations.

A major concern in interorganizational analysis is how organizations with shared interests or forced relations deal with each other in the *absence* of a defined structure of authority (Evan, 1978). Because organizations are reluctant to cede their authority, they attempt to structure and manage conflict and mandated cooperation in a way that assures continued independence. For instance, the doctrine of the separation of powers facilitates limited cooperation in some spheres even as it recognizes and perhaps fosters conflict in others. Division of labor in general serves a similar function. Salesmen, who have an incentive to foster especially friendly relationships with buyers, are not usually assigned the task of drafting contracts. In law, the theory of the adversary process not only recognizes the inevitability of conflict but celebrates it, holding that the legal process functions best when conflict is vigorous.

Much interorganizational conflict, however, is *not* the result of intentional design; it emerges unplanned, as organizations expand their activities and begin to collide with one another. In the words of J. D. Thompson, "organizations do some of the basic things they do because they must—or else!... The concepts of rationality brought to bear on organizations establish limits within which organizational action must take place" (Thompson, 1967:7). Thus, many relationships are forged by necessity, and cooperation—even among the most bitter of enemies—may emerge. Such mixtures of divergent goals and cooperative interactions may take any number of forms.

The standard examples in interorganizational analysis are community charities competing among themselves for contributions, and social service agencies chasing after the same clients. In both situations, what one organization gains another loses. At the same time, if they cooperate, transaction costs can be drastically cut. This paper builds on these examples, although we have expanded the notion of conflict to include divergent goals as well.

There are numerous ways in which autonomous institutions with conflicting and differing goals learn to function effectively, even as they are faced with the reality of divergent interests. If the institutions are forced to deal with one another or will derive mutual advantages if they do, one or more of the following structures is likely to develop: *exchange relationships, conflict-resolution institutions, formal arrangements to cooperate, institutions of coordination* (i.e., federation or expanded authority), the *emergence of boundary-spanning institutions* to bridge the organizational differences by searching for common grounds, and efforts at *organizational imperalism* by one organization seeking domination.

Exchanges

Exchange theory views organizations as complicated networks in which various elements are functionally interdependent upon one another and also depend upon the reciprocity of exchange. This approach minimizes the importance of "formal" organization, and in its extreme form it minimizes the distinction between organization and environment (i.e., an organization is understood to be any system of exchange, rather than some formally designated institution). The value of this approach is its appreciation that few institutions are either self-sufficient or locked in total conflict with other institutions. Many relationships are maintained precisely because of differences of interest that result in mutual advantage.

Some have found the exchange principle helpful in accounting for interorganizational relationships among competing organizations (Levine and White, 1961). Others, however, have criticized it on the grounds that, while useful in accounting for some types of relationships (principally voluntary), it may have less explanatory value for relationships that are officially prescribed (see, e.g., Litwack and Meyer, 1966). These critics argue that to focus on voluntary exchanges minimizes differences by emphasizing areas of agreement and recipcrocity. We also believe that exchange theory in this context is more useful in accounting for interorganizational relationships that involve *joint* decisions (e.g., trades or mutual consent) than for relationships involving *sequential* involvement, particularly those that are mandated by law, such as the relations between police and prosecutors.

Conflict-Resolution Institutions

Organizations that frequently are at odds with each other often institutionalize their relationships in such a way that conflict will be contained. In anticipation of future conflict, some organizations provide adjudication or mediation of disputes in ways that institutionalize settlement of differences at relatively low cost. In some cultures, disputants turn to "trusted authorities" to resolve their conflicts.

These voluntary conflict-resolution institutions tend to be reactive, and are usually invoked after disputes occur. Because of this, organizations that find themselves in recurring conflict with each other are also likely to take measures to prevent or limit conflict before it occurs. Agreement to binding arbitration in the event of dispute is an example.

Coordinating Arrangements

One such institution is the "coordinating" mechanism, a *formal* structure "to order behavior among two or more other formal organizations" (Levine and White, 1961:599). Such coordinating mechanisms may be purely voluntary and emerge almost unplanned as a by-product of other activity (e.g., price fixing among supposedly competitive companies may emerge after a while from periodic meetings among company officers called for the purposes of sharing credit information on their common customers). Or, coordinating "task forces" may be appointed by a trade association or higher authority to seek ways to reduce conflict and better coordinate relationships among competitive agencies. Typically, the division of labor that separates cooperating from competing functions helps manage relations among organizations with divergent goals.

The desire to eliminate conflict among different organizations may lead to coordinating councils comprised of representatives of the various groups who are charged with the task of meeting together on a regular basis. There information is exchanged, mutual concerns are explored, more is learned of each others' goals and problems, and the channels of communication are opened—all devices adopted to reduce friction. At the other extreme may be the emergence of a new super-agency, which slowly acquires authority over institutions it was once only supposed to coordinate. At one time, for example, many suggested that this could be the evolutionary path of the United Nations. The federation is still another type of coordinating institution: a central institution of limited authority is created to coordinate the activities of individual members and to assure that conflict among member organizations will be kept within bounds and pursued through legally prescribed channels.

In each of these cases, the dominant principle of interorganizational interaction is to secure cooperation through increased communication and perhaps subservience under a recognized (although limited) superior. Such formally created arrangements are most likely to develop among interdependent organizations that have standardized, continuing, and repetitious relationships over long periods of time (Levine and White, 1961).

Boundary-Spanning Institutions

Despite formal goals that make them antagonists, organizations may turn to boundary-spanning institutions to mute their differences. Such institutions may be implicit or explicit. They may be vague "environmental" factors, such as a common culture that prescribes the "rules of the game" among adversaries or competitors, or shared cultural values that ameliorate differences. In governmental organizations, two such boundary-spanning institutions, which serve to blunt differences among agencies, are shared values deriving from a common political culture and a strong political party organization. Both can serve to informally mediate and moderate differences that may require formal organizations in other circumstances.

Organizational Imperialism

Still another way to deal with conflict among organizations is to eliminate it through domination and incorporation. The development of the nation-state is largely the history of larger and more powerful principalities swallowing up weaker neighbors. Similarly, in public bureaucracies, there is an ever-present tendency to incorporate through expansion. While absorbing units with divergent goals into one organization will not necessarily resolve tensions, it does create a structure of authority for mediating conflicts.

THE DIFFERING ORGANIZATIONAL REALMS OF POLICE AND PROSECUTORS

The literature just reviewed does not constitute a well-developed theory, nor is the fit between interorganizational theory and the criminal justice system perfect. Nevertheless, the discussion provides an opening in which to study a poorly understood and oft-neglected field within the criminal justice system—the synchronization of work relationships between the relatively autonomous organizations of police and prosecutors. Too often the outputs of these two organizations, which ideally will operate in harmony, have been regarded as anomalous and pathological.

Our perspective of interorganizational relationships leads us to a quite different view from that of most students of the criminal process. We decline to view the separate institutions in the criminal justice system as elements of a single organization. Rather, we characterize them as a system comprised of a number of formally autonomous and often antagonistic agencies pursuing their own goals in the face of conflict and *forced* interdependence and interaction.

Specifically, we propose to examine how criminal cases are disposed of in the court system between arrest and conviction. Reports on this "sieve effect" from many different types of jurisdictions—large and small, old and new—all point to a similar phenomenon: roughly 40 to 60 percent of all arrests are disposed of by something other than conviction, and among those convicted many have their charges reduced. Reformist explanations for this funnel effect focus on either poor police work or poor prosecution—the results of incompetence, overwork or both. Organizational explanations focusing on the courts tend, as we said earlier, to seek explanations in terms of goals displacement among the courtroom work group.

These views have dominated studies of courts for years, as suggested by Felix Frankfurter and Roscoe Pound in the conclusion to their pioneering study of the administration of criminal justice in Cleveland in the 1920s: "A high percentage of cases which fail at various stages is an indication of something wrong in earlier stages" (Pound and Frankfurter, 1968, [1922]:290–292).[2] In a 1977 study of the Washington, D.C., police department researchers asked, "Assuming that it is generally undesirable for the police to arrest a person and for the prosecutor or the court to drop all charges, what can the police do to decrease the rate at which persons arrested are not convicted?" (Promis Research Project, 1977:2).[3] With this question as their guide, they sought to account for differences in conviction rates among officers and to suggest means for improving the police-officers' abilities to obtain names of witnesses, gather evidence, prepare testimony, and make quick and speedy arrests. In fact, according to this study, the quality of the police officer can be determined by these aspects of his or her work:

> It seems reasonable to expect that an officer who is prudent in his exercise of arrest discretion and conscientious about recovering evidence, securing good witnesses, and in general supporting the prosecution of his arrests will have a higher conviction rate for his arrests than an officer who is less prudent and conscientious (Promis Research Project, 1977:48).

More scholarly studies of criminal courts grounded in organization theory have a different explanation, but still tend to regard "drop out" as pathological, the result of goal displacement due to organizational pressures to cope with pressing case loads, self-interest of the courtroom work group, and the like. It is for this reason, we think, that court studies focus primarily on the institution of plea bargaining, and generally give short shrift to the even less visible discretionary practice of prosecutors to drop cases outright.

Few court studies systematically consider both police and prosecutor practices and the interdependencies between these two institutions when trying to account for case dispositions. While organization theory focuses on the concerns generated within the courtroom work group to account for these dispositions, interorganization theory suggests another complementary explanation: they are the result of the interaction of two relatively autonomous institutions with diverging interests. Below, we outline some of these divergences as they pertain to arrest.[4]

Police

Any view that suggests that all or even most arrests should result in convictions needs to first examine the assumption that arrests that fall short of conviction represent a setback for the police or that the successful policeman—according to standards set by the police—makes the most arrests. A preliminary step is to distinguish between the police functions of crime control and order maintenance. While obviously connected, the two activities are conceptually distinct, have different historical antecedents, and are often in direct conflict with one another. Crime control, as we use the term, involves (although it is not limited to) a conscious effort to deter criminal acts and to apprehend law-breakers. It constitutes only a fraction of the time expanded by most police officers. Order maintenance relates to general patrolling activities, often collapsed under the rubric of community relations, and reactive intervention in conflict situations— potential or actual—that pose the possibility of exploding into more serious conduct. The latter function is only loosely connected to the concerns of the courts, while the former is squarely within their orbit.

Order maintenance has long been recognized as a major function of the police (cf. Bittner, 1973), and although it can be pursued vigorously without the need to apprehend citizens, arrest is not inconsistent with the pursuit of these goals. A great many cases are resolved by arrest itself, and when they are, police may not be particularly concerned with subsequent judicial reaction. Court appearances may be regarded by all involved—police, prosecutors, accused, and victim—as something of a bookkeeping ritual with little actual significance of its own, even if the symbols of "legality" may have to be acknowledged in order to legitimize the activity of officials (Balbus, 1973; Feeley, 1979b). In addition, the police possess *de facto* judicial powers and can apply sanctions in their own right. Their power to arrest, detain, set charges, and recommend bail means, in effect, that they can charge, adjudicate, and sentence in an unofficial but very effective fashion. This is particularly true for petty offenses, in which the process itself is often the punishment, but it also applies to more serious incidents as well. Arrest and charge trigger a host of sanctions even if the case is eventually dismissed. Thus, it is ironic that the American police, who explicitly have been denied adjudicatory functions, are in practice able to exercise more adjudicatory functions than many of their European counterparts who have been granted limited adjudicatory powers (cf. Miller, 1977).

When the police arrest an apartment resident who is drunk in response to a neighbor's late-night complaint, there is—in their view—little value in pursuing a court prosecution. The arrest itself immediately resolves the potentially explosive situation. Indeed, an effort to obtain evidence or pursue the necessary steps to obtain a conviction might very well detract from the effort to re-establish order. The community, in the police officer's mind, desires some official response but probably is not sufficiently concerned to pursue the matter beyond arrest. Likewise, in incidents of domestic violence, a spouse may insist upon arrest at the time of the disturbance but may not wish to pursue prosecution afterward for a host of reasons. If the police refuse to make arrests under these circumstances because they believe that prosecution would not ensue or be successful, their order maintenance function would be hampered.

The Vera Institute's study, *Felony Arrests* (1981; cf. Richardson, 1970), makes it abundantly clear that this type of situational justice applies to more serious cases as well. It found that a great many accused felons—in cases involving robberies, assaults, burglaries—knew their victims personally, and were often related to them. The Vera researchers found that, despite strength of evidence, neither the police nor the courts usually regarded these cases as "real" felonies. While the behavior led to arrests, officials had few incentives to invest time and energy in "making" strong cases. Still, arrest and court appearances were perceived as useful by police and prosecutors, even when they led to nolles, dismissals, or pleas of guilty to drastically reduced charges. Officials felt that arrest temporarily separated parties who, if unapprehended, might have escalated their dispute and often taught the disputants "a lesson." In other cases, intervention led to the return of "borrowed" property, payment for destroyed items, and the like—all important aspects of order maintenance functions and situational justice by the police.[5]

In other cases, the police may make illegal arrests to seize narcotics and weapons knowing that the arrests cannot withstand judicial scrutiny, but here seizure should not always be seen as a waste of their efforts. It can be an end in itself, since regardless of outcome, the police retain the contraband and have imposed some situational sanctioning. Similarly, police continue to make illegal arrests of drunks and prostitutes in response to community pressure to remove undesirables from an area. Improper arrests of protesters and picketers are often undertaken for similar reasons. Illegal activity by law enforcement officials against Black Panthers, leftists, and anti-war activities was often unconnected to any hopes of successful prosecution in court, and indeed may even have been spurred precisely because of this (Donner, 1980). The power to arrest also provides police an opportunity to question individuals who might have knowledge of criminal activity. In short, arrest not leading to conviction can serve a number of valued police functions. The leverage of arrest is an important coercive tool in the police armory, whether or not it leads to conviction.

The discrepancy between arrest and conviction rates is not a recent phenomenon, the result of a judiciary more solicitous of the rights of the accused or of a court staggering under unprecedented heavy case loads. In 1866, the New York Police Commissioner pointed out that two-thirds of the defendants arrested and charged with murder, arson, burglary, robbery, and receiving stolen goods were not convicted (Miller, 1977:96). The frustration that the New York police may have experienced with the courts would have been reciprocated. James Richardson reports that in New York in the 1890s, "police often made arrests on suspicion (of theft) without supporting evidence, and after they had the suspect locked up they went out to make a case" (1970:194). At that time, the police had the right to discharge people at the station house after making arrests that were weak, a practice which state senatorial investigators found to be subject to frequent abuse. One New York police justice charged that patrol officers "arrogate to themselves the right to construe the law" (Miller, 1977:71).

From this perspective, it is wrong to assume that police who make more arrests and have higher conviction rates are more competent police officers. To the contrary, an officer's proclivity to make an arrest even if it leads to conviction may at times be taken as a sign of incompetence. No police officer can reasonably pursue a policy of apprehending every known violator. Order maintenance remains the paramount goal—only those who pose a major threat to the peace should be arrested. It also meshes with the police officer's desire as a worker to define his or her duties in a restrictive manner. Police who tried to arrest every known offender and sought accompanying evidence would quickly come to be regarded as nuisances and ineffective by their peers and superiors. Frequent arrests might also suggest that the officer lacked "natural" authority or a sense of reasonableness. One study revealed that police who resolved conflict situations with an arrest often did so only because they were unable to successfully impress youths with their authority by other means (Piliavin and Werthman, 1967). An arrest is a discretionary act, and will be judged as either appropriate or inappropriate for a great many reasons other than upon strength of evidence.

Indeed, arrest may even threaten to destabilize the existing order in many communities. Because police officers in many communities must contend with countervailing moral and social cohesion, it is frequently necessary to ignore "the law." If police officers intervened in every craps game, every act of public drinking or smoking of marijuana or other violation of the criminal statutes, the order of society would be turned into bedlam. Even if the law enforcement function of the police would receive a boost by enforcing the law to the letter, the legitimation function of the police would be irreparably damaged. Bardach and Kagan (1982) report the antipathy and ineffectiveness generated by letter-of-the law inspectors in regulated industries, and we can hypothesize similar responses to efforts to strictly enforce criminal law. An observation on the criminal process in England is apropos of the United States: "The more resources allocated to increasing the efficiency of repressive policing, the more manpower has to be poured into 'community relations' to restabilize the public image of the force" (Cohen, 1979:133).

In still other situations, arrest represents a diversion from the monotonous and time-consuming task of order maintenance. One recent study of police work revealed that British police often legitimize their activities in their own eyes by actively seeking out incidents for arrest. The act of arresting an individual convinced them that they were in fact involved in "real work," rather than in simply humdrum activity:

> For all the men, however, the "event," the prisoner caught in the act or, more commonly, the street brawl, assumed an overriding importance, because these things broke into the dull routine and also because the men had no other clearly defined role as the county men had. These events told them who they were. They became their justification and "raison d'etre." Thus a good pitch to work was one on which crime and fights were frequent (Cain, 1973:65).

However, chase and arrest represent brief interludes in the day-to-day activities of the policeman. The norm is unbroken periods of uneventful patrolling and devising schemes to ward off boredom and work fatigue. The average New York City police officer over the course of a year makes one arrest a month, and only three or four of these are for serious criminal acts (Bittner, 1974:25). Nor is the police officer often responding to reports of criminal activity. As several (Reiss, 1971; Bittner, 1973; Goldstein, 1977) have noted, the vast majority of citizen calls to the police are of a noncriminal nature. Police are involved in aiding in emergency situations, crowd control, resolving minor conflicts on the street, responding to domestic disputes, controlling noise and other nuisances in the community, checking the security of businesses and homes, maintaining high visibility, and a myriad of other functions, which run from delivering babies to brokering landlord–tenant disputes. An officer on New York's polyglot upper west side, in a rare moment of candor, reflected this reality of order maintenance: "We've even changed our name. We're no longer called the police force, but the police service. You have to be more of a diplomat now than a tough guy" (New York Times, 1979:81). Such an attitude is not uncommon among police in Western Europe. Those police reportedly emphasize their general service functions and activities not related to law enforcement, and in many instances think of themselves as social workers (Berkeley, 1969). Actually, the concept of social service work was once prevalent among the American police. Roger Lane writes of this in his report on the Boston police in the 1870s: "For many citizens, the most popular function of the department was the service of free soup in the station house (shoes, coal and medicine were also distributed). Supporters agreed that the police who moved daily among the poor were best qualified to determine who was 'worthy'" (1967:199). With the increasing division of labor, sewer, health, street, and building departments have assumed many of the noncriminal-related tasks of the police. The diminution of these police functions corresponds to the increase in the use of police for crime control.

Today, few police officers who enter the force have the intention of being auxiliary social workers or samaritans. It is no surprise then that domestic disputes and other noncrime-related work are often cited as reasons for demoralization (Reiner, 1978b:176–177). While the reality of the police officer's daily work is still composed of the enforced idleness of routine and passive preventive patrol and social service work, the ideology of professionalization rarely acknowledges it. August Volmer, former police chief and academic spokesman for increased police professionalism, worrried that the domestic dispute "may encroach seriously upon the time at the disposal of the police. Real police work is crime prevention and control, not keeping the peace" (1936:155–156).

While police may positively juxtapose catching criminals to pejorative social work functions, they express little interest in undertaking the necessary effort to assure a conviction. Police officers find the numerous reports and forms they must fill out to satisfy the court unpleasant tasks, which deter them from their real work of catching criminals. So, unless they perceive the violation as a threatening one, and the arrestee as a serious offender, they may not see the need to be diligent in "making" the case.[6] Indeed, the various technical functions that the police must comply with in order to prove the case also serve as an internal means of controlling and supervising the police officer's day. The log book that must be faithfully completed, the various incident reports that should be filed, the reports radioed into the central command to inform them of the patrol's location—each act serves both to document a criminal charge and diminish one of the few pleasures of the job, the freedom from supervision.[7]

There are still other factors that lead to the irony that good police work may contribute to weak cases for prosecutors. Police sometimes view the evidentiary requirements imposed by the courts as unworkable. At the scene of an incident their primary task is to apprehend the suspect as quickly and as safely as possible and to defuse the likelihood of a more violent situation. Furthermore, police experience with the courts encourages the view that evidence or "quality of evidence" is of secondary importance in obtaining convictions. In most urban courts, nearly 90 percent of all convictions are obtained through guilty pleas. While the strength of the evidence is certainly considered by prosecutors and defense counsel, it is usually only considered in the abstract, and *not* actually tested. The prevalence of plea bargaining and the near absence of trials discourage both prosecutor and defense counsel from carefully reviewing each arrest. Likewise, the police officer can be certain that in the typical arrest he or she will not have to have his or her testimony scrutinized by cross-examination, nor be forced to bring witnesses or complainants to court. The arresting officer can be quite certain that the court outcome will be strongly influenced by the arresting officer's complaint or by his or her initial testimony at a preliminary hearing or to a grand jury. A demonstration of probable cause—that, in fact, a crime was committed and that the individual arrested committed it—is therefore often sufficient to achieve a plea of guilty. Under such circumstances, the gathering of additional evidentiary material against the defendant is often seen as superfluous. In fact, in New York City, it is not uncommon for a police officer who did not actually make the arrest to testify in a preliminary hearing or swear out the criminal complaint as a favor to another officer who might have other matters to attend to. In the event that a case proceeds to trial or formal pretrial discovery, documents and cross-examination might reveal discrepancies and result in a dismissal or acquittal, but such events are highly unlikely. Thus, much seemingly dysfunctional police work may appear to be an adaptation to the normal operations of the court. Although jury trials often reveal these police practices, in the police officer's day-to-day work experience the jury trial is the rare exception, and is thus *not* a significant factor in shaping standard practices. Indeed, the likelihood of conviction decreases in some situations as *more* information is supplied by the arresting officer. Witnesses are notoriously unreliable, and supplying the names and addresses of a number of witnesses may invite easy challenge and a refutation of the story recounted by the arresting officer. Sometimes good police work may lead to *not* supplying the names and addresses of witnesses and instead just telling a simple story.

Thus, many arrests only appear to be bad if the criterion is black letter law, but black letter law is not a particularly relevant concern to the police. This is not to deny its importance to the prosecutor, who must operate in an atmosphere of legal formality. The difference between good police and prosecutorial work represents a conflict of organizational standards and needs. What appear to be bad arrests further along the road are often good arrests as determined by the operating norms and concerns of police departments; they are not mistakes but the result of conscious, although informal and often unarticulated, policies for some of the reasons we have suggested above.

Nolles and charge reductions also reflect the fact that two different bureaucracies are responsible for the enforcement and adjudication of the law. If the prosecution drops a case or demonstrates leniency, should it alert the arresting officer about the quality of the case or about the honesty or dishonesty of the district attorney? The rule of law based on legal standards of argument is as apt to give way to the personal discretion of the prosecutor as to the police officer. Thus, when prosecutors fail to pursue cases they often do not send a clear signal to the police; instead of fostering future cooperation they engender conflict and frustration.

Admittedly, police do commit grievous errors that result in clearly unintended acquittals and dismissals. Evidence is destroyed, lost, or mishandled, names and addresses of key witnesses are not taken, proper records are not made, poorly prepared testimony is provided. This we do not deny, but what we wish to emphasize is that the "gap" between the numbers arrested and the numbers convicted, or the "convictability quotient" proposed by INSLAW (Institute for Law and Social Research), is in no way a meaningful measure of these "errors."

Prosecutors

Prosecutors are part of the same state apparatus as the police, but they are influenced by very different goals, pressures, and expectations, which are in turn reinforced by differences of social background, education, and career aspirations. Much of this social and class distance, Allen Silver (1967) argues, was created purposely to gain acceptance for law enforcement among the working classes. Drawing police from a social class different from the one prosecutors are drawn from gave the appearance of a separation of constitutional authority from social and economic dominance. Thus, the police could be seen as a force representing communal interests embodied in the rule of law, and, while police and prosecutors must work together and in theory are part of a team, they exist in a perpetual tension created by differences in perceived functions, reinforced by a host of organizational and social pressures.

For the police, arrest often means an end to a problem—restoration of order, reassertion of authority, administration of summary justice. For the prosecutor it is only a beginning. Unlike the police officer who rarely faces institutionalized opposition in the discretionary decision to arrest (there are, of course, important exceptions), in making a *case* the prosecutor must conform his decisions to the confines of the "law," although he or she too has almost unlimited discretion not to prosecute and to reduce charges. Our point here, however, is that if a prosecutor chooses to make a case, he or she must contend with "the law," and often a defense attorney who seeks to limit if not obstruct many of his or her goals. While trials are rare events, they nevertheless represent a potent weapon in the hands of defendants who can threaten to use them and, in so doing, narrow the range of alternatives for the prosecutor. Negotiations take place in the shadow of the law, and the prosecutor who fails to recognize this rigidity in plea bargaining faces the possibility of an embarrassing loss in pretrial motions and the threat of long, time-consuming jury trials, which may result in acquittal and a public proclamation of total defeat. A conviction obtained through a guilty plea, no matter how great the concession, avoids this possibility, and in the process provides public validation of both the police officer's and the prosecutor's actions. Furthermore, frequently publicized failures to secure convictions are likely to lead to complaints of "lawlessness," allegations of disrespect, and charges of harassment in ways that do not occur with or at least are not taken as seriously as the less visible actions of the police.

Because of these considerations, the prosecutor's strategy is not so much to maximize numbers of convictions as it is to *avoid losing*. Outright *nolles*, adjournments in contemplation of dismissals, and guilty pleas to lesser charges all serve this aim quite well. The practices of dismissing charges and plea bargaining also serve to reinforce a smooth functioning relationship with judges and defense attorneys. Judges view those prosecutors who are unwilling to dismiss weak cases or accept pleas of guilty to lesser charges as overly rigid, and see such "inflexibility" as impeding the important goal of efficient case disposition. Court calendars become backed up and serious cases lose priority to trivial ones. Prosecutors who do not recognize this reality are often faced with the wrath of judges, and important cases worthy of all-out combat may suffer because of misplaced emphasis on less important matters.

In large urban criminal courts, good rapport with defense attorneys, particularly large and well-organized public defender offices, are critical in accomplishing the long-term goals of prosecution. If the prosecutor is too willing to accede to police pressures to prosecute exaggerated or unsubstantiated charges, he or she faces numerous forms of resistance from the organized defense bar, which will intensify the difficulty of his or her job. As professional standards of what constitutes a legitimate criminal charge are increasingly adopted by both district attorneys and public defenders, police officers' wishes for rough justice can only be viewed as clear violations of the legal rules accepted by courtroom work groups. The increased professionalization of the courthouse actors, and the shared understanding of acceptable outcomes among judge, public defender, and prosecutor have led to a diminished role for the police officer in the courtroom. Attempts to extend it only weaken the cooperative bonds established in the courtroom. Whether or not the prosecutor is actually committed to the legal ethos, evidentiary standards and the claim of due process provide him or her with a rationale to refuse to prosecute or reduce charges. There are, of course, prosecutors who see themselves as an extension of the police department, but as prosecutors' offices become more professional and establish themselves as more autonomous organizations, this tendency will decline (cf. Utz, 1978:42).

Career and professional aspirations of prosecutors also militate against adopting an uncompromising stance in disposing of criminal cases. Prosecutors and public defenders usually share similar social backgrounds (Platt and Pollack, 1974; Fishman, 1979). Attorneys from both organizations are usually young and come from the same local law schools. As "criminal lawyers," both defenders and prosecutors share the same disfavored status in the hierarchy of the larger legal community. Since a permanent career in either prosecution or public defense is rarely anticipated, attorneys in both organizations seek to prepare themselves for legal careers in other fields, usually in business-related law. The importance of establishing conciliatory relationships in commercial law is even more highly valued than in criminal law. Even if a prosecutor aspires to a career in criminal law as a judge or chief prosecutor, he or she will do little to advance if he or she establishes a reputation for being overly committed to vigorous prosecution. Talent as an administrator or manager becomes as important as success in combatting crime.

Police, on the other hand, usually remain police officers. Furthermore, there is little mobility within the department. At best, police officers must compete for largely lateral promotions with other officers. In contrast, prosecutors often seek to gain names for themselves in the larger legal community, not just within their organization.

Finally, there are important organizational differences between police departments and prosecutors' offices. Students of American police forces have attributed the relatively unrestrained power of the police to the fact that the prosecutor was democratically elected (Richardson, 1970; Miller, 1977). Thus, unlike the English police who have long been subject to tight discipline within the force and the watchfulness of external agencies, the American police have had to contend only with the guidelines of tradition, court reversal in individual cases, and the decisions of the prosecutor.

In addition to the organizational differences, the form of labor control within the organizations is vastly different. Police departments are hierarchical, bordering on the military model of chain command. Patrol officers have little ability to influence policy decisions. Prosecutors' offices, infused with the ideology of professionalism and the limited form of egalitarianism it cultivates, allow even assistant district attorneys considerable influence in shaping decisions. However, while the police officer does not have the same opportunities to affect policy, he or she has much greater freedom to make independent decisions. The assistant prosecutor usually must follow official guidelines on plea bargaining and case dismissals. Each act of a prosecutor is a matter of formal record that creates a history of his or her activities and constrains his or her decisions. In contrast, the police officer on the beat operates without benefit of a stenographer or court clerk. The officer is comparatively free to disregard the rules and regulations established by superiors that he or she feels are cumbersome. When charges presented by the police are not honored by the prosecutor, it is rarely viewed as a failure by either agency but rather as an expression of these different organizational characteristics.

Diverging Goals

This brief discussion has identified a number of important differences between the functions of police and prosecutors, and has suggested that these two institutions are organized to pursue different and often divergent goals. The dominant concern of the police in connection with an arrest is typically *order maintenance*. As such, arrest is only an incidental, although effective, device for its pursuit. Arrests resulting in conviction are in most cases not of paramount concern in the midst of maintaining order on the street. Furthermore, formal and informal organizational notions of what constitutes acceptable police work do not place a high priority on making convictable arrests; indeed, arrest is often seen as serving additional and more important functions other than conviction. Good police work is frequently defined in terms of internal departmental standards: good attendance, good health, sociability, high arrest and ticket rates. Police officers are thus often not terribly concerned with what outsiders, like judges and prosecutors, may think of them. This is not to say that the police do not want convictions, but only that in a great many situations, assuring convictions is not a high priority to the arresting officer who makes street arrests.

In contrast, the daily work of the prosecutor does not involve him or her directly with order maintenance. Prosecutors are faced with the formality of an "autonomous" legal system, and often confronted with adversaries who are seeking to exploit this. Thus, whatever sympathies the prosecutors harbor for the police, they are confronted with the task of dealing with cases in the refined language of law, not the concerns of order maintenance.[8]

This divergence of organizational goals is reinforced by social distance, career aspirations, and the lack of formal connection between the two organizations. Egon Bittner is not far off the mark when he asserts that police are institutionally independent, controlled neither by the courts nor prosecutors (1973:31–35). The police pursue their agenda irrespective of the directives of the courts. The courts can prescribe the standards for making arrests but ultimately are dependent upon the police to implement them. In contrast, the close proximity, shared power, and need for joint action binds prosecutors, defense attorneys, and judges in ways that limit the power of each and forces them to seriously consider the interests of one another, generate some shared control, and honor the norms of legality. Good prosecution requires this last factor to be considered in ways rarely confronted by the police, who tend to regard legality as a technicality, and by no means as an essential ingredient to good police work.

BRIDGING RELATIONS BETWEEN POLICE AND PROSECUTORS: IMPLICATIONS FOR RESEARCH

Despite differences between police and prosecution, the two organizations do not and cannot reach a state of total breakdown. Legal obligations and structural constraints require a minimum of cooperation even in the face of estrangement. Community support for both organizations would quickly evaporate if there were not visible efforts to cooperate. Thus, the need for mutual understanding, accommodation, and cooperation remains intact even as the two units pursue separate and divergent goals.

Earlier we identified five ways institutions with divergent goals can seek to ameliorate conflict and pursue cooperation. These conflict-reduction and conflict-control devices are the development of exchange relationships, mutual acceptance of conflict-resolution institutions, the adoption of coordinating mechanisms, the emergence of informal boundary-spanning institutions, and institutional imperialism by more powerful organizations. At least three of these types of arrangements are frequently present in police–prosecutor relations, and serve to mediate and moderate institutional differences between them. A variation of the latter is occasionally proffered by reformers who want to promote greater coherence and authority in what they regard as an overly chaotic criminal justice system. Consideration of these types of factors will, we think, lead to more insightful examination of how and why cases are disposed of by criminal courts, and more generally will explore a hitherto neglected area—how police and courts change and make adjustments to each other's organizations.[9]

Exchange is most likely to explain cooperative behavior when that activity involves voluntary behavior and joint decision making, neither of which characterizes the preponderance of police–prosecutor relations. Here the connections are mandated by law, and decision making is independent and sequential rather than joint. Still, a variety of reciprocal relationships have sprung up and function to moderate and manage these differences (Cole, 1970). Even the prosecutors' offices that are most independent of police departments are extremely careful to avoid public actions that appear to challenge or tarnish the image of the police. If a prosecutor finds a police officer's story inherently unbelievable, rarely will he or she say so in open court. Rather, he or she will dispose of the case in a form that does not require judicial approval or detailed explanations.

The prosecutor is spared from having to question the officer's veracity in public, while at the same time drawing out a tacit admission of wrong-doing by the accused and thus symbolically legitimizing the police officer's activity.[10] Furthermore, prosecutors always possess the ultimate power of charging police officers for criminal infractions, a tool they rarely employ.[11]

In turn, police officers accept the constraints of the prosecutors' obligation to due process, and do not openly criticize them for it. While the police must bend to the strictures of black letter law, which prosecu-tors must honor, they also know where prosecutorial discretion can be exercised and are knowledgeable about the ways in which it can be used extra-legally to effect their conceptions of rough justice. Police are often highly successful in pressuring both judges and prosecutors into using the ambiguous bail procedure to achieve ends consistent with the police view, thereby contributing to the police concern with order maintenance (e.g., keeping an irritating person off the streets temporarily) and in applying a type of instant sanctioning of their own. The prevalence of this is sug-gested by widespread recent efforts to change the bail setting process into an "objective" decision, thereby diminishing the possibility of prosecutor and judicial discretion to respond to these pressures. The occasional re-sponse by police to those court officials who do not play by their rules in setting bail (e.g., the case of Judge ["Turn 'em Loose"] Bruce Wright in New York City) is evidence of their power in this area.

Because prosecutors are the dominant members of the police–court transaction, they often attempt to make the police feel a part of the legal process by soliciting officers' advice about the appropriate plea or sen-tence. Prosecutors will often treat police as their clients, meeting and chatting with them about the progression of the case. The frequency and intensity of these approaches is contingent upon some of the following factors: the strength of professional models in the office; the social separation between officer and prosecutor; the commitment to a due pro-cess versus crime control mode; and political relationships between the two agencies. Prior to the acceptance of a plea of guilty, the prosecutor may confer with the arresting officer to see if the arrangements meet with his or her approval. This usually represents more of a gesture than a serious invitation to interfere with the equilibrium of the court, but it does serve to foster good relations. Prosecutors who feel particularly sensitive to maintaining good relations with the police may occasionally even place themselves on record as being opposed to an accord or sentence dis-approved of by the police. This may take the form of an aggressive argu-ment before the judge in order to convince the officer of the prosecutor's sincerity. At times, prosecutors will send weak cases to grand juries or take them into court, practices which transfer the responsibility to others— the grand jury, a superior, or a judge—for dismissing cases. In doing this, prosecutors do not endanger their own personal relationships with the officer insistent on pressing the case.

A great variety of *coordinating* institutions have grown up between the police and prosecutors. They are not so much designed to change the practices of either organization as to effect a smooth transmission of information from one organization to another. Both institutions, for example, have a division of labor that assigns to some of their members the task of translating police arrests into terms useful to the prosecutor. Sometimes detectives perform this function for the police, or initial screenings may be left to prosecutors. W. Boyd Littrell in his study of police–prosecutor relations in a New Jersey court describes how detective bureaus, by transposing police cases into prosecution cases, gain control over final court dispositions (1979:chaps. 4, 6). Some prosecutors' offices deploy prosecutors to supervise booking and charging in the station house itself, whereas others screen cases at a later date in their own offices. However arranged, the purpose is to begin to translate cases from arrests for police purposes to cases for prosecutors, weeding out bad arrests and organizing the strong ones. Almost invariably, those who perform these tasks are placed in positions under competing pressures and loyalties. Detectives assigned to review arrests and specify charges before forwarding them for further consideration by the prosecutor are at times under pressure by their colleagues to treat weak cases seriously. Conversely, prosecutors dealing with police on similar matters also find themselves under pressure by the police to pass along weak cases or to insist on rigorous presentation of those defendants disliked by the police. Thus, prosecutors in the complaint room of criminal court are more easily swayed by police than those at the trial stage. Although the police officers exerting the pressure usually know when they have a weak case, they are often intent on using the legal process for punitive purposes even though dismissal may eventually result. Not surprisingly, police resist prosecutors' moves to establish "early case assessment bureaus," the purpose of which is to weed out weak cases as quickly as possible.[12] Such efforts fail to appreciate many of the functions of arrest from the police perspective.

The incongruence between police and prosecutorial goals is also revealed indirectly in the many recent moves and proposals to assure better communication between the two organizations. Recent years have witnessed a proliferation of coordinating councils whose purpose is to bring the separate components of the criminal justice system together to explore mutual concerns. The growing tendency to appoint police administrators from outside rather than from those who "rose through the ranks" is another example of trying to match the needs of organizational maintenance with legal procedural norms. Of course, this creates new tensions within the police force. This problem is nicely described in a passage from a novel about the English force in the 1960s, written by a rank-and-file police officer:

> ... it was as though there were two police forces. One was real, the one which caught criminals and the other one was the one that existed in some high-up's office in the Yard. The real police force was there to catch criminals the best way it knew how; and if you couldn't get them down according to Judges Rules, you got them down in your own way. The real police force worked in and around police stations; the real police force *worked*.
>
> The other one was the one the Press wrote about, the one the taxpayers believed in. It was full of unsung heroes with blue eyes and honest English faces ... *that* police force helped old ladies across the road, in between spells of taking finger prints and running four-minute miles. That police force gave you a pain in the arse. Not only didn't it exist, it *couldn't*. If it did, the prisons would be empty. And the senior officers knew all about the real police force ... But for some reason, once you got up that end of the ladder you started forgetting what it was like. Police duty as it was done became a dirty word. And let some poor sod get caught out in something—whether it was a bit of exaggeration in a magistrate's court, or laying someone else's old woman— and they all raised their clean little hands in horror. "But this is terrible," they would say, their own dirty skeletons locked out of sight, "to think a policeman could do a thing like this." When what they really meant was, "Some bloody reporter's going to get hold of this and splash it on the front page." (Brock, 1968)

The creation of *boundary-spanning* institutions to bridge separate agencies is another device designed to accomplish greater articulation of functions between police and the courts. While there are a host of formal arrangements (e.g., the deputy mayor for criminal justice in New York City, coordinating councils practically everywhere) designed to mediate and moderate the differences between police and prosecutors, it may be informal arrangements that have emerged as by-products of other concerns that are most effective in moderating differences and managing conflict. Political culture and political organizations clearly serve such functions. Culture provides and promotes a shared sense of substantive justice or morality among the various and disparate officials in the criminal justice system; and the organizations nourish a common loyalty among separate agencies that can moderate and broker differences.

James Q. Wilson (1968) and Martin Levin (1977) have both produced important studies that convincingly detail the connection between a community's political culture and organizations and its institutions of criminal justice. Both show that traditional, machine-dominated political communities tend to produce "traditional" police (Wilson) and traditional bargain-oriented courts (Levin), whereas "progressive," good-government communities dominated by "reform" politics rather than ethnic machines tend to produce "professional" and legalistic criminal justice institutions. Traditional institutions are characterized by particularism, bargaining, and a belief in "rough justice," whereas "professional" institutions are characterized by adherence to "legalistic" rountines, universalism, and "due process."

Surprisingly, neither Wilson, Levin, nor anyone else has sought to examine *both* police and courts in the same set of communities to determine if their findings for one institution (either police or courts) characterized all the criminal justice agencies. Given the nature of their arguments, we would expect that this would be the case. If so, then the political culture would tend to moderate in important ways differences in orientations between the police and courts. A community producing a "traditional" police force is likely to produce a "traditional" court system as well, and a community with a "professional" court system is likely to also have a "professional" police department, thereby minimizing the likelihood of the disjuncture between the two institutions.

More specifically, political organizations may serve, in effect, as "sponsoring institutions," which can coordinate practices and mediate differences between conflicting organizations. Although in the United States neither are subject to the direct formal control of the same political authority, as they are in some inquisitorial systems, differences between police and prosecutors may be managed through informal political authority. Such an informal authority is not likely to eliminate or significantly reduce basic differences between these institutions, but it may serve to mediate and contain institutional feuds and to reduce the likelihood that disagreements over policy will pop up in the newspapers. It may also increase the likelihood of recruiting like-minded people for both police and courtroom positions. Certainly the history of law enforcement seems to indicate that when there is a discrepancy between police authority and political power, pressures are slowly generated to force the former into conformity with the larger political system (Bayley, 1976).

Organizational Imperialism

The continued tension between police and prosecutors has led some to suggest that the two agencies be integrated. One proposal, inspired by the continental model, has been to place police under the direct supervision of prosecutors (Weinreb, 1977). This approach seeks to resolve the tensions between the two groups by making police subordinate to prosecutors. Understandably, it has been resisted by the police. Still, while not official policy in any jurisdiction, it has gained informal recognition in some jurisdictions from time to time. Some U.S. attorneys have actively sought to exercise control over the FBI and to employ them as investigators for their offices and their priorities. Elsewhere, it has become common practice to loan detectives to prosecutors' offices for investigative and case review purposes. However, the continued existence of two separate organizations—police and prosecutors—is likely to forestall any major shift to the European model of direct prosecutorial control.

IMPLICATIONS FOR FUTURE RESEARCH

The aim of this paper has been to explore differences between the organizational interests of police and prosecutors. We have argued that the institutional objectives of the police and prosecutors force the two organizations to regard the nature and function of arrest quite differently. Furthermore, it is crucial to examine how the police view and structure arrests if one is to understand how these arrests are subsequently handled in the courts. The initial police characterization of a case in many instances determines its outcome in the courts. Nevertheless, our review of the literature on both the police and the courts has revealed that rarely is there a focus on how these police practices affect the courts, and examinations of the courts rarely address the role of the police in shaping case outcomes. On the one hand, this silence reinforces our argument that the two institutions are relatively independent of each other; yet on the other, the silence reveals a failure to show how these two institutions affect each other.

The failure to investigate the relations of the police and prosecutors and to analyze how arrests are or are not made into cases gives rise to exaggerated expectations and misunderstandings. We have already suggested, for instance, that it can lead to the belief that the purpose of arrest is conviction. We feel that focusing more closely on the interdependencies and interactions of these two organizations will lead to a fuller understanding of how they perform their own autonomous goals and affect each others' actions. Let us close out discussion with some specific illustrations.

Discussions of the process of case disposition in criminal courts often emphasize the organizational goals and interests of the participants, showing the various ways these goals displace the more formal concerns of their offices. Surprisingly, little attention has been directed to how (and why) the police shape these decisions. Although "police over-charging" is often identified, systematic investigation of the police role in transforming an arrest into a case is missing. As a consequence, dismissals and charge reductions are often explained in terms of the interests of the courtroom participants, with police over-charging or carelessness offered as unexamined residual explanations. In fact, they may be due to clues, information, or lack thereof provided by the police. What is needed is careful study to distinguish between functional and purposeful carelessness on one hand and unintended error on the other. We also need to know what the officer expects and wants when he or she takes a suspect into custody; that intent may be a signal of how the case is characterized ("made") and what will happen at the later stages of the criminal process. We have excellent descriptive studies of decisions whether or not to take a suspect into custody. Each has revealed that a host of extra-legal factors come into play. What we need now is a set of parallel studies detailing *how* a suspect is taken into custody, and for what purposes. Such an inquiry would go a long way toward clarifying the nature of the sieve effect. Stated another way, what happens to the accused in court may be determined in large measure by what it is that the police want to happen and how they "make" their cases. Such factors will be systematically ignored as long as the current division of labor in research enterprises continues. Those focusing on the incentives of court officials are likely to find answers within the courtroom work group and to ignore the importance of the police. Similarly, those who seek to understand the operations of the police without examining them in light of the courts' impact on their activities are likely to overstress intraorganizational factors and ignore interorganizational factors. In extreme situations, the interrelations between the two units are obvious and undeniable (e.g., in making and handling arrests in riot and blackout situations or in highly publicized felony cases), but the same interconnections are also present under more ordinary, although less visible, conditions as well.

While numerous studies acknowledge and briefly examine the connections between police and courts, and some deal with the relation of detectives and prosecutors, few treat the connection between arresting officers and the courts as their central focus. The best empirical investigation of this issue that we know of is the recent book by Ericson and Baranek (1982), who follow the fates of suspects from arrest to adjudication. Their study supports our contention that police and, particularly the arresting officer, order the nature of justice in the courtroom and elsewhere in significant and systematic ways. Ericson and Baranek expand the organizational paradigm that has guided much empirical research on the courts in recent years, and we hope that it will become a model for future research in this area.

A number of others have also produced valuable discussions of this topic. Donald McIntyre (1968, 1975, 1977) has written extensively and coauthored an important study with Lippman (1970) on the subject. McDonald (1982) has surveyed a number of police departments and prosecutors' offices, described the tensions inherent in their relationships, and identified a variety of practices that moderate these tensions. Greenspan (1982) has approached the problem in comparative perspective and contrasted police-prosecutor relationships in Canada, England and the United States.

Another implication of our proposed interorganizational perspective deals with changes over time in the roles of police and prosecutors. Historically, the evolutionary expansion of the right to counsel and the increased professionalism and legalization of the courts, especially of the lower courts, have meant that the police cannot so easily assume that the courts will back them up in their efforts to render rapid, rough justice. Given the increased procedural formalities of the courts, how have the police responded? How has their use of the courts to help pursue their order maintenance functions and to secure rough justice been altered in light of this? How, for instance, have the police responded to court decisions to routinely dismiss charges against prostitutes and drunks? To what extent have these same behaviors been reclassified to fit more acceptable legal categories?

The relationship and responsiveness of both police and prosecutors to broader political authority is also of interest. If the prosecutor's office and the police department are subservient to the same political constituency, it is likely that operational and policy differences will be minimized or more easily resolvable. However, a prosecutor's office whose political jurisdiction extends beyond that of the various police departments, which funnel cases to it, would be able to operate with greater autonomy from the constraints generated by the law enforcement community. The professional values sustained by the ideology of the law and the requirements of cooperative courtroom relationships would then face fewer obstacles from the police.

This hypothesis is given support in Pamela Utz's (1978) examination of the Alameda County prosecutor's office. The local governments that supported the several police departments were lacking in strength. In contrast, the prosecutor's office enjoyed a county-wide staff and was highly centralized, and throughout the history of the office the chief district attorneys were chosen from within the organization. This broad jurisdiction and sense of continuity served to strengthen the professional elan of the office and increase its resistance to "law-and-order" groups (Utz, 1978:115). This independence in turn permitted it to institute a case-weighting system, which encouraged "under-charging" in nonserious cases and permitted intensive concentration on serious cases. This action was also successful in countering police resistance to "tightened charging" (1978:110). San Francisco, right next door, provided a stark contrast. There the prosecutor's office and the police department were under the direct control of combined city-county government, and whenever the city administration embarked on a campaign against crime, both the prosecutor's office and police department were drafted. Mass arrests by police were followed by prosecutors' adopting "tough and indiscriminate charging, game-like bargaining, and opportunistic adaptations to volume pressure" (1978:114). More generally, Utz's provocative study suggests the value of comparative and historical studies that trace different ways police and prosecutors cope with charges in each other's policies.

CONCLUSIONS

During the past few years, organization theory has become the dominant model for guiding research on criminal courts. We do not dispute the value of this approach. Although organization theory has never been systematically applied and tested, nevertheless, it has served to structure investigations and to sensitize researchers to nonobvious issues. It has led researchers to explore how seeming adversaries become well-integrated work groups, how apparent inefficiencies serve useful functions, how self-interest and institutional concerns foster goal displacement, how standard operating procedures emerge. In so doing, this approach has sought to account for practices in the courthouse in terms of the interests and concerns of the major figures in the courtroom work group—the prosecutor, defense attorney, and judge.

This paper has proposed a modest expansion of this tradition. It has argued for an interorganizational perspective, specifically, one that would prominently include the police in the study of how cases are handled in the courts. Our contention is that the police play a major, although unobtrusive, role in shaping outcomes in the courts. This is most obvious in examining reasons for dismissals, nolles, "no-papering," and the like, but it also affects charge reductions and other decisions. Further, we have argued that the division of labor between police and the courtroom work group—even the prosecutor—yields divergent and conflicting goals. This tension is reinforced by distance in social backgrounds, the salience of legal culture, and other factors. Interorganizational theory explores how organizations with conflicting goals, which still must deal with each other, learn to structure their relationships and to moderate tension and divergent interests. We have reviewed the tension between police and prosecutors' roles, and suggested some of the ways they learn to cope with one another. Our hope is that this review will lead to a greater appreciation of the police role in structuring outcomes in criminal courts and will encourage greater interest in the systematic investigation of the relations between police and prosecutors and the nature of the bridging institutions that emerge to moderate differences between them.

NOTES

1. We also recognize that there are a great many different ways cases get into court. Our primary concern here is with "street arrests." Our discussion is less relevant to arrests made after investigation and issuance of warrants, white collar crimes, juvenile arrests, the work of specialized law enforcement units, and the work of the FBI. While we think that an interorganizational analysis can profitably be used to explore these types of activities as well, here we focus on only one type—the dominant type —of police–prosecutor arrest practices.

2. Compare also Packer, 1968; and Skolar, 1977.

3. One early notable exception to this view is the now classic work by Jerome H. Skolnick, *Justice Without Trial: Law Enforcement in a Democratic Society* (1966). While his work generally accepts the view of police as being essentially crime fighters, he recognizes that arrests in violation of the exclusionary rule that will not result in convictions are not undesirable from the police vantage point. Skolnick writes (p. 224):
Consequently, all these reasons—the norm of police alertness; the requirement that police confiscate illegal substances; the tendency toward a presumption of the legality of the search once the illegal substance is found; the fact that in a "small pinch" the policeman is usually not interested in an arrest but in creating an informant; the fact that the defense will be impressed by the presence of incriminating evidence; the sympathy of police superiors so long as policemen act in conformity with administrative norms of police organization; the difficulty of proving civil suits for false arrest; the denial of fact by the exclusionary rule; and the problematic character of what behavior is permitted when justification may appear to a court to be "uniquely present"—militate against the effectiveness of the exclusionary rule. In short, the norms of the police are fundamentally pragmatic. Since the policeman has everything to gain and little to lose when he uses the "reasonableness of the search and seizure" standard in small cases, he does so, even though this is not the prevailing legal standard.

4. What follows is not intended as an exhaustive catalogue of the interests and activities of these two institutions. Our point is to emphasize the most salient differences between the treatment of arrests by police and prosecutors.

5. That the process is the punishment has a long history in American law enforcement is underscored by this advice of a New York City sergeant to a patrolman in the 1890s: "Now let me tell you something. They may beat you in court, the complainant may not show up, they may jump their bail, politicians may interfere, there are several ways they can beat you, but this [and he pointed to the marks and bruises] they've got, and make no damned mistake about it" (Richardson, 1970:190).

6. For an unusual examination of how police departments have enormous flexibility in "constructing" criminal cases, see Littrell (1979), especially chapters 2 and 3.

7. Considering that police are employees as well as agents of law enforcement, it is unusual how few studies examine them within the sociology of the labor process literature. One notable exception to this lack has been Robert Reiner. He begins with a simple premise: "But before the policeman can be a labeller, peace-keeper, philosopher, guide and friend, he first has to turn up for work" (Reiner, 1978b:167).

8. Here, too, there are exceptions; political trials and urban disorders are only two examples, but these events continue to represent exceptional moments in American criminal justice.

9. There are encouraging signs that this concern is becoming more generally recognized within the past few years. See, for example, work by William

F. McDonald (1982), Richard Ericson and Patricia Baranek (1981), and Rosann Greenspan (1982).

10. A study of police-prosecutor relations in England and Wales reveals the extreme pressure upon prosecutors by police to process even weak cases. According to Sanders, prosecutors do this because "they wish to maintain good relations with the police with whom they have to work" (1980:17).

11. Even if a prosecutor should take this most unusual step, he or she still may choose not to pursue it with enthusiasm. During racial disturbances in Miami it was alleged by some that police officers charged with the murder of a black man were not aggressively prosecuted (Levin, 1980).

12. Stanko (1979:21) demonstrates the tremendous antagonism between prosecutors and police engendered by early case assessment bureaus: "Just before I completed my series of observations, I witnessed a scuffle between a police officer and an A.D.A. (Assistant District Attorney). Both the A.D.A. and the police officer were loudly arguing, which then escalated into pushing and shoving. Although this incident did not result in a physical contest, the discussion ended with both parties squared off. I could not help thinking that perhaps this would be a continuous stance between the police and prosecutorial organizations as well." We would caution, however, against extrapolating from this situation to police-prosecutor relations in general. Skolnick writes of the relationship as being almost nonproblematic: "He [the prosecutor] is perceived in a fashion similar to that in which the captain of a team or a higher military officer would be viewed—possibly will some resentment, but with clear acknowledgment of his right (and duty) to correct errors. At the superior court level the policeman and the district attorney become part of the same team" (1966:202). See also McIntyre (1968), McIntyre and Lippman (1970), and McDonald (1982).

10

Epilogue: Ways to Organize the Study of Courts

Lynn Mather

In the 1960s, trial courts in America were called upon to solve a variety of social and economic problems. The poor, through their newly funded legal service lawyers, began to challenge unfair landlord practices, exploitation by commercial businesses, and arbitrary actions by government bureaucracies. Blacks—and later, other minorities—used new constitutional and statutory law to litigate for equal treatment and an end to discrimination. Crime became a political issue: defendants demanded greater procedural rights, judges began to enforce restrictions on police discretion, and communities (often led by law enforcement officials) expressed their outrage at rising crime rates—and at courts. Given all of this politically important activity occurring in local courts, concern grew for a better understanding of their actual operation. *Task Force Report: The Courts* by the President's Commission on Law Enforcement and Administration of Justice (1967) is an interesting early example of empirical research arising from this concern, which then grew enormously through the support of the Law Enforcement Assistance Administration (LEAA) and in response to specific policy concerns.

At the same time, social scientists began turning their attention to legal processes and institutions with newly developed approaches and methodologies. Political scientists investigated the behaviors and processes involved in appellate court decision making rather than simply reviewing the opinions and doctrines articulated by judges. Studies of *trial* court decision making were the next logical step for political scientists specializing in legal processes. Similarly, the fields of sociology and anthropology saw major efforts toward explaining and analyzing the behaviors of legal officials, litigants, and others interacting with legal institutions. Some scholars of the law *per se* also devoted considerable energy to empirical description and explanation of legal phenomena. Collaborative interdisciplinary research on law was then boosted in the mid-1960s through the formation of the Law and Society Association and the publication of *Law and Society Review*.

With the impetus of both reform and social science, researchers discovered a great deal about courts. The most striking fact was the acknowledgement that—for the vast majority of civil and criminal cases—the traditional model of court as a judge-dominated, formal adversary process of adjudication did not hold. The question then became: How *do* we explain courts once the traditional model has been proved inadequate? The essays in this volume each examine a portion of the empirical research on courts in an effort to develop theoretically based explanations for phenomena observed in courts.

One of the most significant aspects of these essays is the extent to which the authors question the usefulness of a theory of courts, with courts as the key unit of analysis. Indeed, some of the authors so reconceptualize the nature of courts that the hallowed halls in which Perry Mason might argue cases are barely recognizable. Other contributors accept the centrality of courts (as commonly perceived in the United States in our time) and work to refine the concepts and perspectives used to understand them. In view of the title of this volume—*Empirical Theories About Courts*, a phrase penned some years ago—it seems appropriate here to organize my concluding comments on the eight essays according to the implicit direction suggested by each for theory-building about courts. In so doing, I continue a theme suggested in the introduction to this book, and make more explicit the differences and similarities we can expect to see in future theoretical research on courts.

The two essays in Part III most directly address questions about trial courts themselves and their internal processes. Courts are taken as they are conventionally defined in the United States: formal, public, dispute-processing institutions. What needs to be explained then is how these courts accomplish their work. The explanatory concepts and ideas for both essays are found in theories of organizations. Thus, courts are simply interesting examples (with their own peculiar characteristics) of a much wider range of phenomena known as organizations. Some of the explanations and generalizations developed about other organizations can be profitably applied to courts, the authors argue. Herbert Jacob reviews a number of issues within organizational theory and analyzes their applicability to courts. For example, questions about decision making, distribution of power, and patterns of communication are discussed with reference to existing empirical studies of court processes. Jacob points out that it is unfortunate that most of the research has been done on criminal courts and consequently our understanding of the organizational entity of the civil court is still quite limited. The argument Jacob advances is also more persuasive in its examination of individual court systems than it is in providing linkage between the court system and its wider social (not just organizational) environment.

Organizational theory correctly helps us move beyond the judge, as the key decision maker, to include other participants in the courtroom work group. The relation between this work group and another key participant—the police—is clarified in the essay by Malcolm Feeley and Mark Lazerson. Their focus is much narrower than that of Jacob: the interaction of police and prosecutors within the criminal courts. Interorganizational theory provides the perspective and concepts for analyzing the specific interaction of these two legal actors. The argument of the police-prosecutor essay builds nicely on Jacob's discussion of communication patterns within courts in which he asks for more research on how the nature of communication of information affects the outcomes of cases. Feeley and Lazerson focus on the information provided by the arresting officer in the arrest report. This information indicates in part what the police officer *intended* by the arrest. Was the arrest the result of police discretion in an order maintenance situation, or was it intended to lead to full prosecution and, hopefully, conviction? As the literature on police behavior makes quite clear, police operate within their very specific working environment, where multiple meanings and motives can be associated with an arrest. This environment is quite different from that of prosecutors, where arrests are "supposed" to lead to convictions. By comparing the organizational realms of police and prosecutors, examining the empirical studies of case disposition (especially data on case drop-off), and considering the impact of the arrest report on later actions, Feeley and Lazerson argue that the arresting officer's view of the case heavily influences the outcome of many cases in court. Their essay represents a significant broadening of the domain of court study with the suggestion that the police officer may actually play the pivotal role in court disposition.

While Jacob and Feeley and Lazerson help us to organize our thinking about how courts do their work, they offer much less about what it is that courts do. The other essays, however, address that question in various ways. One approach to understanding the nature of court activity is to *count* what goes in and out of courts, and then to compare these various numbers across courts and over time. Empirical research is always vastly easier when quantifiable data are available, and thus the existence of case load data for courts offers a tantalizing opportunity for social scientists. Unfortunately, as Samuel Krislov suggests in his essay, the actual meaning of case load data is often obscure and the results of case load studies to date have been disappointing. Krislov outlines four general theoretical approaches to the study of courts that have used case load data: utilitarian, functional, systems or organizational, and a norm or value approach. He argues that, in each of these approaches, case load data are used as substitutes for other concepts. What is needed is an explicit articulation of what those other concepts are. Another problem with case load data for courts is typically the lack of comparable data (or else the lack of consideration of such data) on cases taken to alternative dispute processing institutions, such as arbitration. The importance of looking at these "by-pass" institutions to explain changes in the litigation rates of courts is emphasized in Lawrence Friedman's essay. Like Krislov, Friedman sees value in these quantitative data, but only if they are used carefully.

Friedman provides a broad historical overview of trends in court activity over the last 100 years or so, focusing primarily on empirical studies of courts in the United States. For example, he describes shifts in the content of tort law doctrine, in the rise of Constitutional law issues (especially in the federal courts), and in the replacement of private prosecution with public enforcement and prosecution for criminal cases. The theoretical concepts are far less distinctly defined in Friedman's essay than they are, for example, in Black and Baumgartner's essay, but Friedman offers a rich and suggestive review of a vast number of historical studies of courts.

The study of courts in other cultures, especially in tribal and village settings, raises a host of important issues about what it is that courts do and what, in fact, defines them as courts. In the beginning of his essay Friedman presents the conventional model of courts and legal evolution in which forms of dispute settlement are associated with levels of social development. Courts, as coercive third party institutions imposing their judgments on litigants, are said to emerge with a certain level of complex social structure. In contrast, Barbara Yngvesson and Lynn Mather reject this tribal/modern paradigm of dispute processing. Their essay reviews some of the literature on which the paradigm is based, in addition to pointing to other critical discussions of the tribal/modern model. They pay particular attention to anthropological studies of dispute processing and of tribal and village social organization. The authors urge greater recognition of the similarities between processes in modern courts and tribal moots.

Having identified a wide range of practices for dispute processing in diverse sociocultural settings, Yngvesson and Mather explain the concept of dispute transformation as a theoretical focus for explaining the role of courts in conflict management. When individuals and groups take their disputes to third parties, the object of the dispute is frequently redefined through the participation and involvement of others. Through these changes—or transformations—in the dispute, significant others (whether friends, witnesses, lawyers, witch-doctors, judges, audiences, etc.) influence the outcome of individual disputes, while simultaneously shaping and reinforcing broader patterns of social order. The process of dispute transformation does not occur in identical ways everywhere, however,

248 / *Epilogue: Ways to Organize the Study of Courts*

and the essay suggests several contextual variables (e.g., involving physical and cultural accessibility) useful for distinguishing dispute processing fora.

Instead of investigating the changes that occur as quarrels are redefined within the dispute processing arena (Yngvesson and Mather), Keith Boyum takes a step further "back," and asks how those quarrels and claims are initially created. Boyum's concern is with the etiology of claims —the precursors to cases in court (or to well-defined disputes brought to other third parties). His essay develops several critical variables to explain the process by which one comes to focus on and define a circumstance that might lead to a claim. These theoretical ideas are then applied to existing empirical studies on legal needs, providing an interesting reinterpretation of data found in them.

Where Boyum focuses on the initial process by which claims emerge, and where Yngvesson and Mather examine changes in the definition of disputes during the process of dispute management, Marc Galanter looks at the influences flowing *outward* from the dispute processing institution. Specifically, he argues for a richer understanding of what courts do through an investigation of the endowments (or bargaining chips) provided by courts and of the general and specific effects of court action. By examining courts in this perspective, Galanter makes explicit the continuity between the conflict resolution (disputing) and social control (regulating) functions performed by courts, a continuity that is also developed through the concept of dispute transformation. Galanter's essay further elaborates the argument against legal centralism and calls for a theory of courts that recognizes their role as but one part of a complex system of public and private regulation and disputing.

The three essays just discussed see courts simply as examples of a wide range of dispute processing institutions; courts, as we commonly name them, may have particularly interesting properties, but an empirical *theory* of courts would place them in a much broader framework of conflict management (see Shapiro, 1980). Similarly, the essay by Black and Baumgartner envisages a general theory of conflict management, with no special role for courts in such a theory. The critical unit for analysis for them is the behavior of the third party. Thus, their essay develops a typology that examines the nature and degree of third party intervention in the conflicts of others. Noteworthy in their discussion is their inclusion of various support roles (informers, advocates, surrogates, etc.) as well as the more conventional settlement roles (mediator, arbitrator, judge, etc.). Although they carefully define and illustrate these individual third party roles, they pay little attention to the interactions among the various roles. Black and Baumgartner's approach stands in stark contrast then to that of Jacob or Feeley and Lazerson, whose primary focus is on interrelations among individuals and their tasks within the organization of the court.

In sum, these essays suggest that the study of courts will proceed along various paths, some complementary and others indifferent to one another. Courts raise complex issues for theory building because their boundaries and essences can be defined in such different ways. The division between public and private dispute processing is hard to maintain; the nature of what goes into courts affects the nature and operation of the court process, while court actions in turn influence dispute processing and the normative order beyond the court; and finally, the relevant participants to be observed in order to understand courts include a wide range of third parties, litigants, and relevant audiences. These essays organize and comment on some of the paths that look most promising in the development of empirical theory about courts.

Bibliography

Abel, Richard L. (1979) "Western Courts in Non-Western Settings: Patterns of Court Use in Colonial and Neo-Colonial Africa," in S. B. Burman and B. E. Harrell-Bond (eds.), *The Imposition of Law*. New York: Academic Press.
────── (1978) "From the Editor," *Law & Society Review* 12:33.
────── (1974) "A Comparative Theory of Dispute Institutions in Society," *Law & Society Review*, 8:217.
Abel-Smith, Brian, Michael Zander, and Rosalind Brooke (1973) *Legal Problems and the Citizen: A Study in Three London Boroughs*. London: Heinemann.
Addiss, Penny (1980) "The Life History Complaint Case of Martha and George Rose: 'Honoring the Warranty'," in Laura Nader (ed.), *No Access to Law: Alternatives to the American Judicial System*. New York: Academic Press.
Administrative Office of the United States Courts (1977) *Annual Report of the Director*. Washington, DC: U.S. Government Printing Office.
Akers, Ronald L. (1968) "The Professional Association and the Legal Regulation of Practice," *Law & Society Review* 2:462.
Alinsky, Saul D. (1969) *Reveille for Radicals*. New York: Vintage Books.
Allison, Graham T. (1971) *Essence of Decision*. Boston: Little, Brown and Co.
Alpert, Lenore (1981) "The Judicial Career: Patterns of Socialization on the Bench." Unpublished Ph.D. Dissertation, Department of Political Science, Northwestern University, Evanston, Illinois.
Alschuler, Albert W. (1979) "Plea Bargaining and Its History," *Law & Society Review* 13:211.
American Law Institute (1934) *A Study of the Business of the Federal Courts, Part II: Civil Cases*. Philadelphia: The American Law Institute.
Andenaes, Johannes (1966) "The General Preventive Effects of Punishment," *University of Pennsylvania Law Review* 114:949.
Arno, Andrew (1979) "A Grammar of Conflict: Informal Procedure on an Island in Lau, Fiji," in Klaus-Friedrich Koch (ed.), *Access to Justice, Vol 4, The Anthropological Perspective*. Milan: Guiffre.
Aubert, Vilhelm (1963) "Competition and Dissensus: Two Types of Conflict and of Conflict Resolution," *Journal of Conflict Resolution* 7:26.
Auerbach, Jerold S. (1976) *Unequal Justice: Lawyers and Social Change in Modern America*. New York: Oxford University Press.
Bailey, Frederick S. (1971) "Gifts and Poison," in F. S. Bailey (ed.), *Gifts and Poison*. New York: Schocken Books.
Balandier, Georges (1970) *Political Anthropology*. New York: Random House.
Balbus, Isaac (1973) *The Dialectics of Legal Repression*. New York: Russell Sage.

Baldick, Robert (1965) *The Duel: A History of Duelling.* London: Chapman and Hall.

Ball, Milner S. (1975) "The Play's the Thing: An Unscientific Reflection on Courts under the Rubric of Theater," *Stanford Law Review* 28:81.

Bard, Morton and Joseph Zacker (1976) *The Police and Interpersonal Conflict: Third-Party Intervention Approaches.* Washington, DC: Police Foundation.

Bardach, Eugene and Robert Kagan (1982) *Going by the Book.* Philadelphia: Temple University Press.

Barkun, Michael (1968) *Law Without Sanctions.* New Haven: Yale University Press.

Barnard, Chester I. (1938) *The Functions of the Executive.* Cambridge: Harvard University Press.

Barry, Donald D. and Harold J. Berman (1968) "The Soviet Legal Profession," *Harvard Law Review* 82:1.

Barton, John (1975) "Behind the Legal Explosion," *Stanford Law Review* 27:567.

Barton, Roy Franklin (1969) [1919] *Ifugao Law.* Berkeley: University of California Press.

Baum, Lawrence, Sheldon Goldman, and Austin Sarat (1978) "Transformations in Appellate Activity: A Look at the Business of Three United States Courts of Appeals, 1895–1975." Presented at the annual meeting of the American Political Science Association, New York, 1978.

Baumgartner, M. P. (1981) "Social Control in a Suburban Town: An Ethnographic Study." Unpublished Ph.D. Dissertation, Department of Sociology, Yale University, New Haven, Connecticut.

Bavelas, A. (1950) "Communication Patterns in Task-Oriented Groups," *Journal of the Acoustical Society of America* 22:725.

Baxi, Upendra (1974) "Comment—Durkheim and Legal Evolution: Some Problems of Disproof," *Law & Society Review* 8:645.

Bayley, David H. (1976) *Forces of Order: Police Behavior in Japan and the United States.* Berkeley: University of California Press.

Becker, Gary and George Stigler (1974) "Law Enforcement Malfeasance and Compensation of Enforcers," *Journal of Legal Studies* 3:1.

Becker, Howard (1963) *Outsiders: Studies in the Sociology of Deviance.* New York: Free Press.

Becker, Theodore L. and Malcolm M. Feeley (eds.) (1973) *The Impact of Supreme Court Decisions* (2nd ed.). New York: Oxford University Press.

Beiser, Edward N. (1973) "The Rhode Island Supreme Court: A Well-Integrated Political System," *Law & Society Review* 8:167.

Berger, Raoul (1940a) "From Hostage to Contract: Part One," *Illinois Law Review* 35:154.

——— (1940b) "From Hostage to Contract: Part Two," *Illinois Law Review* 35:281.

Berkeley, George E. (1969) *The Democratic Policeman.* Boston: Beacon Press.

Berkowitz, Leonard and Nigel Walker (1967) "Laws and Moral Judgments," *Sociometry* 30:410.

Berkson, Larry and Susan Carbon (1978) *Court Unification: History, Politics and Implementation.* Washington, DC: U.S. Government Printing Office.

Berman, Harold J. (1978) "The Background of the Western Legal Tradition in the Folklaw of the Peoples of Europe," *University of Chicago Law Review* 45:553.

Berman, Jesse (1969) "The Cuban Popular Tribunals," *Columbia Law Review* 69:1318.

Best, Arthur and Alan Andreasen (1977) "Consumer Response to Unsatisfactory Purchases: A Survey of Perceiving Defects, Voicing Complaints, and Obtaining Redress," *Law & Society Review* 11:701.

Bittner, Egon (1974) "Florence Nightingale in Pursuit of Willie Sutton," in Herbert Jacob (ed.), *The Potential for Reform of Criminal Justice*. Beverly Hills: Sage Publications.

———— (1973) *The Functions of the Police in Modern Society*. Washington, DC: NIMH Center for Studies of Crime and Delinquency.

———— (1967) "Police Discretion in Emergency Apprehension of Mentally Ill Persons," *Social Problems* 14:278.

Black, Donald (1980) *The Manners and Customs of the Police*. New York: Academic Press.

———— (1976) *The Behavior of Law*. New York: Academic Press.

———— (1972) "The Boundaries of Legal Sociology," *Yale Law Journal* 81:1086.

Black, Robert A. (1967) "Hopi Grievance Chants: A Mechanism of Social Control," in Dell H. Hymes and William E. Bittle (eds.), *Studies in Southwestern Ethnolinguistics: Meaning and History in the Languages of the American Southwest*. The Hague: Mouton.

Blankenburg, Erhard (1975) "Studying the Frequency of Civil Litigation in Germany," *Law & Society Review* 9:307.

Blau, Peter M. (1963) [1955] *The Dynamics of Bureaucracy: A Study of Interpersonal Relations in Two Government Agencies*. Chicago: University of Chicago Press.

———— (1956) *Bureaucracy in Modern Society*. New York: Random House.

Blau, Peter M. and W. Richard Scott (1962) *Formal Organizations*. San Francisco: Chandler Publishing Co.

Blaustein, Albert and Roy Mersky (1978) *The First One Hundred Justices*. Hamden, CT: Archon Books.

Blegvad, Britt-Mari, P. O. Bolding, and Ole Lando (1973) *Arbitration as a Means of Solving Conflicts*. Copenhagen: New Social Science Monographs.

Bloch, Maurice (1964) [1940] *Feudal Society. Vol. 2: Social Classes and Political Organization*. Chicago: University of Chicago Press.

———— (1964b) [1939] *Feudal Society. Vol. 1: The Growth of Ties of Dependence*. Chicago: University of Chicago Press.

Blumberg, Abraham (1970) *The Scales of Justice*. Chicago: Aldine Publishing Co.

———— (1967a) *Criminal Justice*. Chicago: Quadrangle Books.

———— (1967b) "The Practice of Law as a Confidence Game: Organizational Cooptation of a Profession," *Law & Society Review* 1:15.

Bohannan, Paul (1965) "The Differing Realms of Law," in Laura Nader (ed.), *The Ethnography of Law*, Special issue, *American Anthropologist* 67:33. Reprinted in P. Bohannan (ed.), (1967) *Law and Warfare: Studies in the Anthropology of Conflict*. Garden City, NY: The Natural History Press.

———— (1957) *Justice and Judgment among the Tiv*. London: Oxford University Press.

Bolton, Ralph (1974) "To Kill a Thief: A Kallawaya Sorcery Session in the Lake Titicaca Region of Peru," *Anthropos*, 69:191.

Bond, Carroll T. (1927) "The Maryland Practice of Trying Criminal Cases by Judges Alone, Without Juries," *American Bar Association Journal* 11:699.

—— (1928) *The Court of Appeals of Maryland, A History*. Baltimore: Barton-Gillett Co.

Bonn, Robert L. (1972a) "Arbitration: An Alternative System for Handling Contract Related Disputes," *Administrative Science Quarterly* 17:254.

—— (1972b) "The Predictability of Nonlegalistic Adjudication," *Law & Society Review*. 6:563.

Bourdieu, Pierre (1977) *Outline of a Theory of Practice*, (Richard Nice, transl.). Cambridge: Cambridge University Press.

Boyum, Keith and Samuel Krislov (eds.) (1980) *Forecasting the Impact of Legislation on Courts*. Washington, D.C.: National Academy Press.

Brantley, James R. and Marjorie Kravitz (compilers) (1979) *The Etiology of Criminality: Nonbehavioral Science Perspectives. A Definitive Bibliography*. Washington, DC: National Criminal Justice Reference Service, U.S. Department of Justice.

Brock, E. (1968) *The Little White God*. London: Allyn & Unwin.

Brown, Theodore J. (1979) "The Tennessee County Courts under the North Carolina and Territorial Governments: The Davidson County Court of Pleas and Quarter Sessions, 1783–1796, as a Case Study," *Vanderbilt Law Review* 32:349.

Buckle, Suzann R. Thomas and Leonard G. Buckle (1977) *Bargaining for Justice: Case Disposition and Reform in the Criminal Courts*. New York: Praeger.

Burman, Sandra B. and Barbara E. Harrell-Bond (eds.) (1979) *The Imposition of Law*. New York: Academic Press.

Cain, Maureen (1979) "The General Practice Lawyer and the Client: Towards a Radical Conception," *International Journal of the Sociology of Law* 7:331.

—— (1973) *Society and the Policeman's Role*. London: Routledge and Kegan Paul.

Canon, Bradley C. and Lawrence A. Baum (1980) "Patterns of Adoptions of Tort Law Innovations: An Application of Diffusion Theory to Judicial Doctrines." Presented at the annual meeting of the Law and Society Association, Madison, Wisconsin, June, 1980.

Canon, Bradley C. and Dean Jaros (1979) "The Impact of Changes in Judicial Doctrine: The Abrogation of Charitable Immunity," *Law & Society Review* 13:969.

—— (1970) "External Variables, Institutional Structure and Dissent on State Supreme Courts," *Polity* 3:175.

Caplovitz, David (1974) *Consumers in Trouble: A Study of Debtors in Default*. New York: Free Press.

Cappelletti, Mauro and Bryant Garth (1978) "Access to Justice: The Worldwide Movement to Make Rights Effective. A General Report," in M. Cappelletti and B. Garth (eds.), *Access to Justice. Vol. 1: A World Survey*. Leyden: Sijthoff, and Milan: Guiffre.

Carlin, Jerome E. (1962) *Lawyers on Their Own: A Study of Individual Practitioners in Chicago*. New Brunswick, NJ: Rutgers University Press.

Carter, Lief H. (1979) *Reason in Law*. Boston: Little, Brown.
——— (1974) *The Limits of Order*. Lexington, MA: Lexington Books.
Cavanagh, Ralph and Austin Sarat (1980) "Thinking about Courts: Toward and Beyond a Jurisprudence of Judicial Competence," *Law & Society Review* 14:371.
Chagnon, Napoleon A. (1977) [1968] *Yanomamö: The Fierce People*. New York: Holt, Rinehart and Winston.
Chalidze, Valery (1977) *Criminal Russia: Essays on Crime in the Soviet Union*. New York: Random House.
Chayes, Abram (1976) "The Role of the Judge in Public Law Litigation," *Harvard Law Review* 89:1281.
Christie, Nils (1977) "Conflicts as Property," *British Journal of Criminology* 17:1.
Chroust, Anton-Hermann (1954a) "The Legal Profession in Ancient Athens," *Notre Dame Lawyer* 29:339.
——— (1954b) "The Legal Profession in Ancient Republican Rome," *Notre Dame Lawyer* 30:97.
Church, Thomas, Jr., Alan Carlson, Jo-Lynn Lee, and Teresa Tan (1978) *Justice Delayed: The Pace of Litigation in Urban Trial Courts*. Williamsburg, VA.: National Center for State Courts.
Clark, Charles E. and Harry Shulman (1937) *A Study of Law Administration in Connecticut*. New Haven: Yale University Press.
Clark, Cornelia Anne (1979) "Justice on the Tennessee Frontier: The Williamson County Circuit Court 1810–1820," *Vanderbilt Law Review* 32:413.
Clark, David S. (1981) "Adjudication to Administration: A Statistical Analysis of Federal District Courts in the Twentieth Century," *Southern California Law Review* 55:65.
Clynch, Edward J. and David W. Neubauer (1981) "Trial Courts as Organizations," *Law and Policy Quarterly* 3:69.
Cohen, Michael D., James G. March, and Johan P. Olsen (1972) "A Garbage Can Model of Organizational Choice," *Administrative Science Quarterly* 17:1.
Cohen, Phil (1979) "Policing the Working-Class City," in Bob Fine et al. (eds.), *Capitalism and the Rule of Law*. London: Hutchinson.
Cohn, Bernard S. (1965) "Anthropological Notes on Disputes and Law in India," in Laura Nader (ed.), *The Ethnography of Law*, Special issue, *American Anthropologist* 67:82.
——— (1959) "Some Notes on Law and Change in North India," *Economic Development and Cultural Change* 8:79.
Cohn, Norman (1975) *Europe's Inner Demons: An Enquiry Inspired by the Great Witch-Hunt*. New York: Basic Books.
Cole, George F. (1971) "Criminal Justice as an Exchange System," *Camden Law Review* 3:18.
——— (1970) "The Decision to Prosecute," *Law & Society Review* 4:313.
Coleman, James S. (1974) *Power and the Structure of Society*. New York: W. W. Norton & Co.
Collier, Jane F. (1973) *Law and Social Change in Zinacantan*. Stanford, CA: Stanford University Press.
Collier, Jane F. and Michele Z. Rosaldo (1981) "Politics and Gender in Simple Societies," in Sherry Ortner and Harriet Whitehead (eds.), *Sexual Meanings*. Cambridge: Cambridge University Press.

Colombatos, John (1969) "Physicians and Medicare: A Before-After Study of the Effects of Legislation on Attitudes," *American Sociological Review* 34:318.

Colson, Elizabeth (1974) *Tradition and Contract: The Problem of Order*. Chicago: Aldine.

―――― (1969) "Spirit Possession among the Tonga of Zambia," in John Beattie and John Middleton (eds.), *Spirit Mediumship and Society in Africa*. New York: Africana Publishing Corporation.

Columbia Journal of Law and Social Problems (1970) "Rabbinical Courts: Modern Day Solomons," *Columbia Journal of Law and Social Problems* 6:49.

Comaroff, John L. and Simon A. Roberts (1977) "The Invocation of Norms in Dispute Settlement," in I. Hamnett (ed.), *Social Anthropology and Law*. New York: Academic Press.

Cross, Harry M. (1973) "The College Athlete and the Institution," *Law and Contemporary Problems* 38:151.

Crowe, Patricia W. (1978) "Complainant Reactions to the Massachusetts Commission Against Discrimination," *Law & Society Review* 12:217.

Cumming, Elaine, Ian Cumming, and Laura Edell (1965) "Policeman as Philosopher, Guide and Friend," *Social Problems* 12:276.

Curran, Barbara A. (1977) *The Legal Needs of the Public: The Final Report of a National Survey*. Chicago: American Bar Foundation.

Curtis, George B. (1977) "The Colonial County Court, Social Forum and Legislative Precedent, Accomack County, Virginia, 1633–1639," *Virginia Magazine of History and Biography* 85:274.

Damaska, Mirjan (1978) "A Foreign Perspective on the American Judicial System," in T. J. Fetter (ed.), *State Courts: A Blueprint for the Future*. Williamsburg, VA: National Center for State Courts.

―――― (1975) "Structures of Authority and Comparative Criminal Procedure," *Yale Law Journal* 84:480.

Danelski, David J. (1961) "The Influence of the Chief Justice in the Decisional Process," in Walter F. Murphy and C. Herman Pritchett (eds.), *Courts, Judges, and Politics*. New York: Random House.

Daniels, Stephen (1981) "The Trial Courts of 'Spoon River': Patterns and Changes, 1870 to 1963." Presented at the annual meeting of the Law and Society Association, Amherst, Massachusetts, June, 1981.

Danzig, Richard (1978) *The Capability Problem in Contract Law: Further Readings on Well-Known Cases*. Mineola, NY: Foundation Press.

―――― (1973) "Toward the Creation of a Complementary, Decentralized System of Criminal Justice," *Stanford Law Review* 26:1.

Danzig, Richard and Michael J. Lowy (1975) "Everyday Disputes and Mediation in the United States: A Reply to Professor Felstiner," *Law & Society Review* 9:675.

Davies, Thomas Y. (1980) "The Limits of Appellate Justice: A Case Study of the Organizational Basis for the Distribution of Legal Sanctions and Benefits in a California Court of Appeal." Unpublished Ph.D. Dissertation, Department of Political Science, Northwestern University, Evanston, Illinois.

Daynard, Richard (1971) "The Use of Social Policy in Judicial Decision-Making," *Cornell Law Review* 56:919.

Dickens, Charles (1859) *Tale of Two Cities*. London: Chapman and Hall.

Dimond, Alan J. (1960) *The Superior Court of Massachusetts, Its Origin and De-*

velopment. Boston: Little, Brown and Co.

Diver, Colin S. (1979) "The Judge as Political Powerbroker: Superintending Structural Change in Public Institutions," *Virginia Law Review* 65:43.

Dolbeare, Kenneth M. and Phillip E. Hammond (1971) *The School Prayer Decisions: From Court Policy to Local Practice*. Chicago: University of Chicago Press.

Donner, Frank J. (1980) *The Age of Surveillance: The Aims and Methods of America's Political Intelligence System*. New York: Alfred A. Knopf.

Doo, Leigh-Wai (1973) "Dispute Settlement in Chinese-American Communities," *American Journal of Comparative Law* 21:627.

Dore, Ronald P. (1978) *Shinohata: A Portrait of a Japanese Village*. New York: Pantheon Books.

Douglass, Paul F. (1933) *The Mayor's Court of Hamilton County, Ohio*. Baltimore: Johns Hopkins Press.

Ducat, Craig R. and Victor E. Flango (1976) *Leadership in State Supreme Courts: Roles of the Chief Justice*. Beverly Hills: Sage Publications.

Dunlop, John (1975) "The Limits of Legal Compulsion," *John Herlings' Labor Letter*. 25:48–49.

Durkheim, Emile (1964) [1893] *The Division of Labor in Society* (George Simpson, transl.). New York: Free Press.

Dworkin, Ronald (1977) *Taking Rights Seriously*. Cambridge: Harvard University Press.

Eckhardt, Kenneth (1968) "Deviance, Visibility, and Legal Action: The Duty to Support," *Social Problems* 15:470.

Eckhoff, Torstein (1966) "The Mediator, the Judge and the Administrator in Conflict-Resolution," *Acta Sociologica* 10:148. Reprinted in B. M. Blegvad (ed.), *Contributions to the Sociology of Law*. Copenhagen: Munksgaard.

Edgerton, Robert B. (1979) *Alone Together: Social Order on an Urban Beach*. Berkeley: University of California Press.

Edgerton, Robert B. and Francis P. Conant (1964) *"Kilapat:* The 'Shaming Party' among the Pokot of East Africa," *Southwestern Journal of Anthropology* 20:404.

Ehrlich, Eugen (1936) *Fundamental Principles of the Sociology of Law*, (Moll transl.). New York: Russell & Russell.

Eisenberg, Melvin A. (1976) "Private Ordering through Negotiation: Dispute Settlement and Rulemaking," *Harvard Law Review* 89:637.

Eisenstein, James and Herbert Jacob (1977) *Felony Justice: An Organizational Analysis of Criminal Courts*. Boston: Little, Brown and Co.

Ekvall, Robert B. (1954) "Mi sTong: The Tibetan Custom of Life Indemnity," *Sociologus* 4:136.

Engel, David M. (1980) "Legal Pluralism in an American Community: Perspectives on a Civil Trial Court," *American Bar Foundation Research Journal* 1980:425.

——— (1978) *Code and Custom in a Thai Provincial Court: The Interaction of Formal and Informal Systems of Justice*. Tucson: University of Arizona Press.

Engel, David M. and Eric H. Steele (1979) "Civil Cases and Society: Process and Order in the Civil Justice System," *American Bar Foundation Research Journal* 1979:295.

Enker, Arnold (1967) "Perspectives on Plea Bargaining," *Task Force Reports: The Courts*, Task Force on the Administration of Justice, The President's Commission on Law Enforcement and Administration of Justice. Washington, DC: U.S. Government Printing Office.

Ennis, Philip H. (1967) *Criminal Victimization in the United States*, Field Surveys II, The President's Commission on Law Enforcement and the Administration of Justice. Washington, D.C.: U.S. Government Printing Office.

Ericson, Richard V. and Patricia M. Baranek (1982) *The Ordering of Justice: A Study of Accused Persons as Defendants in the Criminal Process*. Toronto: University of Toronto Press.

Erikson, Kai T. (1966) *Wayward Puritans: A Study in the Sociology of Deviance*. New York: John Wiley & Sons, Inc.

Etzioni, Amitai (1975) *A Comparative Analysis of Complex Organizations*. New York: The Free Press.

Evan, William M. (1978) *Inter-Organizational Relations*. Philadelphia: University of Pennsylvania Press.

——— (1962) "Public and Private Legal Systems," in William Evan (ed.), *Law and Sociology*. New York: The Free Press of Glencoe.

Evans-Pritchard, E. E. (1940) *The Nuer: A Description of the Modes of Livelihood and Political Institutions of a Nilotic People*. Oxford: Clarendon Press.

——— (1937) *Witchcraft, Oracles and Magic among the Azande*. Oxford: Clarendon Press.

Federal Judicial Center (1978) *Central Legal Staffs in the United States Courts of Appeals*. Washington, DC: Federal Judicial Center.

Feeley, Malcolm M. (1979a) "Pleading Guilty in Lower Courts," *Law & Society Review* 13:461.

——— (1979b) *The Process Is the Punishment*. New York: Russell Sage.

——— (1976) "The Concept of Laws in Social Science: A Critique and Notes on an Expanded View," *Law & Society Review* 10:497.

Fehrenbacher, Don E. (1978) *The Dred Scott Case: Its Significance in American Law and Politics*. New York: Oxford University Press.

Feifer, George (1964) *Justice in Moscow*. New York: Simon and Schuster.

Felstiner, William L. F. (1974) "Influences of Social Organization on Dispute Processing," *Law & Society Review* 9:63.

Felstiner, William L. F., Richard L. Abel, and Austin Sarat (1981) "The Emergence and Transformation of Disputes: Naming, Blaming, Claiming . . . ," *Law & Society Review* 15:631.

——— (1980) "The Emergence and Transformation of Disputes." Presented at the annual meeting of the Law and Society Association, Madison, Wisconsin, June, 1980.

Ferdinand, Theodore N. (1981) "Boston's Courts: 1814–1850." Presented at the annual meeting of the Law and Society Association, Amherst, Massachusetts, June, 1981.

——— (1967) "The Criminal Patterns of Boston since 1849," *American Journal of Sociology* 73:184.

Ferguson, Charles A. (1971) *Language Structure and Language Use: Essays by Charles A. Ferguson*, Anwar S. Dill (ed.). Stanford, CA: Stanford University Press.

Field, Oliver (1941a) "Unconstitutional Legislation in Indiana," *Indiana Law Journal* 17:101.
—— (1941b) "Unconstitutional Legislation in Minnesota," *American Political Science Review* 35:898.
Firth, Raymond (1936) *We, the Tikopia: A Sociological Study of Kinship in Primitive Polynesia*. New York: American Book Company.
Fisher, Eric A. (1975) "Community Courts: An Alternative to Conventional Criminal Adjudication," *American University Law Review* 24:253.
Fishman, James (1979) "The Social and Occupational Mobility of Prosecutors: New York City," in William F. McDonald (ed.), *The Prosecutor*. Beverly Hills: Sage Publications.
Fitzgerald, Jeffrey and Richard Dickins (1981) "Disputing in Legal and Non-Legal Contexts: Some Questions for Sociologists of Law," *Law & Society Review* 15:681.
Fitzgerald, Jeffrey M., David C. Hickman, and Richard L. Dickins (1980) "A Preliminary Discussion of the Definitional Phase of the Dispute Process." Presented at the annual meeting of the Law and Society Association, Madison, Wisconsin, June, 1980.
Fogelson, Robert (1978) *Big-City Police*. Cambridge: Harvard University Press.
Foster, George M. (1965) "Peasant Society and the Image of Limited Good," *American Anthropologist* 67:293.
—— (1960) "Interpersonal Relations in Peasant Society," *Human Organization* 19:174.
Frank, John P. (1948) "Historical Bases of the Federal Judicial System," *Law and Contemporary Problems* 13:3.
Fried, Jacob (1953) "The Relation of Ideal Norms to Actual Behavior in Tarahumara Society," *Southwestern Journal of Anthropology* 9:286.
Friedman, Lawrence M. (1979) "Plea Bargaining in Historical Perspective," *Law & Society Review* 13:247
—— (1975) *The Legal System: A Social Science Perspective*. New York: Russell Sage.
—— (1974) "Notes Toward a History of Americal Justice," *Buffalo Law Review* 24:111.
—— (1973) *A History of American Law*. New York: Simon and Schuster.
—— (1969) "On Legal Development," *Rutgers Law Review* 14:11.
—— (1967) "Legal Rules and the Process of Social Change," *Stanford Law Review* 19:786.
—— (1966) "On Legalistic Reasoning: A Footnote to Weber," *Wisconsin Law Review* 1966:148.
Friedman, Lawrence M., Robert Kagan, Bliss Cartwright, and Stanton Wheeler (1981) "State Supreme Courts: A Century of Style and Citation, *Stanford Law Review* 33:773.
Friedman, Lawrence M. and Jack Ladinsky (1967) "Social Change and the Law of Industrial Accidents," *Columbia Law Review* 67:50.
Friedman, Lawrence M. and Robert V. Percival (1981) *The Roots of Justice: Crime and Punishment in Alameda County, California, 1870–1910*. Chapel Hill, North Carolina: University of North Carolina Press.

Friedman, Lawrence M. and Robert V. Percival (1976) "A Tale of Two Courts: Litigation in Alameda and San Benito Counties," *Law & Society Review* 10:267.

Fuller, Lon L. (1978) "The Forms and Limits of Adjudication," *Harvard Law Review* 92:353.

——— (1971) "Mediation—Its Forms and Functions," *Southern California Law Review* 44:305.

——— (1969) "Human Interaction and the Law," *The American Journal of Jurisprudence* 14:1.

——— (1968) *Anatomy of the Law*. New York: Praeger.

——— (1964) *The Morality of Law*. New Haven: Yale University Press.

——— (1934) "American Legal Realism," *University of Pennsylvania Law Review* 82:429.

Galanter, Marc (1975) "Afterword: Explaining Litigation," *Law & Society Review* 9:347.

——— (1974a) "The Future of Law and Social Sciences Research," *North Carolina Law Review* 52:1060.

——— (1974b) "Why the 'Haves' Come Out Ahead: Speculations on the Limits of Legal Change," *Law & Society Review* 9:95.

——— (1968) "The Displacement of Traditional Law in Modern India," *Journal of Social Issues* 24:65.

——— (1966) "The Modernization of Law," in M. Weiner (ed.), *Modernization: The Dynamics of Growth*. New York: Basic Books.

Galanter, Marc, Frank S. Palen, and John M. Thomas (1979) "The Crusading Judge: Judicial Activism in Trial Courts," *Southern California Law Review* 52:699.

Galtung, Johan (1965) "Institutionalized Conflict Resolution: A Theoretical Paradigm," *Journal of Peace Research* 2:349.

Geerken, Michael and Walter R. Gove (1975) "Deterrence: Some Theoretical Considerations," *Law & Society Review* 9:497.

Gessner, Volkmar (1976) *Recht und Konflikt*. Tubingen: J. C. B. Mohr.

Getman, Julius G. (1979) "Labor Arbitration and Dispute Resolution," *Yale Law Journal* 88:916.

Gibbs, Jack P. (forthcoming) "Punishment, Deterrence, and Retribution," in *Law and the Social Sciences* (provisional title). To be published under the sponsorship of the Social Sciences Research Council.

——— (1975) *Crime, Punishment and Deterrence*. New York: Elsevier Scientific Publishing Co.

Gibbs, James L. (1963) "The Kpelle Moot: A Therapeutic Model for the Informal Settlement of Disputes," *Africa* 33:1.

——— (1962) "Poro Values and Courtroom Procedures in a Kpelle Chiefdom," *Southwestern Journal of Anthropology* 18:341.

Gibson, James L. (1978) "Judges' Role Orientations, Attitudes, and Decisions: An Interactive Model," unpublished paper, University of Wisconsin (Milwaukee).

Giddings, Jane (1975) "Soviet Legal Consultation," *Review of Socialist Law* 1:161.

Gillin, John (1956) "The Making of a Witch Doctor," Psychiatry 19:131.

――― (1948) "Magical Fright," Psychiatry 11:387

Ginnell, Laurence (1924) [1894] The Brehon Laws: A Legal Handbook. Dublin: P. J. O'Callaghan.

Glick, Henry R. (1971) Supreme Courts in State Politics: An Investigation of the Judicial Role. New York: Basic Books.

Glick, Henry R. and Kenneth N. Vines (1973) State Court Systems. Englewood Cliffs, NJ: Prentice-Hall.

Gluckman, Max (1968) Politics, Law and Ritual in Tribal Society. New York: Mentor Books

――― (1967) [1955] The Judicial Process among the Barotse of Northern Rhodesia. Manchester: Manchester University Press.

――― (1963) "Gossip and Scandal," Current Anthropology 4:307.

Goebel, Julius and T. Raymond Naughton (1944) Law Enforcement in Colonial New York: A Study in Criminal Procedure 1664–1776. New York: The Commonwealth Fund.

Goffman, Erving (1969) "The Insanity of Place," in Erving Goffman (ed.), Relations in Public: Microstudies of the Public Order. New York: Basic Books.

Goldberg, Victor P. (1976) "Regulation and Administered Contracts," The Bell Journal of Economics 7:426.

Goldstein, Herman (1977) Policing a Free Society. Cambridge, MA: Ballinger Publishing Co.

Gould, Leroy C., Andrew L. Walker, Lansing E. Crane, and Charles W. Lidz (1974) Connections: Notes from the Heroin World. New Haven: Yale University Press.

Gouldner, Alvin W. (1960) "The Norm of Reciprocity: A Preliminary Statement," American Sociological Review 25:161.

Goutal, Jean Louis (1974) "The Dynamics of Justification: A Comparative Study of Reasons in Civil Judgments." Unpublished J. S. D. Thesis, Stanford University Law School.

Gray, Robert F. (1969) "The Shetani Cult among the Segeju of Tanzania," in John Beattie and John Middleton (eds.), Spirit Mediumship and Society in Africa. New York: Africana Publishing Corporation.

Greenberg, Douglas (1974) Crime and Law Enforcement in the Colony of New York, 1691–1776. Ithaca, NY: Cornell University Press.

Greenspan, Rosann (1982) Prosecutors, Police and Charging: Relationships. Manuscript on file at the Jurisprudence and Social Policy Program, School of Law, University of California, Berkeley.

Griffiths, John (forthcoming) "The Division of Labor in Social Control," in Donald Black (ed.), Toward a General Theory of Social Control, New York: Academic Press.

――― (1981) "What Is Legal Pluralism," presented to the annual meeting of the Law and Society Association, Amherst, Massachusetts, June, 1981.

Groot, Roger D. (1971 "The Effects of an Intermediate Appellate Court on the Supreme Court Work Product: The North Carolina Experience," Wake Forest Law Review 7:548.

Gross, E. (1968) "Universities as Organizations: A Research Approach," American Sociological Review 33:519.

Gross, Jan Tomasz (1979) *Polish Society under German Occupation: The General-gouvernement, 1939–1944.* Princeton, NJ: Princeton University Press.

Grossman, Joel (1970) "The Supreme Court and Social Change: A Preliminary Inquiry," *American Behavioral Scientist* 13:535.

Grossman, Joel B. and Mary H. Grossman (1971) "Introduction," in J. B. Grossman and M. H. Grossman (eds.), *Law and Change in Modern America.* Pacific Palisades, CA: Goodyear Publishing Co.

Grossman, Joel B. and Austin Sarat (1975) "Litigation in the Federal Courts: A Comparative Perspective," *Law & Society Review* 9:321.

Guetzkow, Harold and W. R. Dill (1957) "Factors in the Organizational Development of Task-Oriented Groups," *Sociometry* 20:175.

Guice, John D. (1972) *The Rocky Mountain Bench: The Territorial Supreme Courts of Colorado, Montana, and Wyoming, 1861–1890.* New Haven: Yale University Press.

Gulliver, Philip H. (1979) *Disputes and Negotiations: A Cross-Cultural Perspective.* New York: Academic Press.

——— (1977) "On Mediators," in Ian Hamnett (ed.), *Social Anthropology and Law.* London: Academic Press.

——— (1973) "Negotiations as a Mode of Dispute Settlement: Towards a General Model," *Law & Society Review* 7:667.

——— (1969) "Introduction to Case Studies of Law in Non-Western Societies," in L. Nader (ed.), *Law in Culture and Society.* Chicago: Aldine.

——— (1963) *Social Control in an African Society: A Study of the Arusha, Agricultural Masai of Northern Tanganyika.* Boston: University Press.

Gurr, Ted R. and Peter N. Gabosky (1976) *Rogues, Rebels and Reformers: A Political History of Urban Crime and Conflict.* Beverly Hills, CA: Sage Publications.

Gutierrez, Carlos Jose (1979) *El Funcionamento del Sistema Juridico.* San Jose, Costa Rica: Editorial Juricentro.

Hagan, John (1974) "Extra-Legal Attributes and Criminal Sentencing: An Assessment of a Sociological Viewpoint," *Law & Society Review* 8:357.

Hager, Philip (1979) "'Complaint-Mobile': Wheels of Justice; DA's Office-in-a-Van Handles Consumer Gripes in San Francisco," *The Los Angeles Times,* June 10, Part I, pp. 3 ff.

Haley, John Owen (1978) "The Myth of the Reluctant Litigant," *Journal of Japanese Studies* 4:359.

Haller, Mark H. (1979) "Plea Bargaining: The Nineteenth-Century Context," *Law & Society Review* 13:273.

Harris, Silas A. (1933) *Appellate Courts and Appellate Procedure in Ohio.* Baltimore: Johns Hopkins Press.

Hart, H. L. A. (1961) *The Concept of Law.* Oxford: Clarendon Press.

Hart, Henry M., Jr., and Albert M. Sacks (1958) *The Legal Process: Basic Problems in the Making and Application of Law.* Cambridge: Harvard Law School (second tentative edition, first tentative edition, 1957).

Hartog, Hendrik (1976) "The Public Law of a County Court: Judicial Government in Eighteenth-Century Massachusetts," *American Journal of Legal History,* 20:282.

Haskins, George (1960) *Law and Authority in Early Massachusetts.* New York: Macmillan.

Hasluck, Margaret (1954) *The Unwritten Law in Albania*. Cambridge: Cambridge University Press.

Hay, Douglas (1975) "Property, Authority, and the Criminal Law," in D. Hay et al. (eds.), *Albion's Fatal Tree: Crime and Society in Eighteenth-Century England*. New York: Pantheon.

Heiberg, Robert A. (1969) "Social Backgrounds of the Minnesota Supreme Court Justices: 1858–1968," *Minnesota Law Review* 53:901.

Heinz, John P. and Edward O. Laumann (1978) "The Legal Profession: Client Interests, Professional Roles and Social Hierarchies," *Michigan Law Review* 76:1111.

Henderson, Dwight F. (1971) *Courts for a New Nation*. Washington, DC: Public Affairs Press.

Henderson, Thomas A., Randal Guynes, and Carl Baar (1980) "Organizational Design for Courts." Presented at annual meeting of the Southern Political Science Association, November, 1980.

Heumann, Milton (1978) *Plea Bargaining: The Experiences of Prosecutors, Judges, and Defense Attorneys*. Chicago: University of Chicago Press.

—— (1975) "A Note on Plea Bargaining and Case Pressure," *Law & Society Review* 9:515.

Hickman, Martin B. (1954) "Judicial Review of Legislation in Utah," *Utah Law Review* 5:50.

Hindus, Michael S. (1980) *Prison and Plantation: Crime, Justice and Authority in Massachusetts and South Carolina, 1767–1878*. Chapel Hill: University of North Carolina Press.

—— (1977) "The Contours of Crime and Justice in Massachusetts and South Carolina, 1767–1878," *American Journal of Legal History* 21:212.

Hindus, Michael S., Theodore M. Hammett, and Barbara M. Hobson (1979) *The Files of the Massachusetts Superior Court, 1859–1959: An Analysis and a Plan for Action*. Boston: G. K. Hall and Company.

Hirschman, Albert O. (1970) *Exit, Voice and Loyalty: Responses to Decline in Firms, Organizations and States*. Cambridge: Harvard University Press.

Hoebel, E. Adamson (1961) *The Law of Primitive Man: A Study of Comparative Legal Dynamics*. Cambridge: Harvard University Press.

—— (1940) *The Political Organization and Law-Ways of the Comanche Indians*. Memoirs of the American Anthropological Association, Number 54. Menasha: American Anthropological Association.

Homans, George C. (1958) "Social Behavior as Exchange," *American Journal of Sociology* 63:597.

—— (1950) *The Human Group*. New York: Harcourt, Brace and World.

Horowitz, Donald L. (1977) *The Courts and Social Policy*. Washington, DC: Brookings.

Horwitz, Allan V. (1982) *The Social Control of Mental Illness*. New York: Academic Press.

Hufstedler, Shirley (1971) "New Blocks for Old Pyramids: Reshaping the Judicial System," *Southern California Law Review* 44:901.

Hunting, Roger Bryant and Gloria S. Neuwirth (1962) *Who Sues in New York City? A Study of Automobile Accident Claims*. New York: Columbia University Press.

Hurst, J. Willard (1956) *Law and the Conditions of Freedom in the Nineteenth-*

Century United States. Madison: University of Wisconsin Press.

Ireland, Robert M. (1972) *The County Courts in Antebellum Kentucky.* Lexington: The University of Kentucky.

Jackson, R. M. (1971) *Enforcing the Law.* Harmondsworth: Penguin Books.

—— (1937) "The Incidence of Trial by Jury during the Past Century," *Modern Law Review* 1:132.

Jacob, Herbert (1969a) *Debtors in Court: The Consumption of Government Services.* Chicago: Rand-McNally.

—— (1969b) "Judicial and Political Efficacy of Litigants: A Preliminary Analysis," in Joel B. Grossman and Joseph Tanenhaus (eds.), *Frontiers of Judicial Research.* New York: John Wiley and Sons.

Johnson, Charles A. (1979) "Judicial Decisions and Organization Change: Some Theoretical and Empirical Notes on State Court Decisions and State Administrative Agencies," *Law & Society Review* 14:27.

Johnson, Earl, Jr. (1978) *Justice and Reform: The Formative Years of the American Legal Services Program.* New Brunswick: Transaction Books.

Johnson, Earl, Jr., and Ann Barthelmes Drew (1978) "This Nation Has Money for Everything—Except Its Courts," *Judges Journal* 17:8.

Johnson, Earl, Jr., Valerie Kantor, and Elizabeth Schwartz (1977) *Outside the Courts: A Survey of Diversion Alternatives in Civil Cases.* Williamsburg, VA: National Center for State Courts.

Jones, Harry W. (1969) *The Efficacy of Law.* Evanston, IL: Northwestern University Press.

Jones, Schuyler (1974) *Men of Influence in Nuristan: A Study of Social Control and Dispute Settlement in Waigal Valley, Afghanistan.* New York: Seminar Press.

Judicial Conference of the United States (1976) *Reports of the Proceedings of the Judicial Conference of the United States Held at St. Paul, MN. April 7, 1976, and Washington, D.C., September 23–24, 1976, and Annual Report of the Director of the Administrative Office of the United States Courts, 1976.* Washington, DC: U.S. Government Printing Office.

Kagan, Richard L. (1981) *Lawsuits and Litigants in Castile, 1500–1700.* Chapel Hill: University of North Carolina Press.

Kagan, Robert, Bliss Cartwright, Lawrence M. Friedman, and Stanton Wheeler (1978) "The Evolution of State Supreme Courts," *Michigan Law Review* 76:961.

—— (1977) "The Business of State Supreme Courts, 1870–1970," *Stanford Law Review* 30:121.

Kahn, D. and D. Katz (1953) "Leadership Practices in Relation to Productivity and Morale," in D. Cartwright and D. Zander (eds.), *Group Dynamics.* Evanston, IL: Row, Peterson.

Kalven, Harry and Hans Zeisel (1966) *The American Jury.* Boston: Little, Brown.

Kaupen, Wolfgang and Etienne Langerwerf (1980) "The Comparative Analysis of Litigation Rates," unpublished paper.

Kelly, J. M. (1966) *Roman Litigation.* Oxford: Clarendon Press.

Kelsen, Hans (1945) *General Theory of Law and State.* Cambridge: Harvard University Press.

Kennedy, Duncan (1973) "Legal Formality," *Journal of Legal Studies* 2:351.

Kidder, Robert (1981) "The End of the Road? Problems in the Analysis of Disputes," *Law & Society Review* 15:717.

—— (1979) "Toward an Integrated Theory of Imposed Law," in S. B. Burman and B. E. Harrell-Bond (eds.), *The Imposition of Law*. New York: Academic Press.

—— (1978) "Western Law in India: External Law and Local Response," in Harry M. Johnson (ed.), *Social System and Legal Process: Theory, Comparative Perspectives, and Special Studies*. San Francisco: Jossey-Bass Publishers.

—— (1975) "Afterword: Change and Structure in Dispute Processing," *Law & Society Review* 9:385.

—— (1974) "Formal Litigation and Professional Insecurity: Legal Entrepreneurship in South India," *Law & Society Review* 9:11.

—— (1973) "Courts and Conflicts in an Indian City: A Study in Legal Impact," *Journal of Commonwealth Political Studies* 11:121.

Kimball, Edward (1965) "Criminal Cases in a State Appellate Court, 1839–1959," *American Journal of Legal History* 9:95.

Klein, Carol, David M. Horton, and Marjorie Kravitz (compilers) (1980) *Bibliographies in Criminal Justice: A Selected Bibliography*. Washington, DC: National Criminal Justice Reference Service, U.S. Department of Justice.

Koch, Klaus-Friedrich (1979) "Introduction," in K.–F. Koch (ed.), *Access to Justice, Volume IV: The Anthropological Perspective*. Alphen aan den Rijn: Sijthoff and Noordhoff.

—— (1974) *War and Peace in Jalémó: The Management of Conflict in Highland New Guinea*. Cambridge: Harvard University Press.

Konig, David L. (1979) *Law and Society in Puritan Massachusetts, Essex County, 1629–1692*. Chapel Hill: University of North Carolina Press.

Kopytoff, Igor (1961) "Extension of Conflict as a Method of Conflict Resolution among the Suku of the Congo," *Journal of Conflict Resolution* 5:61.

Kroeber, A. L. (1926) "Law of the Yurok Indians," in *Proceedings of the 22nd International Congress of Americanists* 2:511.

Kurczewski, Jacek and Kazimierz Frieske (1978) "The Social Conciliatory Commissions in Poland: A Case Study of Nonauthoritative and Conciliatory Dispute Resolution as an Approach to Access to Justice," in Mauro Cappelletti and John Weisner (eds.), *Access to Justice, Volume II: Promising Institutions*. Milan: Giuffre and Alphen aan den Rijn: Sijthoff and Noordhoff.

Kurland, P. B. and D. W. M. Waters (1959) "Public Prosecutions in England, 1854–1859: An Essay in English Legislative History," *Duke Law Journal* 1959:493.

Kutler, Stanley I. (1971) *Privileges and Creative Destruction: The Charles River Bridge Case*. Philadelphia: Lippincott.

Ladinsky, Jack (1976) "The Traffic in Legal Services: Lawyer-Seeking Behavior and the Channeling of Clients," *Law & Society Review* 11:207.

Landes, William and Richard Posner (1975) "The Private Enforcement of Law," *Journal of Legal Studies* 4:51.

Lane, Roger (1979) *Violent Death in the City: Suicide, Accident and Murder in 19th Century Philadelphia*. Cambridge: Harvard University Press.

—— (1969) "Urbanization and Criminal Violence in the 20th Century: Massachusetts as a Test Case," in H. D. Graham and Ted R. Gurr (eds.),

Violence in America: Historical and Comparative Perspectives. New York: Bantam Books.

———— (1967) *Policing the City: Boston 1822–1885.* Cambridge: Harvard University Press.

Langbein, John (1979) "Land without Plea Bargaining: How the Germans Do It," *Michigan Law Review* 78:204.

———— (1978) "The Criminal Trial Before the Lawyers," *University of Chicago Law Review* 45:263.

Langerwerf, Etienne (1978) "The Influence of Industrialization on the Activities of the Belgian Civil Courts from 1835 to 1970." Presented at the 9th World Congress of Sociology meeting, Uppsala, Sweden, August, 1978.

Laurent, Francis W. (1959) *The Business of a Trial Court: 100 Years of Cases.* Madison: University of Wisconsin Press.

Law & Society Review (1980–81) "Special Issue on Dispute Processing and Civil Litigation," *Law & Society Review* 15:395.

———— (1979) "Plea Bargaining," *Law & Society Review* 13:189.

Lea, Henry Charles (1892) [1878] *Superstition and Force: Essays on the Wager of Law—The Wager of Battle—The Ordeal—Torture.* Philadelphia: Lea Brothers.

Lempert, Richard O. (1981) "Grievances and Legitimacy: The Beginnings and End of Dispute Settlement," *Law & Society Review* 15:707.

———— (1978) "More Tales of Two Courts: Exploring Changes in the 'Dispute Settlement Function' of Trial Courts," *Law & Society Review* 13:91.

———— (1976) "Mobilizing Private Law: An Introductory Essay," *Law & Society Review* 11:173.

Lepawsky, Albert (1932) *The Judicial System of Metropolitan Chicago.* Chicago: University of Chicago Press.

Levi, Edward II, (1948) *An Introduction to Legal Reasoning*, Chicago: University of Chicago Press.

Levin, Martin A. (1977) *Urban Politics and the Criminal Courts.* Chicago: University of Chicago Press.

Levin, Tamar (1980) "Did Miami DA's Blow Case?" *National Law Journal.* 2:1.

Levine, Felice J. and Elizabeth Preston (1970) "Community Resource Orientation Among Low Income Groups," *Wisconsin Law Review* 1970:80.

Levine, James P. (1970) "Methodological Concerns in Studying Supreme Court Efficacy," *Law & Society Review* 4:583.

Levine, Sol and Paul E. White (1961) "Exchange as a Conceptual Framework for the Study of Interorganizational Relationships," *Administrative Science Quarterly* 15:583.

Levitan, Sar (1969) *The Great Society's Poor Law: A New Approach.* Baltimore: Johns Hopkins University Press.

Lewis, I. M. (1966) "Spirit Possession and Deprivation Cults," *Man* 1:307.

———— (1961) *A Pastoral Democracy: A Study of Pastoralism and Politics among the Northern Somali of the Horn of Africa.* London: Oxford University Press.

———— (1959) "Clanship and Contract in Northern Somaliland," *Africa* 29:274.

Li, Victor (1977) *Law Without Lawyers.* Stanford: Stanford Alumni Association.

———— (1971) "The Evolution and Development of the Chinese Legal System," in John M. H Lindbeck (ed.,), *China: Management of a Revolutionary Society.* Seattle: University of Washington Press.

Littrell, W. Boyd (1979) *Bureaucratic Justice: Police, Prosecutors and Plea Bargaining*. Beverly Hills, CA: Sage Publications.

Litwack, Eugene and Harry J. Meyer (1966) "A Balance of Coordination Between Bureaucratic Organizations and Community Primary Granges," *Administrative Sciences Quarterly* 11:31.

Llewellyn, Karl (1960) *The Common Law Tradition: Deciding Appeals*. Boston: Little, Brown and Co.

—— (1950) "Remarks on the Theory of Appellate Decision and the Rules or Canons about How Statutes Are to Be Construed," *Vanderbilt Law Review* 3:395.

Llewellyn, Karl and E. Adamson Hoebel (1941) *The Cheyenne Way: Conflict and Case Law In Primitive Jurisprudence*. Norman: University of Oklahoma Press.

Macaulay, Stewart (1979) "Lawyers and Consumer Protection Laws," *Law & Society Review* 14:115.

—— (1977) "Elegant Models, Empirical Pictures, and the Complexities of Contract," *Law & Society Review* 11:507.

—— (1966) *Law and the Balance of Power: The Automobile Manufacturers and Their Dealers*. New York: Russell Sage.

—— (1963) "Non-Contractual Relations in Business: A Preliminary Study," *American Sociological Review* 28:55.

Mac Collum, Spencer (1967) "Dispute Resolution in an American Supermarket," in P. Bohannan (ed.), *Law and Warfare*. Garden City, NY: The Natural History Press.

Mac Lachlan, Colin M, (1974) *Criminal Justice in Eighteenth-Century Mexico: A Study of the Tribunal of Acordada*. Berkeley: University of California Press.

Maguire, John M. (1928) *The Lance of Justice: A Semi-Centennial History of the Legal Aid Society, 1876–1926*. Cambridge: Harvard University Press.

Maine, Sir Henry S. (1963) [1861] *Ancient Law: Its Connections with the Early History of Society and Its Relation to Modern Ideas*. Boston: Beacon Press.

Malone, Wex S. (1965) "The Genesis of Wrongful Death," *Stanford Law Review* 17:1043.

—— (1948) "The Formative Era of Contributory Negligence," *Illinois Law Review* 4:151.

Mann, Bruce H. (1980) "Rationality, Legal Change, and Community in Connecticut," *Law & Society Review* 14:187.

Manning, Bayless (1977) "Hyperlexis: Our National Disease," *Northwestern University Law Review* 71:767.

Mansfield, Seymour J. (ed.) (1978) *Judgment Landlord: A Study of Eviction Court in Chicago*. Chicago: Chicago Council of Lawyers.

March, James G. and Johan P. Olsen (1976) *Ambiguity and Choice in Organizations*. Bergen, Norway: Universitetsforlaget.

March, James G. and Herbert A. Simon (1958) *Organizations*. New York: John Wiley and Sons.

Marks, F. Raymond, Robert Paul Hallauer, and Richard R. Clifton (1974) *The Shreveport Plan : An Experiment in the Delivery of Legal Services*. Chicago: The American Bar Foundation.

Marshall, L. C. (1932) *Judicial Criminal Statistics in Maryland, 1931*. Baltimore: Johns Hopkins University Press.

Mather, Lynn M. (1979a) "Comments on the History of Plea Bargaining," *Law & Society Review* 13:281.

——— (1979b) *Plea Bargaining or Trial? The Process of Criminal Case Disposition*. Lexington, MA: Lexington Books.

——— (1974) "The Outsider in the Courtroom: An Alternative Role for the Defense," in Herbert Jacob (ed.), *The Potential for Reform in Criminal Justice*. Beverly Hills, CA: Sage Publications.

Mather, Lynn and Barbara Yngvesson (1981) "Language, Audience, and the Transformation of Disputes," *Law & Society Review* 15:775.

Maybury-Lewis, David (1967) *Akwē-Shavante Society*. Oxford: Clarendon Press.

Mayhew, Leon H. (1971) "Stability and Change in Legal Systems," in Bernard Barber and Alex Inkeles (eds.), *Stability and Social Change*. Boston: Little, Brown and Co.

Mayo, E. and G. F. F. Lombard (1944) *Teamwork and Labor Turnover in the Aircraft Industry of Southern California*. Boston: Harvard University Graduate School of Business Administration.

McCain, Paul M. (1954) *The County Court in North Carolina before 1750*. Durham, NC: Duke University Press.

McCormack, Albert E., Jr. (1977) "Rule Enforcement and Moral Indignation: Some Observations on the Effects of Criminal Antitrust Convictions upon Societal Reaction Processes," *Social Problems* 25:30.

McDonald, William F. (1982) *Police-Prosecutor Relationships in the United States: Final Report*. Washington, D.C.: National Institute of Justice.

McGillis, Daniel and Joan Mullen (1977) *Neighborhood Justice Centers: An Analysis of Potential Models*. Washington, D.C.: U.S. Government Printing Office.

McIntosh, Wayne V. (1981) "150 Years of Litigation and Dispute Settlement: A Court Tale," *Law & Society Review* 15:823.

——— (1978) "Litigation and Private Dispute Settlement in the St. Louis Circuit Court, 1820–1970: A Preliminary Analysis." Presented at the annual meeting of the American Political Science Association, New York, New York, August-September, 1978.

McIntyre, Donald M. (1977) "Police-Prosecutors: Relationship," in John Jay Douglass (ed.), *Prosecutorial Relationships in Criminal Justice*. Houston: National College of District Attorneys.

——— (1975) "Impediments to Effective Police-Prosecutor Relationships," *American Criminal Law Review* 13:201.

——— (1968) "A Study of Judicial Dominance in the Charging Process," *Journal of Criminal Law, Criminology and Police Science* 59:463.

McIntyre, Donald M. and David Lippman (1970) "Prosecutors and Early Disposition of Felony Cases," *American Bar Association Journal* 56:1154.

Mentschikoff, Soia (1961) "Commercial Arbitration," *Columbia Law Review* 61:846.

Merry, Sally Engle (forthcoming) "Toward a General Theory of Gossip and Scandal," in Donald Black (ed.), *Toward a General Theory of Social Control*. New York: Academic Press.

—— (1982) "The Social Organization of Mediation in Non-Industrial Societies: Implications for Informal Community Justice in America," in Richard L. Abel (ed.), *The Politics of Informal Justice*, Vol. 2. New York: Academic Press.

—— (1979) "Going to Court: Strategies of Dispute Management in an American Urban Neighborhood," *Law & Society Review* 13:891.

Merryman, John H. (1977) "Toward a Theory of Citations: An Empirical Study of the Citation Practice of the California Supreme Court in 1950, 1960, and 1970," *Southern California Law Review* 50:381.

—— (1954) "The Authority of Authority: What the California Supreme Court Cited in 1950," *Stanford Law Review* 6:613.

Merryman, John H., David S. Clark, and Lawrence M. Friedman, (1979) *Law and Social Change in Mediterranean Europe and Latin America*. Dobbs Ferry, New York: Oceana Publications.

Miller, E. Richard and Austin Sarat (1981) "Grievance, Claims, and Disputes: Assessing the Adversary Culture," *Law & Society Review* 15:525.

Miller, Wilbur R. (1977) *Cops and Bobbies: Police Authority in New York and London, 1830–1870*. Chicago: University of Chicago Press.

Mintzberg, Henry (1979) *The Structuring of Organizations*. Englewood Cliffs, NJ: Prentice-Hall, Inc.

Mnookin, Robert H. and Lewis Kornhauser (1979) "Bargaining in the Shadow of the Law: The Case of Divorce," *Yale Law Review* 88:950.

Mohr, Lawrence B. (1976) "Organizations, Decisions, and Courts," *Law & Society Review* 10:621

—— (1973) "The Concept of Organizational Goal," *American Political Science Review* 67:470.

Moley, Raymond (1932) *Tribunes of the People: The Past and Future of the New York Magistrates' Courts*. New Haven: Yale University Press.

—— (1929) *Politics and Criminal Prosecution*. New York: Minton, Balch.

Monkkonen, Eric (1975) *The Dangerous Class: Crime and Poverty in Columbus, Ohio, 1860–1885*. Cambridge: Harvard University Press.

Moore, Sally Falk (1980) "Legal Systems of the World: Types and Typologies," unpublished manuscript, University of Southern California.

—— (1978) *Law as Process: An Anthropological Approach*. London: Routledge & Kegan Paul.

—— (1977) "Individual Interests and Organizational Structures: Dispute Settlements as 'Events of Articulation'," in I. Hamnett (ed.), *Social Anthropology and Law*. New York: Academic Press.

—— (1973) "Law and Social Change: The Semi-Autonomous Social Field as an Appropriate Object of Study," *Law & Society Review* 7:719.

—— (1972) "Legal Liability and Evolutionary Interpretation: Some Aspects of Strict Liability, Self-Help and Collective Responsibility," in M. Gluckman (ed.), *The Allocation of Responsibility*. Manchester: Manchester University Press.

Morgenstern, Oskar (1963) *On the Accuracy of Economic Observations*. Princeton, NJ: Princeton University Press.

Morris, Thomas R. (1975) *The Virginia Supreme Court: An Institutional and Political Analysis*. Charlottesville: University of Virginia Press.

Muir, William Ker, Jr. (1977) *Police: Streetcorner Politicians*. Chicago: University of Chicago Press.

—— (1967) *Prayer in the Public Schools*. Chicago: University of Chicago Press.

Murphy, Walter F. (1964) *Elements of Judicial Strategy*. Chicago: University of Chicago Press.

Myers, Martha A. and John Hagan (1979) "Private and Public Trouble: Prosecutors and the Allocation of Court Resources," *Social Problems* 26:439.

NACCA Law Journal (1954) 13:282.

Nadel, S. F. (1953) "Social Control and Self-Regulation," *Social Forces* 31:265.

Nader, Laura (ed.) (1980) *No Access to Law: Alternatives to the American Judicial System*. New York: Academic Press.

—— (1969a) *Law in Culture and Society*. Chicago: Aldine.

—— (1969b) "Styles of Court Procedure: To Make the Balance," in L. Nader (ed.), *Law in Culture and Society*. Chicago: Aldine.

Nader Laura and Harry F. Todd, Jr. (eds.) (1978) *The Disputing Process: Law in Ten Societies*. New York: Columbia University Press.

Nagel, Stuart S. and Lenore J. Weitzman (1972) "Double Standard of American Justice," *Transaction* 9:18.

Nardulli, Peter F. (1978) *The Courtroom Elite: An Organizational Perspective on Criminal Justice*. Cambridge, MA: Ballinger Publishing Co.

National Center for State Courts (1978) *State Court Caseload Statistics: The State of the Art*. Washington, DC: U.S. Government Printing Office.

—— (1975) *State Court Caseload Statistics: Annual Report, 1975*. Washington, DC: U.S. Government Printing Office.

National Institute of Law Enforcement and Criminal Justice (1979a) *Comparative Research on the Organization of State Court Systems*. Washington, DC: U.S. Department of Justice, Law Enforcement Assistance Administration.

—— (1979b) *Analysis of Practices and Behavior that Affect the Pretrial Process*. Washington, DC: U.S. Department of Justice, Law Enforcement Assistance Administration.

Nelson, Margaret V. (1947) *A Study of Judicial Review in Virginia, 1789–1928*. New York: Columbia University Press.

Nelson, William E. (1981) *Dispute and Conflict Resolution in Plymouth County, Massachusetts, 1725–1825*. Chapel Hill: University of North Carolina Press.

—— (1967) "Emerging Notions of Modern Criminal Law in the Revolutionary Era: An Historical Perspective," *New York University Law Review* 42:450.

New York Times. October 11, 1980, p. 21.

—— December 1, 1979, B. 1.

—— November 3, 1979, p. 23, 44.

—— October 20, 1978, p. 380.

Newman, Donald J. (1966) *Conviction: The Determination of Guilt or Innocence without Trial*. Boston: Little, Brown and Co.

—— (1956) "Pleading Guilty for Considerations: A Study of Bargain Justice," *Journal of Criminal Law, Criminology and Police Science* 46:780.

Nonet, Philippe (1969) *Administrative Justice: Advocacy and Change in Government Agencies*. New York: Russell Sage.

Nonet, Philippe and Philip Selznick (1978) *Toward Responsive Law*. New York: Octagon Books.

Noonan, John T., Jr. (1976) *Persons and Masks of the Law: Cardozo, Holmes, Jefferson, and Wythe as Makers of the Masks*. New York: Farrar, Straus, & Giroux.

Oberg, Kalervo (1934) "Crime and Punishment in Tlingit Society," *American Anthropologist* 36:145.

O'Connell, Jeffrey and Rita J. Simon (1972) *Payment for Pain and Suffering: Who Wants What, When and Why*. Champaign-Urbana, IL: Insurors' Press.

Otterbein, Keith F. and Charlotte Swanson Otterbein (1965) "An Eye for an Eye, a Tooth for a Tooth: A Cross-Cultural Study of Feuding," *American Anthropologist* 67:1470.

Packer, Herbert L. (1968) *The Limits of the Criminal Sanction*. Stanford, CA: Stanford University Press.

Palen, Frank S. (1979) "Media Ombudsmen: A Critical Review," *Law & Society Review* 13:799.

Parsons, Talcott (1949) *The Structure of Social Action*, 2nd ed. Glencoe, IL: The Free Press.

Pennock, J. Roland and John W. Chapman (eds.) (1967) *Equality*, vol. IX: *Yearbook of the American Society for Political and Legal Philosophy*. New York: Atherton Press.

Perry, J. A. G. (1977) "Law Codes and Brokerage in a Lesotho Village," in Ian Hamnett (ed.), *Social Anthropology and Law*. London: Academic Press.

Peters, E. Lloyd (1972) "Aspects of the Control of Moral Ambiguities: A Comparative Analysis of Two Culturally Disparate Modes of Social Control," in M. Gluckman (ed.), *The Allocation of Responsibility*. Manchester: Manchester University Press.

—— (1967) "Some Structural Aspects of the Feud among the Camel-Herding Bedouin of Cyrenaica," *Africa* 37:261.

Phillips, David (1977) *Crime and Authority in Victorian England*. London: Croom, Helm.

Piliavin, Irving and Carl Werthman (1967) "Gang Members and the Police," in David J. Boruda and Albert Reiss (eds.), *The Police: Six Sociological Essays*. New York: John Wiley and Sons.

Platt, Anthony and Randi Pollack (1974) "Channelling Public Defenders," *Issues in Criminology* 9:1.

Pollock, Sir Frederick and Frederic William Maitland (1898) [1895] *The History of English Law: Before the Time of Edward I*, 2 vols. Cambridge: Cambridge University Press, 1968.

Posner, Richard A. (1980) "A Theory of Primitive Society, with Special Reference to Law," *Journal of Law and Economics* 23:1.

—— (1976) *Anti-Trust Law: An Economic Perspective*. Chicago: University of Chicago Press.

—— (1972) "A Theory of Negligence," *Journal of Legal Studies* 1:29.

Pospisil, Leopold J. (1971) *Anthropology of Law: A Comparative Perspective*. New York: Harper & Row.

—— (1958) *Kapauku Papuans and Their Law*. New Haven: Yale University Publications in Anthropology, No. 54.

The Pound Conference (1976) *Federal Rules Decisions* 70:79.

Pound, Roscoe (1953) *The Lawyer from Antiquity to Modern Times: With Particu-

lar Reference to the Development of Bar Associations in the United States. St. Paul, MN:West.

—— (1930) *Criminal Justice in America*. Cambridge: Harvard University Press.

—— (1917) "The Limits of Effective Legal Action," *International Journal of Ethics* 27:150.

Pound, Roscoe and Felix Frankfurter (eds.) (1968) [1922] *Criminal Justice in Cleveland: Reports of the Cleveland Foundation Survey of the Administration of Justice in Cleveland*. Cleveland: The Cleveland Foundation. Reprinted, Montclair, NJ: Patterson-Smith.

President's Commission on Law Enforcement and the Administration of Justice (1967) *Task Force Report: The Courts*. Washington, DC: U.S. Government Printing Office.

Promis Research Project (1977) *Highlights of Interim Findings and Implications*, Publication No. 1. Washington, DC: Institute for Law and Social Research.

Rabin, Robert L. (1979) "Impact Analysis and Tort Law: A Comment," *Law & Society Review* 13:987.

Randall, Richard S. (1968) *Censorship of the Movies: Social and Political Control of a Mass Medium*. Madison: University of Wisconsin Press.

Rattray, R. S. (1979) [1927] *Religion and Art in Ashanti*. New York: AMS Press.

Rawls, John A. (1971) *A Theory of Justice*. Cambridge, MA: Belknap Press of Harvard University Press.

Reay, Marie (1974) "Changing Conventions of Dispute Settlement in the Minj Area," in A. L. Epstein (ed.), *Contention and Dispute: Aspects of Law and Social Control in Melanesia*. Canberra: Australian National University Press.

Rees, Alwyn D. (1961) *Life in a Welsh Countryside*. Cardiff: University of Wales Press.

Reid, John Phillip (1970) *A Law of Blood: The Primitive Law of the Cherokee Nation*. New York: New York University Press.

Reiner, Robert (1978a) *The Blue-Coated Worker*. Cambridge: Cambridge University Press.

—— (1978b) "The Police in the Class Structure," *British Journal of Law and Society* 5:160.

Reiss, Albert (1971) *The Police and the Public*. New Haven: Yale University Press.

Renfrew, Charles B., et al. (1977) "The Paper Label Sentences: An Evaluation," *Yale Law Journal* 86:590.

Rheinstein, Max (ed.) (1954) *Max Weber on Law in Economy and Society*. Cambridge: Harvard University Press.

Richardson, James F. (1974) *Urban Police in the United States*. Port Washington, NY: Kennikat Press.

—— (1970) *The New York Police: Colonial Times to 1901*. New York: Oxford University Press.

Rohde, David W. and Harold J. Spaeth (1976) *Supreme Court Decision Making*. San Francisco: W. H. Freeman.

Rosenberg, Maurice (1972) "Let's Everybody Litigate?" *Texas Law Review* 50:1349.

Rosenthal, Douglas E. (1974) *Lawyer and Client: Who's in Charge?* New York: Russell Sage Foundation.

Rosett, Arthur and Donald Cressey (1976) *Justice by Consent.* Philadelphia: Lippincott.

Ross, H. Laurence (1970) *Settled out of Court: The Social Process of Insurance Claims Adjustments.* Chicago: Aldine.

Rubinstein, Jonathan (1973) *City Police.* New York: Farrar, Straus & Giroux.

Ruffini, Julio L. (1978) "Disputing over Livestock in Sardinia," in Laura Nader and Harry F. Todd, Jr. (eds.), *The Disputing Process—Law in Ten Societies.* New York: Columbia University Press.

Ruhnka, John C. and Steven Weller, with John A. Martin (1978) *Small Claims Courts: A National Examination.* Williamsburg, VA: National Center for State Courts.

Ryan, John Paul, Allan Ashman, Bruce D. Sales, and Sandra Shane-Dubow (1980) *American Trial Judges.* New York: The Free Press.

Sahlins, M. D. (1963) "Poor Man, Rich Man, Big Man, Chief: Political Types in Melanesia and Polynesia," *Comparative Studies in Society and History* 5:285.

Sander, Frank, E. S. (1976) "Varieties of Dispute Processing," *Federal Rules Decisions* 70:111.

Sanders, Andrew (1980) "Criminal Prosecution in England and Wales: Decision-Making by Police and Prosecutors." Presented to the annual meeting of the Law and Society Association, Madison, Wisconsin, June, 1980.

Santos, Boaventura de Sousa (1977) "The Law of the Oppressed: The Construction and Reproduction of Legality in Pasargada," *Law & Society Review* 12:5.

Sarat, Austin (1977a) "Judging in Trial Courts: An Exploratory Study," *Journal of Politics* 39:380.

——— (1977b) "Studying American Legal Culture: An Assessment of Survey Evidence," *Law & Society Review* 11:427.

——— (1976) "Alternatives in Dispute Processing: Litigation in a Small Claims Court," *Law & Society Review* 10:339.

Sarat, Austin and Joel Grossman (1975) "Courts and Conflict Resolution: Problems in the Mobilization of Adjudication," *American Political Science Review* 69:1200.

Schachter, S., et al. (1953) "An Experimental Study of Cohesiveness and Productivity," in D. Cartwright and D. Zander (eds.), *Group Dynamics.* Evanston, IL: Row, Peterson.

Schattschneider, Elmer E. (1960) *The Semisovereign People.* New York: Holt, Rinehart and Winston.

Scheiber, Harry N. (1973) "Property Law, Expropriation and Resource Allocation by Government: The United States, 1789–1910," *Journal of Economic History* 33:232.

Schubert, Glendon (1974a) *Judicial Policy Making* (revised ed.). Glenview, IL: Scott, Foresman.

——— (1974b) *The Judicial Mind Revisited: Psychometric Analysis of Supreme Court Ideology.* New York: Oxford University Press.

——— (1965) *The Judicial Mind.* Evanston, IL: Northwestern University Press.

——— (1964) *Judicial Behavior: A Reader in Theory and Research.* Chicago: Rand McNally.

——— (1959) *Quantitative Analysis of Judicial Behavior.* Glencoe, IL: The Free Press.

Schulman, Mark A. (1979) *A Survey of Spousal Violence against Women in Kentucky*. Washington, DC: U.S. Department of Justice.

Schwartz, Richard D. (1974) "Legal Evolution and the Durkheim Hypothesis: A Reply to Professor Baxi," *Law & Society Review* 8:653.

———— (1954) "Social Factors in the Development of Legal Control: A Case Study of Two Israeli Settlements," *Yale Law Journal* 63:471.

Schwartz, Richard D. and James C. Miller (1964) "Legal Evolution and Societal Complexity," *American Journal of Sociology* 70:159.

Seashore, S. E. (1954) *Group Cohesiveness in the Industrial Work Group*. Ann Arbor: University of Michigan, Survey Research Center.

Selznick, Phillip, with Philippe Nonet and Howard M. Vollmer (1969) *Law, Society and Industrial Justice*. New York: Russell Sage Foundation.

Shapiro, Martin (1980) *Courts: A Comparative and Political Analysis*. Chicago: University of Chicago Press.

———— (1975) "Courts," in F. Greenstein and N. Polsby (eds.), *Handbook of Political Science*, Vol. 5. Reading, PA: Addison-Wesley.

———— (1972) "From Public Law to Public Policy, or the 'Public' in 'Public Law'," *P. S.: Political Science* 5:410.

———— (1964) "Stability and Change in Judicial Decision-Making: Incrementalism or Stare Decisis?" *Law in Transition Quarterly* 2:134.

Shearman, Thomas G. and Amasa A. Redfield (1869) *A Treatise on the Law of Negligence*. New York: Baker, Voorhis & Co.

Shepard, H. A. (1954) "The Value System of a University Research Group," *American Sociological Review* 19:456.

Sherrill, George P. (1930) *Criminal Procedure in North Carolina, as Shown by Criminal Appeals since 1890*. Chapel Hill: University of North Carolina Press.

Silberman, Matthew (1978) "The Study of Legal Change: The Survey and Related Methods." Presented at the annual meeting of the Law and Society Association, Minneapolis, Minnesota, May, 1978.

Silver, Alan (1967) "The Demand for Order in a Civil Society," in David J. Boruda and Albert Reiss (eds.), *The Police: Six Sociological Essays*. New York: John Wiley and Sons.

Silverman, Robert (1980) *Law and Urban Growth: Civil Litigation in the Boston Trial Courts, 1880–1900*. Princeton, NJ: Princeton University Press.

Simmel, Georg (1960) [1908] *The Sociology of Georg Simmel* (Kurt H. Wolff, ed.). New York: Free Press.

Simon, Herbert A. (1957) *Administrative Behavior*. New York: Macmillan.

Simon, Herbert A., Donald W. Smithburg, and Victor A. Thompson (1959) *Public Administration*. New York: Alfred A. Knopf.

Skolar, Daniel L. (1977) *Organizing the Non-System*. Lexington, MA: Lexington Books.

Skolnick, Jerome H. (1967) "Social Control in the Adversary System," *Journal of Conflict Resolution* 11:59.

———— (1966) *Justice Without Trial: Law Enforcement in a Democratic Society*. New York: John Wiley.

Smigel, Erwin O. (1964) *The Wall Street Lawyer: Professional Organization Man?* Bloomington: Indiana University Press.

Spindel, Donna J. (1981) "The Administration of Criminal Justice in North Carolina, 1720–1740," *American Journal of Legal History* 25:141.

Spiro, Melford E. (1961) "Social Systems, Personality, and Functional Analysis," in Bert Kaplan (ed.), *Studying Personality Cross-Culturally*. Evanston, IL: Row, Peterson & Co.

Spitzer, Steven (1975) "Punishment and Social Organization: A Study of Durkheim's Theory of Penal Evolution," *Law & Society Review* 9:613.

Stanko, Elizabeth (1979) "The Arrest Versus the Case." Unpublished manuscript, Clark University, Worcester, Massachusetts.

Starr, June (1978) *Dispute and Settlement in Rural Turkey*. Leiden Netherlands: E. J. Brill.

Starr, June and Barbara Yngvesson (1975) "Scarcity and Disputing: Zeroing-in on Compromise Decisions," *American Ethnologist* 2:553.

Steele, Eric H. (1977) "Two Approaches to Contemporary Dispute Behavior and Consumer Problems," *Law & Society Review* 11:667.

Stein, Peter (1979) *Legal Evolution: The Story of an Idea*. New York: Cambridge University Press.

Stevens, Robert B. (1978) *Law and Politics: The House of Lords as a Judicial Body*. Chapel Hill: University of North Carolina Press.

Stone, Thomas (1979) "The Mounties as Vigilantes: Perceptions of Community and the Transformation of Law in the Yukon," *Law & Society Review* 14:83.

Stone, L. (1979) *Marriage, Sex and the Family in England*. London: Oxford University Press.

Sudnow, David (1965) "Normal Crimes: Sociological Features of the Penal Code in a Public Defender Office," *Social Problems* 12:255.

Swindler, William F. (1969) *Court and Constitution in the Twentieth Century: The Old Legality, 1889–1931*. Indianapolis, IN: Bobbs Merrill.

Sykes, Gresham M. (1969) "Legal Needs of the Poor in the City of Denver," *Law & Society Review* 4:255.

—— (1958) *The Society of Captives*. Princeton, NJ: Princeton University Press.

Tachau, Mary K. Bonsteel (1978) *Federal Courts in the Early Republic: Kentucky, 1789–1816*. Princeton, NJ: Princeton University Press.

Tanner, Nancy (1970) "Disputing and the Genesis of Legal Principles: Examples from Minangkabau," *Southwestern Journal of Anthropology* 26:375.

Thoden Van Velzen, H. U. E. and W. Van Wetering (1960) "Residence, Power Groups and Intra-Societal Aggression: An Enquiry into the Conditions Leading to Peacefulness within Non-Stratified Societies," *International Archives of Ethnography* 49:169.

Thomas, Keith (1971) *Religion and the Decline of Magic*. New York: Charles Scribner's Sons.

Thompson, Edward P. (1975) *Whigs and Hunters: The Origin of the Black Act*. New York: Pantheon.

Thompson, Hunter S. (1966) *Hell's Angels: A Strange and Terrible Saga*. New York: Random House.

Thompson, James D. (1967) *Organizations in Action*. New York: McGraw-Hill.

Tobias, John Jacob (1979) *Crime and Police in England, 1700–1900*. New York: St. Martin's Press.

Toharia, Jose Juan (1974) *Cambio Social y Vida Juridica en Espana*. Madrid: Edicusa.

—— (1973) "Economic Development and Litigation: The Case of Spain." Presented to the Conference on the Sociology of the Judicial Process, University of Bielefeld, F. R. G., September, 1973.

Tonnies, Ferdinand (1957) *Community and Society* [Gemeinschaft und Gesellschaft] (Charles P. Loomis, ed.). East Lansing: Michigan State University Press.

Trubek, David M. (1981) "The Construction and Deconstruction of a Disputes-Focused Approach: An Afterword," *Law & Society Review* 15:727.

——— (1972) "Max Weber on Law and the Rise of Capitalism," *Wisconsin Law Review* 1972:720.

Trubek, David and Marc Galanter (1974) "Scholars in Self-Estrangement: Some Reflections on the Crisis in Law and Development Studies in the United States," *Wisconsin Law Review* 1974:1062.

Tumin, Melvin M. (1952) *Caste in a Peasant Society: A Case Study in the Dynamics of Caste*. Princeton, NJ: Princeton University Press.

Turnbull, Colin M. (1965) *Wayward Servants: The Two Worlds of the African Pygmies*. Garden City, NY: Natural History Press.

Uhlman, Thomas M. (1977) "The Impact of Defendant Race in Trial Court Sanctioning Decisions," in John Gardiner (ed.), *Public Law and Public Policy*. New York: Praeger.

Uhlman, Thomas M. and Herbert Kritzer (1976) "Sisterhood in the Courtroom," unpublished manuscript, University of Missouri (St. Louis).

Utz, Pamela J. (1978) *Settling the Facts: Discretion and Negotiation in Criminal Court*. Lexington, MA: Lexington Books.

Van der Sprenkel, Sybille (1962) *Legal Institutions in Manchu China: A Sociological Analysis*. New York: Humanities Press.

Van Maanen, John (1976) "Breaking in: Socialization to Work," in Robert Dubin (ed.), *Handbook of Work: Organization and Society*. Chicago: Rand McNally.

Van Velsen, J. (1964) *The Politics of Kinship: A Study in Social Manipulation among the Lakeside Tonga*. Manchester: Manchester University Press.

Veith, Ilza (1965) *Hysteria: The History of a Disease*. Chicago: University of Chicago Press.

Vera Institute of Justice (1981) *Felony Arrests: Their Prosecution and Disposition in New York City's Courts*, revised ed. New York: Longman Inc.

Vernier, C. G. and Philip Selig, Jr. (1928) "The Reversal of Criminal Cases in the Supreme Court of California," *Southern California Law Review* 2:21.

Volmer, August (1936) *The Police and Modern Society*. Berkeley: University of California Press.

Walker, Samuel (1980) *Popular Justice: A History of American Criminal Justice*. New York: Oxford University Press.

Wanner, Craig (1975) "The Public Ordering of Private Relations, Part Two: Winning Civil Court Cases," *Law & Society Review* 9:293.

——— (1974) "The Public Ordering of Private Relations, Part One: Initiating Civil Cases in Urban Trial Courts," *Law & Society Review* 8:421.

Wanous, John P. (1977) "Organizational Entry," *Psychological Bulletin* 84:601.

Warren, Charles (1922) *The Supreme Court in United States History*. Boston: Little, Brown and Co.

Wasby, Stephen L. (1970) *The Impact of the United States Supreme Court: Some Perspectives*. Homewood, IL: Dorsey Press.

Weber, Max (1958) *From Max Weber: Essays in Sociology*. (translated by H. H.

Gerth and C. W. Mills) New York: Oxford University Press.

———— (1954) *On Law in Economy and Society* (Max Rheinstein, ed.). Cambridge: Harvard University Press.

Wechsler, Herbert (1959) "Toward Neutral Principles of Constitutional Law," *Harvard Law Review* 73:1.

Weinreb, Lloyd L. (1977) *Denial of Justice.* New York: Free Press.

Wetter, J. Gillis (1960) *The Styles of Appellate Judicial Opinions: A Case Study in Comparative Law.* Leyden, Netherlands: A. W. Sythoff.

Wherry, William M. (1931) *A Study of the Organization of Litigation and of the Jury Trial in the Supreme Court of New York County.* Brattleboro, VT: Vermont Printing Co.

Whitford, William C. (1968) "Law and the Consumer Transaction: A Case Study of the Automobile Warranty," *Wisconsin Law Review* 1968:1006.

Wildhorn, Sorrel, et al. (1976) *Indicators of Justice: Measuring the Performance of Prosecution, Defense and Court Agencies Involved in Felony Proceedings.* Santa Monica, CA: Rand Corporation.

Williams, Jack Kenny (1959) *Vogues in Villainy: Crime and Retribution in Ante-Bellum South Carolina.* Columbia: University of South Carolina Press.

Wilson, James Q. (1968) *Varieties of Police Behavior: The Management of Law and Order in Eight Communities.* Cambridge: Harvard University Press.

Wimberly, Howard (1973) "Legal Evolution: One Further Step," *American Journal of Sociology* 79:78.

Wishingrad, Jay (1974) "The Plea Bargain in Historical Perspective," *Buffalo Law Review* 23:499.

Witty, Cathie J. (1980) *Mediation and Society: Conflict Management in Lebanon.* New York: Academic Press.

Wunder, John R. (1979) *Inferior Courts, Superior Justice: A History of the Justices of the Northwest Frontier, 1853–1889.* Westport, CT: Greenwood Press.

Yankelovich, Skelly & White, Inc. (1978) *The Public Image of Courts.* Williamsburg, VA: National Center for State Courts.

Yngvesson, Barbara (forthcoming) "What Is a Dispute About?" in Donald Black (ed.), *Towards a General Theory of Social Control.* New York: Academic Press.

———— (1978) "Leadership and Consensus: Decision-Making in an Egalitarian Community," *Ethnos* 1–2:73.

———— (1977) "Law in Preindustrial Societies," *Sociological Inquiry* 47:128.

———— (1976) "Responses to Grievance Behavior: Extended Cases in a Fishing Community," *American Ethnologist* 3:353.

Yngvesson, Barbara and Patricia Hennessey (1975) "Small Claims, Complex Disputes: A Review of the Small Claims Literature," *Law & Society Review* 9:219.

Zablocki, Benjamin (1971) *The Joyful Community: An Account of the Bruderhof, A Communal Movement Now in Its Third Generation.* Baltimore, MD: Penguin Books.

Zald, Mayer N. and Feather Davis Hair (1972) "The Social Control of General Hospitals," in Basil Georgopoulos (ed.), *Organization Research on Health Institutions.* Ann Arbor: University of Michigan, Institute for Social Research.

Zaltman, Gerald, Robert Duncan, and Jonny Holbek (1973) *Innovations and Organizations*. New York: John Wiley and Sons.

Zeisel, Hans, Harry Kalven, Jr., and Bernard Buchholz (1959) *Delay in the Court*. Boston: Little, Brown and Co.

Index

Llewellyn, Karl, 34
Long-linked technology, 204

Macro-studies, 10
Magnitide of change in
  circumstance, 146–148
Maine, Sir Henry, 10–11, 60
Maintenance, order, 223, 225–226,
  232
Malpractice law, 29
Marginal roles of third parties,
  107–111
Mather, Lynn, 3, 209, 247
McIntosh, Wayne, 21
Mediating technology, 204
Mediation, 11–12
  passive, 101–102
  in tribal society, 56–59
Mediators, 100–102
Mobilization, 126
Modern society, 51–53, 61–63
  dispute transformation in, 75–80

National Institute of Justice, vii–viii
National Institute of Law
  Enforcement and Criminal
  Justice (NILECJ), vii, 212
National legal systems, 130
Negotiations, 121
  relation of courts to, 141
Negotiators, 108–109
NILECJ (National Institute of Law
  Enforcement and Criminal
  Justice), vii, 212
Nominalists, 2, 163, 165–166
Normative evolution notion,
  181–182
Normative validation, 125
Norms, social, 150, 180–181

Open arenas, 66, 68, 81
Opposition roles, 97–98
Order maintenance, 223, 225–226,
  232

Organization complexity, 67, 69,
  72–73, 81, 82
Organization theories, 170–171
Organizational concepts, 214–215
Organizational imperialism, 221,
  237–238
Organizational realms, differing, of
  police and prosecutors, 221–233
Organizational research, 203
Organizations
  boundaries of, 198–200
  communication patterns within,
    200–201
  "core technology" of, 204
  courts as, 191–215
  decision making in, 201–207

Pacification, repressive, 106–107
Packer, Herbert, 40–41
Partisans, 85
Passive mediation, 101–102
Patterns, communication, within
  organizations, 200–201
Peacemakers
  friendly, 99–100
  repressive, 106–107
Peters, E. Lloyd, 69–73
Plea bargaining, *see* Bargaining
  entries
Police, 11, 223–229
Police-prosecutor relations,
  216–243
  differing organizational realms
    in, 221–233
  diverging goals, 232–233
  implications for research,
    233–240
  intraorganization theory,
    217–221
Policy questions, 5
Political process, 202
Pound, Roscoe, 40
Power(s)
  basis of, in courts, 197